Ethics, Rationality, and Economic Behaviour

Ethics, Rationality, and Economic Behaviour

Edited by

FRANCESCO FARINA, FRANK HAHN,
AND STEFANO VANNUCCI

CLARENDON PRESS · OXFORD
1996

Oxford University Press, Walton Street, Oxford OX2 6DP
Oxford New York
Athens Auckland Bangkok Bombay
Calcutta Cape Town Dar es Salaam Delhi
Florence Hong Kong Istanbul Karachi
Kuala Lumpur Madras Madrid Melbourne
Mexico City Nairobi Paris Singapore
Taipei Tokyo Toronto
and associated companies in
Berlin Ibadan

Published in the United States
by Oxford University Press Inc., New York

British Library Cataloguing in Publication Data
Data available

Library of Congress Cataloging-in-Publication Data
Ethics, rationality, and economic behaviour/edited by Francesco Farina, Frank Hahn, and Stefano Vannucci.
Papers presented at a conference held in Sieena in 1991.
Includes bibliographical references.
1. Economics—Moral and ethical aspects—Congresses. I. Farina, Francesco. II. Hahn, Frank. III. Vannucci, Stefano.
HB72.E786 1996 95 41186
174′.4—dc20
ISBN 0–19–828981–2

1 3 5 7 9 10 8 6 4 2

Typeset by Pure Tech India Limited, Pondicherry
Printed in Great Britain
on acid-free paper by
Biddles Ltd, Guildford & King's Lynn

Contents

III. FAIRNESS IN DISTRIBUTION

IV. THE ETHICAL DIMENSION OF RATIONAL DECISIONS

V. STRATEGIC INTERACTION AND MORAL ANALYSIS

List of Contributors

JOHN BROOME, Professor of Economics, Department of Economics, University of Bristol

FRANCESCO FARINA, Professor of Economics, Department of Political Economy, University of Siena

DAVID GAUTHIER, Professor of Philosophy, Department of Philosophy, University of Pittsburgh

FRANK HAHN, Professor of Economics, Department of Political Economy, University of Siena

PETER J. HAMMOND, Professor of Economics, Department of Economics, Stanford University

JOHN C. HARSANYI, Professor of Economics, Department of Economics, University of California at Berkeley

STEVEN LUKES, Professor of Political Science, European University Institute, Florence

HERVÉ MOULIN, Professor of Economics, Department of Economics, Duke University, Durham, NC

JOHN E. ROEMER, Professor of Economics, Department of Economics, University of California at Davis

PIER LUIGI SACCO, Professor of Economics, Department of Economics, University of Florence

AMARTYA K. SEN, Lamont University Professor, and Professor of Economics and Philosophy, Harvard University

ROBERT SUGDEN, Professor of Economics, School of Economic and Social Studies, University of East Anglia

STEFANO VANNUCCI, Professor of Economics, Department of Political Economy, University of Siena

PHILIPPE VAN PARIJS, Chaire Hoover d'étique économique et sociale, Faculté des sciences économiques, sociales et politiques, Université Catholique de Louvain

MENAHEM E. YAARI, Professor of Economics, President of the Open University of Israel, Tel Aviv

BERNARD WILLIAMS, Professor of Philosophy, Corpus Christi College, Oxford University

STEFANO ZAMAGNI, Professor of Economics, Department of Economics, University of Bologna

Introduction

Most of us would probably find it disturbing to concede that the prescriptions of rationality may well contradict the requirements of moral 'rightness' and vice versa. In fact, a few most influential contemporary approaches to ethics advocate decision-theoretic or game-theoretic foundations of some sort for moral principles, while several economic theorists are now prepared to take into serious account the ethical dimension of rational decisions. As a result, it appears that economics and ethics are somehow inextricably linked through theories of rational decision-making. The essays included in the present volume provide a detailed analysis of these connections between ethics and economics as viewed from several different—sometimes conflicting—perspectives.

The five papers included in the first section of this volume address some foundational issues regarding ethics, rational choice theory, and normative economics. The scope and significance of utilitarianism is bound to be an issue of central concern when venturing into that territory. This is so at least since Harsanyi's celebrated 'aggregation theorem' made it clear that any unanimity-respecting rule aggregating individual expected utilities into a 'social' expected utility function is representable by an utilitarian-like weighted sum of individual utility functions.

Indeed, the basic tenet of modern utilitarianism is that moral choice can be reduced to maximization of a social welfare functional which is in turn a 'sum' of suitable indicators of individual well-being (such indicators are usually constructed as representations of individual rational preferences or choices). This typically requires the feasibility of a full description of all relevant consequences of every action profile, the completeness and transitivity of social welfare evaluations on the part of the relevant moral actor, and the availability of reasonably 'hard' information in the right format (say, comparable interval scales) concerning individual preferences or utilities. Now, the contributions by Sen, Lukes, and Williams point to the inescapable multidimensionality and incompleteness of ethical evaluations by arguing for the irreducible plurality of values and reasons, while both Hahn's and Sen's papers insist on the limited reliability of preferences as ultimate indicators of individual well-being. Thus, Hahn, Lukes, Sen, and (less explicitly) Williams advance—*inter alia*—several critical arguments against various aspects of utilitarianism. In contrast, Harsanyi offers a spirited defence of utilitarian principles.

Indeed, Hahn's contribution ('Some Economical Reflections on Ethics') forcefully stresses a basic difficulty of any ethical doctrine which—as modern utilitarianism sometimes does—treats the preferences or choices of a rational agent as the fundamental indicator of his/her own individual well-being. Namely, any such doctrine is forced to assess the goodness of the relevant alternatives (e.g. allocations, policies, or institutional arrangements) by means of criteria which are arguably moulded by the prevailing state of affairs. Hahn points out that the standard ('welfarist') approach to normative economics can be salvaged only under the assumption that preferences are highly separable to the effect that preferences on some subdomain of the space of relevant alternatives (e.g. allocations of certain physical goods) are comparatively persistent, and are not affected by the more volatile preferences on other subdomains (e.g. basic institutions or ethical norms).

Harsanyi's chapter ('Morality and Incentives') provides a bold restatement and defence of utilitarianism, based upon the Harrodian distinction between 'rule utilitarianism' and 'act utilitarianism' and the endorsement of the former as an optimal moral code. He argues that a right action must be consistent with a right moral code, and the latter must simply be (according to his theorem on utilitarianism mentioned above) a social utility maximizing rule. Of course, 'act utilitarianism' amounts to a particular rule, so that 'rule utilitarianism' will typically result in a greater amount of 'social utility'. In particular, as Harsanyi stresses, 'rule utilitarianism' may well accommodate non-consequentialist evaluation criteria (e.g. the respect of 'morally protected rights') and some suitable incentive schemes (e.g. payment according to performance) which may not be consistent, in his view, with rival accounts of moral choice such as those embodied in the Rawlsian principles of justice. It is worth noting that Harsanyi's argument raises, without addressing, the general issue of infinite regress in social choice which is now being tackled by a slowly growing body of literature: in fact, why not consider rules to choose among rules for choosing rules, and so on? Why truncate at the very first step this chain of increasingly complex objects of moral choice?

Lukes's chapter ('On Trade-Offs between Values') insists on plurality of values, but argues that some of the alleged conflicts between them (e.g. liberty versus equality, or efficiency versus equity) are the result of misconceived assumptions. In particular, equality has several dimensions, and some of them may be interpreted in terms of positive liberty. In fact, the first concern of many egalitarians is to equalize liberties, so that the alleged conflict and trade-off between liberty and equality is, as such, untenable. To be sure, there are genuine conflicts between different values. Lukes submits, however, that the solutions of these conflicts call for choices that do not necessarily involve trade-offs: in some cases conflicts between values can not be reduced to cost-benefit problems, and the reasons underlying choices between them may be best expressed in a Kantian language (i.e. choosing in a manner which is not consistent with a certain value may amount to a 'sacrifice' which does not deny the dignity of the neglected value as an end in itself).

A detailed criticism of 'welfarism' and a strong defence of the plurality of values, with the ensuing irreducible incompleteness of moral evaluations are presented in Sen's chapter ('On the Foundations of Welfare Economics: Utility, Capability, and Practical Reason'). Sen provides a critical survey of the main themes of the debate concerning the foundations of welfare analysis, ranging from the issue of interpersonal comparisons to the contrast between utilitarian and non-utilitarian or non-welfarist views on ethics. Sen's attempt at reconciling ethics and welfare economics starts from restoring the significance of interpersonal welfare comparisons, contrary to the Arrowian axiomatization of social choice problems and to the older Robbinsian tradition. Indeed, he advocates an even broader enlargement of the informational basis of welfare judgements beyond the strictures of 'welfarism'—namely, the inclusion of the functionings and capabilities of individuals among the basic indicators of individual well-being. However, Sen points out very explicitly that even such enlargements of the informational basis of welfare analysis call for value-ridden choices, and cannot therefore evade the irreducible plurality of values and the radical incompleteness of overall welfare judgements.

The focus of Williams's chapter ('Values, Reasons, and the Theory of Persuasion') is on the proper interpretation of the statement 'agent A has reason to—'. Williams's thesis is that only 'internal' reasons (i.e. the agent's preferences, evaluations—including possibly moral ones—and other sorts of psychological states) count as proper reasons for action: no appeal has to be made to 'external' reasons (i.e. those usually introduced by the prefix 'there is reason to—'). In particular, Williams addresses the fact that a 'justifier' is sometimes introduced by rational choice theorists to the effect of guaranteeing rational intelligibility of preferences in terms of values when trying to restore consistency between actual behaviour and some basic Bayesian-rationality postulate (e.g. transitivity or the 'sure-thing' principle). He insists that appealing to those 'justifiers' does not contradict his 'internalist' thesis since after all the invoked values are (some of) the agent's values. However, 'internal' reasons are not necessarily summarized by preferences, let alone complete preferences: generally speaking, ambiguity and incompleteness can not be evaded. Moreover, 'internal' reasons do not rule out external decision aid, and—on Williams's account—even call for public discussion of some sort, whence the inescapable role of persuasion and power in analysing individual rational decision-making.

Some very general arguments in favour of a broadly utilitarian view of ethics are offered by the papers included in the second section of the volume.

Broome's chapter ('Economic Analysis and the Structure of Good: Transferring Utility Theory from Preferences to Betterness') advocates an extensive use of economic methods in the analysis of the basic 'at least as good as'—or 'betterness'—relation (to be distinguished from more specific preference relations). Broome also suggests that Harsanyi's theorem concerning the utilitarian representability of any Pareto optimal aggregation of expected utilities needs a radical reinterpretation in terms of betterness relations, in order to ensure its meaningfulness. His argument runs as follows. A probability-relative 'betterness' relation does make sense, but only under a fixed probability distribution. In contrast, preference relations over uncertain prospects involve personal assessments of probabilities which are typically different from each other. Drawing upon the so-called 'probability agreement' theorem, Broome argues that Harsanyi's 'utilitarian' aggregation theorem does only make sense when the relevant interval scales are interpreted as representations of (individual and social) betterness—as opposed to preference—relations. While Broome's theory of good is general enough to admit a non-utilitarian interpretation (e.g. by dispensing with the standard interpretation of the individual betterness relations in terms of, say, satisfaction-based preferences or desire-fulfilling choices), it retains the formal additive structure of the utilitarian functional, due to its reliance on interval scales for both the input and the output of the aggregation exercise resulting in the comparative evaluation of the good attached to alternative states of affairs.

Hammond's chapter ('Consequentialist Decision Theory and Utilitarian Ethics') offers an argument for a generalized version of utilitarianism, couched in terms of a set of decision-theoretic axioms for a 'social norm' concerning social choice problems represented by suitable finite decision trees with chance moves. Hammond's argument is as follows. He first shows—using a former result of his own—that the requirements of 'universal domain' (i.e. versatility), 'subtree consistency' (a version of the familiar backward induction principle), continuity and 'consequentialism' (i.e. the social norm must prescribe the same choice sets for any two decision trees having the same feasible set of contingent consequences) entail representability of the prescriptions of the 'social norm' by means of expected utility maximizing behaviour (EUM) with respect to a suitable von Neumann-Morgenstern utility function. Moreover, if two further requirements are imposed (namely, a weak unanimity-respecting axiom called 'individualistic consequentialism' and a condition establishing that the welfare of a uniquely affected individual is the only one to count) then the 'social norm' must be representable by an utilitarian-like additive social welfare function. Hammond carefully points out that his 'social norm' may well admit interpretations of individual and social welfare which are quite different from the received utilitarian view. However, his argument has a distinctly utilitarian flavour: it suggests that, under the assumptions mentioned above, 'consequentialism' entails '(generalized) utilitarianism'. Intuitively, this is so because in that setting 'consequentialism' implies that the 'social norm' is EUM which in turn implies interpersonal cardinal comparability of individual scales. Therefore, in view of the 'unanimity-respecting' axiom mentioned above, the 'consequentialism entails generalized utilitarianism' thesis follows from a fundamental theorem of measurement theory concerning the characterization of weighted arithmetic means.

It is well known that utilitarianism has been strongly criticized on egalitarian grounds. Obviously, any version of egalitarianism amounts to the basic contention that (at least) some inequalities are ethically wrong and should therefore be corrected or compensated for. A naïve egalitarian might perhaps insist that every inequality can and should be compensated for: however, he would have to face strong objections concerning both the feasibility of his project, and its predictably adverse incentive effects. Other versions of egalitarianism contend that the advancement of knowledge should make it possible to draw at least some plausible distinctions between two basic kinds of inequalities. Namely, it should sometimes be possible to distinguish between certain inequalities which are 'clearly' brought about by circumstances that lay beyond the control of the involved agents (e.g. genetic endowments, or cultural factors imputable to general and/or persistent traits of the relevant social environment), and other inequalities which are 'clearly' to be imputed to personal choices (the undeniable fact that in some cases such distinctions are apparently difficult to draw does not rule out the possibility of reaching a reasonable degree of consensus in other relevant cases). The suggestion of such more sophisticated versions of egalitarianism is obviously that only inequalities of the first kind are eligible for compensation. Indeed, one of the basic tenets of the egalitarian criticism of utilitarianism alluded to above may be summarized by a principle and a presumption. The principle is that individuals should be compensated for all those inequalities that arise from circumstances for which they cannot reasonably be held responsible: to put it in bolder terms, 'no fair inequality without responsibility'. The presumption is that choices and preferences are largely affected by that sort of circumstances, and cannot therefore be taken as the ultimate source of information in order to determine the good, or the right, thing to do. More often than not, this egalitarian and anti-utilitarian contention has been recently formulated in terms of a critique of 'welfarism', and using a procedural approach couched in the language of 'rights' (but see Sen's contribution on this). However, it should be noticed that this broadly egalitarian approach can be articulated in different ways, and is fully consistent with a heavy reliance on informational bases which include preference or welfare data. Furthermore, as we shall see in a moment, it turns out that for certain fair division problems, an egalitarian-like solution can be advocated even conceding full responsibility of agents for their own preferences, and replacing the 'no inequality without responsibility' principle with a milder looking principle of uniform treatment under mutual responsibility.

The contributions of the third section provide in fact three different applications of several variants of those egalitarian principles to some specific problems of fair distribution.

In his chapter ('Stand Alone and Unanimity Tests: A Re-examination of Fair Division') Moulin offers a critical survey of some recent results concerning anonymous and Pareto optimal methods of fair division of common non-marketed resources (e.g. mineral resources in international waters, or broadcasting frequencies). Here, the informational base is the standard one of economic theory consisting of ordinal non-comparable preferences or utilities, and individual rights are expressed as welfare guarantees or bounds. The focus of Moulin's analysis is on two 'new' criteria. The first one is the 'stand alone' criterion, which requires that, at any preference profile, the externality brought about by the presence of other agents affects the utility level of any agent in the same direction (either everyone is sorry not to be alone or everyone is happy not to be alone). The second criterion is the 'unanimity test', which similarly requires that at any preference profile either everyone be sorry to disagree or everyone be happy to disagree with other agents. This amounts to requiring that—since every agent is equally responsible for the externality produced by disagreement—everyone be uniformly affected. The ethical stance underlying such criteria is the following: it is implicitly assumed that every agent is fully responsible for his/her own preferences, and that externalities for which the agents are mutually responsible are not to affect them in a completely different manner. This amounts to a horizontal equity counterpart to the 'no inequality without responsibility' principle, which could be phrased as a 'no grossly differential treatment without differential responsibility' principle. It turns out that both criteria are satisfied by a suitable egalitarian-equivalent mechanism (i.e. a mechanism that selects allocations which everyone regards as welfare equivalent to an egalitarian—possibly unfeasible—allocation). Hence—as anticipated above—one may end up with an egalitarian-like solution to fair division problems even starting from the mild-looking 'no grossly differential treatment without differential responsibility' principle and conceding full responsibility for personal preferences.

Roemer's contribution ('On a Mechanism for Implementing Egalitarianism with Responsibility') fully endorses the 'no inequality without responsibility' principle. In order to explore some of its (re)distributive consequences, Roemer provides a suitable formulation of this principle in terms of a functional to be maximized by an egalitarian social planner when choosing an optimal tax policy in pursuit of 'equality of opportunity'. He suggests that the population be partitioned into a finite number of types (as defined by level of income, occupation, gender, etc.). The social planner is allowed to consider eligible for compensation only those inequalities for which individuals can not be held responsible (as opposed to those inequalities which are to be imputed to different personal strategies—e.g. educational choices—chosen by people within the same type). The proposed mechanism results in a tax policy whose redistributive effects are typically weaker than those of its Rawlsian counterpart.

Van Parijs's chapter ('Free-Riding Versus Rent-Sharing: Should Even David Gauthier Support An Unconditional Basic Income?') offers an application of a version of the same 'no inequality without responsibility' principle mentioned above to the problem of distribution of co-operative benefits as formulated in a standard bargaining model. This author's concern is the compatibility of the favoured Gauthier's solution (i.e. the maximin-of-relative-benefits rule)—and of his treatment of factor rent—with the introduction of an unconditional basic income as advocated by Van Parijs himself. Van Parijs claims that—under his interpretation—Gauthier's solution is in fact consistent with such a basic 'citizenship' income unrelated to work. His argument revolves around the proper assessment of the relevant opportunity costs. Van Parijs submits that the true opportunity costs are determined by the benefits achievable by each individual when standing alone with his/her own talent and a fair share of external resources. All the rest is factor rent, i.e.—according to Gauthier's own broadest definition—return on scarcity (as opposed to individual talents). Now, scarcity results from the operation of supply and demand hence, ultimately, from the terms of social interaction: thus, factor rent has to be fairly shared. Hence, in Van Parijs's view, even the maximin-of-relative-benefits rule—when properly stated—can accommodate significant redistributions, including a basic unconditional income.

The interplay between rational choice, fairness, and ethics is obviously an ubiquitous theme in the present volume. The three contributions collected in the fourth section are, however, explicitly devoted to discussing some of its several facets. Their common theme is the theoretical explanation of behavioural attitudes which both contradict the orthodox view of rational choice and are apparently influenced by ethical motivations. Their focus is, respectively, on the relationship between individual rational decisions and the conditions for social choice to take into account equity; on the scope for rational commitment and reciprocity in dynamic choice; and on the emergence of conventions which bring about success to the co-ordination enterprise.

In fact, Farina's chapter ('Social Preferences, Equity and Non-Expected Utility Theory') explores the feasibility of an individualistic and equity-concerned aggregation of rational personal preferences. He argues that, since violations of Bayesian rationality in individual decisions under uncertainty should also apply to social preferences as determined by an ethical decision-maker, the social ordering resulting from aggregation will typically be different from the one advocated by Harsanyi's utilitarianism. However, when the violation of the 'sure-thing' principle due to the 'common consequence effect' is applied to interpersonal distributions, the behavioural shift of the ethical decision-maker towards 'inequality aversion' (similar to the change towards 'risk aversion' in individual decisions between lotteries) turns out to be counter-intuitive. In fact, when individuals are exposed to the worst possible outcomes, no social preference reversal to the most equitable interpersonal distributions is likely to occur. Farina then maintains that equity-concerned social judgements will be more properly represented by considering equity not as a desirable general feature of interpersonal distributions but as an individual value which enters into the welfare assessment of each position to be occupied in the relevant society. He submits that this view of equity as an individual value might be best conveyed—in the vein of non-expected utility theory—by 'disappointment'-sensitive utility functions.

In his chapter ('Commitment and Choice: An Essay on the Rationality of Plans') Gauthier suggests a rational choice-theoretic argument for the ability to commit to plans. His argument is based upon the role of resolute choice in achieving successful personal and interpersonal co-ordination in sequential decision problems. Contrary to the subgame perfection principle, Gauthier maintains that a rational agent can always regiment his/her *ex post* choice to the *ex ante* evaluation of plans. In particular, a resolute rational planner will discipline his/her choices this way whenever the chosen plan is deemed to be at any stage the most advantageous amongst the available *ex ante* plans. Moreover, Gauthier suggests that in interactive decisions the commitment of an agent to reciprocate in the future will induce the opponent to co-operate so that interpersonal co-ordination may obtain. In fact, Gauthier submits that precisely this role of commitment as a co-ordination device might explain the strict connection between commitment and moral behaviour: thus, under his view, the ethical dimension of decisions is somehow subsumed to the rationality of the commitment to co-operate.

Sugden's contribution ('Rational Co-ordination') is focused on the appraisal of the comparative success of standard game-theoretic rational behaviour and moral-like behaviour in solving one-shot pure co ordination problems. Sugden's project aims at bridging the persistent explanatory gap between the standard rational choice paradigm and the fairly high degree of successful co-ordination achieved in practice. His argument suggests a somewhat unconventional view on the emergence of 'spontaneous order' through the establishment of social conventions. In fact, he argues—through a careful scrutiny of several views on 'salience' and 'focal points'—that successful (i.e. efficient) co-ordination can not be justified through a standard rational choice-theoretic argument. On the contrary, one-shot efficient co-ordination can only follow from a joint maximization approach on the part of the players as prescribed by a suitable convention. But this amounts to the introduction of a piece of moral-like, team-style reasoning which is apparently beyond the reach of conventional rational choice arguments: thus, on Sugden's account, success as measured in terms of individual preferences is achieved by deviating from standard rational behaviour.

The theme of efficient co-ordination and its prerequisites—along with other topics concerning ethics and rational interaction—is further reprised in the papers of the last section.

Sacco and Zamagni's chapter ('An Evolutionary Dynamic Approach to Altruism') explores this possibility to provide an evolutionary justification of altruism, using a simple one-shot contribution game. Sacco and Zamagni contend that an all-encompassing notion of self-interest is misleading, and that a firm distinction between self-interested and altruistic behaviour is therefore called for. Moreover, they offer a taxonomy of a few possible types of altruistic and egoistic behaviour as defined in terms of preferences over the relevant outcomes of the contribution game. The comparative performance of alternative types of egoists and altruists is assessed by studying the stationary distribution of types of a suitably defined replicator dynamics starting from the relevant two-type population, and relying on Nash equilibrium behaviour. It is shown that while some types of altruism are more resilient than others and can resist invasion by 'regretful egoists', only an extreme form of altruistic behaviour can survive against 'pure egoists'.

Hence, while genuinely altruistic preferences may well be something more than an inexplicable curiosum from an evolutionary perspective, it seems that in several cases purely egoistic preferences are likely to prove one of those facts one had better learn to live with. By studying to what extent rational strategic behaviour can be harnessed through clever mechanism design in order to induce socially desirable outcomes whatever the individual preferences, implementation theory is of considerable interest in that connection.

Vannucci's chapter ('Social Ethics and Implementation Theory') is a critical survey of some results concerning implementability of social norms by several alternative game-theoretic solution concepts of the 'eductive'—as opposed to 'evolutive'—variety. The focus is on social norms for democratic and efficient collective decision-making and for a fair distribution of the benefits from co-operation. The surveyed results clearly show that—in principle—such social norms are by and large implementable whatever solution concept is advocated. Since implementability amounts to a test of consistency between the prescriptions of social ethics and those of rational strategic behaviour, one may conclude that such prescriptions can be made consistent with each other through clever mechanism design. However, some kinds of game forms or mechanisms are better (i.e. more robust) than others at doing the job. In particular, drawing on the surveyed results,

Vannucci submits that consensual procedures are more effective than majoritarian ones in implementing democratic and efficient collective decisions.

Thus, implementation theory brings about both a positive message concerning the consistency of rational strategic behaviour and (certain) prescriptions of social ethics, and some valuable information concerning the nature of successful mechanisms. However, are we sure that we are employing the right notion of rationality? Why stick to 'eductive' solution concepts? What about the relationship between rationality and moral behaviour when the former is represented by solution concepts in a more 'evolutionary' vein?

Yaari's chapter ('Remarks on Rationality and Morality') offers a preliminary exploration of the possible import of 'evolutionary' theories of rational behaviour in explaining the emergence of co-operative and moral modes of behaviour. Yaari addresses the growing evidence of systematic 'co-operative' departures from Nash equilibrium behaviour in strategic interactions. He shares the Humean view according to which 'self-interest rationality' is compelling solely within the State of Nature. Moreover, he rejects the explanations of co-operation in terms of bounded rationality recently put forward by some game theorists: in his view, the institutional change towards the Humean 'civilized society' can not be modelled as the outcome of a mere 'imperfection' inserted into the State of Nature. Yaari outlines an alternative way out of 'co-operation' paradoxes. His approach, while calling for a fictitious 'referee' who combines the 'reaction functions' submitted by the players (and sorts out the relevant outcomes), avoids the difficulties inherent to the 'common knowledge' hypothesis, and results in a game in response functions which may or may not admit Nash response functions as its reasonable solutions. In fact, Yaari suggests that rationality be regarded as a relative notion, depending on the given evolving initial environment, so that an evolutionary approach is likely to prove best suited for explaining the emergence of a Humean 'civilized society'.

F.F.
F.H.
S.V.

I

FOUNDATIONAL ISSUES

1

Some Economical Reflections on Ethics

FRANK HAHN

I am not a philosopher, let alone a moral philosopher. Even worse, I have always had 'doubts' concerning arguments of welfare economists. So what follows is both idiosyncratic and ill-informed by a vast literature. I have thought on some of the main issues often for a considerable time, and this is the only inducement which I can offer to the reader to follow what I now have to say.

1

It would be nice to have a well-founded positive theory of ethics in the sense of providing an explanation rather than a justification of the prevailing values of a society. Of course there have been attempts at such a theory—certainly by evolutionists like Spencer and by what are sometimes called functionalists. But what I know of such theories does not inspire confidence. However, economists and especially game theorists have also made efforts in this direction.

A well-known procedure (Kurz) is to think of society as represented by a game and its ethical rules as an equilibrium of such a game. This equilibrium requires all participants to act according to the equilibrium rules. This is achieved by well-calibrated punishments for deviations. This does not strike one as very deep even when all the game-theoretic paraphernalia is displayed. For one thing it does not offer an account of the 'internalization' of the rules which often inhibits deviation independently of possible punishments. More technically—this theory takes 'pay-offs' as independently given. But apart from that there are many other problems. We are not told why one particular game rather than another is chosen. There may be many equilibria for any particular game (notoriously very many for this sort), so that at best we get an account of why people stick to the rules rather than an explanation of why these are what they are.

Recent work has much improved on these theories by giving an account of processes by which social norms are formed. These are learning and/or evolutionary theories formulated stochastically. One establishes stochastic convergence to an equilibrium of a game. This may itself be represented by a distribution over agents who make different choices. The processes need not be ergodic, so that detailed histories are required to account for any one outcome. (The interested reader should consult the literature, especially Canning (1989; 1990) and Peyton-Young (1993: 57–84). It is not possible to give very convincing verbal accounts, let alone proofs.)

I have been not only impressed by what has so recently been achieved but I have also been pleased to see economists sticking to their comparative advantage, which is bringing precision to imprecise questions. This, however, does not mean that I am unaware that all these efforts, however far they are taken, will always only provide very partial, albeit suggestive, answers. Theories of 'Society' whatever they are meant to accomplish are not a goal for reasonable men and women. What has been shown is that it is possible, in a more or less special setting, to study the evolution of social norms with not implausible results.

The status of ethical arguments in the light of these 'partial' theories is now of some interest. If these provide some account of how our ethical beliefs have been formed, then presumably they ought also to account for how we argue about them. The process which took us there is 'history', but even if we are not aware of it, can we, as it were, step outside? I am sure that this question is not new and I also have little doubt that I have no qualifications to attempt an answer. Indeed I suspect that very few economists are qualified for this task. Certainly, since I suppose that the question has considerable bearing on arguments supporting a 'relativistic ethic', it is not unimportant.

But for economists this 'philosophical' question is, I think, of minor importance. They are in quite another kind of fix. It can easily be stated. For much of economics concerned with 'ought' questions, one form or another of utilitarianism is the organizing principle. But what if citizens are not utilitarians? For instance, history may have left them with absolute religious foundations of right and wrong. Would not the underlying principle that it is the individual's assessment of his or her own satisfaction count against the application of a utilitarian ethic?

2

The first point to settle is the description of the domain of preferences if for the moment we grant that people do have preferences in the sense in which economists define them. There has been a good deal of confusion which arose from going straight to preferences before considering their domain (see Sen 1977: 317–44). The question ending the previous section can be formulated as: should the social and ethical norms of a society be included in the domain of preferences?

If the answer were to be 'no', the utilitarian economist would be in the somewhat strange situation of first claiming the primacy of preferences in ethical judgement and then that only preferences on a subdomain 'should count'. This attitude may be justified on certain grounds which I shall give. But it cannot be justified by the curious move made by Harsanyi (1982) who, in defence of a utilitarian ethic, urges us to ignore 'anti-social' preferences. That move begs far too many questions and certainly does so in a defence of a utilitarian ethic.

The defence of ignoring parts of the preference system might be called the 'pragmatic' defence. Thus it might be arguable that to some useful extent preferences are separable. For instance those between different kinds of foodstuffs *may* be independent of preferences over norms. (But think of orthodox Jews and Muslims for a mental test of the plausibility of this hypothesis.) Separability entails that orderings in one subspace of the domain are independent of where the agent is in other subspaces. If one is really pragmatic one could replace this by 'sufficiently independent' so that changes in the position in one space which are small leave the ordering in others unaffected. That is, 'local separability' may suffice.

Suffice for what? Suffice for a utilitarian resolution of some of the problems welfare economics studies. That is, it may suffice because it does not itself directly beg the question of why only part of individual preferences 'should count'. For instance, there may be neighbourhood around the existing norms such that for all such norms in that neighbourhood Pareto improvements accomplished in the commodity space are preferred by all citizens. What this means is that citizens might have utilitarian norms in one subspace or for certain neighbourhoods in that space without being utilitarian *tout court*. It is a defence which appeals to those of us who are willing to be traditional welfare economists when it comes to parking meters and indeed when pure Pareto improvements are contemplated but not prepared for this without serious doubts concerning logical coherence when it comes to grander matters.

A good example is provided by the utilitarian approach to income distribution. The proposal that high marginal utility of income citizens should receive transfers from those with low marginal utilities requires Benthamite ethics for its justification. Clearly there will be citizens who will not subscribe to this. Indeed, even in the 'initial position', there is no reason to expect agreement to this policy. For the initial position is described as leading to choices which are already in terms of utility. Why can we exclude the possibility that in that position some agents may not care about the utility which will go with one or the other of their identities, but only about the adopted rule being consonant with the will of God? And why should arguments from the initial position have any particular standing when it is possibly a historical and evolutionary process which provides us with the norms relevant to today's decision. For instance one might agree to slavery as an institution having carefully considered the utilities of being slave or master but disagree with it in the light of norms one knew nothing of in 'the initial' position.

But it is the lack of separability which the income distribution problem particularly illuminates. It could be argued that egalitarian societies will, or may, themselves change social norms—that is, separability will fail. Indeed many who have never heard of marginal utilities support greater equality on these grounds. They claim that more equal distributions go with norms in which benevolence and kindness between people is raised in the social ranking. They may be wrong, but it is noteworthy that the appeal is based on the dependence of subspace preferences on each other.

But there is another aspect of the pragmatic defence to which I have already alluded implicitly: the separability of instruments. I do not think that this point needs labouring. For instance the arguments for changing from a command to a market economy will not be able to appeal to separability. In such an argument the utilities of secret policemen and of functionaries may be ignored. But it is hard to see a utilitarian justification for this. That is, the change is such that it will have to be evaluated in the whole domain.

A similar problem arises in almost all applied welfare economic exercises which are confined to a single country. There is no immediately obvious utilitarian justification for ignoring the utilities of foreign agents. But since for instance every decision to increase expenditure on, say, public goods in a country means that there is less available for transfer to poor countries (with presumably higher marginal utilities of income), the question of how to take account of these utilities is not a remote one. One suspects that unstated social norms such as 'charity begins at home' need to be added to the kind of utilitarian calculations which are usual in welfare economics.

Indeed that this is the case is recognized in the literature on social welfare functions. The Benthamite sum of utilities as representing this function is required simply to leave out of the sum the utilities of those the welfare economist has decided not to consider. But there are welfare functions which run in terms of weighted utility sums. (For instance some American economists engage in welfare arguments on the basis of a 'representative agent' whose utility function is actually a weighted utility sum where the weights reflect the actual distribution of wealth.) But whatever is done, when we add or compare utilities we require a cardinalization, and the cardinalization adopted cannot in any straightforward way be provided by utilitarian arguments.

One famous attempt to do this none the less is by Harsanyi (1955: 309–21) who uses a version of the 'initial position' and utilizes the well-known von Neumann–Morgenstern cardinalization arising from attitudes to risk. This requires an assumption that agents' 'basic' preferences are the same, in the sense that they are representable by the same function. One certainly may permit oneself some doubt concerning this hypothesis. But even when that is suppressed the brute fact remains that a support for a particular cardinalization cannot find its justification on purely utilitarian grounds. It is not a closed system of ethics and at the very least needs some meta-utilitarian arguments to complete it. I return to this 'more philosophical' aspect later.

3

I think it is easy to agree that in any ethical judgement utilities 'matter' although this is some way from saying that they are decisive. But I want to re-emphasize the complexity and high dimension of the domain of utilities. Suppose that you are offered a sum of money by the secret police in an authoritarian state to betray your friend. What mental processes can we take to represent you as going through in deciding on your utilitarian answer? Certainly the loss in utility of your friend if betrayed by you is relevant. The secret policy may not be all that terrible. It is possible that the utility weight of the money on offer is also considered. But it would be surprising if the principle, 'it is wrong to betray a friend', were given no utility weight. The social norm will surely be given weight in the calculation. Indeed you may regard the estimate of the utility loss of the betrayed friend as hard to assess but one element of this loss will be that he has been betrayed by you, a friend. The social norm or the non-utilitarian prescription, it is wrong to betray a friend, can be expressed in utility terms but it is not clear that it will not lead to error or tautology. The error occurs if one supposes that 'every man has his price' since we know that to be false from numerous instances. The tautology is courted if one makes the *ad hoc* postulate that utility is bounded above in the direction of money (goods) but not, or differently, in the direction of the social norm. These specifications would add nothing to the argument and obscure the underlying reality.

I shall shortly draw some lessons from these considerations. But it is a little too early to leave fundamentals. In particular I have so far neglected questions of information and questions of 'mental power'.

Moral philosophers frequently make their case with reference to the thoughtful, reflective, and reasonable individual. It so happens that very many people are not of this sort. It seems non-utilitarian to proceed on the basis of utilities agents would have if indeed they were thoughtful, etc. This is a well-known problem and it is often discussed with reference to children. But there are millions who are unaccustomed to moral reflections and indeed could not carry them very far. That does not mean that they do not act morally, but they do so by accepting without analysis prevailing social norms. Of course that is not universally true. But in any case the fine properties of moral trade-offs may simply be beyond them.

The temptation is, as I have said, not to use actual but virtual utility functions to represent these agents. It hardly needs emphasizing that it is pretty *ad hoc* and that different 'thoughtful, etc.' manufacturers of virtual functions will derive different ones. These matters were and are at the centre of arguments concerning democracy. On the one hand one can point to the danger of the inept and inexperienced and indeed poorly informed possibly having a decisive say. On the other there are the dangers of (possibly just as inept) agents dictating the outcome. Some years ago these problems came to the fore on the mini-stage of universities. Should students, by definition as yet only poorly in command of their subject, have a voice in the appointment of professors or should it be done by those whose competence is already certified by their holding of university posts? Answers here were neither simple nor agreed. In particular there were differences of opinion amongst those who had been designated as competent to participate in the process on the grounds of their academic status. Norms of equity of personal respect and of efficiency were in conflict and eventually resolved by power. Utilitarian calculations in any of the more obvious meanings played little part.

It has always seemed to me that moral philosophers often leave their arguments uncompleted when they argue in terms of the thoughtful, etc. agent. At least they leave it uncompleted for anyone concerned with public and social policy and the design of institutions. For instance, the following Robertsonian argument is not often discussed. Precisely because moral choices are very hard to make in a 'thoughtful' way and because many people lack the mental equipment for doing so, institutions should be designed which minimize the need for such judgement. (They inevitably will still leave quite enough occasions for such judgements.) Thus it is far too hard to choose a career on the basis of its contribution to the 'good', or to decide on pricing or employment on this basis. It is of course this, much more than just efficiency, which is a powerful argument in favour of market economies. In its idealization there is no need to calculate the 'just' price or moral obligations to society when making economic decisions. This connection between this aspect and the argument that market economies promote liberty is too obvious to merit comment.

Of course market economies do not conform to the ideal and will in any case generate a host of 'moral' problems. The point to be made here is that these are almost all in the public domain. They are not of the sort: will I betray my friend for money?', but rather: is the distribution of income and wealth morally tolerable? or: should freedom be restricted for the sake of the environment or for the sake of children? etc. These questions are quite different from 'how should I live?' although no doubt one could establish a connection. Inevitably these 'public questions' will be the concern of public bodies like governments and committees of experts. They will also be argued by academics and by those with immediate relevant knowledge. For the majority the interest will lie largely in how they themselves are affected, although in the case of important social norms it may go beyond that. If these matters are to be decided on utilitarian grounds it is at best that virtual, or, even worse, guessed at, utilities will need to be employed. This seems to me as important a matter as whether utilitarian considerations should figure at all. Evidently a great deal of attention would need to be paid to the status of such 'pseudo-utilitarianism'.

It is somewhat depressing to find how little attention has been paid to matters of information and mental capacities by utilitarians and until recently by welfare economists. So far I have had the 'ideal thoughtful reflective' agent as my target. But there is a quite general question of the role of the expert in moral judgements. Welfare economists have a stylized picture. The expert announces what the possible choices are and then the moral agent the form a government with a social welfare function chooses amongst these possibilities. It must be rare for this scenario to be applicable. Importantly in many instances the expert does not know the possibilities but at best has beliefs concerning these, perhaps expressed in probabilities. Experts may differ over these. So the 'government's' social welfare function must include 'social risk attitudes'.

But now we notice that individual agents who are to be represented by the social welfare functions also have beliefs which concern outcomes of particular policies. These beliefs may be quite different from those of the experts. Does utilitarian ethic commit us to represent all of these beliefs as well as preferences in the social welfare function? It seems to me that the logic of the matter requires an affirmative answer. But that is surely not a comfortable conclusion: after all one would expect most beliefs to be inexpertly based and indeed sometimes to involve logical contradiction. It is surprising that relatively little attention has been paid to this matter. A distinction has been made between *ex ante* and *ex post* efficiency but there are no decisive arguments in favour of either.

In this connection Arrow's Impossibility Theorem is an interesting instance of my complaint. Of course it is a splendid intellectually satisfying result. But the vast literature which it has spawned rarely, perhaps never, discusses the question whether, if the theorem were not valid, we would care to act on the social preference ordering it would yield. That is, whether we would care to embody ignorance and false beliefs in this ordering. Perhaps the question is too 'élitist' and offends a prevailing norm that one must adhere to the fiction that all agents are equally capable of mental effort.

Returning to where I started in this section, I conclude that even very little reflection leads one to large unresolved complexities. In their light, the question, 'are you a utilitarian?', is not one which can be sensibly answered since one does not know how the questioner proposes to deal with conundrums in his definition.

4

I have left to the end a well-known problem: how should a utilitarian decide on what kind of preferences to encourage and what kind to discourage (say by means of education)? One answer might be that a utilitarian has no business with this problem: it is his contention that actual preferences give all the moral authority required. The difficulty with that answer is simply that it would be a dishonest answer, as will be obvious to the utilitarian when he observes himself in the role of parent. Moreover utilitarians like everyone else are ready to label some people as of 'bad' character and others as having a good one, and they surely do not employ these labels only by reference to externalities generated by one person in the utility of some others.

There are various more respectable answers which I have already touched upon in my discussion of virtual utilities. The question is whether these answers are derivable from a utilitarian ethic. In the final analysis it would seem that this can only be done in a literal Benthamite way: utility function *A* is a more efficient means to happiness than is utility function *B*. But this answer seems to commit one to a position which simply is not in accordance with our social norms. Thus for instance if, as is often maintained, the ignorant are happier than are the educated, then *cet. par.* we would wish to discourage a preference for education. And so on. No doubt there are some who will wish to distinguish between 'true' and 'superficial' happiness, but such a move is profoundly question-begging. My view is that there is no utilitarian answer to moral preferences over preferences in particular since possible ideas of 'choosing one's preferences' ultimately seem incoherent.

It would now seem that I have been arguing that traditional welfare economics has pretty shaky foundations. Indeed I have. But it would be wrong to conclude that I therefore advocate doing without it, or that I consider it worthless. On the contrary, it seems to me to provide some of the only firm ground in a swamp. The reason for this view is simple. Welfare economics provides arguments which are internally consistent and, above all, unambiguous. It thus provides a starting-point from which to venture forth in judging how secure a basis, *in that particular instance*, welfare economics provides. I have already compared its power in the case of, say, parking meters or road pricing with its much more feeble contribution to a debate on the desirability of market economies. But, as I have asserted before, welfare economic arguments are almost always a relevant ingredient without always being decisive. Certainly they are a considerable defence against all sorts of ideological foolishness.

On the other hand economists are, as the saying goes, 'only human'. That is, they find it as difficult as the next man to keep reasoned doubts firmly in the forefront. This often results in moral illiteracy best exemplified by the almost universal confusion between Pareto efficiency and social optimality. Far more than semantics is involved here as will be evident to, say, readers of Barro. But of course the trouble goes beyond that confusion, as it is bound to do when a closed ethical system is adopted. (Was it an accident that Bentham invented his beastly Panopticon?) So it may be that these sceptical notes will contribute a little to reducing the certainties of welfare economist which, as far as I can see, would be pretty desirable.

REFERENCES

Canning, D. (1989), 'Social Equilibrium', mimeo (Pembroke College, Cambridge University).

—— (1990), 'Social Equilibrium', Economic Theory Discussion Paper No. 152, (University of Cambridge).

Harsanyi, J. C. (1982), 'Utilitarianism', in A. K. Sen and B. Williams (1982), *Utilitarianism and Beyond* (Cambridge: Cambridge University Press).

—— (1955), 'Cardinal Welfare, Individualistic Ethics and Interpersonal Comparison of Utility', *Journal of Political Economy*, 63: 309–21.

Peyton Young, H. (1993), 'The Evolution of Conventions', *Econometrica*, 61/1: 57–84.

Sen, A. K. (1977), 'Rational Fools: A Critique of the Behavioural Foundations of Economic Theory', *Philosophy and Public Affairs*, 6: 317–44.

2

Morality and Incentives

JOHN C. HARSANYI

1. Particularistic individuals vs. universalistic morality

One of the basic concepts of economic theory is that of personal preferences, assumed to govern our everyday behaviour. As is well known, if a person's preferences satisfy certain rationality requirements then they can be represented by an ordinal utility function. If they satisfy some even stronger rationality requirements (in choosing between alternative lotteries) such as the von Neumann–Morgenstern (= vN–M) axioms (see von Neumann and Morgenstern 1953), then they can be represented also by vN–M utility functions. The latter have the nature of cardinal utility functions because they permit meaningful comparisons, not only between the relevant person's utility levels in different situations, but also between his various utility differences in moving from one situation to another. In what follows, I shall assume that people's preferences satisfy the vN–M axioms.[1]

Economists sometimes assume that people's preferences are completely selfish. But we all know that this is an oversimplification. First, many people and perhaps most people display considerable altruism, at least in dealing with members of their family and with their close friends. Indeed, they are often quite willing to provide some help and do some favours for many other people, including complete strangers, as long as this costs them only a little in time, effort, and money. But even if most people's preferences are not completely selfish, they are particularistic in the sense of giving more weight to their own interests and to those of their family members and friends than to those of other people.

In contrast, our moral value judgements are, or at least are expected to be, universalistic in the sense of impartially giving the same weight to everybody's interests. This fact can be expressed also by saying that our moral value judgements are guided by our moral preferences, defined as the preferences we would have if we made a special effort to look at social situations from an impersonal and impartial point of view.

[1] For justification of this assumption, see Harsanyi (1987: 545–58).

Adam Smith pointed out that the moral point of view is basically that of a sympathetic but impartial observer. (He actually spoke of a 'spectator' rather than an 'observer'.) In other words, the moral point of view is originally that of an outsider, not that of a direct participant. When people have conflicting interests, each of them will be tempted to judge the situation from his or her[2] one-sided, and often quite biased, perspective. Only an outsider, whose personal interests are not affected, will tend to take an impartial point of view. Any directly interested party will do so only if he makes a special effort to look at the situation with the eyes of an outside observer.

Thus, we live in a world where people's personal preferences are particularistic yet where most people's moral values are universalistic. One of the basic problems of ethics is how to induce people with highly particularistic natural inclinations to comply with the requirements of a universalistic morality. The need for economic (and non-economic) incentives is part of this more general problem.

I shall discuss both problems from the point of view of utilitarian and, more particularly, rule utilitarian theory because, for reasons I shall indicate, I am a supporter of this theory, and also because the latter provides a very clear picture of how universalistic and particularistic considerations interact in ethics.

More specifically, as we know, each individual's particularistic personal preferences are represented by his individual utility function. Utilitarian theory uses a social utility function (also called a social welfare function) to represent society's common interests as an embodiment of universalistic considerations. In the next section, I shall argue that this social utility function should be defined as the arithmetic mean of all individual utilities.[3]

2. An equi-probability model for a social utility function

Suppose that somebody tells me that he strongly prefers our capitalist system to a socialist system. When I ask him why he feels this way, he gives as his reason that in our present capitalist system he is a millionaire and has a very interesting and satisfying life whereas in a socialist system in all probability he would have a badly paid and utterly boring job in some branch of government bureaucracy. If he is right about his prospects in a socialist system then his strong preference for our present capitalist system is no doubt a rational preference from his own personal point of view. But

[2] In what follows, for stylistic reasons, in similar phrases I shall omit the female pronoun.

[3] Some utilitarian authors define the social utility function as the arithmetic mean of individual utilities, as I propose to do. Others define it as the sum of these utilities. In contexts where the number of individuals can be regarded as constant (which means that in all contexts other than discussions of optimal population policies), these two definitions are mathematically equivalent because, by maximizing one of these two quantities, one automatically maximizes the other as well.

it will be merely a personal preference based on self-interest, and obviously will not be a moral preference based on impersonal and impartial considerations.

On the other hand, suppose he would state his preference between the capitalist and the socialist system without knowing what his own social position would be in either social system. Indeed, suppose he would have to assume that he would end up with the same probability $\frac{1}{n}$ in any one of the n available social positions in either system. Then, his preference could not any longer be based on self-interest but could be based only on impersonal and impartial considerations and, therefore, would now fully qualify as a moral preference.

More particularly, suppose that society consists of n individuals. Let U_i be the vN–M utility function of individual i ($i = 1, \ldots, n$) so that his utility level in any given social situation S would be $U_i(S)$. (Of course, in our example, S can take only the values 'capitalist system' and 'socialist system'.) Let j be the individual trying to decide what his preference should be between the two social systems. Then, under our assumptions, j's expected utility for any given social situation S (or social system S) will be:

$$W_j(S) = \frac{1}{n} \sum_{i=1}^{n} U_j(S) \tag{1}$$

Moreover, according to the vN–M theory (and, indeed, according to any version of Bayesian decision theory), j will always choose that one of two social situations for which his expected utility, i.e. the quantity $W_j(S)$ takes the higher value; and, as I have argued, under the postulated conditions, his choice will always express his moral preference for the situation he chooses. This in turn means that j will use the quantity $W_j(S)$—defined by equation (1) as the arithmetic mean of all individual utilities $U_i(S)$—as his social utility function for evaluating alternative social situations, in accordance with utilitarian theory.

Of course, equation (1) will make sense only if j is able to make interpersonal comparisons of utility. This is necessary because the quantities $U_i(S)$ occurring on the right-hand side of the equation can be added up only if they are expressed in the same utility unit, and this can be done only if the various individuals' utilities are comparable (at least in terms of 'unit comparability') (see Harsanyi 1977: 51–60).

Now suppose that two different individuals j and j' both try to compute the social utility function. Since both of them will use equation (1) for this purpose, they will arrive at the same social utility function $W_j(S) = W_j{}'(S) = W(S)$, provided that they both know the various individuals' utility functions $U_j(S)$. They can disagree about the mathematical form of this social utility function only if one or both of them have insufficient information about the individual utility functions $U_i(S)$. In what follows, unless otherwise indicated, by the social utility function I shall always mean that one that a well-informed individual j would use.

3. Act utilitarianism and rule utilitarianism

There are two versions of utilitarianism, called act utilitarianism and rule utilitarianism. (The two terms are due to Brandt (1959) but the distinction itself goes back to Harrod (1937).) Since both of these are utilitarian theories, both agree that, in some suitable sense, the goal of all morality must be to serve the common interests of society by maximizing social utility or, more exactly, by maximizing expected social utility.[4]

Act utilitarianism is the view that a morally right action is simply one that would maximize expected social utility in the existing situation. In contrast, rule utilitarianism is the view that a morally right action must be defined in two steps. First, we must define the right moral rule as the moral rule whose acceptance would maximize expected social utility in similar situations. Then, we must define a morally right action as one in compliance with this moral rule.

Actually, reflection will show that in general we cannot judge the social utility of any proposed moral rule without knowing the *other* moral rules accepted by the relevant society. Thus, we cannot decide what the moral obligations of a father should be towards his children without knowing how the moral obligations of other relatives are defined towards these children. (We must ensure that somebody should be clearly responsible for the well-being of every child. On the other hand, we must not give conflicting responsibilities to different people with respect to the same child.)

Accordingly, it seems to be preferable to make society's moral code, i.e. the set of all moral rules accepted by the society, rather than individual moral rules, the basic concept of rule utilitarian theory. Thus, we may define the optimal moral code as the moral code whose acceptance would maximize expected social utility, and may define a morally right action as one in compliance with this moral code.

How should we interpret the term 'social acceptance' used in these definitions? Realistically, we cannot interpret it as full compliance by all members of the society with the accepted moral code (or moral rule). All we can expect is partial compliance, with a lesser degree of compliance in the case of a very demanding moral code. (Moreover, we may expect much more compliance in the moral judgements people make about each other's behaviour than in their actual behaviour.)

How will a rational utilitarian choose between the two versions of utilitarian theory? It seems to me that he must make his choice in terms of

[4] Here the adjective 'expected' is short for 'the mathematical expectation of'. We must speak of expected social utility rather than of social utility as such because we are considering the social effects of various individual actions as well as those of various moral rules and of various moral codes, and such effects are always highly uncertain.

the basic utilitarian choice criterion itself: he must ask whether a rule utilitarian or an act utilitarian society would enjoy a higher expected level of social utility.

Actually, the problem of choosing between the rule utilitarian and the act utilitarian approaches can be formally regarded as a special case of the rule utilitarian problem of choosing among alternative moral codes according to their expected social utility. For, when a rule utilitarian society chooses among alternative moral modes, the act utilitarian moral code (asking each individual to choose the social-utility maximizing action in every situation) is one of the moral codes available for choice.

Note that this fact already shows that the social-utility level of a rule utilitarian society, one using the optimal rule utilitarian moral code, must be at least as high as that of an act utilitarian society, using the act utilitarian moral code. Indeed, I shall argue that the social-utility level of a rule utilitarian society would be actually much higher than that of an act utilitarian society. I shall also discuss how the problem of economic and of non-economic incentives would be resolved in a rule utilitarian society.

4. The social effects of a socially accepted moral code

When a society accepts a given moral code, the most obvious effects of this will be the benefits people will obtain by other people's (and by their own) compliance with this moral code. These effects I shall call positive compliance effects.

Yet, compliance with any moral code—together with the fact that this compliance will always be somewhat incomplete—will give rise also to some social costs. These include the efforts needed to comply with specific injunctions of the moral code, in particular in some difficult situations; the guilt feelings and the social stigma that may follow non-compliance; loss of respect for the moral code if people see widespread non-compliance; and the efforts needed to inculcate habits consistent with the moral code in the next generation (see Brandt 1979: 287–9). These effects I shall call negative compliance effects. They will be particularly burdensome in the case of a very demanding moral code and may make adoption of such a moral code unattractive even if it would have very attractive positive compliance effects.

Another important group of social effects that a moral code will produce are its expectation effects. They result from the fact that people will not only themselves comply with the accepted moral code to some degree but will expect *other* people likewise to comply with it. This expectation may give them incentives to socially beneficial activities, and may give them some assurance that their interests will be protected. Accordingly, I will divide the expectation effects of a moral code into incentive effects and assurance effects. As we shall see, these two classes of expectation effects are extremely important in determining the social utility of any moral code. It is all the more surprising that so far they have received hardly any attention in the literature of ethics.

5. The negative compliance effects of act utilitarian morality

In section 1 I argued that people's personal preferences are particularistic because they tend to give much greater weight to their own, their family members', and their closest friends' interests than they tend to give to other people's interests; but that they often make moral value judgements based on universalistic criteria, giving the same weight to everybody's interests. As a result, the utility function U_i of any individual i will be quite different from its social utility function W_j since the former will be particularistic while the latter will be universalistic. A world like ours where people's personal preferences and their utility functions are particularistic I shall call a particularistic world.

In contrast, imagine a world where even people's personal preferences and their utility functions would be universalistic. In such a world, each individual's utility function U_i would be *identical* with his social utility function W_j. Indeed, assuming that different individuals would define their society's interests in the same way, different individuals' social utility functions would be likewise identical. Such an imaginary world I shall call a universalistic world.

In a universalistic world, people would have no difficulty in following the act utilitarian moral code. To be sure, the latter would require them in every situation to choose the action maximizing social utility. But since for them maximizing social utility would be the same thing as maximizing their own individual utility, they could easily comply with this requirement without going against their own natural inclinations.

Yet things are very different in our own particularistic world. Even those of us who try to comply with some moral code will tend in each situation to choose, among the actions permitted by our moral code, the one maximizing our individual utility. But act utilitarian morality would require a radical shift in our basic attitudes and in our everyday behaviour. It would require complete replacement of maximizing our individual utility by maximizing social utility as our choice criterion for all our decisions.

Clearly, this would amount to suppressing our particularistic personal preferences, our personal interests, and our personal commitments to our family and our friends, for the rigidly universalistic principles of act utilitarian morality. Such a complete suppression of our natural inclinations could be done, if it could be done at all, only by extreme efforts and at extremely high psychological costs. In other words, act utilitarian morality would have intolerably burdensome negative compliance effects.

In contrast, compliance with a rule utilitarian moral code would not pose any such problems. The latter would be basically a greatly improved and much more rational version of conventional morality, and compliance with it would require much the same effort as compliance with conventional morality does. No doubt, it would require us in many cases to give precedence to other people's interests and to society's common interests over our personal preferences, concerns, and interests. But in most cases it would let us follow our own preferences, concerns, and interests.

6. The value of free individual choice

One aspect of the negative compliance effects of act utilitarian morality would be its social-utility maximization requirement in every situation, that is, its insistence on the highest possible moral performance at every instant of our life. We would not be permitted to relax, or to do what we would like to do, even for one moment. If I were tempted to read a book or to go for a leisurely walk after a tiring day, I would always have to ask myself whether I could not do something more useful to society, such as doing some voluntary work for charity (or perhaps trying to convert some of my friends to utilitarian theory) instead. This of course means that, except in those rare cases where two or more actions would equally produce the highest possible social utility, I would never be permitted a free choice between alternative actions.

This also means that act utilitarian theory could not accommodate the traditional, and intuitively very appealing, distinction between merely doing one's duty and performing a supererogatory action going beyond the call of duty. For we would do only our duty by choosing an action maximizing social utility, and by doing anything else we would clearly fail to do our duty.

In contrast, a rule utilitarian moral code could easily recognize the intrinsic value of free individual choice. Thus, suppose I have a choice between action A, yielding the social utility α, and action B, yielding the social utility β, with $\alpha > \beta$. In this case, act utilitarian theory would make it my duty to choose action A. But a rule utilitarian moral code could assign a procedural utility to free moral choice. This would make me morally free to choose between A and B as long as $\beta + \gamma \geq \alpha$. Nevertheless, because $\alpha > \beta$, A would remain the morally preferable choice. Thus, I would do my duty both by choosing A and by choosing B. Yet, by choosing the morally preferable action A, I would go *beyond* merely doing my duty and would perform a supererogatory action.

7. Morally protected rights and obligations, and their expectation effects

The moral codes of civilized societies recognize some individual rights and some special obligations[5] that cannot be overridden merely because by

[5] By special obligations I mean moral obligations based on one's social role (such as one's obligations as a parent, or as a teacher, or as a doctor, or as a citizen, etc.) or on some past

overriding them one could here and now increase social utility—except possibly in some very special cases where fundamentally important interests of society are at stake. I shall describe these as morally protected rights and obligations.

As an example of individual rights, consider a person's property rights over a boat he owns. According to our accepted moral code (and also according to our legal rules), nobody else can use this boat without the owner's permission in other than some exceptional cases (say, to save a human life). The mere fact that use of the boat by another person may increase social utility (because he would derive a greater utility by using the boat than the owner would) is not a morally acceptable reason for him to use the boat without the owner's consent.

Even though, as we have seen, the direct effect of such property rights will often be to prevent some actions that might increase social utility, their indirect effects, namely their expectation effects, make them into a socially very useful institution. They provide socially desirable incentives to hard work, saving, investment, and entrepreneurial activities. They also give property owners assurance of some financial security and of some independence of other people's goodwill. (Indeed, as a kind of assurance effect benefiting society as a whole, widespread property ownership contributes to social stability, and is an important guarantee of personal and political freedom.)

As an example of special obligations, consider a borrower's obligation to repay the borrowed money to the lender, except if this would cause extreme hardship. In some cases, in particular when the borrower is very poor whereas the lender is very rich, by repaying the money the borrower will substantially decrease social utility because his own utility loss will greatly exceed the lender's utility gain (since the marginal utility of money to very poor people tends to be much higher than the marginal utility of money to very rich people). Nevertheless, it is a socially very beneficial moral (and legal) rule that loans must be repaid (even in the case of very poor borrowers and very rich lenders) because otherwise people would have a strong incentive not to lend money. Poor people would particularly suffer by being unable to borrow money if it were known that they would not have to repay it. The rule that loans must be repaid will also give lenders some assurance that society's moral code will protect their interests if they lend money.

Since a rule utilitarian society would choose its moral code by the criterion of social utility, it would no doubt likewise choose a moral code recognizing many morally protected rights and obligations, in view of their very beneficial expectation effects. But an act utilitarian society could not do this. This is so because act utilitarian morality is based, not on choosing

event (such as having made a promise or a contract, or on having incurred an obligation of gratitude to a benefactor, and so on).

between alternative moral codes, but rather on choosing between alternative individual actions in each situation. Therefore, the only expectation effects to which it could pay attention would be those of individual actions and not those of entire moral codes. Yet, normally an individual action will have negligibly small expectation effects. If people know that their society's moral code does protect, or does not protect, property rights, this will have a substantial effect on the extent to which they will expect property rights to be respected in the future. In contrast, an act utilitarian society would know that violation of somebody's property rights in one particular case would have little or no effect on people's expectations. Hence, an act utilitarian society would have no reasons to respect property rights and, more generally, to recognize morally protected rights and obligations.

Yet, in fairness to act utilitarian theory, a consistent act utilitarian would not really regret the absence of morally protected rights and obligations from his society. For he would not really mind if what we would consider to be his individual rights were violated, or if what we would consider to be special obligations owed to him were infringed, if this were done to maximize social utility—because maximization of social utility would be the only thing he would actually care about.

8. The advantages of the rule utilitarian approach

To conclude, most of us would very much prefer to live in a rule utilitarian society rather than in an act utilitarian society. For one thing, we would very much prefer to live in a society whose moral code permitted us within reasonable limits to make our own choices, and to follow our own personal preferences and interests as well as our personal commitments to the people we most cared for. In other words, we would prefer to live under a moral code with much less burdensome negative compliance effects than the act utilitarian moral code would have.

For another thing, we would much prefer to live in a society whose moral code recognized individual rights and special obligations that may not be overridden for social-expediency considerations, except possibly in some rare and special cases. We would feel that in such a society our interests would be much better protected, and that society as a whole would benefit from the desirable expectation effects of such a moral code.

The fact that most of us would definitely prefer to live in a rule utilitarian society is a clear indication that most of us would expect to enjoy a much higher level of individual utility under a rule utilitarian moral code than under an act utilitarian moral code. Yet, social utility can be defined as the arithmetic mean (or as the sum) of individual utilities. Therefore, we have very good reasons to expect that the level of social utility would be likewise much higher in a rule utilitarian society than it would be in an act utilitarian society.

Both act utilitarianism and rule utilitarianism are consequentialist theories because both of them define morally right behaviour ultimately in terms of its consequences with respect to social utility. This gives both versions of utilitarianism an important advantage over non-consequentialist theories because it gives them a clear and readily understandable rational criterion for the solution of moral problems—something that non-consequentialist theories of morality altogether lack, and that they have to replace by vague references to our 'moral intuitions' or to our 'sense of justice' (see e.g. Rawls 1971: 48–51). As I have tried to show, even though both versions of utilitarianism are based on the same consequentialist choice criterion, the rule utilitarian approach has important advantages over the act utilitarian approach. At a fundamental level, all these advantages result from the much greater flexibility of the rule utilitarian approach. As we have seen, whereas the rule utilitarian approach is free to choose its moral code from a very large set of possible moral codes, the act utilitarian approach is restricted to one particular moral code within this set.

Yet this means that act utilitarianism is committed to evaluate each individual action directly in terms of the consequentialist utilitarian criterion of social-utility maximization. In contrast, rule utilitarianism is free to choose a moral code that judges the moral value of individual actions partly in terms of non-consequentialist criteria if use of such criteria increases social utility. Thus, it may choose a moral code that judges the moral value of a person's action not only by its direct social-utility yield but also by the social relationship between this person and the people directly benefiting or directly damaged by his action, by this person's prior promises or other commitments, by procedural criteria, and so on. Even if consequentialist criteria are used, they may be based not only on the social consequences of one individual action but also on the consequences of a morally approved social practice of similar behaviour in all similar cases. This greater flexibility in defining the moral value of individual actions will permit adoption of moral codes with significantly higher social utility.

This completes my general comments about the nature of rule utilitarian theory. Now I propose to discuss the problem of incentives, and the approach used both by rule utilitarian theory and by conventional morality to deal with this problem.

9. The problem of incentives

Presumably, in a universalistic world, people would need no special incentives to do their jobs properly and, more generally, to act in accordance with society's best interests. But in our own particularistic world, many socially important jobs would be left undone or would be done in a very unsatisfactory manner if society did not appeal to people's own particularistic personal interests by providing economic (and non-economic) incentives to good performance.

There is a particular need for adequate incentives in activities requiring special effort, in the form of very hard work, careful thinking, initiative, and imagination, or a willingness to take risks, and so on. The same is true about activities requiring special abilities, whether native or acquired, not only to ensure high performance by people already engaged in these activities but also to encourage other people with the required talents and skills to participate in them.

A dramatic illustration for the importance of adequate economic incentives was the remarkable upsurge in agricultural production in mainland China and in Hungary (which at that time was still a communist country) when farmers were permitted to sell their produce at free markets and to retain most of their earnings. Many farmers responded by working much harder and often for very long hours, by taking the initiative in adopting better farming methods, and by investing a sizeable proportion of their still very low incomes in making their work more productive.

Of course, it depends on a society's basic moral attitudes as expressed in its moral code whether it can provide the needed incentives. For this to be feasible:

(1) Its moral code must approve and admit the justness of remuneration strongly dependent on performance.

(2) Its moral code (as well as its legal system) must recognize individual rights and special obligations that will give rise to suitable incentive effects and assurance effects (see section 7 above). For instance, both the moral code and the legal system must protect people's right to personal safety, must enforce property rights, contractual obligations, and at least a minimum level of honesty in economic transactions.

(3) Society's moral code must require the government to ensure an acceptable standard of living for everybody, if necessary by redistributing income from the relatively well-to-do to the poor, without unduly weakening economic incentives, *either* for the well-to-do, who have to pay higher taxes to defray the costs of such policies, *or* for the poor who are the beneficiaries of such policies. Indeed, these policies must be implemented in a way providing strong incentives for these poor people to improve their own social and economic positions both by their own effort and by making better use of the educational, vocational-training, medical, and other social services available to them.[6]

It is easy to see that the act utilitarian moral code fails to satisfy requirement (1) because it is a maximalist moral code, requiring all of us to

[6] To be sure, in many countries the more fundamental problem is the inadequacy of the educational and other social services available. Yet, even in such cases, this problem is further aggravated by our inability to motivate the people most in need of these services to make better use of what is in fact available.

put forward the highest possible performance all the time, even in the absence of any special rewards (see sections 5 and 6). (Further reflection will show that it fails to satisfy also requirement (2).) In contrast, both the rule utilitarian moral code and conventional common-sense morality satisfy all three requirements. On the other hand, many conservatives and libertarians (see e.g. Nozick 1974, *passim*) oppose any form of income redistribution, which means that their moral attitudes fail to satisfy requirement (3).

Finally, one of the leading American moral philosophers, John Rawls, has proposed a new interpretation of the concept of justice, inconsistent with requirement (1). I shall discuss Rawls's theory in section 10.

10. Rawls's theory of justice

According to the traditional common-sense conception of justice, which Rawls calls the 'system of liberal equality' (Rawls 1971: 65–6),[7] not only social expediency, based on the common interests of society, but also justice itself require us to reward people making superior contributions to our common good by social recognition and in many cases also by more tangible benefits. They deserve such rewards regardless of whether their superior contributions were based on their special abilities, native or acquired, or were based on their special efforts, or both.

Rawls rejects this view, obviously because he considers it to be insufficiently egalitarian. Instead, he proposes a novel conception of justice, which he calls the system of democratic equality (ibid.). He admits that, as a matter of social expediency, we should reward people making superior contributions so as to give them an incentive to continued high performance. But he insists that they do not deserve any special rewards strictly as a matter of justice.

According to Rawls, the reason is that people do not deserve even moral credit for their superior contributions. For if what enabled them to make these contributions were their special talents then they do not deserve moral credit because they owe their talents, not to personal merit, but rather to their good luck of having a favourable genetic endowment. But even if their contributions were based on their special efforts, they do not deserve moral credit. For what enabled them to make these efforts was their good character, which again they do not owe to personal merit but rather to the good luck of having been brought up in a favourable social environment (ibid. 100–4).

This is a very strange doctrine indeed. No doubt, talented people do not deserve any moral credit for their native talents as such. But they surely deserve moral credit for developing their talents, and for using them for the benefit of society.

[7] All my references in this section will be to Rawls (1971).

By the same token, people who have good character do deserve moral credit for their character, and for the efforts they make, and for the other desirable activities they perform owing to their good character. No doubt, a favourable social environment makes it much easier for us to acquire good character. Nevertheless, even for people brought up under very favourable social conditions, having good character is an important personal achievement, which is clearly to their moral credit.

When Rawls tries to deny this, he is implicitly denying that people have free will and are morally responsible for their actions and for their character; and he is adopting some form of 'hard' determinism,[8] without saying so, and without offering any argument in favour of this, rather unusual, philosophic position.

By denying that people with special talents and/or with good character deserve any moral credit and any social recognition for their valuable services to society, he is first of all very unfair to them. At the same time, he also sends them the socially very undesirable message that society does not really appreciate their contributions and would actually prefer it if the comfortable quiet of a Philistine acceptance of general mediocrity were never disturbed by upsetting instances of individual excellence and of superior performance. At a time when it is vitally important for every country to encourage its citizens, both those with outstanding abilities and those with lesser abilities, to develop their personal talents up to the very limit of their abilities,[9] and to acquire the character traits they need for creditable performance in their jobs, in their other social roles, and in public life, this is clearly the wrong message to send.

It is one of the basic tasks of moral and political philosophy to reconcile respect for the basic equality of all human beings with respect for individual differences and for individual excellence. To perform this task it needs a better balance between a concern for egalitarian considerations and the need for proper incentives to superior performance than provided by Rawls's theory.

11. Conclusion

The incentive problem gives rise to an important dilemma. On the one hand, if society wants to enjoy high levels of economic prosperity, of economic

[8] Determinism is the view that people's behaviour is ultimately determined (at least probabilistically) by their genetic make-up and by their social and natural environment. We speak of soft or of hard determinism according as determinism is or is not considered to be compatible with free will and with moral responsibility.

[9] By encouraging all people to develop their personal talents up to the very limit of their abilities, we may actually increase the difference between the performance of very able and of less able individuals. But we simply cannot afford to adopt educational policies that actually discourage the ablest individuals artificially from reaching their full potential, as many schools now do both in America and in some European countries. We need as many well-educated and creative individuals as we can get.

growth, and of cultural achievements, then it must provide economic (and other) incentives to superior performance. On the other hand, if it does so then it will create some economic and social inequalities—even though relatively small inequalities, probably much smaller ones than we actually have today, might be quite sufficient. (In any case, the existence of very poor, and of very rich people, especially those with inherited wealth and without any socially useful activity, can only weaken socially desirable incentives.)

It seems to me that we cannot avoid the conclusion that society can provide the needed incentives only if people are willing to accept the fact that people who work particularly hard, and those who show initiative and entrepreneurial ability or have other special talents, will often earn higher than average incomes—even without doing anything immoral or illegal or contrary to the public interest. If we can believe the newspapers, then one major obstacle to economic reform in the former Soviet Union is that the general public there is still unwilling to accept this fact.

REFERENCES

Brandt, R. B. (1959), *Ethical Theory* (Englewood Cliffs: NJ Prentice-Hall).

—— (1979), *A Theory of the Good and the Right* (Oxford: Clarendon Press).

Feiwel, G. R. (1987) (ed.), *Arrow and the Ascent of Modern Economic Theory* (New York: New York University Press).

Harrod, R. F. (1937), 'Utilitarianism revised', *Mind*, 45: 137–56.

Harsanyi, J. C. (1977), *Rational Behavior and Bargaining Equilibrium in Games and Social Situations* (Cambridge: Cambridge University Press).

—— (1987), 'Von Neumann–Morgenstern utilities, risk taking and welfare', in Feiwel (1987).

Neumann, J., von and Morgenstern, O. (1953), *Theory of Games and Economic Behavior* (Princeton: Princeton University Press).

Nozick, R. (1974), *Anarchy, State and Utopia* (Oxford: Basic Blackwell).

Rawls, J. (1971), *A Theory of Justice* (Cambridge, Mass.: Harvard University Press).

3

On Trade-Offs between Values

STEVEN LUKES

I begin with three commonplaces, namely: (*a*) that values are plural, (*b*) that plural values may conflict, and (*c*) that choice between conflicting plural values consists in a trade-off between them.

Each of these apparent truisms has, nevertheless, been denied. (*a*) was denied by Plato, or so at least Aristotle thought when he insisted, against the 'Platonists', that 'of honour, wisdom and pleasure, the accounts are distinct and diverse. The good, therefore, is not some common element answering to one Idea'.[1] Some utilitarians deny it, as indeed do all those 'monists' who insist on the descriptive homogeneity of the objects of value. Indeed, its denial used to be a commonplace, but it is so no longer.[2] It now seems increasingly to be accepted as obvious that things, or options, or states of affairs may be valuable in ways that cannot be reduced to a single way. As Max Weber (1948 edn.: 147–8) remarked, we have known since Nietzsche that something can be beautiful, not only in spite of the aspect in which it is not good, but rather in that very aspect. You will find this expressed in the *Fleurs du Mal* as Baudelaire named his volume of poems. It is commonplace to observe that something may be true although it is not beautiful and not holy and not good.

Moreover, within the moral sphere, it is, as Bernard Williams (1973*a*: 183) argues, 'surely falsifying of moral thought to represent its logic as demanding that in a conflict situation one of the conflicting oughts must be totally rejected': one may 'act for the best' and yet commit an uncancelled wrong (which one may rationally regret). And finally, values are not only plural, in the sense of irreducibly diverse: they are also internally so. Even simple pleasures consist in diverse component aspects.

(*b*) arises when alternatives instantiating different values are mutually incompatible: when one excludes the other or more of one means less of the other. Professor Hirschman has labelled this the 'jeopardy thesis', seeing it

[1] Aristotle (1954 edn.: 9–10). I do not mean to take sides here on the controversial issue of whether Aristotle was an ethical 'pluralist'.

[2] See e.g. the various writings of Sir Isaiah Berlin, Nagel (1979), Williams (1985), Taylor (1982), MacIntyre (1981), Stocker (1990), Raz (1986).

as a typical component of the 'rhetoric of reaction': examples are 'Democracy imperils Liberty' and 'The Welfare state imperils Liberty and Democracy or both'. In characterizing it, Hirschman recalls the famous chapter heading of Victor Hugo's *Notre Dame de Paris*, 'Ceci tuera cela', and he attributes its appeal to what he calls a 'stubborn "zero-sum mentality" ' (Hirschman 1991: 85, 121, 122). One way of denying (*b*) in particular cases is to propose that the alternatives in question may not conflict, but rather, in various ways, mutually support one another: to argue, in other words, 'that an already established reform or institution A would be strengthened rather than weakened (as in the jeopardy claim), by projected reform or institution B, that B's enactment is required to give robustness and meaning to A, that B is needed as a complement to A' (Hirschman 1991: 124). Or the conflict may be illusory: it may be possible to advance along both fronts.[3] These kinds of argument are typical of left-wing and progressive rebuttals of the jeopardy thesis. But there is another way of calling (*b*) into question: by suggesting that the values instantiated by incompatible alternatives are not themselves incompatible but rather, in various ways, interdependent. That is the line of thought I shall develop in the first part of what follows.

(*c*) asserts that when a choice must be made between incompatible alternatives instantiating different values, such a choice is best described by using the metaphor of a 'trade-off': that the market provides an appropriate model for understanding decision-making in such cases.[4] I shall argue that it is not always appropriate and try to say something about when it is and when it is not.

I shall, therefore, take (*a*) for granted. I shall suggest that (*b*) does not adequately describe central cases thought to exemplify it. And I shall argue that where values do conflict, (*c*) can be a poor way to think about how we make sense of some of our choices and a poor guide to how we should make them.

1. Interdependence of values

When values clash, this may be because they are mutually inconsistent, or it may be because they yield incompatible alternatives for action, given the way the world is. The latter is, for example, what Sir Isaiah Berlin had in mind when he wrote that 'ends may clash irreconcilably':

> Should democracy in a given situation be promoted at the expense of individual freedom, or equality at the expense of artistic achievement, or mercy at the expense

[3] See Blinder (1987: 31): 'For decades, economists have emphasised the fundamental trade-off between equity and efficiency . . . for the most part, I ignore such painful trade-offs in this book . . . our present policies are so far from right that the need to trade equity for efficiency disappears. Most of the policies advocated in this book enhance both efficiency and equity.' But see below on this particular alleged trade-off.

[4] See Macpherson (1985). Macpherson's argument is different from that advanced here.

of justice, or spontaneity at the expense of efficiency, or happiness, loyalty, innocence at the expense of knowledge and truth? The simple point which I am concerned to make is that when alternative values are irreconcilable, clear-cut solutions cannot in principle be found. (Berlin 1969: pp. xlix–1)

But where the latter relation holds, it may turn out that the 'values' said to be in conflict—the goods that alternative options embody—are interdependent. Consider the cases of equality versus efficiency and equality versus liberty

Equality vs. efficiency[5]

The idea that these two values are in conflict and must therefore be traded off has long been a commonplace among economists. Arthur Okun, Chairman of the Council of Economic Advisers under President Johnson, published his book *Equality and Efficiency: The Big Tradeoff* in 1975, in which he described it as 'our biggest socio-economic tradeoff, one which 'plagues us in dozens of dimensions of social policy' (Okun 1975: 2)—words quoted in recent editions of Samuelson's *Economics* (Samuelson 1989: 804) to support the idea that there is a tension between democracy and market capitalism. 'For decades', according to Alan Blinder (1987: 31), 'economists have emphasised the fundamental trade-off between equity and efficiency'. But is it, after all, so clear what is to be traded for what, and, in particular, whether 'efficiency' can be understood as conflicting, and thus tradeable, with equality or equity? (In the following discussion I shall not distinguish between 'equality' and 'equity', since for this purpose the distinction between them does not matter. The question is: can 'efficiency' be traded off against either?)

Efficiency, on its most natural interpretation, is a secondary objective. It is, one might say, an adverbial quality: one pursues this or that goal more or less efficiently. I can, of course, speak of efficiency as such and value it in, say, a person or a certain way of organizing production or a bureaucracy, but only because what they are efficient *at* is understood. So, for this remarkably simple reason, I agree with Le Grand (1990: 560) when he writes that 'efficiency is not an objective in the sense in which equity is an objective, rather it is a secondary objective that only acquires meaning with reference to primary objectives such as equity'. To speak of a conflict or trade-off between equality or equity and efficiency makes little sense if one's primary objectives include equality and equity. More generally, the very idea of 'efficiency' is, as philosophers used to say, 'parasitic': it presupposes an objective or set of objectives. Professor Atkinson (1991: 14) has suggested that it could be interpreted as meaning 'making the best use of scarce resources' and thus be treated as a fundamental objective. But how can we escape the need for an objective or set of objectives that define what the 'best' uses or

[5] The argument of this section is much indebted to Le Grand (1990: 554–68).

resources consists in? I think that Le Grand (1990: 560) is right in saying that 'efficiency can be defined only in relation to the ability of forms of social and economic organisation to attain their primary objectives and that therefore efficiency cannot itself be one of those primary objectives'.

Often, however, 'efficiency' is really a code for one of those objectives—usually aggregate economic growth. I suspect that this is most often what is meant when the trade-off in question is referred to, as in the case of Okun's book. But why not then speak directly about a trade-off between growth and equality or equity? I suspect that there may be some rhetorical advantage in using the language of efficiency instead. Perhaps it is that doing so suggests both that economic growth is in itself most efficient in securing a range of implicit social values, such as individual want satisfaction, social stability, technical progress, democracy, and, perhaps, equity, and that welfare programmes and redistributive policies are relatively inefficient, and even counter-productive, at doing so.

There are other possible interpretations of 'efficiency'. One is Pareto optimality. In that case, the suggestion is that the conflict, and thus trade-off, occurs between equal or equitable outcomes and Pareto-optimal ones. But Pareto optimality is a welfarist idea, embodying a social welfare function, ruling out non-welfarist objectives, such as those based on freedom or rights, or invoking merit or desert. Indeed, as Le Grand (1990: 566) has suggested, investigations of the trade-off between various interpretations of equity Pareto optimality are not really concerned with the trade-off between equity and efficiency at all. Instead, they are investigating what is, at least in part, actually a trade-off between two different kinds of equity: that whose properties are being explored and that embodied in the Pareto social welfare function. From which I conclude that this famous, supposed trade-off between equality or equity and efficiency is never quite what it seems to be. It is either incoherent or else it is a coded way of referring to other trade-offs between equality or equity and other values, which may well include other conceptions of equity.

Equality vs. liberty[6]

It is often said that equality and liberty must conflict, and that more of one must mean less of the other. Libertarians typically claim that more equality means less liberty, but this thought is widespread, as is its apparent corollary that they must be traded off or weighed against one another. Thus Sir Isaiah Berlin (1969: 170) observed that 'the extent of a man's, or a people's liberty to choose to live as they desire must be weighed against the claims of many other values, of which equality, or justice, or security, or public order are perhaps the most obvious examples'.

[6] See Lukes (1991).

But the question is: are equality and liberty related in this way? The idea that they are relies on the following picture: that these are discrete, free-standing, and independently characterizable values the extent of whose realization can in any case be measured according to some scale that enables the agent engaged in evaluation to express a preference between such 'extents' or else indifference between them. How plausible is this picture?

The answer depends on how one answers Amartya Sen's famous question: 'Equality of What?' (1982*a*). The simplest, and most naïve answer, is welfare or utility, whether conceived as happiness or the satisfaction of desire, but this answer fails, as Rawls and other have shown, above all in the face of the objection that it would unjustly compensate those with expensive tastes for which they could be held responsible. All the other, more plausible accounts of what is fundamental to equality—of what those who seek more equality seek to equalize—include various liberties as an essential, constitutive part of the equalizandum. Surveying recent discussions, this is true of Rawls's primary goods (1972: 62, 92), Dworkin's resources (1981: 303), Sen's basic capabilities (1983: 5, 16, 21), Arneson's opportunity for welfare (1989: 77–93), and Cohen's access to advantage (1989: 906–44). In short, all plausible answers to Sen's question include as central components those aspects of the circumstances of persons that maintain or expand their range of significant choices, and almost all focus explicitly on the notion of opportunity. Indeed, Sen himself describes his favoured notion of a person's 'capabilities'—'the various alternative functioning bundles he or she can achieve through choice'—as 'the natural candidate for reflecting the idea of freedom to do'. His central concern is with those human interests he calls 'advantage', as opposed to 'well-being'. 'Advantage', he writes, is a notion which deals with 'a person's real opportunities compared with others' and is a "freedom" type notion' (Sen 1983: 27, 5, 6). All these accounts—and, I submit, all plausible accounts—of what is to be equalized see freedom, meaning the availability of significant options of choice, as integral to equality. In short, egalitarians largely seek to equalize liberties.

So what is at issue here is, in large part, a change from one distribution of (some set of) liberties to another. There are plainly liberties, such as freedom of speech, that can be seen as public goods, used by all in such a way that use by one does not detract from use by another, and others, such as freedom of association, that require use by others to be effective. But suppose that the postulated relation holds. There are then six possibilities. As (some set of) liberties for all becomes more equal, there will be a reduction in (1) the same liberties of some, (2) other liberties of some, (3) the overall liberty of some, (4) the same liberties of all, (5) other liberties of all, and (6) the overall liberty of all. Possibility (1) describes the case of effective property rights or use rights, where previous owners or users lose their exclusive rights. (6) describes the extreme Hayekian thesis of 'the road to serfdom'. But the important point is that in all these cases—except for the extreme case of (6)—the verdict on the prospects for liberty after equalization remains open. This is so, even if, as here assumed, equalization reduces the liberties asserted in (1)–(5), since these at most show the existence of a trade-off between the liberties indicated. The verdict on liberty awaits an assessment of all those liberties which survive or are unaffected by the postulated trade-offs. And of course egalitarians urge that the equalization of conditions, including liberties, often enhances the scope of, and gives reality to, other liberties that would otherwise be worth little.

I conclude that the alleged conflict, and trade-off, between equality and liberty also turns out to be other than it seems—a conflict between alternatives that this formula fails to capture. The choice in question is rather between particular distributions of various goods, including various liberties. Equalizing policies will equalize some of these, at the cost, or to the benefit, of others.

2. Choice as trade-off

When faced with a choice between alternatives, trade-offs occur when one is exchanged for another because they are taken to be equal in value. But what if the alternatives in question instantiate plural and conflicting values? Le Grand (1990: 556) has usefully distinguished between two kinds of trade-off that are relevant here: a production trade-off and a value trade-off. In the former, what is at issue is 'production-substitutability', that is, 'the ability of a welfare programme or of other aspects of the economic and social system to deliver different combinations of objectives'. This idea is an extension of the idea of productive capacity to produce goods and services: what combinations of, say, equity and economic growth can a certain type of economy (given the distribution and structure of actors' objectives) produce? In a value trade-off, there is 'value-substitutability', the idea of which has been expounded by Brian Barry (1965: 6) as follows:

> The fundamental idea . . . is that although two principles need not be reducible to a single one, they may normally be expected to be to some extent substitutable for one another. The problem of someone making an evaluation can thus be regarded as the problem of deciding what mixture of principles more or less implemented out of all the mixtures which are available would be, in his own opinion, best.

On this, Le Grand (1990: 556) comments that 'the idea that in making social evaluations people might be indifferent between various combinations of objectives or principles, just as in making their consumption decisions they might be indifferent between various combinations of goods, seems eminently sensible. But does it?

Sen (1987: 65) has suggested that where there are several objects of value, one alternative course of action may be more valued in one respect and less so in another. There are then three different ways of dealing with the problem. One is in terms of trade-offs: 'to examine the appropriate "trade-offs" and to decide whether *on balance* one alternative combination of objects is superior to another'. This is to establish a 'balanced complete ordering' specifying which combinations of objects are superior to others. Such an approach, Sen argues, is appropriate for institutional public policy, which requires unambiguous instructions (and, one might add, public justification). Hence the need for consistent and complete social welfare functions or complete social choice functions, specifying non-empty choice sets for all non-empty sets of alternatives to choose from (Sen 1987: 67).

The other two ways involve 'incompleteness' and 'overcompleteness' respectively. The former 'permits incompleteness in the partial order emerging from plural evaluation' (Sen 1987: 66). The latter drops the requirement of consistency and, 'faced with an irreducible conflict of compelling principles . . . may admit both the superiority of one alternative over the other and the converse' (Sen 1987: 66). Sen maintains that the recognition of the diversity of goods with unclear trade-off is peculiarly relevant to personal judgements and decisions (Sen 1987: 68). I fully agree with his suggestion that the first model of 'balanced complete ordering' may be 'unrealistic and deeply deceptive for description and prediction of behaviour, in addition to being possibly unreasonable in substantive ethics' (Sen 1987: 70). I also endorse his suggestion that the context of decision-making makes a difference here, though, as I shall argue later, I think that his distinction between 'institutional public policy' and 'personal judgements and decisions' is too crude for the purpose at hand.

Other writers have resisted the first answer by appealing to the notion of 'incommensurability' of values. Thus Charles Taylor writes of values that are 'incommensurably higher': 'integrity, charity, liberation, and the like stand out as worthy of pursuit in a special way, incommensurable with other goods we might have, such as the pursuit of wealth, or comfort, or the approval of those who surround us'. Such values establish what Taylor (1982: 236–40) calls 'qualitative contrasts'. They are values of a special kind with a protected status. They are sacred in a given culture, evoking special emotions, such as admiration and sometimes reverence; they are values with which certain other values cannot be compared without evoking contempt or even horror or outrage.

Joseph Raz (1986: 345–6, 355–6) invokes the incommensurability of values in a different way. He writes of 'constitutive incommensurabilities', which obtain when agents normally refuse to forgo one option for another, where the options have 'a special significance for people's ability to engage in certain pursuits or relationships' and the refusal to trade one for the other is 'a condition of the agent's ability successfully to pursue one of his goals' and where it is typical for people 'to regard the very thought that they may be comparable in value as abhorrent'. Such incommensurabilities play their part in conventions of fidelity to relationships and pursuits. Being engaged in a relationship or a pursuit includes belief that certain options are not comparable in value.

Thus 'certain judgements about the non-comparability of certain options and certain attitudes to the exchangeability of options are constitutive of relations with friends, spouses, parents, etc.'. So, for instance, 'only those who hold the view that friendship is neither better nor worse than money, but is simply not comparable to money or other commodities are *capable* of having friends'. Rankings that treat all options as commensurate 'do not represent people's actual evaluations'. Projects and relationships that constitute human well-being 'depend on a combination of incommensurability with a total refusal even to consider exchanging one incommensurate option for another' (Raz 1986: 352, 348).

Finally, Pildes and Anderson (1990: 2146) write of 'hierarchical incommensurability' which occurs where the incomparably higher regard for one value over the other is expressed by refusing certain types of trade-offs between the two. Social choice theory cannot represent the relations of hierarchically incommensurable values because an individual's attitude towards them cannot be captured in terms of a single consequentialist preference ranking. Any description of options in terms of their consequences alone, apart from their expressive significance, will exclude some of the concerns individuals have that influence their choices.

Thus 'subtle legal and social processes' express 'the higher worth of some values by protecting them against certain kinds of trade-off against lower values. When higher values are at stake, particular kinds of comparisons with lower values are considered inappropriate, immoral, or unjust—comparisons that would express a degradation or depreciation of the higher values (Pildes and Anderson 1990: 2150).

This last approach's focus on the different contexts of choice seems to me promising. To see where it may lead, let us examine a value with a strong *prima facie* claim to protected status within our culture.

The value of life

What is it worth to save a human life? Is doing so tradeable off against the expenditure incurred in doing so, or against the value of other uses to which that expenditure might be put? One view relies on Kant's distinction between price and dignity. According to Kant, in the Kingdom of Ends, 'everything has either a price or a dignity. If it has a price, something can be put in its place as an equivalent; if it is exalted above all price and so admits of no equivalent, then it has a dignity' (Kant 1956 edn.: 102). On this view, the value of human life is 'incommensurably higher' than that of its putative equivalents: to suppose that they could be traded off is, in Kant's very words, 'a profanation of its sanctity' (Kant 1956 edn.: 103).

Another view is that we do it all the time. Thus James Griffin (1986: 82) writes:

> An individual human life has no equivalent. But that is not to say that nothing can be ranked with, let alone outrank, a human life. The French government knows that each year several drivers lose their lives because of the beautiful roadside avenues of trees, yet they do not cut them down. Even aesthetic pleasure is (rightly) allowed to outrank a certain number of human lives. It is easy here to move imperceptibly from Kant to cant.

Each of these views seems right, though neither seems *quite* right. Yet they contradict one another. How can this be?

The first (call it 'Kantian') view identifies a principle central to our legal and moral culture that accords a special kind of respect to persons and their inviolability, and a means from within that culture to condemn its frequent violation. Durkheim (1969: 14–30) spoke of this as the religion of individualism, in which the individual as such becomes the focus of sacredness. We think of the right to life as the most basic of rights. We honour those who save lives at great risk to their own; we condemn those who coolly or ruthlessly calculate to gain by the deaths of others; and we devote vast sums to the saving or the prolonging of lives that contribute little or nothing to the general utility and of those that derive little or none from continuing. It seems that refusing to contemplate a trade-off between the worth of a life and other values (especially monetary or material advantage) is constitutive of taking the value of life seriously. Only someone, we are inclined to think, who has the disposition to treat such trade-offs as unthinkable can claim to treat human life, or by extension human dignity, with appropriate respect. (I leave aside the question of abortion here, because, it seems to me, both sides are likely, in this sense, to be Kantians, differing rather over when a human life or personhood begins. I have not heard anyone defending abortion as justified killing.)

And yet we certainly do not treat the right to life or the value of saving it as always and everywhere overriding—as 'trumping' or as lexically prior or as insurmountable moral 'side constraints'. It is easy to think of examples that fall far short of what Robert Nozick (1974: 30 n.) has called 'catastrophic moral horror' in which choices are made that sacrifice, say, a margin of safety for other benefits, or that distribute risks among different categories of people, or allocate scarce medical resources that benefit some at the cost, sometimes fatal, of others. This is the stuff of decision-making in the use and disposal of dangerous materials, in industrial safety, flood control, transport policy, and medical administration and practice. The second (call it 'anti-Kantian') view rightly insists on this last point. We do engage in such trade-offs, or rather we expect our public institutions to do so.

When we do so, we do not normally see the decisions they make as violating Kantian respect, for various reasons. In the first place, they typically concern not the lives of identifiable individuals but rather statistical lives. Second, they are made professionally and impersonally. Third, they are not made from a moral point of view. Often they are made from an economic point of view, from which a life-saving decision foreseen to result in a certain number of deaths can be viewed as a 'practical judgement—a consumer choice—by the members of society about what it is worth to reduce the risk of death' (Schelling 1984*a*: 114). As Schelling has argued in a famous essay, the value of life is, from that point of view, its worth 'to the people who may die, or who may lose somebody who matters to them' (Schelling 1984*a*: 113). It may, he suggests, be possible to approximate an answer to the difficult question of what that is by using evidence as to what people will pay to avoid their own deaths or the deaths of those who matter to them, by direct enquiry techniques, or else by some vicarious professional or paternalistic judgement. The first two techniques, he suggests, may lead us to an answer based on the scaling of risks that relies on consumers actual choices, where the risk can be perceived directly:

> The gravity of decisions about lifesaving can be dispelled by letting the consumer (taxpayer, lobbyist, questionnaire, respondent) express himself on the comparatively unexciting subject of small increments in small risks, acting though as he has preferences even if in fact he has not. People do it for life insurance; they could do it for lifesaving. The fact that they may not do it well, or may not quite know what they are doing as they make the decision, may not bother them and need not disenfranchise them in the exercise of consumer-taxpayer sovereignty. (Schelling 1984*a*: 145)

Schelling's answer, in short, is that the economic point of view is sometimes the right one from which 'to enlighten the issues involved in public programs to save lives' (Schelling 1984*b*: 148) for the avoidance of death is not a 'wholly different kind of objective from others to promote the general welfare' (Schelling 1984*a*: 143).

So perhaps it is true, as Sen suggests, that the trade-off is an appropriate metaphor for analysing and guiding institutional decisions—decisions in the market-place concerning, for instance, the marketing of dangerous products? The answer seems to be: sometimes yes, and sometimes no. We allow tobacco companies to sell cigarettes and the marketing of cars without passive restraint systems (permitting safety belts not to be worn). Yet sometimes cost-benefit calculations are inadmissible, as in the case of the Ford-Pinto car.

In the late 1970s Ford discovered that the location of the Pinto's petrol tank subjected passengers and drivers to substantially greater average risks of burn injuries and death in low-speed rear-end collisions. Ford investigated the possibility of investing to rectify the problem and made a cost-benefit analysis, *à la* Schelling, in which a human life was assigned the value of $200,000. Calculating the total cost of repairs for all vehicles at $11 per vehicle, Ford concluded the repair costs would be substantially greater than the benefits of avoiding deaths and burn injuries, and decided against making any repairs the revelation of this story provoked public outrage and court cases in which substantial damages were awarded against Ford (including large punitive damages) and the Pinto was eventually withdrawn.

What this case shows is that, under certain conditions, trade-offs are inadmissible because of what they are taken to mean. As Pinto and Anderson have put it, in respect of the Pinto story:

The complaint was that, given the background of social and legal understandings against which Ford executives had acted, Ford's particular trade-off expressed contempt for human life. Other trade-offs of safety against cost need not do so. The Pinto trade-off was especially offensive because the Pinto's problem resulted from a design defect, known to Ford but not disclosed to customers, which Ford's electives took no action to correct. To market deliberately or refuse to recall a dangerously defective good expresses contempt for human life; that contempt is, of course, heightened when the defect is concealed from consumers.[7]

Marketing cars without mandatory seat belts might involve an identical or even less favourable trade-off of safety against economy, but, Pildes and Anderson argue, conventions mark out the Pinto decision as inadmissible because of 'culturally contingent reasons' such as 'expressive concerns about autonomy and personal responsibility'. What principles govern admissibility here? One seems to be that the chain leading from the decision in question to eventual death should run through informed choices of all the actors concerned, or, perhaps, choices that could be so informed.

If conventions mark out admissible from inadmissible private institutional trade-offs, the same must be true for public institutional policy-making. It is by no means always clear, or agreed, what these are or what principles underlie them. Thus the legal regulations governing the US OSHA (Occupational Health and Safety Administration) agency are mutually contradictory, and much doubt and controversy surrounds their operation.[8] Further analysis of the principles governing the admissibility of trade-offs in both public and private policy-making is, it seems to me, much needed.

If we are sometimes Kantians and sometimes not in our (public and private) institutional lives, what of our 'personal' judgements and decisions? Here too the picture is more complex than it may seem. For one thing, these may also be private or public. Consider the following two stories, each of which has two stages.

Suppose a close relative of a sick person who stands to benefit materially from the latter's death is faced with the questions of whether and how much

[7] Pildes and Anderson (1990: 2151). My account of the Pinto story relies on theirs.

[8] On these issues, see Calabresi and Bobbitt (1985), and Rhoads (1980). See also the brief discussion of the doubts of a senior analyst working at OSHA about the use of standard economic techniques to determine acceptable trade-offs between the high costs of safe technology and risks to human life in Bellah *et al.* (1991: 27–9).

to care for that person. To treat such questions as a trade-off is anathema. Whether to care, how much to care, or how much to pay for care are not, we think, matters for cost-benefit calculation in such a context. Yet suppose the illness worsens and the costs of care increase. Would we expect a family, one of whose members is, it appears, incurably sick, to go on pouring its resources away in search of a miracle cure, at the expense, say, of the children's education?[9]

Or consider an example suggested by Schelling (1984*b*: 151). A member of a small fishing community is lost at sea. It may have been agreed in advance to be uneconomical and probably fruitless to search for more than one day in such cases, yet it will not be easy to curtail the rescue. Indeed, 'one more day and another and another may be irresistible, though we damn ourselves for wasting our resources, not at all reconciled by the thought that, when it is our turn to be lost at sea, others will waste their time in a fruitless search for us' (Schelling (1884*b*: 151)). And yet, if the search beyond a certain distance requires aircraft, we may agree not to acquire the aircraft which, let us suppose, would impose a crippling burden on the community's resources.

On a Griffin-like anti-Kantian account, trade-offs are occurring at all stages in these two stories, for the absolute priority given to care (in the first) and to rescue (in the second) already presupposes a cost-benefit analysis of the limits within which it can operate. On a Kantian account, however, *neither* stage of the two stories is a trade-off. In the first stage, the question is simply rejected, Raz-wise, as inadmissible. In the second, a cost is eventually contemplated which appears insupportable because incompatible with the very basis of the family or community. The refusal to pay such a cost need not mean that a corresponding value is set on the benefit forgone. It *may* do so, but to suppose that it *must* is to assume that valuation is identical with revealed preference.

My suggestion is that the actors in these stories may be *either* Kantians *or* anti-Kantians, and that it is dogmatic to assume that they must be one or the other. If they are Kantians, they will refuse, and indeed attach importance to refusing, the trade-off in question. To fail to see this is to misunderstand what they do. At stage two of each story, we need a religious, not an economic metaphor: the choice they make is a sacrifice, not a trade-off. They do not take the alternatives between which they choose to be equivalent, i.e. equal in value. Least of all are they indifferent between them.

Trade-offs, I conclude, are widespread: they characterize much of our choice-making in both our institutional and our personal lives. But there are areas of both in which choice-making does not take this form, or does so at the cost of violating conventions that we hold to be important. There is no

[9] I owe this example to Jon Elster.

good reason for assuming that all our choices are to be understood as trade-offs. To assume this is to subscribe to a dogma which deflects us from paying attention to the ethical and explanatory significance, in personal and institutional life, of choices that are not trade-offs.

REFERENCES

Aristotle (1954 edn.), *The Nicomachean Ethics*, 1. 6. 1096^b 23 ff. trans. and introd. Sir David Ross (London: Oxford University Press, World Classics).

Arneson, R. (1989), 'Equality and Equality of Opportunity for Welfare', *Philosophical Studies*, 55: 77–93.

Atkinson, A. B (1991), 'Il trade-off fra equità ed efficienza', in Lugaresi and Pennacchi (1991).

Barry, B. (1965), *Political Argument* (London: Routledge and Kegan Paul).

Bellah, R. N., *et al.* (1991), *The Good Society* (New York: Knopf).

Berlin, I. (1969), *Four Essays on Liberty* (Oxford: Oxford University Press).

Blinder, A. S. (1987), *Hard Heads. Soft Hearts* (Reading, Mass.: Addison-Wesley).

Calabresi, G., and Bobbitt, P. (1985), *Tragic Choices* (New York: Norton).

Cohen, G. A. (1989), 'On the Currency of Egalitarian Justice', *Ethics*, 99: 906–44.

Durkheim, E. (1969), 'Individualism and the Intellectuals', trans. in *Political Studies* (1969: 14–30).

Dworkin, R. (1981), 'Equality of Resources', *Philosophy and Public Affairs*, 10: 303.

Gerth, H. H., and Mills, C. W. (1948) (tr. and ed.), *From Max Weber* (London: Routledge and Kegan Paul).

Griffin, J. (1986), *Well-being* (Oxford: Clarendon Press).

Hirschman, A. O. (1991), *The Rhetoric of Reaction* (Cambridge, Mass.: The Bellknap Press of Harvard University Press).

Kant, I. (1956 edn.), *The Moral Law* (*Groundwork of the Metaphysic of Morals*), ed. and trans. H. J. Paton, 3rd edn. (London: Hutchinson).

Le Grand, J. (1990), 'Equity versus Efficiency: The Elusive Trade-off', *Ethics*, 100: 554–68.

Lugaresi, S., and Pennacchi, L. (1991) (eds.), *Dilemmi della democrazia e Strategie del Riformismo* (Roma: Editori Riuniti).

Lukes, S. (1991), *Moral Confliet and Politics* (Oxford: Clarendon Press).

MacIntyre, A. (1981), *After Virtue* (London: Duckworth).

Macpherson, C. B. (1985*a*), 'Liberalism as Trade-Offs', in Macpherson (1985*b*).

—— (1985*b*), *The Rise and Fall of Economic Justice and Other Essays* (Oxford: Oxford University Press).

Nagel, T. (1979*a*), 'The Fragmentation of Value', in Nagel (1979*b*) *Mortal Questions* (Cambridge: Cambridge University Press).

—— (1979*b*), *Mortal Questions* (Cambridge: Cambridge University Press).

Nozick, R. (1974), *Anarchy, State and Utopia* (Oxford: Basil Blackwell).

Okun, A. M. (1975), *Equality and Efficiency. The Big Tradeoff* (Washington, DC: The Brookings Institution).

Pildes, R. H., and Anderson, E. S. (1990), 'Slinging Arrows at Democracy: Social Choice Theory, Value Pluralism, and Democratic Politics, *Columbia Law Review*, 90.

Rawls, J. (1971), *A Theory of Justice* (Cambridge, Mass.: Harvard University Press).

Raz, J. (1986), *The Morality of Freedom* (Oxford: Clarendon Press).

Rhoads, S. E. (1980) (ed.), *Valuing Life: Public Policy Dilemmas* (Boulder,: Colo. Westview Press).

Samuelson, P. A., and Nordhaus, W. D. (1989), *Economics* (13th edn., New York: McGraw-Hill).

Schelling, T. C. (1984*a*), 'The Life You Save May Be Your Own', in Schelling, (1984*c*).

—— (1984*b*), 'Strategic Relationships in Dying', in Schelling (1984*c*).

—— (1984*c*), *Choice and Consequence. Perspectives of an Errant Economist* (Cambridge, Mass.: Harvard University Press).

Sen, A. K. (1982*a*), 'Equality of What?,' in Sen, (1982*b*).

—— (1982*b*), *Choice, Welfare and Measurement* (Oxford: Basil Blackwell).

—— (1985), *Commodities and Capabilities* (Amsterdam: North Holland).

—— (1987), *On Ethics and Economics* (Oxford: Basil Blackwell).

—— and Williams, B. (1982) (eds.), *Utilitarianism and Beyond* (Cambridge: Cambridge University Press).

Stocker, M. (1990) *Plural and Conflicting Values* (Oxford: Clarendon Press).

Taylor, C. (1982) 'The Diversity of Goods,' in Sen and Williams (1982).

Weber, M. (1948 edn.), 'Science as a Vocation', in Gerth and Mills (1948).

Williams, B. (1973*a*), 'Ethical Consistency', in Williams (1973*b*).

—— (1973*b*), *Problems of the Self* (Cambridge: Cambridge University Press).

—— (1985), *Ethics and the Limits of Philosophy* (London: Fontana/Collins).

4

On the Foundations of Welfare Economics: Utility, Capability, and Practical Reason[1]

AMARTYA SEN

1. Utility, utilitarianism, and welfare economics

'There is no "royal road" to geometry', Euclid is supposed to have told Ptolemy. A similar remark can be made about welfare economics also. Welfare economics deals with the basis of normative judgements, the foundations of evaluative measurement, and the conceptual underpinnings of policy-making in economics. It is not a modest subject. Given the variety of problems and the diversity of concerns that are inevitably included in this broad field, it would have been amazing had there been some simple—and already chosen—'royal road' directing us on how to make these judgements, evaluations, and decisions. Pluralism and variety would be hard to avoid in this important field—characterized as it is by heterogeneity of problems and diversity of normative concerns.

However, for a long time—for well over a century—welfare economics was dominated by one particular approach, to wit, utilitarianism, initiated in its modern form by Jeremy Bentham, and championed by such economists as Mill, Edgeworth, Sidgwick, Marshall, and Pigou. Utilitarianism has been the 'official' theory of welfare economics in a thoroughly unique way, and standard welfare economics is still largely utilitarian. The pretension of utilitarianism of being *the* 'royal road' to welfare economics was, I believe, hard to justify, but this did not weaken the firmness with which its claims to unique superiority were presented, nor the seriousness with which the profession took these claims.

Utilitarians, such as Bentham, or Edgeworth, or Marshall, or Pigou, saw no great difficulty in asserting that the ranking of social goodness and the

[1] This chapter was presented as a paper at the Summer School on 'Ethics and Economics' held by the International School of Economic Research (Department of Economics, University of Siena), Certosa di Pontignano, Siena, July 1991. It draws on an earlier paper presented at the University of Economics and Business in Athens. Research support from the National Science Foundation is gratefully acknowledged.

selection of what is to be chosen must be done simply on the basis of the *sum* of individual welfares. They also took individual welfare as being represented by individual pleasure or utility.[2] To take social welfare to be exclusively dependent on individual utilities is often called 'welfarism'. To aggregate the utilities simply by summing them together (an arithmetic addition) is called 'sum-ranking'. Utilitarianism is a species of *welfarism* that relies also on *sum-ranking*.

Welfarism in general—including the particular approach championed by the utilitarians—yields a very special approach to social ethics.[3] One of the major limitations of this approach lies in the fact that the same collection of individual welfares may go with very different social arrangements, opportunities, freedoms, and consequences. For example, in one case it may involve violations of accepted individual rights, but not in another. Or it may involve denial of some important individual freedoms in one case but not in another. No matter what happens in these other respects, welfarism would still demand that those differences be given no intrinsic importance in the ultimate assessment.

The neglect applies both to 'overall' freedoms (sometimes called 'positive' freedoms) which may entail claims on others or on the state (e.g. the right to free elementary education, right to unemployment insurance, or to basic health care), and to 'negative' freedoms which demand non-interference by others (e.g. the rights to personal liberty).[4] The indifference of welfarism to negative freedoms (such as libertarian immunities) is obvious enough, but the overall (or positive) freedoms are also quite different from individual welfare achievements. Welfarism implies a rather limited view of normative evaluation and welfare economics, and I shall have to consider how substantive note may be taken of considerations of freedom in assessing social arrangements.

Second, the informational limitation is made even stronger by the particular utilitarian interpretation of individual welfare, seeing it simply in terms of pleasures or desires. This can be particularly restrictive when making interpersonal comparisons of deprivation. Comparisons of pleasures, or of fulfilments of desires, can be very misleading as a guide to interpersonal contrasts of well-being, since our desires and pleasure-taking abilities adjust to circumstances, particularly to make life bearable in adverse situations.

2 The definition of utility has varied over the years. While Bentham's hedonistic view of utility as pleasure still survives in welfare economics and in political philosophy, other ways of seeing utility have also become common, including desire fulfilment and preference satisfaction, and various alternative formulations of preference-based utilities (see e.g. Arrow (1951), Harsanyi (1976), Hahn (1982), Hammond (1982), Mirrlees (1982), Griffin (1986), Broome (1991), Sen (1991)).

3 I have tried to discuss some of the limitations in Sen (1970; 1982; 1987).

4 The use of this distinction in welfare economics tends to be rather different from the classic contrast outlined by Isaiah Berlin (1969) whose focus was on the difference between *internal* and *external* constraints on a person's ability to do things. On these distinctions, see Sen (1992*a*). See also Sugden (1981; 1986).

The utilitarian calculus can be deeply unfair to those who are persistently deprived: for example, traditional underdogs in stratified societies, oppressed minorities in intolerant communities, precarious sharecroppers living in a world of uncertainty, sweated workers in exploitative industrial arrangements, subdued housewives in deeply sexist cultures. The hopelessly deprived people may lack the courage to desire any radical change and often tend to adjust their desires and expectations to what little they see as feasible. They train themselves to take pleasure in small attainments. Such adjustments in chronically deprived positions are easy to understand, but they also have the incidental effect of distorting the scale of utilities. In terms of pleasure or desire-fulfilment, the disadvantages of the hopeless underdog may, thus, appear to be much smaller than what would emerge on the basis of a more objective analysis of the extent of their deprivation and unfreedom.[5]

Third, there are special limitations of utilitarianism related to 'sum-ranking', i.e. the procedure of aggregating collections of utilities simply by addition. Utilitarianism cannot differentiate between two distributions of the same total utility. For example, it makes no difference in utilitarian evaluation whether one person has 100 units of utility and another has 2, or both have 51 units of utility each. This lack of concern with the distribution of welfares is a further limitation of utilitarianism.

2. Non-comparable utilities and Paretian economics

The subject of welfare economics suffered a big blow in the 1930s when economists came to be persuaded by arguments presented by Lionel Robbins and others (influenced by 'logical positivist' philosophy) that interpersonal comparisons of utility have no scientific basis and cannot be sensibly done. Robbins invoked Jevons in finding 'no means whereby such comparisons can be accomplished. 'Every mind is inscrutable to every other mind and no common denominator of feelings is possible' (see Robbins 1932 and 1938: 636).

Since economists came largely to be convinced that there was indeed something methodologically wrong in using interpersonal comparison of utilities, the fuller version of the utilitarian tradition soon gave way, in the 1940s and the 1950s, to a kind of mutilated welfarism—what came to be known as 'the new welfare economics'. This largely took the form of continuing to rely on utilities only, but to dispense with interpersonal comparisons altogether. The 'informational basis' of welfare economics remained narrowly confined to utilities, but the permitted ways of using the

[5] The general need for taking note of perceptual adjustments in making ethical assessments has been discussed in Sen (1985*a*). Adaptation of perceptions tends to play a particularly major part in the perpetuation of social inequalities, including the relative deprivation of women (on this see Sen 1985*b*; 1990).

utility information were further restricted by the ban on interpersonal comparisons. Welfarism without interpersonal comparisons is, in fact, a very restrictive informational basis for social judgements.

An important part of the new welfare economics used only one criterion of social improvement, namely the Pareto criterion, which relied on taking note of utilities of each person separately without any interpersonal comparisons. According to this criterion, social state x is better than social state y if at least one person has more utility in x than in y and everyone has at least as much utility in x as in y. A state is described as 'Pareto optimal' if and only if there is no other feasible state that is superior to it in terms of the Pareto criterion. A good deal of subsequent welfare economics confines attention to Pareto optimality only, and that practice is very common even today.

It is hard to accept Pareto optimality as an adequate condition for a good society. Pareto optimality only requires that no one's utility can be raised without someone's utility having to be reduced, and thus it is just a limited condition of efficiency in the generation of utilities. Pareto optimality is silent on the distribution of utilities (including inequalities of utilities), and it takes no direct note of anything other than utilities (such as inequalities of incomes, rights, or freedoms). A society in which some people lead lives of great luxury while others live in acute misery can still be Pareto optimal if the agony of the deprived cannot be reduced without cutting into the ecstasy of the affluent. A state can be Pareto optimal and still be sickeningly iniquitous.

It has become, for this reason, more common to argue that Pareto optimality is a necessary condition for social optimality even though not sufficient (see Samuelson 1947 and Arrow 1951). If Pareto optimality is not sufficient (though necessary), we need some *further* criteria to make judgements about different distributions, and the question arises as to how that supplementation may be done. The need for using systematic procedures for this supplementation was discussed by Abram Bergson (1938; 1966), and extensively explored by Paul Samuelson (1947) in his classic treatise *Foundations of Economic Analysis*.

3. Social choice and Arrow's impossibility theorem

It was in the context of the ongoing search for acceptable formulations of social welfare that Kenneth Arrow presented his well-known impossibility theorem, and his book *Social Choice and Individual Values* (published in 1951) launched the new subject of social choice theory. Arrow considered a set of very mild-looking conditions relating the social choices or judgements to the set of individual preferences. Arrow showed that it is impossible to satisfy those conditions simultaneously. The impossibility theorem precipitated a major crisis in welfare economics, and it is, in fact, a landmark in the history of modern social analysis.

In formulating the problem of social choice based on individual preferences, Arrow (1951: 9) took the viewpoint—following what was by then the dominant tradition—that 'interpersonal comparison of utilities has no meaning'. He took the social choice to be determined by the set of individual preferences, and this functional relationship between the set of individual preferences and the social ordering he called the 'social welfare function'. While welfarism was not explicitly invoked as a condition, it is in fact—in a particular form—entailed by the conditions that Arrow imposed.[6]

The combination of this specific welfarism result and the ruling out of interpersonal comparisons of utility makes the resulting system—axiomatized by Arrow—extremely undiscriminating. Let me illustrate. Consider, for example, the problem of choosing between different distributions of a cake between two or more persons. In the informational framework characterized by Arrow, we cannot, in effect, be guided by any equity consideration that would require the identification of the rich *vis-à-vis* the poor. If 'being rich' or 'being poor' is defined in terms of income or commodity holdings, then that is a non-utility characteristic of which we cannot take any direct note in the Arrow system, thanks to welfarism. But nor can we identify 'being rich' or 'being poor' with having high or low utility, since that would involve interpersonal comparison of utilities, which is also ruled out. Equity considerations thus lose their applicability in this framework (see Sen 1982; 1986*b*), and Hammond 1985; 1986).

Other types of discriminating principles also prove to be inviable with such informational limitation. The only acceptable information as specified by welfarism (to wit, utility) has to be used in an extremely limited form because of the insistence on non-comparability of utilities. This leaves us with a class of decision procedures that are really some variant or other of voting methods (like majority decision). Since they do not need any interpersonal comparison, they do remain available in Arrow's informational framework. But these procedures have consistency problems, as was noted more than two hundred years ago by French mathematicians such as Condorcet and Borda. We are left, then, with the unattractive possibility of having a dictatorial method of social judgement, i.e. handing it all over to one person whose preferences determine everything. This is clearly an unacceptable method of decision-making, and indeed is ruled out directly by one of Arrow's conditions (to wit, non-dictatorship). Hence the impossibility.

The exclusions are so total, thanks to the informational lacunae, that we end up with no rule whatever which could be used to make systematic social welfare judgements, or to make systematic social choices. The crisis really arises from demanding welfarism, which is one part of the allegedly 'royal

[6] Formally, a kind of welfarism follows from Arrow's unrestricted domain, independence of irrelevant alternatives, and the Pareto principle; on this see Sen (1982: Essays 11 and 15).

road' of utilitarianism, while—at the same time—ruling out interpersonal comparability of utilities on which utilitarianism in fact relies.

4. Well-being and interpersonal comparisons

There is a vast literature dealing with the significance and robustness of Arrow's result and exploring various ways of getting round the impossibility identified by him.[7] 'Ways out' have been sought in terms of relaxing each of Arrow's conditions, and each alleged solution has some considerable difficulty. I have argued elsewhere that despite the interesting possibilities rightly explored in each direction, the most likely route of escaping the Arrow dilemma in making social welfare judgements lies not in any marginal modification of one of the Arrow axioms, but in the general direction of enriching the informational input into that analysis.[8]

Arrow ruled out not only interpersonal comparison of utilities, but also the use of the so-called 'cardinal' measures of utility, which would permit us to go beyond people's utility rankings to comparisons of such things as utility differences. Cardinal utility can be used for each person separately, without interpersonal comparison, and it can be asked whether an escape from the Arrow impossibility result can be found if we admit cardinal utility. The answer is no. It is, in fact, possible to show (as was demonstrated in Sen 1970: Theorem 8*2) that Arrow's impossibility result will hold even in the case in which cardinal utility measures are fully admitted for each person separately (with interpersonal utility comparisons still ruled out). The real issue is interpersonal comparisons, not cardinality on its own.

It is, in fact, easy to show that all of Arrow's conditions can be fulfilled if the axioms are redefined to admit interpersonal comparison of utilities, even if the comparisons do not admit cardinality. An important example that meets this demand can be derived from the philosopher John Rawls's (1971) Difference Principle.[9] This approach concentrates on making the worst off individual as well off as possible.[10] If stricter interpersonal

[7] The literature is immensely large. General accounts of the main issues and results can be found in Sen (1970; 1982; 1986*a*), Pattanaik (1971), Fishburn (1973), Kelly (1978), Suzumura (1983), Elster and Hylland (1986).

[8] The different possible routes are identified and critically assessed in Sen (1970; 1982), Hammond (1976; 1985; 1986), Arrow (1977), d'Aspremont and Gevers (1977), Maskin (1979), Gevers (1979), Roberts (1980*a*; 1980*b*), Blackorby, Donaldson, and Weymark (1984), d'Aspremont (1985).

[9] It must, however, be noted that Rawls's (1971) own formulation applies to judging individual advantage by holdings of 'primary goods', rather than enjoyment of utilities. Thus, the welfarist recharacterization of the Difference Principle is not strictly a 'Rawlsian' rule.

[10] The lexicographic form of Rawls's Difference Principle, redefined over the space of utilities, meets all of Arrow's conditions provided interpersonal comparisons of levels are admitted; on this see Sen (1970). Formal axiomatizations and proofs of the Difference Principle can take different forms, and the technical reader can be referred to Hammond (1976), Arrow (1977), d'Aspremont and Gevers (1977), Sen (1977), Gevers (1979), Roberts (1980*a*; 1980*b*), Blackorby, Donaldson, and Weymark (1984), d'Aspremont (1985), among others. See,

comparisons are admitted, then other types of social welfare rules also become usable (including, of course, the utilitarian one).

Once interpersonal comparisons are systematically admitted, the problems faced by modern welfare economics change radically. Instead of Arrow's impossibility, we have to face choices over various different rules of social decision (e.g. the utilitarian rule of maximization of sum-total *vis-à-vis* the Rawlsian rule of maximizing the position of the worst off individual).[11] This applies both to the general evaluative frameworks and also to specific welfare-economic exercises, e.g. comparison of inequality or poverty (see Sen 1973; 1982, Atkinson 1983; 1989, Osmani 1982). Instead of being at a loss about how to compare inequalities or poverty levels, we have then various different informational bases for these comparisons, demanding different types of interpersonally comparable information.

The problem of interpersonal comparisons of welfare is, in fact, broader than that of interpersonal comparisons of utility (pleasures, desire-fulfilments, etc.), since there are also other—more interesting—ways of seeing individual welfare. The two questions were not distinguished in traditional and 'new' welfare economics, because, under utilitarian influence, utility and welfare were thoroughly identified. When Lionel Robbins delivered his influential critique of the foundations of welfare economics (to which reference was made earlier), he did not feel the necessity to go beyond disputing the viability of interpersonal comparison of utilities as such. To deny the possibility of interpersonal comparison of welfare, it was adequate for him to argue that 'no common denominator of feelings is possible'.

But comparative assessments of welfare are not just matters of comparison of 'feelings'. The 'rules' that we follow in describing someone as being better off than another have many other elements, and the possibility of welfare comparisons cannot be reduced simply to the scrutability of our feelings. The problem of comparing the well-being of people has to be dissociated from the insistence on sticking to the utilitarian strait-jacket of comparisons of pleasures or desires.

5. Capability comparisons and evaluative weights

One route that some of us have tried to explore relates to Aristotle's pointer, in the *Nicomachean Ethics*, to the achievement of valuable functionings and to the ability to achieve such functionings. This is not the occasion to go

however, Roberts (1980*a*; 1980*b*) on a demonstration that the interpersonal comparison *without* cardinality (in the presence of some standard conditions of aggregation) forces admissible social choices rules to a rather narrow class.

[11] On this see d'Aspremont and Gevers (1977), Gevers (1979), Maskin (1979), Roberts (1980*a*; 1980*b*), Blackorby, Donaldson, and Weymark (1984), d'Aspremont (1985).

into the details of that approach,[12] but I would like to emphasize the fact that the use of interpersonal comparisons of well-being implies neither full utilitarianism, nor even the general format of welfarism.

One of the basic issues in the analysis of effective freedom is the choice of variables in terms of which achievement is to be judged. For example, freedom to buy commodities can be expressed by what economists call a 'budget set', namely, the set of alternative bundles of commodities which are all within one's budget and from which any one bundle can be chosen. But commodity ownership is rarely sought for itself, since commodities are means to other ends. The importance of commodities is typically instrumental rather than intrinsic. For example, having food helps us to be nourished, to enjoy eating, to entertain friends, and so forth. The extent of the different 'functionings' we can achieve with the same bundle of commodities can vary greatly from one person to another. For example, the extent of nourishment that a person is able to get from a given amount of food depends on the person's basal metabolic rate, body size, age, gender, presence of parasitic diseases, climatic conditions, and so on. There is, thus, a need to go beyond commodity holdings or real incomes to judge individual advantage.

Functionings represent parts of the state of a person—in particular the various things that he or she manages to do or be in leading a life. The capability of a person reflects the alternative combinations of functionings the person can achieve, and from which he or she can choose one collection.[13] The assessment of welfares and of freedoms can be related to the functionings achieved and to the capability to achieve them.

Some functionings are very elementary, such as being adequately nourished, being in good health, etc., and these may be strongly valued by all, for obvious reasons. Others may be more complex, but still widely valued, such as achieving self-respect, being socially integrated. Individuals may, however, differ a good deal from each other in the weights they attach to these different functionings—valuable though they may all be—and the assessment of individual and social advantages must be alive to these variations.

In the context of some types of social analysis, e.g. in dealing with extreme poverty in developing economies, we may be able to concentrate, to a great extent, on a relatively small number of centrally important functionings and the corresponding basic capabilities (e.g. the freedom to be well nourished, well sheltered, and in good general health, the capability of escaping

[12] I have presented them elsewhere, e.g. Sen (1980; 1985*a*; 1985*b*; 1992*a*). On related matters, see Nussbaum (1988), Arneson (1989), Cohen (1989; 1990), Van Parijs (1990), Nussbaum and Sen (1993).

[13] There are several technical problems in the representation and analysis of functionings and capability sets, on which see Sen (1985*b*; 1992*a*), and Dreze and Sen (1989). On related matters, see also the papers of Keith Hart, Geoffrey Hawthorn, Ravi Kanbur, John Muellbauer, Bernard Williams, and my rejoinder, in Sen *et al.* (1987). See also Arneson (1989), Cohen (1989; 1990) and Van Parijs (1990).

avoidable morbidity and premature mortality, the ability to move about freely, and so forth).[14] In other contexts, the list may have to be longer and more diverse.

Choices have to be faced in the delineation of the relevant functionings. The format always permits additional 'achievements' to be defined and included. Many functionings are of no great interest to the person.[15] There is no escape from the problem of evaluation in selecting a class of functionings in the description and appraisal of capabilities, and this selection problem is, in fact, one part of the general task of the choice of weights in making normative evaluations.

The need for selection and discrimination is neither an embarrassment, nor a unique difficulty, for conceptualizing functionings and capabilities. Exactly a similar problem exists in evaluating commodity bundles, viz., what weights to use. This valuation is often done in terms of market prices, and it may thus give the impression of being rather unproblematic and objective. But weighting at market prices also involves implicit valuation (namely that the prices provide the right weights for normative evaluation) and that procedure may be misleading for a number of reasons, including the fact that a rich person's dollar may reflect a very different level of urgency compared with a poor person's dollar (this requires systematic correction to market prices, on which see Sen (1976)). In the case of functionings and capabilities, since there are no markets directly involved, the weighting exercise has to be done in terms of explicit valuations, drawing on the prevailing values in a given society (on this see section 3). This explicitness is not, in itself, a bad thing, since it gives the public a clear opportunity to question the values and to debate the decisions. The scope for rational arguments on valuation can be quite considerable, and informed public discussions and debates can be very important for successful use of this approach.[16]

The concentration on functionings and capabilities differs from more commonly used approaches. The explicit valuation of these achievements and freedoms can escape the biases implicit in utility-based valuation, with the serious problem of perceptual distortions, especially related to persistently adverse circumstances (discussed earlier in section 4). There is also a contrast with commodity-based assessment (as in 'real income analysis'), and evaluations based on expenditure data. The capability perspective also differs from the important ethical approach championed by John Rawls (1971) of concentrating on what he calls 'primary goods'. These are general-purpose means for pursuing various different ends, and include such diverse things as 'rights, liberties and opportunities, income and wealth, and

[14] See Sen (1980; 1985*b*; 1992*a*), Griffin and Knight (1989), Dreze and Sen (1989), Dasgupta (1988; 1990), Desai (1990), Hossain (1990), Anand and Ravallion (1993).

[15] On this, see the exchange between Bernard Williams and myself in Sen *et al.* (1987).

[16] On these questions, see also Sen (1985*a*), and Dreze and Sen (1989), among others.

the social bases of self-respect' (see Rawls 1971: 60–5). While this concentration serves Rawls's purpose, holdings of primary goods are neither indicators of well-being, nor of freedom. A disabled or an ill person can quite possibly achieve much less with the same bundle of primary goods than another person without that problem. There are systematic differences related to gender, age, proneness to disease, and so on, and they make the holding of primary goods a bad indicator of a person's advantage. In this respect focusing instead on functionings and capabilities has some obvious merit.[17]

6. Freedom achievement and capability

What are the links between capabilities and functionings, on the one hand, and well-being and freedom on the other? As a first approximation it is plausible to argue that well-being achievement depends only on the achieved functionings, whereas the freedom to achieve well-being is correspondingly associated with the capability to function.

But freedom may have intrinsic importance for a person's well-being also. Acting freely and being able to choose may be directly conductive to well-being, not just because more freedom may make better alternatives available. This view on the direct relevance of freedom is contrary to the one typically assumed in standard economic theory, in which the contribution of a set of feasible choices is judged exclusively by the value of the best element available. Even the removal of all the elements of a feasible set (e.g. of a 'budget set') other than the chosen best element is seen, in that theory, as no real loss, since the freedom to choose does not, in that view, in itself matter.

In contrast, if choosing is seen as a part of living (and 'doing *x*' is distinguished from 'choosing to do *x* and doing it'), then even the achievement of well-being need not be independent of the freedom reflected in the capability set.[18] The 'good life' is partly a life of genuine choice, and not one in which the person is forced into a particular life—however rich it might be in other respects.[19] With this additional consideration, the assessment of well-being as well as that of the freedom to achieve well-being would depend on the person's 'capability set'.

7. Evaluation, rights, and rules

There is nothing methodologically odd about making systematic interpersonal comparisons of welfare. Nor are such comparisons 'meaningless' in

[17] These issues have been discussed in Sen (1980; 1992*a*) and Drèze and Sen (1989).

[18] The constitutive importance of freedom in well-being is discussed in Sen (1985*a*; 1992*a*).

[19] The temptation to see freedom of choice as a luxury of the rich is common enough, but the poor are often more crucially diminished by the absence of freedom in living (on this see Sen 1980; Dasgupta 1988). For an empirical study that *inter alia* shows the importance attached by the Belgian unemployed to the options they have, see Schokkaert and Van Ootegem (1990).

the way the profession came to see them under the 'positivist' philosophical influences which had been so dominant in standard mainstream economics. As Wittgenstein (1953) has taught us, we communicate with each other and understand what others are saying by following certain rules. The rules of communication about welfare are governed by mutually recognized standards, which, for example, permit us to say that a starving wretch is worse off than a healthy, wealthy, and happy person.

Principles underlying such standards have been discussed a great deal in many intellectual traditions. They were, for example, examined in the fourth century bc both by Kautilya in India and by Aristotle in Greece. Agreed rules have also provided the basis of empirical works on standards of living and well-being by such pioneers of economic analysis as Petty, King, Quesnay, Lavoisier, Lagrange, Turgot, Condorcet, and of course Adam Smith (1776; 1790). The tradition of enlightenment that emerged in eighteenth-century Europe made a forceful case for the inescapable necessity of public discussion on social principles and standards.[20]

These issues are indeed central to modern works on social welfare and living conditions, and the recent revival of welfare economics in a broad form has done much to bring them into focus.[21]

Our standards are not always uniform, ambiguities do exist, and there is often much scope for argument about what the standards should be. But communications on interpersonal comparisons of welfare are not hollow utterances devoid of shared intelligibility, as the 'positivist' philosophers and economists have tended to claim.

Similarly, considerations of rights and freedoms, going well beyond the focus on individual well-being, can also be systematically incorporated into welfare-economic evaluation, using rules of procedure that are well understood and open to examination. There are, however, interesting consistency problems in including considerations of liberty and freedom in welfare economics frameworks that tend to give unconditional priority to welfare information (for example, in treating Pareto optimality as a necessary—even if not sufficient—condition of overall optimality).[22] But it is possible to accommodate both types of information if we do not also insist a priori on some inflexible judgement about the uncompromising superiority of the welfare-based criteria such as the Pareto principle.

[20] Emma Rothschild's oral presentation at the 1991 Siena conference provides an analysis of this important intellectual development and its connections with modern social debates.

[21] See e.g. Atkinson (1975; 1983; 1989), Deaton and Muellbauer (1980), Allardt (1981), Sen (1982; 1985*b*), Sen and Williams (1982), Erikson and Aberg (1987), Sen *et al.* (1987), Dasgupta (1988; 1990), Griffin and Knight (1989), Dreze and Sen (1989), Schokkaert and Van Ootegem (1990), Desai (1990), among many other contributions.

[22] On this see Sen (1970; 1983; 1992*b*), Suzumura (1983), Wriglesworth (1985), Riley (1987), Seabright (1989), Gaertner, Pattanaik, and Suzumura (1992). On some related matters involving the connections between welfares and rights, see also Nozick (1974), Buchanan (1975), Dworkin (1977), Sen (1980), Dasgupta (1982), Kanger (1985).

8. A concluding remark

Modern welfare economics has to go more and more in these pluralist and heterodox directions, taking note of a variety of information in making the wide-ranging judgements that have to be made. Welfare economics is a major branch of 'practical reason'. There are no good grounds for expecting that the diverse considerations that are characteristic of practical reason, discussed, among others, by Aristotle, Kant, Smith, Hume, Marx, or Mill, can, in any real sense, be avoided by taking refuge in some simple formula like the utilitarian maximization of utility sums, or a general reliance on optimality, or going by some mechanical criterion of technical efficiency or maximization of the gross national product.

This inadequacy applies even to the informational base of capabilities for which I have tried to argue here (and elsewhere). It is true that the capabilities a person enjoys (depending, as it does, both on personal features and social arrangements) give us considerable understanding of that person's real opportunities and the prospects of actual achievements. But that does not, in any way, 'close' the issue of informational bases of social choice.

First, the ranking of capability sets would often be incomplete and partial, requiring supplementation by other considerations, to yield specific decisions. If the primary purpose of political ethics is to avoid serious injustice (a view to which I am sympathetic), an incomplete ranking may well be adequate enough to identify some situations and arrangements that must be avoided. However, it still could leave open the choice over a range of acceptable—not patently unjust—possibilities. Second, even if one unambiguous interpersonal ranking of capability sets exists, we may still be ill-advised to forget everything else in making social choices. For one thing, the important social value of liberty for which John Rawls makes room, through his 'priority of liberty', suggests that we do not permit liberty to be altogether outweighed by other considerations that may legitimately figure in any general capability ranking. It is appropriate to supplement considerations of liberty by the force of overall freedom to achieve valuable objectives (and thus the capability index to be used must be broad based), but it does not follow from this that the importance of liberty cannot go beyond what is captured in the value of that overall index.[23] There are other consequential and deontological concerns that may compete for attention in social choice, along with the powerful force of capability-based reasoning.

[23] On this question, see Sen (1992*a*). The programme of relying entirely on *one* overall index that covers different considerations would be defective not only in the case of exclusive reliance on capability considerations, but also in proposals to have some other similarly aggregative index (for example, Ronald Dworkin's 1981 system of pursuing 'equality of resources', where liberties figure *inter alia* in the general indexing of resources). On this question, see Sen (1970; 1987; 1992*a*), Rawls (1971; 1993), Dworkin (1981; 1985; 1987).

Third, the conflicting demands of equity and efficiency cannot, obviously, be resolved by any reliance on capability considerations to judge efficiency and equity. The issue of the 'space' in which to characterize efficiency and equity has to be distinguished from the problem of balancing these two basic considerations.

Francis Bacon had said, 'the shortest way is commonly the foulest'. We may not quite agree with that, but nor can we accept any of the aggregative formulae as the 'royal road' to solving deep and complex issues of social evaluation. Searching for some all-purpose simple formula would take us in a different direction altogether from where we have to go. There is, to return to Euclid, no 'royal road' to welfare economics, any more than there is to geometry.

REFERENCES

Allardt, E. (1981), 'Experiences from the Comparative Scandinavian Welfare Study, with a Bibliography of the Project,' *European Journal of Political Research*, 9.

Anand, S., and Ravallion, M. (1993), 'Human Development in Poor Countries: On the Role of Private Incomes and Public Services', *Journal of Economic Perspectives*, 7.

Arneson, R. (1989), 'Equality and Equality of Opportunity for Welfare,' *Philosophical Studies*, 56: 77–93.

Arrow, K. J. (1951), *Social Choice and Individual Values* (New York: John Wiley and Dover; 2nd edn., 1963).

—— (1977), 'Extended Sympathy and the Possibility of Social Choice', *American Economic Review*, 67: 219–25.

—— and Intriligator, M. (1986) (eds.), *Handbook of Mathematical Economics*, iii (Amsterdam: North Holland).

Atkinson, A. B. (1975), *The Economics of Inequality* (Oxford: Clarendon Press).

—— (1983), *Social Justice and Public Policy* (Brighton: Wheatsheaf, and Cambridge, Mass.: MIT Press).

—— (1989), *Poverty and Social Security* (New York: Harvester Wheatsheaf).

Bergson, A. (1938), 'A Reformulation of Certain Aspects of Welfare Economics', *Quarterly Journal of Economics*, 52.

—— (1966), *Essays in Normative Economics* (Cambridge, Mass.: Harvard University Press).

Berlin, I (1969), *Four Essays on Liberty* (Oxford: Oxford University Press).

Blackorby, C., Donaldson, D., and Weymark, J. A. (1984), 'Social Choice with Interpersonal Utility Comparisons: A Diagrammatic Introduction', *International Economic Review*, 25: 327–56.

Broome, J. (1991), 'Utility', *Economics and Philosophy*, 7.

Buchanan, J. M. (1975), *The Limits of Liberty* (Chicago: Chicago University Press).

Cohen, G. A. (1989), 'On the Currency of Egalitarian Justice', *Ethics*, 99: 906–44.

—— (1990), 'Equality of What? On Welfare, Goods and Capabilities,' *Recherches Economiques de Louvain*, 63.

Dasgupta, P. (1982), 'Utilitarianism, Information and Rights', in Sen and Williams (1982).
—— (1988), 'Lives and Well-being', *Social Choice and Welfare*, 5.
—— (1990), 'Well-being and the Extent of Its Realisation in Poor Countries', *Economic Journal*, 100.
d'Aspremont, C. (1985), 'Axioms for Social Welfare Ordering,' in L. Hurwicz, D. Schmeidler, and H. Sonnenschein, *Social Goals and Social Organisation* (Cambridge: Cambridge University Press).
—— and Gevers, L. (1977), 'Equity and Informational Basis of Collective Choice,' *Review of Economic Studies*, 44.
Deaton, A., and Muellbauer, J. (1980), *Economics and Consumer Behaviour* (Cambridge: Cambridge University Press).
Desai, M. J. (1990), 'Poverty and Capability: Towards an Empirically Implementable Measure', mimeo, London School of Economics.
Drèze, J., and Sen, A. (1989), *Hunger and Public Action* (Oxford: Clarendon Press).
Dworkin, R. (1977), *Taking Rights Seriously* (London: Duckworth).
—— (1981), 'What is Equality? Part 1: Equality of Welfare', and 'What is Equality? Part 2: Equality of Resources', *Philosophy and Public Affairs*, 10.
—— (1985), *A Matter of Principle* (Cambridge, Mass.: Harvard University Press).
—— (1987), 'What is Equality? III: The Place of Liberty', *Iowa Law Review*, 73.
Elster, J., and Hylland, A. (1986) (eds.), *Foundations of Social Choice Theory* (Cambridge: Cambridge University Press).
Erikson, R., and Aberg, R. (1987), *Welfare in Transition: A Survey of Living Conditions in Sweden 1968–81* (Oxford: Clarendon Press).
Feiwel, G. (1985) (ed.), *Issues in Contemporary Microeconomics and Welfare* (London: Macmillan).
Fishburn, P. C. (1973), *The Theory of Social Choice* (Princeton: Princeton University Press).
Gaertner, W., Pattanaik, P. K., and Suzumura, K. (1992), 'Individual Rights Revisited', *Economica*, 59.
Gevers, L. (1979), 'On Interpersonal Comparability and Social Welfare Orderings', *Econometrica*, 47.
Griffin, J. (1986), *Well-being* (Oxford: Clarendon Press).
Griffin, K., and Knight, J. (1989) (eds.), 'Human Development in the 1980s and Beyond', Special Number, *Journal of Development Planning*, 19.
Hahn, F. (1982), 'On Some Difficulties of the Utilitarian Economist', in Sen and Williams (1982).
Hammond, P. J. (1976), 'Equity, Arrow's Conditions and Rawls' Difference Principle', *Econometrica*, 44: 793–804.
—— (1982), 'Utilitarianism, Uncertainty and Information,' in Sen and Williams (1982).
—— (1985), 'Welfare Economics', in Feiwel (1985).
—— (1986), 'Consequentialist Social Norms for Public Decisions', in Heller *et al.* (1986).
Harsanyi, J. C. (1976), *Essays in Ethics, Social Behaviour and Scientific Explanation* (Dordrecht: Reidel).
Hayek, F. A. (1960), *The Constitution of Liberty* (London: Routledge and Kegan Paul).

Heller, W. P., Starr, R. M., and Starrett, D. A. (1986) (eds.), *Social Choice and Public Decision-Making: Essays in Honor of Kenneth J. Arrow* (Cambridge: Cambridge University Press).

Hossain, I. (1990), *Poverty as Capability Failure* (Helsinki: Swedish School of Economics, 1990).

Kanger, S. (1985), 'On Realization of Human Rights', *Acta Philosophica Fennica*, 38.

Kelly, J. S. (1978), *Arrow Impossibility Theorems* (New York: Academic Press).

Maskin, E. (1979), 'Decision-making under Ignorance with Implications for Social Choice', *Theory and Decision*, 11.

McMurrin, S. (ed.) (1980), *Tanner Lectures on Human Values*, (Cambridge: Cambridge University Press); reprinted in Sen (1982) and in Rawls *et al.* (1987).

Meade, J. E. (1976), *The Just Economy* (London: Allen and Unwin).

Mirrlees, J. (1982), 'The Economic Uses of Utilitarianism', in Sen and Williams (1982).

Nozick, R. (1974), *Anarchy, State and Utopia* (Oxford: Basil Blackwell).

Nussbaum, M. C. (1988), 'Nature, Function, and Capability: Aristotle on Political Distribution', *Oxford Studies in Ancient Philosophy*, Supplementary Volume.

—— and Sen, A. (1993) (eds.), *The Quality of Life* (Oxford: Clarendon Press).

Osmani, S. R. (1982), *Economic Inequality and Group Welfare* (Oxford: Clarendon Press).

Pattanaik, P. K. (1971), *Voting and Collective Choice* (Cambridge: Cambridge University Press).

Pigou, A. C. (1920), *The Economics of Welfare* (London: Macmillan).

Rawls, J. (1971), *A Theory of Justice* (Cambridge, Mass. Harvard University Press).

—— (1993), *Political Liberalism* (New York: Columbia University Press).

—— *et al.* (1987), *Liberty Equality and the Law* (Cambridge: Cambridge University Press).

Riley, J. (1987), *Liberal Utilitarianism: Social Choice Theory and J. S. Mill's Philosophy* (Cambridge: Cambridge University Press).

Robbins, L. (1932), *An Essay on the Nature and Significance of Economic Science* (London: Macmillan).

—— (1938), 'Interpersonal Comparisons of Utility,' *Economic Journal*, 48.

Roberts, K. W. S. (1980*a*), 'Possibility Theorems with Interpersonally Comparable Welfare Levels', *Review of Economic Studies*, 47.

—— (1980*b*), 'Interpersonal Comparability and Social Choice Theory', *Review of Economic Studies*, 47.

Samuelson, P. A. (1947), *Foundations of Economic Analysis* (Cambridge, Mass.: Harvard University Press).

Seabright, P. (1989), 'Social Choice and Social Theories', *Philosophy and Public Affairs*, 18.

Scanlon, T. M. (1982), 'Contractualism and Utilitarianism', in Sen and Williams (1982).

Schokkaert, E., and Van Ootegem, L. (1990), 'Sen's Concept of Living Standard Applied to the Belgian Unemployed', *Recherches Economiques de Louvain*, 63.

Sen, A. K. (1970), *Collective Choice and Social Welfare* (San Francisco: Holden-Day; Amsterdam: North Holland, 1979).

—— (1973), *On Economic Inequality* (Oxford: Clarendon Press, and New York: Norton).

—— (1976), 'Real National Income', *Review of Economic Studies*, 43; reprinted in Sen (1982).
—— (1977), 'On Weights and Measures: Informational Constraints in Social Welfare Analysis', *Econometrica*, 45; reprinted in Sen (1982).
—— (1980), 'Equality of What?' in McMurrin (1980); reprinted in Sen (1982) and in Rawls *et al.* (1987).
—— (1982), *Choice, Welfare and Measurement* (Oxford: Basis Blackwell, and Cambridge, Mass.: MIT Press).
—— (1983), 'Liberty and Social Choice', *Journal of Philosophy*, 80.
—— (1985*a*), 'Well-being, Agency and Freedom: The Dewey Lectures 1984', *Journal of Philosophy*, 82.
—— (1985*b*), *Commodities and Capabilities* (Amsterdam: North Holland).
—— (1986*a*), 'Social Choice Theory', in Arrow and Intriligator (1986).
—— (1986*b*), 'Information and Invariance in Normative Choice', in Heller, Starr, and Starrett (1986).
—— (1987), *On Ethics and Economics* (Oxford: Basil Blackwell).
—— (1990), 'Gender and Cooperative Conflicts', in I. Tinker, *Persistent Inequalities* (New York: Oxford University Press).
—— (1991), 'Utility: Ideas and Terminology', *Economics and Philosophy*, 7.
—— (1992*a*), *Inequality Reexamined* (Oxford: Clarendon Press, and Cambridge, Mass.: Harvard University Press).
—— (1992*b*), 'Minimal Liberty', *Economica*, 59.
—— *et al.* (1987), *The Standard of Living* (Cambridge: Cambridge University Press).
—— and Williams, B. (1982) (eds.), *Utilitarianism and Beyond* (Cambridge: Cambridge University Press).
Smith, A. (1776), *An Inquiry Into the Nature and Causes of the Wealth of Nations* (republished London: Home University, 1910).
—— (1790), *The Theory of Moral Sentiments*, revised edition (republished Oxford: Clarendon Press, 1975).
Streeten, P., *et al.* (1981), *First Things First: Meeting Basic Needs in Developing Countries* (New York: Oxford University Press).
Sugden, R. (1981), *The Political Economy of Public Choice* (Oxford: Martin Robertson).
—— (1986), *The Economics of Rights Co-operation and Welfare* (Oxford: Basil Blackwell).
Suzumura, K. (1983), *Rational Choice, Collective Decisions and Social Welfare* (Cambridge: Cambridge University Press).
Van Parijs, P. (1990), 'Equal Endowments as Undominated Diversity', *Recherches Economiques de Louvain*, 63.
Wittgenstein, C. (1953), *Philosophische Untersuchungen* (Oxford: Basil Blackwell).
Wriglesworth, J. (1985), *Libertarian Conflicts in Social Choice* (Cambridge: Cambridge University Press).

5

Values, Reasons, and the Theory of Persuasion

BERNARD WILLIAMS

1. Internal and external reasons

The distinction that I shall discuss under this title is not, strictly speaking, a distinction between two kinds of reason, but rather a distinction between two kinds of claim that can be made about what an agent *A* has reason to do. The statement '*A* has reason to *X*' receives an internal interpretation if it is taken to mean '*A* could arrive at a decision to *X* by sound deliberation from his existing *S*', where *S* is *A*'s existing set of desires, preferences, evaluations, and other psychological states in virtue of which he can be motivated to act. An external interpretation does not carry this implication. (Throughout the discussion I adopt the simplifying assumption that '*A* has reason to *X*' means '*A* has more reason to *X* than to do anything else'; additional qualifications would in fact enable one to drop this restriction.) A view that I have expressed elsewhere (Williams 1980; 1989; 1994), and will defend here, is that if '*A* has reason to *X*' has a distinctive sense, then it must receive the internal interpretation; in simplified form, the only reasons for action are internal reasons. I do not deny that '*A* has reason to *X*' can entirely intelligibly be asserted without this implication. The claim is merely that when it is so asserted, it means something that could be expressed by a different kind of sentence, for instance to the effect that it is desirable that *A* should do the thing in question, or that we have reason to desire that *A* should do it. Only the internal interpretation represents the statement as distinctively a statement about *A*'s reasons. Relatedly, if a statement of this kind is true, and *A* declines to do the thing in question, what is called in question is *A*'s capacity in this connection to act rationally or reasonably. It would be too strong, for more than one reason, to say that in such circumstances *A* acts irrationally, but the line of criticism that will be appropriate in these circumstances will address itself to *A*'s performance as a rational or reasonable agent rather than to other deficiencies that he may have.

It is important to emphasize the variety of elements that are, on this view, to be included in the agent's *S*. It does not contain merely inclinations or, again, egoistic motivations, and it can certainly contain dispositions associated with the agent's recognition of various kinds of values. Moreover, it is not the case that everything in the agent's *S* has already to be formed into preferences; and in so far as it is formed into preferences, those preferences do not necessarily have to satisfy formal conditions of completeness. There is no naturalistic reason, based on considerations of psychology or the philosophy of mind, to suppose that these indeterminancies are radically reducible, in particular to preference orderings that can be handled by Bayesian techniques. If there is a demand for such a reduction, it is of a normative, rather than an explanatory, character or, perhaps, the kind that is a fusion of the two, namely a demand that the phenomena should be such that a particular kind of explanation should be possible.

It is not an objection to the internalist account, interpreted in this broad way, that it involves vagueness and indeterminacy. This merely mirrors the truth that statements to the effect that *A* has a reason to do a certain thing are themselves vague and in various ways indeterminate. It would, of course, be an objection if the indeterminacy were such that there were no constraints on statements of this kind; if, for instance, there were no distinction between a situation in which someone, advising an agent, helped that agent to discover what he had reason to do, and the situation in which the adviser made a difference to the agent's *S* and gave him a reason for action which he did not have before. This question of vacuity will come up later in this chapter.

There is another difficulty, which concerns the form of the internalist account. In referring to what the agent would arrive at by a sound deliberative route, it can be taken to imply a claim to the effect that if the agent were to deliberate, and were to deliberate soundly, then he would arrive at this conclusion. This cannot be quite right, since deliberation is itself a psychological process, which has effects.

This means that we cannot necessarily equate '*A* could arrive by a sound deliberative route at the decision to *X*' with '*A* would arrive at that conclusion if he deliberated and did so soundly'. Someone may, indeed, do what he has most reason to do without deliberating and, perhaps, because he did not deliberate. We must not assume that thinking about the question of what to do, rehearsing considerations, and so forth, are simply like perception of an external reality. There is a dynamic process involved. Because of this, the internalist account's reference to arriving at a conclusion by a sound deliberative route has to be taken in an idealized or abstract form, which leaves out distinctive psychological effects of the actual process of deliberation. It is to be conceived in terms of a relation between the agent's *S*, the action in question, and the agent's principles of deliberation in so far as those principles are sound.

This raises the question of what counts as sound principles, and of what counts as a sound deliberative route. It is essential to any adequate account of '*A* has reason to *X*' that it should be normative, and should admit the possibility of *A*'s being shown that he is mistaken in thinking that he has a reason for a certain course of action. The internalist account does leave room for normative correction; it allows, for instance, for the agent to be shown that his deliberation is unsound because it is based upon false information. It may be asked why the agent's deliberative route can, on the internalist account, be shown to be unsound by reference to factual mistakes, while claims that what the agent is doing is immoral or imprudent do not necessarily count as showing that the deliberative route is unsound. The answer to this is, crudely, that an agent is committed in general to acting in the light of sound information, simply by being a rational agent; included in the *S* of every rational agent is a desire not to fail through error. (There are of course complex exceptions to the general working of this desire, but they are necessarily exceptions). Now it may be claimed that prudential, or again moral, polices are similarly involved in what it is to be a fully rational agent, and some philosophers have claimed conclusions of this kind. It may, indeed, to some extent be true, particularly with regard to a modest amount of prudence; if an agent is totally devoid of a concern or the effects of his actions on himself, we may indeed have problems in understanding what could count for him as a sound deliberative route at all. But to the extent that these things are true, then we are being told something about the necessary contents of the *S* of any rational agent.

If the claim is that those contents must include, for instance, moral elements, then we need an argument to that effect, an argument that the philosophers who have made these claims have in some cases tried to provide. When Kant, for instance, claimed that rational agent as such is committed to seeing himself as acting impartially, he constructed an entire philosophy with the intention of delivering that conclusion. It is important that the internalist account in itself does not rule out a conclusion of that kind. It merely demands that the conclusion should be argued, and that it cannot be acquired on the cheap, for instance by pointing out the obvious truth that people often describe unfair conduct as 'unreasonable'. It takes more than ordinary language to deliver large Platonic, Aristotelian, or Kantian conclusions to the effect that virtue and reason will coincide.

2. Rationality: interpretation and value

What then are the criteria of deliberative rationality, in which a rational agent presumably does necessarily have an interest? How far do they go beyond the general desire for true information, and minimal constraints of consistency? In particular, how far do they include the kinds of demands that rational decision theory has tended to place on them? I shall not try to answer this extremely large question, but there is an important aspect of it that I shall disucss, because a consideration in this area may seem to undermine the internalist view. It has been convincingly argued (Hurley 1989; Broome 1991*a*; 1991*b*) that in general we cannot disambiguate an agent's preferences and hence, in particular, assess the coherence of those preferences, without taking the agent to have values, values which must be intelligible to us. This might be thought to undermine the thesis of the internalism of reasons, by requiring that at least at some point 'there is reason to *X*' is prior to '*A* has reason to *X*'.

The argument starts from the familiar point that there are prima-facie counter-examples to even very elementary principles of rational decision theory, and that while it is very easy to save the theory by re-describing these cases, some further constraints are needed if this process is not simply going to render the theory trivial. We may take an example of Broome's (1991*b*: ch. 5), about transitivity. Maurice, when offered the choice between going to Rome and going to the mountains, prefers visiting Rome, because he is frightened by mountaineering. Faced with the choice between staying at home and going to Rome, he prefers to stay at home, because he is anti-culture. Compatibly with these two choices, he can prefer going to the mountains to staying at home. The solution to this failure of transitivity lies in a finer individuation of alternatives: we can distinguish between the option of staying at home when Rome is the only alternative from the option staying at home when mountaineering is the only alternative. (The first of these, Broome claims, Maurice does actually prefer to mountaineering but this is not a practical preference, that is to say, one that is expressed in actual choice. I am not sure that this is an altogether satisfactory solution, and some re-description will be needed if it is rejected; but the general principle of such methods is what concerns us here.) Similar problems, and similar solutions, are familiar from Allais's paradox and the Sure Thing Principle.

The problem now is that such differentiation may seem to be entirely arbytrary, with the result that the theory will be trivialized. Broome's solution is that Maurice is rational in these circumstances if and only if he is justified in having a preference between the two subdivided options that involve his staying at home; this implies that there is no rational principle requiring him to be indifferent between them. This introduces the notion of a 'justifying difference', which Broome interprets in terms of a differentiation with regard to good and bad. This may seem to lead to a rejection of internalism. The alternative, it seems, to there being no rational constraints on what will count as deliberative preference, is that discriminations of the agent should be rationally intelligible in terms of values, considerations that we can understand as intelligibly related to questions of value.

I agree with Broome that there is a need for substantive constraints on the interpretations of preference, but I do not agree that this leads to the rejection of internalism. We need in the first place to distinguish two possible aims that can be ascribed to a rational agent as such:

(i) to arrive at conclusions about what to do by procedures that cannot be faulted for irrationality;
(ii) to do what he has most reason to do.

(i) is neither a sufficient nor necessary condition of (ii). It is not a sufficient condition for the simple reason that he may do everything that could conceivably be demanded of a rational agent, but fail through bad luck, in particular through non-culpable ignorance, and in that sense he will not have done what he actually has most reason to do. (This is the sense in which 'a sound deliberative route', if it is to provide a sufficient condition of what the agent has most reason to do, must consist of more than simply the agent's deliberating as best he can in the circumstances.) Equally, (i) is not a necessary condition of (ii), for the reason already mentioned, that the application of any deliberative methods may itself, in certain circumstances, have psychological effects that get in the way of the agent doing what he has most reason to do. Now the rational agent's aim must be more basically (ii), rather than (i): the idea that (i) is more fundamentally the aim of the exercise than (ii) is, in effect, the notorious defensive civil servant syndrome.

What may mislead one about this is that, as a general policy, we can achieve (ii) only because the thing in question is the rational thing for us to do, and that consideration seems to imply (i). It is not a contingent fact that (i) helps in achieving (ii) but, even so, as we have already seen, (i) does not always need to be pursued in pursuing (ii). Now, supposing an agent seems to be failing in pursuing (ii) because of some deviant relation of his choice to his *S*, for instance through failure of transitivity. (Here, of course, we encounter the familiar problem of what is the ground of irrationality in such a case, for instance whether it is enough to say that a Dutch book could be made against him. It is an important consideration here, and one not always recognized by economic theory, that taking on a best is always an *additional* step; it is always a relevant question to ask 'would you make a Dutch book with this man?'.) The agent's interest is in achieving (ii): he is not passing an examination in practical rationality. So what he has to do is to see whether he can make sense of himself, whether he can understand his *S* in terms that will rationalize his choices to himself. Some fine individuations between objects of preferences are just given, but when there is a real issue of interpretation, we can agree with Broome that further reasons, and indeed further values, may be needed at this point. But they are the agent's values, and not the assessor's. It is those values, moreover, that an external interpreter will invoke if he is making sense of the agent's conduct as rational.

Is this an anti-Humean conclusion? In one sense, perhaps it is, inasmuch as some values have to be invoked in order to make sense of preferences,[1] but it is not anti-internalist, even when we grant a further point, that what counts as an intelligible invocation of a value is a shared matter of interpretation. To some extent, it may well be the case that we can interpret another agent's *S*, and, in particular, values that he may invoke in discriminating his own objects of preference, only by ascribing to him some values that we share ourselves. This indeed leaves untouched the internalist claim that what he has reason to do is a function of his *S*—it merely says something about what it is to understand his *S*.

However, internalist doctrine would be pointless if everyone's values, and everyone's *S*, were the same; in those circumstances, anyone's deliberation could be anyone else's, and the distinction between external and internalism would fade away. But clearly this is not how it is. We need to invoke some values, no doubt, in interpreting other people's preferences and in construing their rationality, but the values that we have to invoke are their values rather than ours. This will be true even if, to a limited extent, we can understand their values only by relating them to ours.

3. How much does the internalist account exclude?

As we have seen, the internalist account is generous with what counts as a sound deliberative route. It rejects the picture by which a determinate and fixed set of preferences is expressed simply in terms of its decision-theoretical rational extensions, and deliberation is construed simply as discovering what these are. The difficulty is that if, in abandoning this false picture, we allow any extension whatsoever of the agent's *S* to count, we have lost hold of the notion of what the agent has reason to do in virtue of his *S*. The problem can be modelled in terms of a shared deliberation, in the sense of a deliberation about what *A* is to do in which *B* takes part, typically by seeing the situation so far possible from the point of view of *A*'s *S*. (Some of the same considerations will apply also to a shared deliberation in the sense of a deliberation by *A* and *B* about what they should collectively do, but this is not the case most relevant to the present issue.) The questions of the limitations on what counts as a sound deliberative expression of the agent's *S* can be put in terms of a distinction between *B*'s helping *A* to arrive at such an expression, as opposed to *B*'s acting in such a way as to change *A*'s *S*. If we give a determinate set of rational deliberative procedures (it is often called an 'algorithmic' conception of deliberation), the danger is, once more, that the idea of 'a sound deliberative route' will have no constraining effect, and any resolution that the agent can psychologically reach 'from' his

[1] Susan Hurley (1989), perhaps misleadingly, describes any position that concedes this a 'objectivist'.

present *S*—that is simply to say, setting out from his present *S*—will equally count.

The traditional account assumed a highly determinate *S*, and a highly constrained set of procedures for arriving at new decisions on the basis of that *S*. In terms of this, one could supposedly determinate what procedures of an adviser or fellow deliberator would count as assisting the agent to discover what he had reason to do, as opposed to giving the agent new reasons or persuading him to do something he originally had no reason to do. To the extent that we lose hold of determinate constraints on 'a sound deliberative route', we shall have problems, too, with these derived descriptions: it will be unclear what counts as deliberative assistance in finding what one has reason to do, as opposed to interventions that come closer to conversion.

A possible suggestion at this point is to reverse the order of explanation, and, in some part, place the constraints on the procedures that are to count as deliberative assistance in contrast to these other interventions. What someone has reason to do will be what he can arrive at by a sound deliberative route; and he can arrive at a conclusion or resolution by a sound deliberative route, perhaps, only if he could be led to it by deliberative assistance that operated within those constraints.

What might those constraints be? What will the helpful deliberative assistant be like? Two necessary conditions perhaps are the following.

(i) The assistant will be truthful, in the sense both of telling the truth and of helping the agent to discover the truth. An application of this is that the assistant will be truthful about his own procedures and motives, with the result that these can be transparent to the agent; the assistant has no hidden agenda in his dealings with the agent.

(ii) The assistant will try to make the best sense of the agent's *S*, and, in particular, if there is a conflict between the assistant's and the agent's interpretations of the agent's *S*, the assistant will have some suitable explanation of the agent's misinterpretation. (This condition is not circular: it does not say that the assistant has to make the best sense of what the agent's reasons are.)

If an assistant acting in this way gets the agent to agree that what he has most reason to do is to *X*, may we say that this is indeed what the agent had most reason to do, in virtue of his original *S*? Not necessarily. Just as, in the purely first-personal construction, we had to allow for new psychological effects of the agent's actually deliberating, so in the two-person situation we have to factor out extraneous effects of the advisory situation itself. Thus the assistant might operate scrupulously within the constraints, and the agent fall in love with her, something which radically modifies his *S*. He is led to new courses of action as a result of shared deliberation within the constraints, but the outcome cannot count as what he originally had reason to do.

In the light of this, it is clear that we cannot leave out altogether retrospective interpretation of the ways in which the decision is related to the agent's original *S*. We still need the notion of the decision being the expression, even if an indirect one, of motivations that the agent had in the first place, and not of motivations which he has acquired in the process, unless those motivations themselves are expressions of what there was before. We cannot put all the weight on the procedural criterion in terms of the way in which an assistant has led, or might lead him to the conclusion. But have we now put any weight on it at all? Do we need the idea of the assistant? I suggest that we do. One reason is that the conception of what such an assistant might do itself plays a part (though only one part) in the interpretation of the way in which the decision is related to the agent's *S*.

The traditional account of rational deliberation leaves no room for the deliberation's introducing radically new material. As one might expect from the picture's resemblance to standard accounts of formal inference, it does not allow for a creative step in deliberation, in the sense of the agent's thinking of a course of action which does not already figure in the beliefs or motivations that he has. The traditional account might be extended from this in what, very loosely, could be called a Popperian way: it might allow new material, but be interested only in its relation to the original base, and not in where it came from—it would regard that as a purely psychological question. But we can hardly leave the matter there. Once we admit the truth that the relation of the decision to the original base cannot be algorithmic, or even very tightly constrained, the question of how the new material got into the deliberation becomes important, and the fact that it was suggested favourably by someone else may itself be thought (at least if it is not related in the most obvious and direct ways to the original base) to count in favour of saying that this is a case of the agent's being given a new motivation by persuasion rather than one of the agent's discovering what he already had reason to do. Constraints on the nature of the other person's intervention can play an important part in overcoming this assumption.

If we reflect on the advice and deliberative assistance, it will help us to see not only what counts as the agent's being helped to discover what he has reason to do, but also why this should not in fact be contrasted with persuasion.

The kinds of constraint that are in question here do not imply that the adviser's activity may not be a form of persuasion: it can be a form of persuasion, one that is truthful and addresses the question from the adviser's best understanding of the wants and interests of the agent. It is therefore not manipulative. But it is still pointful to call it 'persuasion', to remind us that it need not be free from emotional effects, it may work by seizing the agent's imagination, and it may be an expression of a power that could be used for other purposes.

A contrast between reason and persuasion, at both an individual and a political level, goes back at least to Plato, and it is still with us. We have to learn, against this, that the operations of reason, above all in its practical applications, cannot be recognized on formal grounds; and equally, a procedural account that tries to eliminate the dimension of persuasion is certain to be empty. (This point applies, obviously enough, to Habermas's 'ideal speech situation', a topic which is very relevant to the present subject but which I am unable to take up here.) Even when the reasons in question are those of an individual, and hence, on the account I have given, grounded in that agent's *S*, we can see why the two ideas, of the agent's discovering what he has reason to do, and of a sympathetic adviser operating within particular kinds of constraint, are connected. If we pursue such connections, we may be able to see more clearly why even internal individual reasons call for discussion with other people; why also, in hoping that public political discussion should be moderately rational and should address the reasons of individuals and groups, we are not committed to the nonsense of supposing that it could be trascendentally air-lifted out of the world of persuasion and power. Indeed, the internal account of individual reasons particularly brings out the importance of linking the discussion of reason with the theory of persuasion: the failings of an externalist account come out all the more clearly when we reflect on the kind of discussion that might be needed to convince an agent that such a reason applied to him, and how that discussion could hardly fail to be coercive.

REFERENCES

Allais, M. (1979), 'The so-called Allais Paradox and Rational Decision under Uncertainty', in Allais and Hagen (1979).

—— and Hagen, O. (1979) (eds.), *Expected Utility Hypotheses and the Allais Paradox* (Dordrecht: Reidel).

Broome, J. (1991*a*), 'Rationality and the Sure-Thing Principle', in Meeks (1991).

—— (1991*b*), *Weighing Goods* (Oxford: Basil Blackwell).

Harrison, R. (1980) (ed.), *Rational Action* (Cambridge: Cambridge University Press).

Hurley, S. L. (1989), *Natural Reasons* (Oxford: Oxford University Press).

Meeks, G. (1991) (ed.), *Thoughtful Economic Man* (Cambridge: Cambridge University Press).

Williams, B. (1980), 'Internal and External Reasons', in Harrison (1980) (reprinted in B. Williams (1991), *Moral Luck* (Cambridge: Cambridge University Press)).

—— (1989), 'Internal Reasons and the Obscurity of Blame', *Logos* 10 (Santa Clara, Calif.) (reprinted in B. Williams (1995*a*), *Making Service of Humanity* (Cambridge: Cambridge University Press).

—— (1995 *a*), *Making Service of Humanity* (Cambridge: Cambridge University Press).

—— (1995*b*), 'Replies', in a festschrift volume edited by R. Harrison and J. E. J. Altham (eds.), *World, Mind and Morality* (Cambridge: Cambridge University Press).

II

TWO VIEWS ON UTILITARIANISM

6

Economic Analysis and the Structure of Good: Transferring Utility Theory from Preferences to Betterness

JOHN BROOME

1. The structure of good

What can economics do for ethics? No doubt several things, but one of them is this: it can contribute a method for analysing the structure of good.

Philosophers sometimes speak about 'The Good' rather grandly, using capital letters, and that can make it seem mysterious. But what I mean by 'the structure of good' is not at all mysterious. We very commonly discuss which things are better or worse than others. We say that sun is generally better than rain; we wonder whether it would be better to move to a new job or stay in this one; we debate about which is the best way of coping with the sufferings of refugees. Betterness and worseness are common topics of our ordinary conversation. To put it more formally, between different alternatives we may be considering, there is a betterness relation:

——is at least as good as——

where the blanks are to be filled in with alternatives. (I ought to call this an 'at-least-as-goodness relation', but 'betterness relation' sounds better.) When I speak of the structure of good, I really mean the structure of this relation. It is a mundane matter, therefore. Also, it is only relative goodness—betterness—I am concerned with, not absolute goodness, whatever that might be.

It is obvious that the betterness relation has an important role in ethics. Some people—'teleologists' or 'consequentialists'—think betterness amounts to the whole of ethics, because we should always act so as to achieve the best possible result. In this chapter, though, I shall not be discussing the truth of this view, or precisely what is the role of betterness in ethics. My topic is the structure of betterness, whatever its role may be.

But what do I mean by the structure of the betterness relation? Here is an example: the betterness relation is transitive. If *A* is at least as good as *B*, and *B* is at least as good as *C*, then *A* is at least as good as *C*. I think this is a truth of logic. For any property *F*, its weak comparative relation

——is at least as *F* as——

is transitive. I shall not try to justify this claim now, but ask you to test it for yourselves. Try 'at least as wet as', 'at least as beautiful as', and some more. There are also some apparent counter-examples you should test. 'At least as westerly as' is one. Larry Temkin (1987: 138–87) has produced worrying counter-examples to the transitivity of the betterness relation, 'at least as good as', itself. So I do not want to suggest that the transitivity of betterness goes unchallenged. But I am not going to dwell on transitivity.[1] I mention it simply as one example of a structural feature of the betterness relation.

This particular feature derives from logic, and we do not need the methods of economics to discover it. But economics can help with other features, and those are the ones on which I am going to concentrate. I shall start with a sketch of the features I have in mind.

The good in the world comes, as I put it, at different locations. It comes, for instance, to different people; some things are good for you, and some are good for me. People, then, are locations for good. They make up, as I put it, one dimension of locations. Good also comes at different times; so times constitute a second dimension of locations. A third dimension is not quite so obvious: the dimension of states of nature. Suppose we do nothing to control emissions of greenhouse gases. The world may be so constituted that the global average temperature will rise by two degrees over the next century, or it may be so constituted that the temperature will rise by six degrees. Each of these possibilities is a state of nature. If the rise is six degrees, the consequences will be very bad; if two degrees, less bad. So good in one state of nature is different from good in another. We may say that states of nature constitute locations for good, too.

An important question about the structure of good is this: how is good located at different locations aggregated or weighed together to make up overall good? This is a broad question, and there are several parts to it. One is how the good of individuals goes together to make up general good. Suppose, for instance, we are comparing possible distributions of income in a society. Should we judge the distributions by the total of people's good, so that the best is the one with the greatest total? Utilitarians take the view that we should, so I shall set down this view as:

> *UTILITARIAN PRINCIPLE OF DISTRIBUTION.* One alternative is at least as good as another if and only if it has at least as great a total of people's good.

[1] It, and most other topics discussed in this chapter, are examined in more detail in Broome (1991). Transitivity is discussed on pp. 11–12.

Some people disagree with the utilitarian principle, because they think it gives no value to equality in the distribution of good between people: it cares only about the total of good, and not how it is distributed. As an alternative to the utilitarian principle, some people think we should give more weight to the good of worse-off people than we do to the good of the better off (see, for instance, Atkinson and Stiglitz (1980: 340), and Parfit (forthcoming)). We should value distributions, they think, not by the total of good, but by some sort of weighted total. So here is one question: how is one person's good to be weighed against another's? To put it another way, how is good to be aggregated across the dimension of people?

Let me express this question more formally. As well as the general betterness relation

——is at least as good as——

for each person *P* there is an individual betterness relation

——is at least as good for *P* as——

The general betterness relation is in some way made up of the individual relations (and possibly other things as well). Our question is how, precisely, is it made up. This is one question about the structure of the betterness relation.

Here is a corresponding question in a different dimension. We can choose to give up a proportion of the earth's resources to controlling emissions of greenhouse gases, or we can choose not to bother. The benefit from each of these alternatives depends on the state of nature. If greenhouse gases will not actually lead to much global warming, then it is better not to bother. If they will warm the world a lot, then it is better to control them. So the choice between these two policies is a matter of weighing a benefit in one state of nature against a benefit in another. We have to weigh goods across the dimension of states of nature. This, too, is a problem about the structure of the betterness relation.

It is problems like these that the methods of economics can help with. Indeed, theorems from economics can deliver very interesting and significant conclusions that link the aggregation of good across one dimension with its aggregation across another. I shall be mentioning one of these theorems later. The theorems can tell us a lot about the utilitarian principle of distribution, for instance, and help us decide whether we should accept it. But this is not intended to be a chapter on the answers to specific questions about the structure of good, or on the specific conclusions we can come to. It is a chapter on method. I shall describe how the techniques of economics can be turned to analysing the structure of good.

The techniques I have in mind are the techniques of utility theory, in which I include decision theory or expected utility theory.[2] Utility theory

[2] The theorem I find most useful in analysing the structure of good is proved by Gorman (1968: 367–90).

was originally designed as a theory of the structure of preferences. A person *P*s preferences constitute a 'preference relation'

P prefers——to——or is indifferent between them.

By means of axioms and theorems derived from the axioms, utility theory tries to describe the structure of this relation. Formally, the theory is nothing more than the assembly of its axioms and theorems. So it can be applied to any relation that happens to conform to the axioms, not just to preference relations. I think the betterness relation conforms to the axioms, or at least to many of them. So utility theory can be transferred from preferences to betterness. But to make the transfer properly requires a certain amount of work.

2. Probability-relative betterness

One piece of work it requires is this. Expected utility theory is a theory about preferences between uncertain prospects. To extend the theory to betterness, we shall have to make sure that the betterness relation can hold between prospects: that one prospect can be at least as good as another. And a doubt may be raised about that.

A prospect is a state of affairs whose results may be uncertain. For instance, we may be interested in comparing the alternatives of building, or not building, a sea wall around Bangladesh. Each of these alternatives is a prospect; the results of each are uncertain, particularly the results of not building the wall. The results depend on how much the sea level rises over the next few decades, and whether tropical storms become more frequent. If the changes in climate and sea level are not great, then the results of not building the wall will be to allow the present occasional floods to continue. But if the changes are great, the results will be much more frequent flooding.

Clearly, a person may have preferences between uncertain prospects. Her preferences will depend on her views about the likelihood of the various possible results. Expected utility theory aims to describe preferences like this. But it is not so clear what we should say about the relative goodness of uncertain prospects. Suppose, after considering the scientific predictions about sea levels and tropical storms, we were to conclude that it is better to build a wall than not to build one. Suppose, at very great expense, we build one. But then suppose the predictions turn out to be too pessimistic, and the work done on building the wall turns out to have been largely wasted. What will we say then? We originally formed the opinion it was better to build the wall. But, with the benefit of hindsight, we will conclude it was not better to build the wall; it would have been better to leave it unbuilt. Our original opinion, we might now conclude, was false. Indeed, we might conclude we were unjustified in forming this opinion in the first place. We might conclude that opinions about betterness ought never to be based on probabilities. It is what actually happens that determines which action is better, not probabilities of what might happen. When we eventually find out what actually happens, *then* we can tell which alternative is better. But up to that point we cannot. We can judge that building the wall is *probably* better than not building it. But we cannot say it is actually better.

The conclusion of this line of thought is that the betterness relation cannot hold between uncertain prospects. If this is so, expected utility theory could not possibly apply to the betterness relation, and my project of extending the theory to betterness will fail. But, naturally, I think the project can succeed. I think that uncertain prospects can be related by betterness, despite the doubt I have raised. To explain why, I want first to consider, not betterness, but rightness. That is to say, I shall consider the question of what we ought to do, and how that is affected by uncertainty. I shall come back to betterness afterwards.

In the example I gave, many authors would agree that building the wall was not better than not building it (since the scientific predictions turned out to be too pessimistic), but would nevertheless say we were right to build it (see, for instance, Jackson 1986: 351–65). Given the predictions we had available, we acted rightly, even though the wall turned out to be unnecessary in the end. G. E. Moore, however, would have denied even this. It was wrong to build the wall, Moore would have said (Moore 1903: 149). What we ought to do, he thought, is what will have the best results. Building the wall did not have the best results, so we ought not to have done it. Moore thought that, if we do not know what the results of our actions will be, we cannot know what we ought to do. Indeed, in practice, we can never know what we ought to do, because we can never know what the results of our actions will be. At best, we can estimate how we *probably* ought to act, but never how we actually ought to act.

But Moore was certainly wrong. When we have to act, the purpose of practical reasoning is to tell us how to act. Our reasoning must therefore issue in a judgement about how we ought to act. A judgement about how we probably ought to act falls short of what we need. So even if we have to base our judgements on probabilities, we shall nevertheless have to derive from them a conclusion about how we ought to act. Suppose, when deciding whether or not to build a wall around Bangladesh, we have Moore with us. We consider the scientific evidence, which predicts rapidly rising sea levels, and then wonder whether or not to build the wall. We ask Moore what we ought to do. He says we cannot possibly know what we ought to do. Pressed, he says that, in view of the evidence, we probably ought to build the wall. But this is not enough for us. We need to know what to do. To be told that *probably* we should build the wall does not help. Pressed further, Moore would certainly tell us to build the wall. This is not a mere whim on his part. He believes that, given the evidence before us, rationality requires us to build the wall. It would be irrational of us not to build it. And this is simply to say we ought to build it. Since Moore thinks rationality requires us to build the wall, he thinks we ought to build the wall. Officially, he denies this. But nevertheless, that is what he thinks.

The conclusion I draw is that we have a probability-relative notion of rightness, and could not get along without it. Relative to the probabilities we have available at the time, it is right to build the wall. Building it turns out in the end to have been a wasted effort. This means that, relative to what actually happens, it was wrong to build the wall. But we have to act when only probabilities are available. So probability-relative rightness is all we have to act on. We could not possibly act without it.

Indeed, I caught Moore himself using this probability-relative notion of rightness. Speaking of a moral rule, he says at one point: 'Though we may be sure there are cases where the rule should be broken, we can never know which those cases are, and ought, therefore, never to break it' (Moore 1903: 162–3). This looks like a contradiction: there are cases where we ought to break the rule, and there are no cases where we ought to break the rule. But it is not a contradiction. The second 'ought' in Moore's sentence is meant to be understood relative to our probabilities, and the first is not. Not even Moore can get along without a probability-relative notion of rightness.

But if we have a probability-relative notion of rightness, why should we not also have a probability-relative notion of betterness? I am sure that, actually, we do. When we conclude, justifiably, on the basis of probabilities, that we ought to build the wall, we also conclude that it is better to build the wall than not to build it. Relative to what actually happens, it may turn out better not to build it. Nevertheless, there is a perfectly good probability-relative sense in which it is better to build it.

I therefore have no qualms about applying the betterness relation to uncertain prospects. That, at least, removes one obstacle in the way of extending expected utility theory to betterness.

Moreover, I think betterness relations do actually conform to the axioms of expected utility theory. A relation that conforms to the axioms I shall call coherent. Both individual and general betterness are coherent, then. I have no need in this chapter to go into what the axioms are. (And actually, I am overstating my claim. I do not think betterness relations necessarily conform to all the axioms; they may not conform to the completeness axiom. But I think they conform to the others.) Nor, unfortunately, do I have time to produce an argument to show that the betterness relations conform to the axioms. I have an argument (Broome (1991: section 6.3)) but in this chapter I am simply going to ask you to accept the conclusion.

3. The Pareto principle

I think we can extend expected utility theory to betterness, then. But the question many people will ask is: why bother? Many economists are interested in problems of weighing and aggregation like the ones I described in section 1. But they think these problems can be understood and dealt with in terms of preferences. There is no need to think of them in terms of good at all, and so no need to convert utility theory into a theory about good. The theory can do the job that needs to be done within its own home territory of preferences. But actually this is not so. We really do need to concern ourselves with the weighing and aggregation of good. Preferences are not enough. In this section and the next I shall explain why not. There are important ethical discoveries to be made that cannot be made by working with preferences.

The job that needs to be done, as I described it in section 1, is to analyse how good distributed across a number of locations goes to make up overall good. For instance, how is general good made up out of the good of individuals? That is how the question is posed in my terms. How might it be posed in terms of preferences rather than good? Typically, by asking how social preferences are made up out of individual preferences. I shall explain why this is not an adequate way of posing the question.

What does it mean, first of all? 'Social preference' is a technical term, invented by economists, and it can be understood in various ways (see the relevant discussion in Sen (1983: 5–28)). But very often, when an economist says one alternative is socially preferred to another, I think she simply means it is better. I shall mention another possible meaning later. But for the moment, I am going to assume that the social preference relation

——is socially preferred or indifferent to——

is nothing other than the betterness relation

——is at least as good as——.

So the question we are considering is how general betterness is made up of individual preferences. But *is* general betterness made up out of individual preferences? Is the relative goodness of two alternatives determined by the preferences of individuals? I am going to argue that it cannot be. General betterness depends on individual betterness, but not on individual preferences. The idea that betterness depends on the preferences of individuals is captured in this widely accepted principle:

PARETO PRINCIPLE. (*a*) Two alternatives are equally good if everyone is indifferent between them. (*b*) If everyone either prefers the first of two alternatives to the second or is indifferent between the two, and someone definitely prefers the first, then the first is better than the second.

I am going to argue that the Pareto principle is false.

The basis of my argument is a theorem:

PROBABILITY AGREEMENT THEOREM. Suppose each person has coherent preferences, and suppose that the betterness relation is coherent and conforms to the Pareto principle. Then everybody agrees about the probability of every event.

This theorem appears in Hammond (1981: 235–50), but I am sure it was known earlier than that. Once you see the point, the theorem is obvious. Pick a range of alternatives that one person has preferences about, but that everyone else is indifferent about. Alternative consumptions for a single person are an example, if the person cares about her own consumption but no one else does. Over this range, the Pareto principle tells us that the betterness relation mimics the preferences of the one person who cares. That is to say, one of these alternatives is better than another if and only if this person prefers it to the other. But this person's preferences will be determined partly by her own probabilities; a person's preferences between two alternatives depend on what the person thinks will be the likely results of these alternatives. So, over this range of alternatives, the betterness relation, in mimicking the one person's preferences, will reflect that person's probabilities. Now take a second range of alternatives that everyone is indifferent about, except for a different person. Over that range, the betterness relation will have to mimic this second person's preferences, and so it will have to reflect her probabilities. Consequently, if these probabilities differ from the first person's, the betterness relation will have to reflect different probabilities in different areas. But expected utility theory requires a relation to be ordered according to consistent probabilities. Therefore, the betterness relation cannot conform to expected utility theory. The point is that the Pareto principle requires the betterness relation to follow each different person's probabilities in particular areas. So this relation cannot reflect consistent probabilities of its own unless everyone agrees about all probabilities.

Now, actually, people disagree about probabilities. Therefore, as things are, the betterness relation cannot be coherent and also conform to the Pareto principle. To be sure, the theorem seems to offer one hope of escape from this conclusion. One premiss of the theorem is that the preferences of individuals are coherent. So if people do not have coherent preferences, the theorem seems not to apply. But the coherence of individual preferences plays a minor part in the proof. All the proof requires is for individual preferences to display enough coherence to show up the individuals' disagreement about probabilities. And people's preferences do in practice often show up disagreements about probabilities. So there is really no escape from the conclusion: for the betterness relation, coherence and the Pareto principle are incompatible.

It will be useful to have a simple example of the conflict between coherence and the Pareto principle. In Table 6.1, the numbers stand for two

TABLE 6.1

	States of nature			
	Alternative I		Alternative J	
	M	N	M	N
Wealth of P	2	2	3	0
Wealth of Q	2	2	0	3

people's wealth. *M* and *N* are states of nature. *I* and *J* are alternative prospects that we have to compare; perhaps they show the results of alternative government policies. Both people are interested only in their own wealth, and both prefer more wealth to less. Furthermore, both are risk neutral about their wealth: of two alternative prospects, they always prefer the one with the greater expectation of wealth. *P* attaches probability 0.7 to state *M* and 0.3 to *N*. *Q* attaches probability 0.3 to *M* and 0.7 to *N*. Consequently each person finds that prospect *J* gives her a greater expectation of wealth than *I*, calculated according to her own probabilities. So both people prefer *J* to *I*. The Pareto principle therefore says *J* is better than *I*.

Let us make the extra assumption that the distribution (2,2),—two units to each person—is better than both (3,0) and (0,3)—three to one and none to the other. I use this assumption simply for the sake of producing this simple example; neither the probability agreement theorem, nor my argument, depends on it. Nevertheless, it is a very plausible assumption, because (2,2) has a greater total of wealth than either (3,0) or (0,3), and has it equally distributed. It is hard to doubt that (2,2) is better. Now, prospect *I* leads to (2,2) for sure, whereas *J* leads to either (3,0) or (0,3). So, given the extra assumption, the result of *I* is, for sure, better than the result of *J*. If betterness is coherent, it follows that *I* itself must be better than *J*. This is an obvious consequence of expected utility theory; you do not need to know much about expected utility theory to realize that. If one prospect has, for sure, better results than another, according to expected utility theory it is a better prospect. Coherence, then, says *I is* better than *J*.

The Pareto principle says the opposite. This example illustrates the conclusion I drew from the probability agreement theorem: coherence and the Pareto principle for betterness are incompatible. I have already said in section 2 that the betterness relation is coherent. Therefore the Pareto principle is false.

However, in section 2 I produced no argument for the coherence of the betterness relation, merely an announcement. So I do not expect you to be immediately convinced by my conclusion that the Pareto principle is false. In the hope of adding conviction, in the next section I shall try to explain just where the Pareto principle goes wrong.

4. Democracy and the principle of personal good

In the example of Table 6.1, coherence requires that *I* is better than *J*. I think this is correct. But let us ask what is the appeal of the opposite view, which is supported by the Pareto principle? I can see two lines of thought that might draw one to it.

The first is this. Since both people prefer *J* to *I*, in a democratic society *J* is surely the one of the two that should come about if there is a choice. When a democracy is faced with a choice, and the people unanimously prefer one of the alternatives to the other, then surely that one should come about. I shall not deny this view. But the conclusion it leads to is that, if there is a choice between *I* and *J*, *J* should come about. It does not lead to the conclusion that *J* is better than *I*. There is no contradiction in believing that *J* is worse than *I* but that, if there is a choice between *J* and *I*, *J* should come about. It is the inevitable fate of a democrat to find herself sometimes holding beliefs of this form. Inevitably, she will sometimes believe that some alternative *A* is worse than *B* but nevertheless that the electorate prefers *B* to *A*. In that case she believes that the alternative she considers worse is the one that should come about.

So this democratic view does not support the Pareto principle as I have expressed it. It may be that many economists would interpret the Pareto principle differently; they might deliberately intend it to express the democratic view. Let us write the principle in terms of social preference:

> *TRADITIONAL PARETO PRINCIPLE.* (*a*) Two alternatives are socially indifferent if everyone is indifferent between them. (*b*) If everyone either prefers the first of two alternatives to the second or is indifferent between the two, and someone definitely prefers the first, then the first is socially preferred to the second.

Then let us interpret '*A* is socially preferred to *B*' to mean that *A* should come about rather than *B* if there is a choice, and '*A* is socially indifferent to *B*' to mean that it does not matter whether *A* or *B* comes about. This is the alternative interpretation of social preference I mentioned in section 3. Then we may well have a principle that adequately expresses the democratic view, and this principle may well be true. Furthermore, we may be able to deduce important conclusions from it. They would be conclusions about the proper working of society, founded on the political principle of democracy. They would not be conclusions about good. Although they might be true, I do not think they would be the whole truth. I hope to show there are other important truths to be found by pursuing the analysis of good.

In the example of Table 6.1, I said there were two lines of thought that might lead one to think that *J* is better than *I*. The democratic line, I have explained, does not actually lead to this conclusion. The other line is simply this: since both people prefer *J* to *I*, *J* must be better than *I* for both; therefore *J* must be better than *I*.

Now, I agree that if *J* were better for both people than *I*, then it would indeed be better. That would follow from this principle:

> PRINCIPLE OF PERSONAL GOOD. (*a*) Two alternatives are equally good if they are equally good for each person. (*b*) If one alternative is at least as good as another for everyone, and definitely better for someone, then it is better.

I believe the principle of personal good, and I believe it can be defended, though I shall not attempt a defence in this chapter (see Broome 1991: ch. 8 and 9). But this principle does not really yield the conclusion that *J* is better than *I*, because actually *J* is not better than *I* for both people. It is only better for person *P* if state of nature *M* is considerably more probable than *N*. But if *M* is considerably more probable than *N*, then alternative *J* is worse for person *Q* than *I*. So this line of thought fails too. It does not show that *J* is better than *I*, and it does not succeed in supporting the Pareto principle. Both people prefer *J* to *I*, but it cannot be true than *J* is better than *I* for both. This illustrates an important fact about probability-relative betterness. I argued in section 2 that we can understand betterness in a probability-relative way. We can make sense of the question whether *J* is better than *I* for person *P*, and we need not make the answer depend on what actually happens. We can give an answer based on probabilities, without waiting till we know which state of nature actually occurs. If state *M* is considerably more likely than *N*, we can say that *J* is better than *I* for person *P*. But we can only speak of probability-relative betterness in the context of some particular probabilities. This context implicitly remains constant unless we deliberately change it. So to say that *J* is better than *I* for both people would mean that *J* is better than *I* for both people relative to the same probabilities. But there are no probabilities relative to which *J* is better than *I* for both people. So we can say with confidence that *J* cannot be better than *I* for both people. This conclusion does not commit us to thinking that some probabilities are correct and others incorrect. Many Bayesians think there are no such things are correct probabilities, and I have no need to disagree with them.

A person's *preferences* will depend on her own probabilities. Both *P* and *Q* believe that *J* is better for themselves than *I*. That is why they both prefer *J*. But *J* cannot be *better* for both. Relative to *P*s probabilities, *J* is better than *I* for *P*. Relative to *Q*'s probabilities, *J* is better that *I* for *Q*. But we cannot detach these facts from the probabilities and say simply that *J* is better than *I* for both people. So long as people disagree about probabilities, a person's preferences and her betterness cannot coincide. Consider this popular view:

PREFERENCE-SATISFACTION THEORY OF GOOD. One alternative is at least as good for a person as another if and only if the person prefers it or is indifferent between the two.

I have just given one reason why this theory cannot be true. I hope this discussion has revealed what is wrong with the Pareto principle. The Pareto principle makes general *betterness* depend on individual *preferences*. It is an unviable hybrid. Considerations of democracy make what should come about depend on individual preferences. The principle of personal good makes general betterness depend on individual betterness. Both of these connections are sound ones. But the connection between general betterness and individual preference is unsound.

I have already said it may be worth while to take the route of democratic theory, and develop the link between preferences and what should come about. But it is also worth while to develop the link between individual and general good expressed in the principle of personal good. This leads us to an investigation that lies within the structure of good. We have to leave preferences, and work with betterness instead. Utility theory gives us the means to pursue this investigation, but only when it is transferred from the domain of preferences to the domain of betterness. That is why I said in section 3 that this transfer needs to be made.

But to justify this remark fully, I still need to demonstrate that there is something significant to be learnt by doing so. I am going to give just one example. This is a true theorem:

INTERPERSONAL ADDITION THEOREM. If the individual and general betterness relations are coherent, and if the principle of personal good is true, then the general betterness relation can be represented, in the manner of expected utility theory, by a utility function that is the sum of utility functions representing the betterness relations of individuals.

Since I think that individual and betterness relations are coherent, and since I believe the principle of personal good, I think the conclusion of this theorem is true. Interpreting the conclusion is an arduous and complicated task, which I am not going to undertake here (see Broome (1991: ch. 10)). I am not even going to explain, for those who are unfamiliar with it, the idea of 'representing' a relation by a utility function in the manner of expected utility theory. I shall simply say that the theorem can be used to give some—not conclusive—support to the utilitarian principle of distribution stated in section 1. I hope you can see by looking at the theorem's conclusion that this might plausibly be so. So the theorem tells us something about the foundations of utilitarianism. I think that alone is enough to justify the application of economic methods to the structure of good. The interpersonal addition theorem is merely a reinterpretation of a theorem of John Harsanyi's (1955: 309–21):

> *HARSANYI'S THEOREM.* Suppose each person has coherent preferences, and that social preferences are coherent and satisfy the traditional Pareto principle. Then social preferences can be represented, in the manner of expected utility theory, by a utility function that is the sum of utility functions representing individuals' preferences.

Reinterpreted, I think this is an extremely important theorem. But it has no significance as it stands, because its premisses are mutually inconsistent. They are not logically inconsistent, but they cannot all be true given the facts of the world. The premisses of this theorem are exactly the premisses of the probability agreement theorem stated in section 3, if the betterness relation is replaced with the social preference relation. To make this explicit, replacing the betterness relation with the social preference relation gives us:

> *TRADITIONAL PROBABILITY AGREEMENT THEOREM.* Suppose each person has coherent preferences, and that social preferences are coherent and satisfy the traditional Pareto principle. Then everyone agrees about the probability of every event.

So the premisses of Harsanyi's theorem imply that everyone agrees about all probabilities. Since people do not agree about all probabilities, the premisses cannot all be true. Consequently Harsanyi's theorem, as it stands, can tell us nothing significant.

Expressed in terms of preferences, Harsanyi's theorem can tell us nothing. Reinterpreted in terms of betterness, it becomes the interpersonal agreement theorem, which tells us a great deal. This clearly demonstrates the value of working in terms of good. We should take the methods from economics, and transfer them to investigate the structure of good.

5. Good and preferences

To concentrate on good instead of preferences raises some people's hackles. Many economists, particularly, resist it. It smacks to them of illiberal paternalism. But I think most of the resistance arises from misunderstandings. So I want to close with some soothing words.

Many of the people who worry about an analysis in terms of good believe in the preference-satisfaction theory of good. They believe that one alternative is at least as good for a person as another if and only if the person prefers it or is indifferent between the two. 'A person is the best judge of her own interests', these people say, thinking it supports the theory. Now, the preference-satisfaction theory says that a person's preference relation coincides with her betterness relation. If it is true, therefore, betterness will coincide with preference. So the preference-satisfaction theory gives no reason to object to an analysis of betterness. If the theory is true, an analysis of betterness is simply an analysis of preferences. To deal in good rather than preferences is simply to allow for a wider range of possibilities. It allows cases where a person's good coincides with her preferences, and it allows for other cases too.

As it happens, the preference-satisfaction theory is false. I have already given one reason why this is so. A person's preferences will depend on her own probabilities, and probabilities vary from person to person. Betterness, on the other hand, implies a constant context of probabilities, so betterness cannot coincide with preferences. But this point about differing probabilities is a very sophisticated reason for separating betterness from preference. I do not think it should provoke anyone to outrage.

Betterness may come apart from preference in other ways too. For instance, people may sometimes be imprudent. By this I mean that they may give some elements of their good more weight than others, in forming their preferences. For instance, you might prefer to sacrifice a greater amount of your good in the further future for the sake of a smaller amount in the near future. This means you will sometimes prefer, of two alternatives, the one that is less good for you on balance. That is simply what I mean by imprudence; an imprudent person sometimes prefers, of two alternatives, the one that is worse for her. To recognize the possibility of imprudence does not commit one to thinking that imprudent preferences should necessarily be overruled, by the government or anyone else. I have already pointed out that what should come about need not be the same as what is better. No doubt, liberal political principles will be opposed to intervention, even when people are imprudent. To be sure, an analysis of the structure of good would be pointless if it did not eventually connect up with action in some way or other. It must in the end help to determine how people, and the government, ought to act. But the determination need not be direct. It certainly does not imply that a government ought to intervene whenever people's preferences do not coincide with their good.

And, although preferences and betterness sometimes come apart, they are more often closely linked. To a large extent a person's good is determined by her tastes. If you prefer apples to oranges, then normally (if you are not allergic to apples, not in serious need of vitamin C, and so on) apples are better for you than oranges. Speaking of good may sound puritanical to some people. But that is only a superficial appearance.

Two final points need to be made about our knowledge of people's good. I may speak of your good without implying that I know what is good for you better than you do yourself, just as I may speak of your preferences without implying that I know your preferences better than you do. Merely to speak of a person's good does not imply superior knowledge.

Also, I can develop a useful formal analysis of the structure of your preferences without knowing which particular things you prefer to others, and I can develop a useful formal analysis of the structure of your good without knowing which particular things are good for you. Since the 'ordinalist revolution' of the 1930s, economists have felt more secure working with preferences than with good, because preferences are supposed to have some sort of epistemological priority. Perhaps they have; perhaps it is easier to find out what a person's preferences are than to find out what is good for the person. But it does not follow that we cannot usefully make an analysis of good. We can have a useful theory of quarks, even though quarks are harder to track than billiard balls. No doubt, an account of the structure of good would be pointless if we had no epistemological access at all to a person's good. But we are not in that position.

I do not think, then, that economists need resist the idea of applying economic techniques to the structure of good. And there is a lot to be learnt by doing so.

REFERENCES

Atkinson, A. B., and Stiglitz, J. E. (1980), *Lectures on Public Economics* (New York: McGraw-Hill).

Barcan Marcus, R., Dorn, G. J. W., and Weingartner, P. (1986) (eds)., *Logic, Methodology and Philosophy of Science VII* (Amsterdam: Elsevier).

Broome, J. (1991), *Weighing Goods* (Oxford: Basil Blackwell).

Gorman, W. M. (1968), 'The Structure of Utility Functions', *Review of Economic Studies*, 35: 367–90.

Hammond, P. (1981), 'Ex-ante and Ex-post Welfare Optimality under Uncertainty', *Economica*, 48: 235–50.

Harsanyi, J. C. (1955), 'Cardinal Welfare, Individualistic Ethics, and Interpersonal Comparisons of Utility', *Journal of Political Economy*, 63: 309–21.

Jackson, F. (1986), 'A Probabilistic Approach to Moral Responsibility', in Barcan Marcus, Dorn, and Weingartner (1986).

Moore, G. E. (1903), *Principia Ethica* (Cambridge: Cambridge University Press).

Parfit, D. (forthcoming), *On Giving Priority to the Worse Off*.

Sen, A. (1983), 'Liberty and Social Choice', *Journal of Philosophy*, 80: 5–28.

Temkin, L. (1987), 'Intransitivity and the Mere Addition Paradox', *Philosophy and Public Affairs*, 16: 138–87.

7

Consequentialist Decision Theory and Utilitarian Ethics[1]

PETER J. HAMMOND

1. Introduction

Normative social choice theory seems to have started out as a discussion of how to design suitable political systems and voting schemes—as in the work of well-known writers like Borda (1781), Condorcet (1785), Dodgson (1884), Black (1948), and Arrow (1951; 1963). Yet, in its attempt to aggregate individual preferences or interests into some kind of collective choice criterion, it would appear equally suited to the general issue of how to make good decisions which affect several different individuals. This, of course, is the subject of ethics in general, rather than just of political philosophy. After all, the design of suitable political systems is just one particular kind of ethical issue. So is the design of economic systems, and even the adjustment of features like tax rates within an existing system.

This suggests that we should be most interested in a normative social choice theory that seems capable of handling practical ethical problems. My claim will be that a properly constructed form of utilitarianism has the best chance of passing this crucial test. Indeed, there are three main strands of normative social choice theory. The first is based on Arrow's original ideas, while the other two follow from succeeding major developments due to Harsanyi (1953; 1955; 1976; 1977; 1978) and Sen (1970*a*; 1970*b*; 1977; 1982*a*) respectively. Of these three it is only the Harsanyi approach, when suitably and significantly modified, that appears not to create insuperable difficulties for a complete theory of ethical decision-making.

The limitations of Arrow's theory are fairly well understood, not least by Arrow himself. His crucial assumption was the avoidance of interpersonal comparisons—at least until the discussion of 'extended sympathy' in the

[1] This chapter was prepared in May 1991 for presentation at the Summer School on 'Ethics and Economics' held by the International School of Economic Research (Department of Economics, University of Siena), Certosa di Pontignano, Siena, July 1991. Parts of the chapter are based on previous talks to the workshop on Operations Research/Microeconomics Interfaces at the European Institute for Advanced Studies in Management in Brussels, Jan. 1990, and to the Economic Justice Seminar at the London School of Economics in Nov. 1990.

second edition of *Social Choice and Individual Values*, and a later (Arrow 1977) article generously acknowledging the potential usefulness of work that d'Aspremont and Gevers (1977) and I (Hammond 1976) had done in the 1970s, building on Sen's ideas (and those of Suppes 1966). The four axioms of Arrow's impossibility theorem—namely, unrestricted domain, independence of irrelevant alternatives, the Pareto principle, and non-dictatorship—can all be satisfied if the definition of a 'social welfare function' is generalized to allow interpersonal comparisons (Hammond 1976; 1991*a*). It might have been better, however, if Arrow's 'independence of irrelevant alternatives' axiom had been called 'independence of irrelevant personal comparisons' instead, since this can then be weakened to 'independence of irrelevant interpersonal comparisons' when interpersonal comparisons are allowed.

Sen's approach, by contrast, uses 'social welfare functionals' that map profiles of interpersonally comparable utility functions into social orderings. These do allow interpersonal comparisons. The approach therefore does not automatically exclude rules such as Harsanyi's (or classical) utilitarianism and Rawlsian maximin. Indeed, as d'Aspremont and Gevers (1977), Roberts (1980), Blackorby, Donaldson, and Weymark (1984), d'Aspremont (1985: 19–76), and others have pointed out, there are many different possibilities. Actually, this indeterminacy of the social welfare functional could well be regarded as a serious weakness of Sen's approach.

Some other weaknesses of standard social choice theory, however, appear even more serious. For there are also several important questions for any ethical theory of this kind, based as it is on a social ordering, derived from unexplained interpersonal comparisons of personal utility, without making very clear what constitutes personal utility or what interpersonal comparisons are supposed to mean. These weaknesses were also present in much of my own earlier work on social choice theory.

Ultimately, in order to overcome all these defects, it would seem that a social choice theoretic approach to ethical decision problems should be able to provide answers to the following important questions:

(1) Why have a social ordering at all, instead of incomplete preferences such as those which lie behind the Pareto rule, or even some completely unpatterned social choice rule which obeys none of the usual axioms of rational choice?
(2) Which individual preferences, and which individuals' preferences, should be reflected in the social choice rule? (The 'which individuals' issue arises when we consider whether and how to include foreigners, animals, and unborn generations in our social choice rule.)
(3) What method of making interpersonal comparisons, if any, is the right one to use when arriving at the social choice rule, and what are these interpersonal comparisons meant to represent?

(4) What should count in addition to individual preferences (or welfare)? Is it right that society should have preferences over issues like diet or religion which are usually regarded as purely personal? Do such personal issues force us to consider 'non-welfarist' theories?

The theory I shall review in the following pages has grown over the years out of attempts to answer these and related questions. It is a utilitarian theory, but with 'utility' defined in quite a different way from what almost all versions of utilitarianism seem to have used in the past. Indeed, an individual's utility—or rather, 'welfare' as I shall often call it when I want to emphasize the distinction from these earlier concepts of utility—will be regarded as that function whose expected value ought to be maximized by decisions affecting only that particular individual. This implies that welfare acquires purely ethical significance. The relevance of personal tastes, preferences, desires, and happiness to this ethical measure of an individual's welfare then becomes an ethical question, which is exactly what I believe it should be. Moreover, interpersonal comparisons will amount to preferences for different kinds of people—for rich over poor, for healthy over sick, for educated over ignorant, for talented over unskilled, etc. Note carefully that such preferences do not imply a disregard for those individuals who either are or will be unfortunate enough to experience poverty, sickness, ignorance, or lack of skills. Rather, such preferences represent society's present and future gains from enriching the poor, healing the sick, educating the ignorant, and training the unskilled. In addition, there will be a zero level of utility which marks the threshold between the desirability and undesirability of adding an extra individual to the world's population. Finally, utility ratios will represent marginal rates of substitution between numbers of indifferent kinds of individual.

The key motivation for this revised utilitarian theory is its unique ability to treat properly multi-stage ethical decisions, represented as ethical decision trees, while at the same time recognizing that there is some concept of individual welfare which ought to determine ethical decisions. In particular, for decisions which affect only one individual, only that individual's welfare ought to matter. Of course, this excludes non-welfarist ethical theories by assumption. But I am going to claim that everything of ethical relevance to individuals can be included in our measures of the welfare of individuals, and that nothing else should matter anyway.

The first part of this chapter is a review of the consequentialist approach to Bayesian decision theory. Section 2 explains why a new approach may be desirable, especially in connection with ethics and social choice theory. Section 3 considers ethical behaviour norms in finite decision trees under uncertainty and presents the two important axioms of unrestricted domain and consistency in continuation subtrees. Thereafter section 4 explains the motivation for the 'consequentialist' axiom, according to which only the consequences of behaviour in decision trees are relevant to proper decision-making. The next few sections are inevitably rather more technical and cite results proved in Hammond (1988*a*). Section 5 discusses how the three axioms together imply the existence of an ethical preference-ordering over uncertain consequences that satisfies the controversial independence axiom. Section 6 adds an extra continuity axiom which implies expected utility maximization.

The second part of the chapter is much more directly concerned with ethics. Section 7 begins to apply the consequentialist decision theory of the first part of the chapter to ethical decision problems concerning a society of individuals. To do so it introduces personal consequences, so that a social consequence is just a profile of personal consequences. Then section 8 puts forward the hypothesis of individualistic consequentialism, according to which it is only the marginal distribution of each individual's personal consequences which is relevant to ethical decision-making. In other words, it does not matter at all how different individuals' risky personal consequences are correlated—they can always be treated as if they were independently distributed.

While individualistic consequentialism captures one aspect of individualism, it does not give rise to any idea that social welfare arises from the individual welfares of different persons in society. This is remedied in section 9, which introduces the concept of 'individual welfarism'. It is assumed that, just as society has its ethical behaviour norm for social decision trees, so there is an ethical behaviour norm for 'individual decision trees'. Such trees are particular social decision trees in which there is only one individual whose probability distribution of personal consequences can be affected by any decision that is taken. It is required that the social behaviour norm in any such individual decision tree should exactly match the ethical behaviour norm for the relevant individual. Under the consequentialist axioms of sections 3–6, as well as the new conditions set out in sections 7 and 8, individual welfarism implies the existence of a cardinal equivalence class of individual welfare functions for each individual, whose expected values are maximized by decisions corresponding to the individual norm.

Section 10 goes on to show, moreover, that the conditions of Harsanyi's (1955) utilitarian theorem are all satisfied. Thus there exists a cardinal equivalence class of social welfare functions whose expected values are maximized by the social norm, and which can be expressed as the sum of suitably normalized individual welfare functions. So the social welfare functional linking individual and social welfare functions is simply additive, as in classical utilitarianism. As is pointed out in section 10, however, the individual welfare functions which ought to be added have a very different interpretation from the classical concept of utility.

In section 11 the vexed question of optimal population is taken up. It is assumed that individuals who do not exist already can be ignored whenever none of the decisions being contemplated could possibly lead to their coming into existence. Thus, in any individual decision tree where the only individual who could be affected never comes into existence anyway, it does not matter what decision is made. This assumption has the effect of determining a constant individual welfare level corresponding to non-existence. The individual welfare function can then be normalized so that this level is zero. The implication is that it is only necessary to sum the individual welfares of those individuals who do come into existence; all other individuals' welfare levels are zero and so their welfare can be ignored.

A crucial question raised above was how to make sense of the interpersonal comparisons which are needed in any satisfactory resolution of Arrow's impossibility theorem. This is the topic of section 12 which, as promised, shows how the utilitarian objective being propounded here relates interpersonal comparisons to, logically enough, social preferences for different kinds of persons.

The final section 13 contains a concluding assessment of what has and has not been achieved so far in this research project.

2. Bayesian decision theory

How does one make good ethical decisions? This is obviously the main question in any ethical theory which is going to arrive at specific recommendations for action. Moreover, this question is not so different from the general problem of how to make good decisions in general, which is the subject of decision theory. As in that theory, it will be helpful to consider what acts are possible, what consequences those acts lead to, and how those consequences should be evaluated. The only special features of ethical decision theory, in fact, are the kind of consequence which we shall admit as relevant, and the way we think about and evaluate those consequences.

In normative decision theory, a standard axiomatic approach was formulated during the 1940s and 1950s, based upon the major contributions of von Neumann and Morgenstern and Savage in particular. It involved a system of axioms whose implication was that agents should have subjective probabilities about uncertain events, and a (cardinal) utility function for evaluating consequences. Moreover, the best action was that which would maximize expected utility. This is the approach which, following Harsanyi (1978), I shall call Bayesian decision theory.

Even as a normative standard, this theory has come under heavy attack in recent years. Yet, with a few exceptions such as Machina (1989) and McClennen (1990), it seems to me that most of the critics have not really fully understood the theory. In particular, they have often failed to appreciate how adaptable it is, and how it can handle many of the familiar criticisms by a suitable extension of the concept of a relevant 'consequence'. In addition, it must be pointed out that the usual framework in which the axioms of decision theory are presented is very special. Following von Neumann and Morgenstern's recommended procedure, complicated intertemporal decision problems are generally collapsed into their 'normal form', in which the decision-maker makes a single choice of strategy or plan which is intended to cover all possible future contingencies. Yet real decision problems offer the chance to change one's mind in future, since decisions are not usually made as irrevocable commitments to a particular strategy. And, as I have pointed out before (Hammond (1988*c*; 1989)), the main alternatives to Bayesian decision theory, with its criterion of maximizing expected utility, create for the decision-maker the risk that *ex ante* plans will not be carried out but will get revised later, even though nothing unforeseen has happened in the meantime. This is very like the inconsistency phenomenon in dynamic choice which Strotz (1956) was the first to explore formally; it is also related to 'subgame imperfections' of the kind first considered by Selten (1965) in *n*-person game theory.

One of the most fundamental axioms of Bayesian decision theory is the existence of a preference ordering over the space of event-contingent consequences. With the notable exceptions of Levi (1974; 1980; 1986), Seidenfeld (1988*a*; 1988*b*) and Bewley (1989), even most critics of the theory accept this axiom. Yet many ethical theorists do not. Some of these simply claim that nobody has any business constructing a 'social preference ordering' over decisions or the consequences to which they lead. Others claim to find it objectionable that anything as subtle and complicated as ethics could be reduced to something as conceptually simple or crude as the maximization of a preference ordering. This, however, overlooks the obvious point that, though a preference ordering may seem like a simple concept, it could still range over an immensely complicated space of ethically relevant consequences. As an analogy, the original Zermelo (1913) theory of two-person games with complete information shows how each player has an optimal strategy in chess, specifying what move should be made in each possible position. It is inconceivable that the optimal strategy could even be found, however, because chess is far too complicated and subtle a game (and the Japanese game of Go, to which the same argument applies, is perhaps even more so).

In an attempt to meet all these cogent objections, I have therefore been developing a different justification for Bayesian decision theory. The standard axioms emerge as implications of what may seem less objectionable 'consequentialist' axioms. Rather than assume that there is a preference ordering, the new theory *proves* that behaviour must reveal such an ordering. Under an additional minor but necessary continuity axiom, it also proves that there exists a unique cardinal equivalence class of utility functions whose expected value is maximized. Of course, the proofs of such results do rely on other axioms, but they may seem less unnatural or open to criticism than many have found the standard axioms to be.

3. Decision trees and ethical theories

The approach I have adopted begins by recognizing that there are multistage decision problems which can be described by means of decision trees. The typical decision tree will be denoted by T. It has a set of nodes N. To avoid unnecessary technical complications, I shall work only with finite trees—i.e trees for which N *is* finite. Among the nodes in N is a subset N^* of decision nodes, at which the decision-maker is offered the choice of several different possible actions.

To represent uncertainty, there will also be a set N^0 of chance nodes at which 'nature makes a decision' outside the decision-maker's control. Really we should now follow the argument presented in Hammond (1988*a*) and discuss decision theory in the absence of probabilities, seeing what assumptions are needed in order to ensure the existence of at least subjective probabilities. Rather than do so here, however, it will simply be assumed that at each chance node $n \in N^0$ there is always an associated probability distribution $\pi(n' \mid n)$ over the finite set $N_{+1}(n)$ of nodes n' which immediately succeed n. To avoid problems that arise in continuation subtrees which are only reached with probability zero, it will be assumed here that any node $n' \in N_{+1}(n)$ for which $\pi(n' \mid n) = 0$ gets 'pruned' from the decision tree, along with the set $N(n')$ of all succeeding nodes. Then only nodes n' for which $\pi(n' \mid n)$ is positive will remain, and so we can indeed assume that $\pi(n' \mid n) > 0$ whenever $n \in N^0$ and $n' \in N_{+1}(n)$.

Any decision tree T starts at an initial node n_0, which could be either a decision node or a chance node. Since the tree is finite, it must also have a set X of terminal nodes at which everything has been resolved. Then N must be the union $N^* \cup N^0 \cup X$ of the three disjoint sets N^*, N^0, and X.

Nature's 'choices' of events and the decision-maker's choices of acts will combine to determine a unique path through the decision tree, starting at the initial node n_0 and ending at some terminal node $x \in X$. In fact there is an obvious one-to-one correspondence between paths through the tree and terminal nodes. Along any such path, it is assumed that there is a history of ethically relevant consequences which can be summarized as just a consequence y in some domain of consequences Y. It does no harm then to think of there being a unique consequence attached to each terminal node of the tree—in other words, there is a function $\gamma: X \to Y$ mapping each terminal node x of the decision tree into the consequence $\gamma(x)$ of following through the tree the unique path which ends at x. It is assumed that ethical decisions should depend only on their different consequences y in a fixed consequence domain Y; consequences outside Y are ethically irrelevant.

Each path through the decision tree also corresponds to a unique sequence of choices by nature, which then determines a history of events. Since the probabilities $\pi(n' \mid n)$ of these successive choices have been specified, there is a corresponding probability $\xi(x)$ of reaching any given terminal node $x \in X$ and then of getting the consequence $\gamma(x)$. In fact decisions will give rise to probability distributions of consequences, in a way to be explained in section 5 below.

One last crucial ingredient is needed for an ethical theory. This is the concept of a behaviour norm. Behaviour at any decision node $n \in N^*$ can be regarded as selecting some non-empty set of nodes from $N_{+1}(n)$, the set of nodes immediately succeeding n. Note that multiple choices at n are allowed, just as economic theory allows consumers to be indifferent between two or more options. Moreover, there is no reason to think that only one decision at each decision node is ethically acceptable. Thus a behaviour norm is formally defined as a function β, which specifies a non-empty behaviour set $\beta(T, n) \subset N_{+1}(n)$ of decisions which are ethically appropriate, or recommended, at each decision node n of each decision tree T in the tree domain τ.

An ethical theory will then consist of the following three items:

(i) a consequence domain Y of possible ethical consequences;
(ii) a tree domain τ of finite decision trees whose terminal nodes $x \in X$ are mapped into consequences $\gamma(x) \in Y$;
(iii) a behaviour norm $\beta(T, n)$ defined for every decision node $n \in N^*$ of each decision tree T in the tree domain τ.

Two important axioms will now be imposed upon such an ethical theory. The first is that of an unrestricted domain: it is required that the tree domain τ should consist of all logically possible finite decision trees, each with its own mapping $\gamma: X \to Y$ from terminal nodes to appropriate ethical consequences. Any theory which applies to only a restricted domain of decision trees will not be able to handle some ethical decision problems which might conceivably arise, or which a complete theory should be able to handle even if the problem is entirely hypothetical. Thus, having an unrestricted domain seems necessary for a complete ethical theory.

The second axiom is consistency in continuation subtrees (or 'consistency' for short). At any node n of a decision tree T, there is a corresponding continuation subtree $T(n)$ which is obtained by pruning T just before the node n, and retaining what gardeners would call a 'cutting' consisting of both that node and all its successors in T. This subtree is, of course, a decision tree in its own right with an initial node n which is just after the cut and the set of nodes $N(n)$ which is a subset of N, the set of nodes in the original tree. The subtree's set of terminal nodes is $X(n)$, the set of those terminal nodes $x \in X$ of the original decision tree which succeed the initial node of the subtree—i.e. $X(n) = X \cap N(n)$. The terminal nodes $x \in X(n)$ in the subtree are still mapped by γ into consequences—that is, $\gamma(x)$ remains well defined for all $x \in X(n)$.

Because of the unrestricted domain assumption, any such continuation subtree $T(n)$ *is* in the tree domain τ. So the behaviour norm β is defined at each decision node $n \in N^*(n) = N^* \cap N(n)$ of the continuation subtree $T(n)$. Yet each such node is identical to a decision node $n \in N^*$ of the original tree. All that has happened in passing from tree T to tree $T(n)$ *is* that time has progressed, so that the set of possible courses of history has become narrowed. This is inevitable. So the description of behaviour, $\beta(T, n')$ at each decision node n' of the continuation subtree should be the same, regardless of whether we think of n' as a node of the subtree $T(n)$ or as a node of the original tree T. Since the behaviour norm must describe possible behaviour, it is therefore required to specify the same set of decisions $\beta(T(n), n')$ at each decision node $n' \in N^*(n)$ of the continuation subtree as it does at the corresponding node of the full tree. In other words, $\beta(T(n), n') = \beta(T, n')$ whenever $n \in N$ and $n' \in N^*(n)$. This is (continuation) consistency, which the second axiom requires.

In a sense, this consistency condition is almost tautological. For, when a specific decision node $n \in N^*$ *is* reached, the decision-maker is really faced only with the continuation subtree $T(n)$ starting at that node. What counts, therefore, is the behaviour set $\beta(T(n), n)$ which the norm prescribes for that decision node in the continuation tree. If this differs from $\beta(T, n)$, which was prescribed for the same decision node in the earlier and larger decision tree T, then this earlier recommendation really carries no force (unless it is recalled as an ethically relevant resolution to behave in a certain way, but then the history of consequences should be expanded to include such resolutions and whether they become honoured or not). In which case we might as well define the behaviour set $\beta(T, n)$ at each decision node $n \in N^*$ of a decision tree T as the value of the behaviour set $\beta(T(n), n)$ at node n in the continuation tree $T(n)$ which starts at that node. The result will then be a behaviour norm which is automatically consistent because one will have $\beta(T(n), n') = \beta(T(n'), n') = \beta(T, n')$ whenever $n \in N$ and $n' \in N^* \cap N(n)$.

4. Consequentialism

A fundamental postulate of decision theory is that behaviour should be entirely explicable by its consequences. Indeed, this is so fundamental that standard decision theories such as that due to Savage (1954) have even defined an act as a mapping from states of the world into consequences. Obviously then, for Savage and other decision theorists, two acts which give rise to identical patterns of state contingent consequences are completely equivalent.

In ethics, the doctrine that an act should be judged by its consequences has been much more controversial. The idea can be traced back to Aristotle, who wrote:

If, then, there is some end of the things we do, which we desire for its own sake (everything else being desired for the sake of this), and if we do not choose everything for the sake of something else (for at that rate the process would go on to infinity; so that our desire would be empty and vain), clearly this must be the good and the chief good. (Aristotle, *Nicomachean ethics*, 1094*a*: 18)

Later, St Thomas Aquinas sought to refute Aristotelian doctrine, and effectively defined consequentialism by defining its negation: 'A consequence cannot make evil an action that was good nor good an action that was evil.'

More recently, Mill (see Warnock (1962) and Moore (1912: 121)) can be counted among those who thought that consequences are what matter about acts. The term 'consequentialism' itself, however, seems rather recent—it was used by Anscombe (1958) to describe a doctrine she wished to criticize. The attacks have continued. Williams (1973) sought to rebut not only utilitarianism, but also consequentialism of which it is a special case. In Williams (1985), he dismisses it in barely half a sentence as merely an elementary error. Sen and Williams (1982) had chosen 'Beyond Utilitarianism' as the provisional title of the volume they edited until it was pointed out that some contributors were reluctant even to step beyond utilitarianism, let alone beyond the broader doctrine of consequentialism.

Sen (1987: 74–8; and the articles cited there) has also remained a critic, even though his attacks may have become muted over the years. In fact, he has recognized the argument (which Williams had made earlier) that one could extend the domain of consequences until it incorporated everything relevant to the ethical merits of any act. What remains at issue, then, is included in the following passage from Sen (1987: 75–6):

> Consequentialism . . . demands, in particular, that the rightness of actions be judged entirely by the goodness of consequences, and this is a demand not merely of taking consequences into account, but of ignoring everything else. Of course, the dichotomy can be reduced by seeing consequences in very broad terms, including the value of actions performed or the disvalue of violated rights. I have tried to argue elsewhere (Sen (1982*b*; 1983)):
> 1. that such broadening is helpful, even essential; but
> 2. that nevertheless even after fully fledged broadening, there can remain a gap between consequentialist evaluation and consequence-sensitive deontological assessment.

Moreover, Sen (1982*b*; 1983) points out that most of the concepts of 'consequence' used in the past have been too narrow, because they pay too little attention to rights and to who performs what action. I agree too that how consequences are evaluated, and perhaps how they are even defined, can depend on who does the evaluation. After all, the world might be a better place if we all demanded higher ethical standards of ourselves than we do of others. I therefore prefer the wider concept of consequence which Sen prefers to call a 'consequence-based evaluation'.

In the end, however, I disagree with Sen (and Regan (1983)) because I do not see any 'gap between consequentialist evaluation and consequence-sensitive deontological assessment'. I claim that any apparent gap can be closed by expanding the domain of consequences even further, if necessary, in order to embrace all possible results of any 'deontological assessment' which were not included in the original domain of consequences. As Williams recognized, this makes consequentialism become a tautology. In the past, the tautology has sometimes been described as 'meaningless'. I am perfectly willing to admit that consequentialism does only acquire meaning with reference to some specific domain of consequences, in which case the tautology has been removed. But I would rather that future debates could be about what consequences really should be included in the domain because they are ethically relevant, instead of about the appropriateness of a doctrine which can be made into a tautology anyway. And if the term 'consequence' remains anathema, perhaps we can change it to something else like 'assessment'. By doing so, however, we sever the convenient link to the standard terminology of decision theory. Accordingly, I prefer to stick to 'consequentialism'.

5. Consequentialist choice

Let us proceed, then, to consider what it means for our ethical theory if actions are judged entirely by their consequences. Obviously, it must mean that our apparatus of decision trees whose terminal nodes have consequences is sufficient to describe the ethical decision problems which they represent. If two decision trees are identical, they represent the same decision problem. There is no need to concern ourselves with differences between the two problems when the consequences that are available in the decision tree and also in each continuation subtree are entirely equivalent. Behaviour should be equivalent at each (equivalent) division node of the two equivalent trees, and lead to an identical pattern of state-contingent consequences.

In fact the consequentialist hypothesis is stronger than this, but not too dissimilar in spirit. What it adds is the idea that not even the structure of the decision tree is important (unless it somehow affects the consequences which the decision maker has available). The hypothesis requires that the (choice set of) consequences of prescribed behaviour should be entirely explicable by the (feasible set of) consequences of possible behaviour. To explain this properly requires a somewhat careful construction of the feasible set and the associated choice set.

Take the feasible set $F(T)$ first. Its members are precisely those probability distributions $p(y)$ over the consequence domain Y that can result from some decision strategy which is available in the tree T—i.e. from some rule specifying a unique action $\alpha(n) \in N_{+1}(n)$ at every decision node $n \in N^*$ of T. Write $\Delta(Y)$ for the set of all probability distributions over Y which attach positive probability to only a finite subset of Y (this finite subset is usually called the support of the distribution). Then every decision strategy results in a unique probability distribution $p(.) \in \Delta(y)$. Indeed, *if* $\xi_\alpha(x)$ $(x \in X)$ denotes the probability distribution over terminal nodes in X that is induced by the actions $\alpha(n)$ $(n \in N^*)$, then

$$p(y) = \sum_{x \in \gamma^{-1}(y)} \xi_\alpha(x)$$

is the probability of consequence y, for each $y \in Y$. That is, the probability of y is the total probability of all the different terminal nodes x for which $\gamma(x) = y$.

Actually, the feasible set $F(T)$ can be constructed by backward recursion, starting at terminal nodes $x \in X$ where only a single determinate consequence $\gamma(x) \in Y$ *is* possible. There

$$F(T(x)) = \{\chi_{\gamma(x)}\}$$

i.e. the only member of $F(T(x))$ is the degenerate probability distribution $\chi_{\gamma(x)}$ which attaches probability one to the particular consequence $\gamma(x)$.

At any previous node n of the tree T, the feasible set $F(T(n))$ can be constructed from the collection of sets $F(T(n'))$ at the immediately succeeding nodes $n' \in N_{+1}(n)$ as follows. First, in the case when n *is* a decision node in N^*, the feasible set $F(T(n))$ *is* the union $\cup_{n' \in N_{+1}(n)} F(T(n'))$. This is because the decision-maker's next move to $n' \in N_{+1}(n)$ determines which set $F(T(n'))$ of this union will still be possible after that move. In the case when n *is* a chance node in N^0, however, the feasible set satisfies

$$F(T(n)) = \sum_{n' \in N_{+1}(n)} \pi(n' \mid n)\, F(T(n'))$$

$$= \left\{ p \in \Delta(Y) \mid \exists p_{n'} \in F(T(n'))\ (n' \in N_{+1}(n)) \colon p = \sum_{n' \in N_{+1}(n)} \pi(n' \mid n) . p_{n'} \right\}$$

That is, $F(T(n))$ consists of all possible probability distributions which result from combining into a compound lottery in an appropriate way one member selected from each of the respective feasible sets $F(T(n'))$ $(n' \in N_{+1}(n))$. The explanation is that nature's next move will determine which term $F(T(n'))$ of the sum will be the next appropriate feasible set, and these different terms occur with probabilities $\pi(n' \mid n)$.

It can easily be shown by backward induction on n that $F(T(n)) \subset \Delta(Y)$ for each $n \in N$. Moreover, since the tree is finite, the backward recursion must eventually terminate at the initial node n_0 of the tree, and yield the appropriate feasible set of contingent consequences $F(T) = F(T(n_0))$ for the tree T as a whole.

The choice set $\Phi_\beta(T)$, on the other hand, will consist of those random consequences which can result from some prescribed decision strategy $\alpha(n)$—i.e. a strategy which, at each decision node $n \in N^*$ of the given tree, selects a single member $\alpha(n)$ of the behaviour set $\beta(T, n) \subset n' \in N_{+1}(n)$

which the ethical behaviour norm prescribes for that node. This set can be constructed by backward recursion just as the feasible set was. The only difference is obvious: at each decision node $n \in N^*$, the choice set $\Phi_\beta(T(n))$ consists of the union $\cup_{n' \in \beta(T,n)} \Phi_\beta(T(n'))$ of the choice sets at only those immediately succeeding nodes $n' \in \beta(T, n)$ which could result from prescribed behaviour at node n; at each chance node $n \in N^0$, on the other hand, the choice set $\Phi_\beta(T(n'))$ consists, as before, of the probability weighted sum

$$\sum_{n' \in N_{+1}(n)} \pi(n' \mid n)\, \Phi_\beta\, (T(n'))$$

of all the choice sets $\Phi_\beta\,(T(n'))$ at the immediately succeeding nodes $n' \in N_{+1}(n)$. This backward recursion again terminates at the initial node, and yields the appropriate choice set $\Phi_\beta\,(T) = \Phi_\beta\,(T(n_0))$ of contingent consequences which could result from following the prescribed behaviour norm β throughout the whole decision tree T. Obviously, this choice set is a non-empty subset of the feasible set $F(T)$—as is easily proved by considering each step of the backward recursion in turn and using mathematical induction. The choice set $\Phi_\beta(T)$ could consist of the whole feasible set, it should be remembered.

After these necessary preliminaries, the crucial hypothesis of consequentialist behaviour can be formally stated. It requires that, whenever two decision trees T and T' have identical feasible sets of contingent consequences $F(T) = F(T')$, the two choice sets $\Phi_\beta\,(T) = \Phi_\beta\,(T')$ must also be equal. If this hypothesis is true, the ethical theory is said to be consequentialist. In fact it obviously implies that there is a 'revealed' consequentialist choice function C_β mapping each non-empty finite feasible set $F \subset \Delta(Y)$ of random consequences $p(y) \in \Delta(Y)$ into the choice set $C_\beta\,(F)$, which is some non-empty subset of the feasible set F. This revealed choice function must satisfy $\Phi\,(T) = C_\beta\,(F(T))$ for all finite decision trees $T \in \tau$.

So far, then, the following three axioms have been formulated for normative behaviour in decision trees: (i) unrestricted domain; (ii) consistency in continuation subtrees; (iii) consequentialism. Following the arguments presented elsewhere (Hammond 1988*a*), these three axioms imply that there exists a (complete and transitive) revealed preference ordering R_β on the set R_β with the property that

$$C_\beta\,(F) = \{p \in F \mid q \in F \Rightarrow pR_\beta q\}$$

whenever $\emptyset \neq F \subset \Delta(Y)$ and F is finite.

Moreover, one other very important property also follows from these same three axioms. This is the controversial independence condition, according to which the revealed preference ordering R_β on $\Delta(Y)$ must satisfy

$$[\alpha p + (1 - \alpha)\bar{p}]\; R_\beta\; [\alpha q + (1 - \alpha)\bar{p}] \Leftrightarrow pR_\beta q$$

whenever $p, \bar{p}, q \in \Delta(Y)$ and $0 < \alpha \leqslant 1$.

As pointed out in Hammond (1988*a*), however, these are the only restrictions on behaviour which the three axioms imply. That is, given any preference ordering R satisfying the independence condition, behaviour whose set of random consequences always maximizes this preference ordering in each possible finite decision tree will certainly satisfy the three axioms.

Although the independence condition is both implied by expected utility maximization and is usually formulated as one of the axioms implying expected utility maximization, the three axioms enunciated here do not on their own imply expected utility maximization. The reason is that the revealed preference ordering R_β could still be discontinuous and not admit any utility representation at all. Indeed, consider the case when Y consists of three different members y_k ($k = 1, 2, 3$). Then an ordering satisfying the independence axiom is given by

$$pR_\beta q \Leftrightarrow [p(y_1) > q(y_1)] \text{ or } [p(y_1) = q(y_1) \text{ and } p(y_2) \geqslant q(y_2)]$$

This is a lexicographic preference ordering, of course, giving priority first to increasing the probability of y_1 but then, if this probability can be increased no further, recognizing as desirable increases in the probability of y_2 (and so, since probabilities sum to one, decreases in the probability of y_3).

6. Continuity and expected utility

Such discontinuous preferences are easily excluded by imposing an additional axiom of continuity on behaviour norms in decision trees. Specifically, let T^m ($m = 1, 2, \ldots$) be any infinite sequence of decision trees which all have the same sets of decision nodes N^*, chance nodes N^0, and terminal nodes X, the same sets $N_{+1}(n)$ of nodes immediately succeeding each node $n \in N$, and the same mapping $\gamma: X \to Y$ from terminal nodes to consequences. The only way in which the trees T^m differ is in the probability distributions $\pi^m(n' \mid n)$ ($n' \in N_{+1}(n)$) attached to each chance node $n \in N^0$. Moreover, assume that $\pi^m(n' \mid n) \to \pi(n' \mid n)$ as $m \to \infty$, where $\pi(n' \mid n) > 0$ (all $n \in N^0$, $n' \in N_{+1}(n)$). Then the behaviour norm $\beta(T, n)$ is said to be continuous if, whenever $n \in N^*$ and $n' \in \beta(T^m, n)$ for all large m, then $n' \in \beta(T, n)$. Mathematical economists will recognize this as upper hemi-continuity of the behaviour correspondence as probabilities vary.

It is not difficult to prove that this additional continuity axiom implies that the revealed preference ordering R_β is continuous as well, in the sense that for all $\bar{p} \in \Delta(Y)$ the two preference sets

$$\{\bar{p} \in \Delta(Y) \mid p\ R_\beta\ \bar{p}\}, \quad \{\bar{p} \in \Delta(Y) \mid \bar{p}\ R_\beta\ p\}$$

are both closed sets of $\Delta(Y)$. Then the ordering R_β can certainly be represented by a utility function U defined on $\Delta(Y)$, in the sense that

$pR_\beta q \Leftrightarrow U(p) \geqslant U(q)$ for all pairs $p, q \in \Delta(Y)$. Moreover the independence condition implies (Herstein and Milnor 1953) that $U(p)$ can be chosen so that it takes the expected utility form

$$U(p) = \sum\nolimits_{y \in Y} P(y)\, v(y) = E_p\, v(y)$$

for some unique cardinal equivalence class of von Neumann–Morgenstern utility functions (NMUFs) v defined on Y.

7. Social norms and personal consequences

Having developed the basic decision theory, the next stage of the argument is much more directly concerned with ethical decisions whose consequences can affect many individuals simultaneously. To represent such consequences, the domain Y will now be given much more structure.

As in social choice theory, assume that there is some basic set A of possible social states $a \in A$. The membership M of a society is just the set of individuals i in that society. Given any $i \in M$, write A_i for a copy of the set A whose members a_i are i's personalized social states. *As* in the theory of public goods (Foley 1970: 70; Milleron 1972, etc.) it helps to imagine that we can choose different social states $a_i \neq a_j$ for individuals i and j whenever they are different members of M, even though this may well be impossible in practice.

In addition to social states in the conventional sense, it will be convenient to consider also for each $i \in M$ a space of personal characteristics $\upsilon_i \in \Theta_i$. Such characteristics determine i's preferences, interests, talents, and everything else (apart from the social state) which is ethically relevant in determining the welfare of individual i. In section 11 below, will even indicate whether individual υ_i ever comes into existence or not.

For each individual i, a personal consequence *is* a pair $z_i = (a_i, \upsilon_i)$ in the Cartesian product set $Z_i := A_i \times \Theta_i$ of personalized social states a_i and personal characteristics υ_i. Then, in a society whose membership M is fixed, a typical social consequence consists of a profile

$$z^M = (z_i)_{i \in M} \in Z^M := \prod\nolimits_{i \in M} Z_i$$

of such personal consequences—one for each individual member of society (both actual and potential). The consequence domain $Y = Z^M$ will then consist of all such social consequences, with typical member $y = z^M$.

The four consequentialist axioms given in sections 3, 5, and 6 above can now be applied to a social behaviour norm $\beta(T, n)$ defined at all decision nodes n of all decision trees T in the domain of finite decision trees with consequences in Z^M. These axioms obviously imply the existence of a unique cardinal equivalence class of von Neumann-Morgenstern social welfare functions $w(y) \equiv w(z^M)$, defined on the space of social consequences, such that the social behaviour norm β always results in consequences that maximize the expected value $w(z^M)$ in every social decision tree. Thus, the only difference so far from section 6 is that the consequence domain has become one of social consequences. What is most important, however, is the idea that each personal consequence $z_i \in Z_i$ captures everything of ethical relevance to individual i—by definition, nothing else, including no other individual's personal consequences, can possibly be relevant to i's welfare.

8. Individualistic consequentialism

A general random social consequence is some joint probability distribution $p \in \Delta(Z^M)$ over the product space Z^M of different individuals' personal consequences. Such personal consequences could be correlated between different individuals, or they could be independent. The extent of this correlation should be of no consequence to any individual, however. For, provided that everything relevant to individual $i \in M$ really has been incorporated in each personal consequence $z_i \in Z_i$, all that really matters to i is the distribution $p_i \in \Delta(Z_i)$ of these consequences. This leads to the individualistic consequentialism hypothesis that any two lotteries $p, q \in \Delta(Z^M)$ are to be regarded as equivalent random consequences whenever, for every individual $i \in M$, the marginal distributions $p_i = q_i \in \Delta(Z_i)$ of i's consequences are the same. This means in particular that if any such pair $p, q \in F(T)$ for any decision tree T in the domain, then

$$p \in \Phi_\beta (T) \Leftrightarrow q \in \Phi_\beta (T)$$

Considering the case when $F(T) = \{p, q\}$ shows that, when individualistic consequentialism is combined with the other consequentialist axioms of sections 3, 5, and 6, then

$$p_i = q_i \text{ (all } i \in M) \Rightarrow E_p\, w(z^M) = E_q\, w(z^M)$$

—i.e. p and q must be indifferent according to the relevant expected utility criterion whenever the personal marginal distributions are all equal.

Succinctly stated, individual consequentialism amounts to requiring that only each individual's distribution of personal consequences be relevant to any social distribution. There is no reason to take account of any possible correlation between different individuals' personal consequences.

9. Individual welfarism

The second individualistic axiom which I shall use is that there is an individual welfare behaviour norm defined for all 'individualistic' decision trees. The latter are trees for which there is only one individual whose distribution of personal consequences is affected by any decision within the tree. Thus, if $i \in M$ denotes the only individual affected in the tree T, then there must be a profile

$$\bar{p}_{-i} \in \prod_{h \in M \setminus \{i\}} \Delta(Z_h)$$

of fixed lotteries $\bar{p}_h \in \Delta(Z_h)$ $(h \in M \setminus \{i\})$ for each individual h other than i, as well as a set $F_i(T) \subset \Delta(Z_i)$ of feasible lotteries over personal consequences for individual i, such that the set $F(T)$ of lottery profiles which are feasible in the tree T satisfies $F(T) = F_i(T) \times \{\bar{p}_{-i}\}$. A decision tree with this property will be called an individualistic decision tree. If $i \in M$ is the only individual affected by decision in the tree T, then T can be called an i-decision tree. Let τ_i denote the set of all such trees.

The crucial hypotheses to be introduced now is that there is an individual welfare behaviour norm $\beta_i\,(T, n)$ defined for every individual $i \in M$ and every decision node n of every i-decision tree $T \in \tau_i$. It is this norm which, by definition, should represent ethical behaviour when only i is affected by whatever decision is taken. Moreover, it is natural to require β_i to satisfy the consequentialist axioms stated in sections 3, 5, and 6 above, and even to do so in a way which is independent of the profile $\bar{p}_{-i}$ of fixed lotteries $\bar{p}_h$ for all unaffected individuals $h \in M \setminus \{i\}$. This last independence property is the key hypothesis here. The motivation is that, if only consequences to i are affected by any decision, the fixed consequences to all other individuals are ethically irrelevant—assuming, as I do, that everything relevant to ethical decision-making is already included in the consequences, and that only (distributions over) personal consequences matter.

Given any individual $i \in M$ and i-decision tree $T \in \tau_i$, the assumption of individual welfarism requires that the social norm β and the individual norm β_i should be identical at all decision nodes of T. Equivalently, in any i-decision tree $T \in \tau_i$ with $\bar{p}_{-i}$ as a fixed profile of random consequences for individuals $h \neq i$, the two sets $\Phi_\beta(T)$ and $\Phi_{\beta_i}(T)$ of social consequences and of i's personal consequences which are revealed as chosen by β and β_i respectively should satisfy $\Phi_\beta\,(T) = \Phi_{\beta_i}\,(T) \times \{\bar{p}_{-i}\}$. Thus, whenever there is 'no choice' in the personal consequences of other individuals, the social norm becomes identical to the only affected individual's welfare norm. Note especially that individual welfarism poses no restrictions on what is allowed to count as part of a personal consequence and so to affect each individual's welfare. All it says is that, in 'one-person situations', social welfare is effectively identified with that one person's individual welfare.

In combination with the other consequentialist axioms, individual welfarism obviously implies the existence of a unique cardinal equivalence class of individual welfare functions $w_i\,(z_i)$ for each $i \in M$. These have the property that each individual i's welfare norm β_i will always yield in every i-decision tree T the set of random consequences $\Phi_{\beta_i}(T)$ that maximize with respect to $p_i \in \Delta(Z_i)$ the expected value $E_{p_i} w_i(z_i)$ of w_i over the set $F_i(T) \subset \Delta(Z_i)$ of feasible probability distributions over i's personal consequences.

10. Utilitarianism

Individual welfarism has a much more powerful implication, however, when it is combined with individualistic consequentialism as defined in section 8. For suppose that the two lotteries $p, q \in \Delta(Z^M)$ are such that $E_{p_i} w_i(z_i) = E_{q_i} w_i(z_i)$ for all $i \in M$, where $p_i = q_i \in \Delta(Z_i)$ denote the respective marginal distributions over just i's personal consequences. Now order the individuals $i \in M$ so that $M = \{i_1, i_2, \ldots, i_r\}$, where r is the total number of individuals. We shall prove by induction on the integer s that, if w denotes a social welfare function as defined in section 7, then the equation $E_s(p, q)$ expressed by

$$E_{p_{i_1}, p_{i_2}, \ldots, q_{i_{s-1}}, p_{i_s}, p_{i_{s+1}}, \ldots, q_{i_r}} w(z^M)$$
$$= E_{p_{i_1}, p_{i_2}, \ldots, p_{i_{s-1}}, q_{i_s}, q_{i_{s+1}}, \ldots, q_{i_r}} w(z^M)$$

or by

$$\sum_{z_{i_1}} \cdots \sum_{z_{i_{s-1}}} \sum_{z_{i_s}} \sum_{z_{i_{s+1}}} \cdots \sum_{z_{i_r}} p_{i_1}(z_{i_1}) \ldots p_{i_{s-1}}(z_{i_{s-1}}) [p_{i_s}(z_{i_s}) - q_{i_s}(z_{i_s})]$$
$$q_{i_{s+1}}(z_{i_{s+1}}) \ldots q_{i_r}(z_{i_r})\, w(z_{i_1}, \ldots, z_{i_{s-1}}, z_{i_s}, z_{i_{s+1}}, \ldots, z_{i_r}) = 0$$

must be true for $s = 1$ to r. Note that the expectations in this equation are taken with respect to two distributions having identical marginal distributions for all individuals except i_s.

Indeed, to show that the equation $E_S(p, q)$ is true, it suffices to consider an i_s-decision tree T in which:

$$F(T) = \prod_{t=1}^{s-1} \{p_{i_t}\} \times \{p_{i_s}, q_{i_s}\} \prod_{t=s+1}^{r} \{q_{i_t}\}$$

Then, since $E_{p_{i_s}} w_{i_s}(z_{i_s}) = E_{q_{i_s}} w_{i_s}(z_{i_s})$ by hypothesis, it must be true that

$$\Phi_{\beta_{i_s}}(T) = \{p_{i_s}, q_{i_s}\}$$

Hence individual welfarism implies that

$$\Phi_\beta(T) = \prod_{t=1}^{s-1} \{p_{i_t}\} \times \Phi_{\beta_{i_s}}(T) \times \prod_{t=s+1}^{r} \{q_{i_t}\} = F(T)$$

and so the equality above does indeed follow.

Stringing all the r equations $E_S(p, q)$ ($s = 1$ to r) together then implies that $E_p\, w(z^M) = E_q\, w(z^M)$. Thus it has finally been proved that

$$E_{p_i}\, w_i(z_i) = E_{q_i}\, w_i(z_i) \text{ (all } i \in M) \Leftrightarrow E_p\, w(z^M) = E_q\, w(z^M)$$

Yet this is precisely the crucial 'Pareto indifference' hypothesis of Harsanyi's (1955) utilitarian theorem. Indeed, given the Cartesian product structure of the social consequence domain

$$Z^M = \prod_{i \in M} Z_i$$

there is not even any need here to amend Harsanyi's original proof. The implication of this theorem is that there must exist an additive constant δ_i and a set of multiplicative constants ($i \in M$) such that

$$w(z^M) \equiv \alpha + \sum_{i \in M} \delta_i\, w_i(z_i)$$

Moreover, individual welfarism implies that maximizing $E_p\, w(z^M)$ must be equivalent to maximizing $E_{p_i}\, w_i(z_i)$ in any i-decision tree, where p_i is the marginal distribution $\text{marg}_{Z_i}\, p$. So $w(z^M)$ and $w_i(z_i)$ must be cardinally equivalent when $w(z^M)$ is regarded as a function of z_i alone. This evidently implies that each constant δ_i ($i \in M$) is actually positive. Then, however, since the individual and social welfare functions are only unique up to a cardinal equivalence class, for each ($i \in M$) we can replace the individual welfare function $w_i(z_i)$ by the cardinally equivalent function $\bar{w}(z_i) := \delta_i\, w_i(z_i)$, and the social welfare function $w(z^M)$ by the cardinally equivalent function $\tilde{w}(z^M) := w(z^M) - \alpha$. The result is that

$$\tilde{w}(z^M) := w(z^M) - \alpha = \sum_{i \in M} \delta_i\, w_i(z_i) = \sum_{i \in M} \tilde{w}(z_i)$$

and so one is back to simple addition of individual 'utilities', once these have all been suitably normalized. Because of this possible normalization, I shall assume in future that

$$w(z^M) \equiv \sum_{i \in M} w_i(z_i)$$

Note, however, that these utilities are by no means the same as those in other more traditional versions of utilitarianism. They are merely representations of appropriate ethical decisions in individualistic decision trees, without any necessary relationship to classical or other concepts of utility such as happiness, pleasure, absence of pain, preference satisfaction, etc. This is a major difference from Harsanyi's (1955) utilitarian theory. On the other hand, as in that theory, the additive structure arises because independence as regards revealed preferences over lotteries is combined with independence of each individual's welfare norm from the (fixed) lotteries faced by all other individuals. The latter independence property is an implication of individual welfarism, as defined in section 9.

11. Variable population

So far the set of individuals M has been treated as though it were fixed. Yet many ethical issues surround decisions which affect the set of individuals who come into existence—both the number and the composition of the set M. Thus, it would seem that M itself should be treated as a variable consequence along with z^M, as indeed it was in Hammond (1988*b*).

A simpler alternative, however, is to treat 'non-existence' for any individual $i \in M$ as a particular personal characteristic $\theta_i^0 \in \Theta_i$ which i could have, and then to define M as the set of all potential rather than actual individuals. Thus M is divided into the two sets $M^* := \{i \in M \mid \theta_i \neq \theta_i^0\}$ of actual individuals who do come into existence, and $M^0 := \{i \in M \mid \theta_i = \theta_i^0\}$ of individuals whose potential existence never comes about in practice. Actually, not much is lost by doing this. Assuming that only a finite number of individuals can ever be born before the world comes to an end (as seems quite reasonable, despite economists' models of steady state growth etc.), one can regard each $i \in M$ as just an integer used to number each individual who comes into existence, more or less in order of date of birth. Everything that is really relevant about an individual i, including date of birth, can be included in i's individual characteristic θ_i. Thus every individual who is ever born certainly gets numbered. But we can also consider the (finite) maximum number N^* of individuals who could ever be born, and then let $M = \{1, 2, \ldots, N^*\}$. Then, unless all N^* individuals do actually come into existence, there will be 'unused' numbers which refer to potential rather than actual individuals.

For those individuals $i \in M^\circ$ who never come into existence, the concept of individual welfare hardly makes any sense. In decision-theoretic terms, this means that non-existent individuals are not affected by social decisions—all social decisions are the same to them (except for decisions causing them to come into existence, of course). Consider now any i-decision tree T with the property that $p \in F_i(T)$ only if $p(A_i \times \{\theta_i^0\}) = 1$—i.e. the probability of i not existing is always 1, no matter what decision is taken in the tree T. Since all decisions in T are the same to this certainly non-existent individual, it follows that at all decision nodes n in this tree, individual i's welfare norm $\beta_i(T, n)$ can be allowed to make any decisions on i's behalf. Therefore $\beta_i(T, n) = N_{+1}(n)$ and so $\Phi_{\beta_i}(T) = F_i(T)$ whenever T is an i-decision tree like this. What this means is that for some constant w_i^0 the individual welfare function $w_i(z_i)$ should satisfy $w_i(a_i, \theta_i^0) = w_i^0$ for all $a_i \in A_i$. Thus w_i^0 can be regarded as the constant 'utility of non-existence', which is entirely independent of the social state or any aspect of any social consequence in which i never exists.

Assuming this to be true, one more useful normalization of individuals' welfare functions is possible. We can replace each $w_i(z_i)$ by the cardinally equivalent function

$$\tilde{w}_i(z_i) := w_i(z_i) - w_i^0$$

because a constant is merely being subtracted. Then, of course, $\tilde{w}_i(a_i, \theta_i^0) = 0$ for all $a_i \in A_i$. This implies that $\tilde{w}_i(z_i) = 0$ whenever $i \in M^0$.

We can also replace

$$\tilde{w}(z^M) \equiv \sum_{i \in M} w_i(z_i)$$

by

$$\tilde{w}(z^M) \equiv w(z^M) - \sum_{i \in M} w_i^0$$

for exactly the same reason. Then, however,

$$\tilde{w}(z^M) \equiv \sum_{i \in M} [w_i(z_i) - w_i^0] \equiv \sum_{i \in M} \tilde{w}_i(z_i) \equiv \sum_{i \in M^*} \tilde{w}_i(z_i)$$

where M^* is the set of individuals who come into existence. So only individuals in the set M^* need be considered when adding all individuals' welfare levels.

Once again, it will be assumed from now on that this normalization has been carried out. Therefore one has

$$w(a^M, \theta^M) = w(z^M) \equiv \sum_{i \in M^*} w_i(z_i) = \sum_{i \in M^*} w_i(a_i, \theta_i)$$

where

$$M^* := \{ i \in M \mid \theta_i \neq \theta_i^0 \}.$$

Note that this is formally identical to classical utilitarianism. But, as pointed out in section 10, the resemblance is only formal because the individual welfare functions $w_i(z_i)$ mean something quite different. In particular, the zero level of this function is, by its very construction, just that level of individual welfare at which it is ethically appropriate for the individual to come into existence. This does much to dilute the strength of Parfit's (1984) 'repugnant conclusion', which is that classical utilitarianism recommends creating very many extra individuals who are barely able to live above a subsistence level set so low that anyone who was forced to live below it would prefer not to have been born at all. Here we can escape the repugnant conclusion because there is nothing to prevent the ethical values embodied in the function $w_i(z_i)$ from making w_i positive only if individual i would actually be quite well off if allowed to come into existence. The fact that the personal consequence (z_i) makes individual i glad to be alive is not enough by itself to make $w_i(z_i)$ positive.

Note too that having $w_i(z_i)$ positive would only be a sufficient condition on its own for wanting i to exist if i's existence could somehow be brought about without interfering with anybody else. Yet children cannot exist without having (or having had) parents. So the personal benefits (and costs) to i of coming into existence have to be weighed against any costs (or benefits) to other individuals, especially i's parents, etc. Some further discussion of such issues occurs in Hammond (1988*b*).

12. Interpersonal comparisons

In the introduction I criticized Sen's social welfare functional approach to social choice theory on the grounds that it never made explicit the interpersonal comparisons on which it was based. It is now my duty to explain how the utilitarian theory expounded above remedies this defect.

In fact, as pointed out in Hammond (1991*b*: ch. 7, 200–54), there are interpersonal comparisons embodied in the social welfare function

$$w(z^M) = \sum_{i \in M^*} w_i(z_i)$$

These comparisons also meet Myerson's (1985: ch. 8, 229–59) criticism that interpersonal comparisons have no decision-theoretic significance. For $w_h(z_h) > w_i(z_i)$ means that society is better off creating individual h with personal consequence z_h rather than individual i with personal consequence z_i. And $w_h(z_h) - w_h(z_h') < w_i(z_i') - w_i(z_i)$, which is of course equivalent to $w_h(z_h) + w_i(z_i) < w_h(z_h') + w_i(z_i')$, really does mean that moving h from z_h to z'_h and i from z_i to z_i' produces a benefit to society (if nobody else is affected) because any loss to h is outweighed by the gain to i, or vice versa. Indeed, even welfare ratios acquire meaning. For $w_h(z_h)/w_i(z_i)$ can be regarded as the marginal rate of substitution between individuals like h facing personal consequence z_h and individuals like i facing personal consequence z_i. If this ratio is greater than 1, for instance, then society could gain by creating more individuals like h and fewer like i.

Thus we have a 'cardinal ratio scale' measure of individual welfare, with 'cardinal full comparability' of both welfare levels and differences, as well as a clearly defined zero level of welfare. Yet, of all the social welfare functionals considered by Roberts (1980) which have this property, only the simple sum is ethically appropriate—according to the theory expounded above. So the social welfare functional is no longer left indeterminate, as usually happens in this approach to social choice theory. Of course, this extra determinacy of the functional form comes at a price, since now all the indeterminacy has been displaced into the individual welfare function. In Sen's version of the theory, as well as in Harsanyi's version of utilitarianism, one could argue that the utility measure had some objective reality which was independent of any particular values; here the individual welfare measure has instead been defined so that it embodies certain relevant ethical values.

13. Concluding assessment

In the introductory section 1 there were four questions which, I suggested, any social choice theoretic approach to ethics should be able to answer. The reader is invited to review them once again, along with the succeeding paragraph which summarized the (admittedly still incomplete) answers that I promised to provide.

The theory has been based upon the idea of a social behaviour norm, defined for decision trees in which multi-stage decisions and compound lotteries combine to give random social consequences. The social consequences to be considered amount to interpersonal profiles of personal consequences, with each personal consequence summarizing everything which is ethically relevant to the corresponding individual. There should be a social norm for society as a whole, and also individual welfare norms specifying what decisions are ethically acceptable when there is only one individual whose personal consequences can be affected by the decision. The relevant individual's welfare norm should coincide with the social norm in all such 'one person situations'.

Four axioms were imposed upon such behaviour norms. The first was unrestricted domain, requiring the norm to be defined for all finite decision trees in which only positive probabilities could occur at any chance node. The second was consistency in continuation subtrees, requiring the same behaviour to be acceptable at any decision node of a tree regardless of whether that node is regarded as belonging to the whole tree or to only a continuation subtree. The third 'consequentialist' axiom was the crucial one—that knowledge of the feasible set of consequence lotteries arising from a decision tree would always suffice to determine the 'revealed choice set' of all consequence lotteries which could possibly result from recommended behaviour. Later on this was further strengthened so that, in society, only the profile of marginal probability distributions over different individuals' personal consequences was relevant to recommended behaviour. A fourth technical axiom of continuity was finally imposed which had the effect of ruling out lexicographic preferences.

From these four axioms, applied to the social norm and so to the individual welfare norms which represent the social norm in one-person situations, there follows a form of classical utilitarianism which is close in spirit to that of Harsanyi (1955), even if the interpretation of individual utilities is quite different. This gives a unique cardinal equivalence class of 'von Neumann–Morgenstern social welfare functions' whose expected values society should maximize. Moreover, each such social welfare function can be expressed as the sum of suitably normalized individual welfare functions whose expected values it is right to maximize in one-person situations where only one individual's personal consequence lottery is affected by any decision that could be made.

Finally, on the assumption that decisions affecting individuals who never come into existence regardless of what decision is made do not matter, and so can be made arbitrarily, it was shown that individuals' welfare levels could be normalized to zero for individuals who never exist. Then it is enough to sum the welfare levels of all individuals who do come into existence, and even to use this criterion to determine who should come into existence—exactly as with classical utilitarianism. The obvious defects of that ethical theory are avoided, however, by interpreting individual welfare as a purely ethical concept representing what behaviour *ought* to maximize in decision trees affecting the personal consequences of only one individual.

In the end, the theory that has been sketched here determines completely the formal structure of the ethical decision criterion. Yet this formal structure remains an empty shell, to be completed by substantive ethical statements concerning what should count as an ethically relevant consequence, and even about what decisions really would be right in certain practical decision problems. The real work in ethics may only just be beginning. It promises to be much more interesting than the rather dry arguments about whether or not utilitarianism or consequentialism are appropriate. I have set out such arguments here only to explain why I personally regard the issue as virtually settled.

REFERENCES

Anscombe, G. E. M. (1958), 'Modern Moral Philosophy', *Philosophy*, 33: 1–19.

Arrow, K. J. (1951) *Social Choice and Individual Values* (New York: John Wiley and Dover; 2nd edn., 1963).

—— (1977), 'Extended Sympathy and the Possibility of Social Choice', *American Economic Review, Papers and Proceedings*, 67: 219–25, reprinted as ch. 11 of Arrow (1983).

—— (1983), *Collected Papers of Kenneth J. Arrow, i. Social Choice and Justice* (Cambridge, Mass.: The Belknap Press of Harvard University Press).

Bewley, T. (1989), *Knightian Uncertainty* (Evanston, Ill.: Northwestern University).

Black, D. (1948), 'On the Rationality of Group Decision-Making', *Journal of Political Economy*, 56: 23–34.

Blackorby, C., Donaldson, D., and Weymark, J. A. (1984), 'Social Choice with Interpersonal Utility Comparisons: A Diagrammatic Introduction', *International Economic Review*, 25: 327–56.

Borda, J. C. de (1781), 'Mémoire sur les elections au scrutin', *Mémoires de l'Academie Royale des Sciences*, 657–65; trans. A. de Grazia (1953) in *Isis*, 44: 42–52.

Condorcet, M. J. A. N. C., Marquis de (1785), *Essai sur l'application de l'analyse a la probabilité des decisions rendues a la pluralité des voix* (Paris: Imsize 4^ primerie Royale).

d'Aspremont, C. (1985), 'Axioms for Social Welfare Orderings', in Hurwicz, Schmeidler, and Sonnenschein (1985).

—— and Gevers, L. (1977), 'Equity and the Informational Basis of Collective Choice', *Review of Economic Studies*, 44: 199–209.

Dodgson, C. L. (1884, 5), *The Principles of Parliamentary Representation* (London: Harrison).

Elster, J., and Roemer, J. E. (1991), *Interpersonal Comparisons of Well-Being* (Cambridge: Cambridge University Press).

Foley, D. K. (1970), 'Lindahl's Solution and the Core of an Economy with Public Goods', *Econometrica*, 38: 66–72.

Hammond, P. J. (1976), 'Equity, Arrow's Conditions, and Rawls' Difference Principle', *Econometrica*, 44: 793–804.

—— (1988*a*), 'Consequentialist Foundations for Expected Utility', *Theory and Decision*, 25: 25–78.

—— (1988*b*), 'Consequentialist Demographic Norms and Parenting Rights', *Social Choice and Welfare*, 5: 127–45.

—— (1988*c*), 'Orderly Decision Theory: A Comment on Professor Seidenfeld', *Economics and Philosophy*, 4: 292–7.

—— (1989), 'Consistent Plans, Consequentialism, and Expected Utility', *Econometrica*, 57: 1445–9.

—— (1991*a*), 'Independence of Irrelevant Interpersonal Comparisons', *Social Choice and Welfare*, 8: 1–19.

—— (1991*b*), 'Interpersonal Comparisons of Utility: Why and How They Are and Should Be Made', in Elster and Roemer (1991).

—— (1991*c*), 'Harsanyi's Utilitarian Theorem: A Simpler Proof and Some Ethical Connotations', European University Institute, Working Paper ECO 91/32; forthcoming in R. Selten (ed.), *Essays in Honour of John Harsanyi* (Berlin: Springer-Verlag).

Harsanyi, J. C. (1953), 'Cardinal Utility in Welfare Economics and the Theory of Risk-Taking', *Journal of Political Economy*, 61: 434–35.

—— (1955), 'Cardinal Welfare, Individualistic Ethics, and Interpersonal Comparisons of Utility', *Journal of Political Economy*, 63: 309–21.

—— (1976), *Essays in Ethics, Social Behaviour, and Scientific Explanation* (Dordrecht: Reidel).

—— (1977), *Rational Behaviour and Bargaining Equilibrium in Games and Social Situations* (Cambridge: Cambridge University Press).

—— (1978), 'Bayesian Decision Theory and Utilitarian Ethics', *American Economic Review, Papers and Proceedings*, 68: 223–8.

Herstein, I. N., and Milnor, J. (1953), 'An Axiomatic Approach to Measurable Utility', *Econometrica*, 21: 291–7.

Hurwicz, L., Schmeidler, D., and Sonnenschein, H. (1985) (eds.), *Social Goals and Social Organisation: Essays in Memory of Elisha Pazner* (Cambridge: Cambridge University Press).

Levi, I. (1974), 'On Indeterminate Probabilities', *Journal of Philosophy*, 71: 391–418.

—— (1980), *The Enterprise of Knowledge* (Cambridge, Mass.: MIT Press).

—— (1986), *Hard Choices: Decision Making under Unresolved Conflict* (Cambridge: Cambridge University Press).

McClennen, E. F. (1990), *Rationality and Dynamic Choice: Foundational Explorations* (Cambridge: Cambridge University Press).

Machina, M. J. (1989), 'Dynamic Consistency and Non-Expected Utility Models of Choice under Certainty', *Journal of Economic Literature*, 27: 1622–68.

Milleron, J. C. (1972), 'Theory of Value with Public Goods: A Survey Article', *Journal of Economic Theory*, 5: 419–77.

Moore, G. E. (1912), *Ethics* (London: Home University Library, Williams and Norgate).

Myerson, R. B. (1985), 'Bayesian Equilibrium and Incentive Compatibility: An Introduction', in Hurwicz, Schmeidler, and Sonnenschein (1985).

Parfit, D. (1984), *Reasons and Persons* (Oxford: Oxford University Press).

Regan, D. H. (1983), 'Against Evaluator Relativity: A Response to Sen', *Philosophy and Public Affairs*, 12: 93–112.

Roberts, K. W. S. (1980), 'Possibility Theorems with Interpersonality Comparable Welfare Levels', *Review of Economic Studies*, 47: 409–20.

Savage, L. J. (1954), *The Foundations of Statistics* (New York: John Wiley and Dover; 2nd rev. edn., 1972).

Seidenfeld, T. (1988*a*), 'Decision Theory without "Independence" or without "Ordering": What is the Difference', *Economics and Philosophy*, 4: 267–90.

—— (1988*b*), 'Rejoinder', *Economics and Philosophy*, 4: 309–15.

Selten, R. (1965), 'Spieltheoretische Behandlung eines Oligopolrnodells mit Nachfragetragheit [Game Theoretical Treatment of an Oligopoly Model with Demand Inertia]', *Zeitschrift fur die gesamte Staatswissenschaft*, 121: 301–24 and 667–89.

Sen, A. K. (1970*a*), *Collective Choice and Social Welfare* (San Francisco: Holden Day).

—— (1970*b*), 'Interpersonal Aggregation and Partial Comparability', *Econometrica*, 38: 393–409; reprinted with correction in Sen (1982*a*).

—— (1977), 'On Weights and Measures: Informational Constraints in Social Welfare Analysis', *Econometrica*, 45: 1539–72.

—— (1982*a*), *Choice, Welfare and Measurement*. (Oxford: Basil Blackwell and Cambridge, Mass.: MIT Press).

—— (1982*b*), 'Rights and Agency', *Philosphy and Public Affairs*, 11: 3–39.

—— (1983), 'Evaluator Relativity and Consequential Evaluation', *Philosophy and Public Affairs*, 12: 113–32.

—— (1987), *On Ethics and Economics* (Oxford: Basil Blackwell).

—— and Williams, B. (1982) (eds.), *Utilitarianism and Beyond* (Cambridge: Cambridge University Press).

Smart, J. J. C., and Williams, B. (1973), *Utilitarianism For and Against* (Cambridge: Cambridge University Press).

Strotz, R. H. (1956), 'Myopia and Inconsistency in Dynamic Utility Maximisation', *Review of Economic Studies*, 23: 165–80.

Suppes, P. (1966), 'Some Formal Models of Grading Principles', *Synthese*, 6: 284–306.

Warnock, M. (1962), (ed.) *Utilitarianism: Selections from the Writings of Jeremy Bentham, John Stuart Mill, and John Austin* (London: Collins, the Fontana Library in Philosophy).

Williams, B. (1973), 'A Critique of Utilitarianism', in Smart and Williams (1973).
—— (1985), *Ethics and the Limits of Philosophy* (London: Collins, the Fontana Library in Philosophy).
Zermelo, E. (1913), 'Uber eine Anwendung der Mengenlehre auf die Theorie des Schachspiels [On an Application of Set Theory to the Theory of the Game of Chess]', *Proceedings of the Fifth International Conference of Mathematicians*, 2: 501–4.

III

FAIRNESS IN DISTRIBUTION

8

Stand Alone and Unanimity Tests: A Re-Examination of Fair Division

HERVÉ MOULIN[1]

1. Fair Division of non-marketed resources

Problems of Fair Division address a fundamental challenge of distributive justice. A given set of resources (the traditional story is manna dropped from heaven; see below the discussion of real-life examples) must be distributed among a given set of agents. Those agents have equal rights on the resources (these are the common property of the group) but different preferences. Thus an equal split of the resources, although a fair outcome, is generally not efficient (Pareto optimal). The challenge is to define an efficient solution that, despite giving unequal shares, fulfils our intuition of fairness.

Two essential caveats in most of the Fair Division literature will be retained here. They are (*a*) that only ordinal data on preferences can be used to define a solution (cardinal measurements of utility levels are not available) and (*b*) that the resources to be divided are to be consumed here and now by our agents, who do not have access to a market where those goods can be traded. Of course in an environment where all goods to be divided are competitively exchanged, an equal split would yield the fair and efficient solution because every agent could trade his or her share at the competitive price.

A third assumption is responsibility for one's preferences, which logically follows the Leibnizian 'de gustibus non disputamus'. As Rawls (1971) puts it: 'as moral persons citizens have some part in forming and cultivating their final ends and preferences.' Also Cohen (1990): 'people with expensive tastes could have chosen otherwise, and if and when they press for compensation, then others are entitled to insist that they themselves bear the cost of their lack of foresight or self discipline.' But notice that we also assume responsibility for one's preferences in the context of production activities; there, differences in preferences may not reflect differences in skills and natural

1 Detailed comments by William Thomson on an earlier draft of this chapter are gratefully acknowledged.

abilities (as when a handicapped person experiences a higher disutility for labour), but rather a voluntary choice of the opportunity uses of inputs and outputs (as when a manager chooses the capital/labour ratio in a division of the firm). My Unanimity test extends the idea of responsibility of one's preference into that of mutual responsibility for the difference in our preferences. If differences in our 'gustibus' are of no ethical relevance, the test says that we should bear jointly the costs or benefits accruing from those differences. More on this in section 5 below.

2. Fair Division in the economic literature

Examples of common property resources abound, from the mineral riches on the deep sea bed to broadcasting frequencies, fishing and hunting grounds, and irrigation water (see the survey by Ostrom 1989). Not all of those can be modelled as the traditional cake division story where a given vector of consumption goods is to be divided into non-negative shares. For instance, fishing in common property waters is better described as a (decreasing returns) technology that the agents exploit co-operatively (each agent contributing a share of the labour-input and receiving a share of the fish-output). Yet another fair division model is the provision of a public good problem (how much of the public good to produce and how to share its cost?).

Our general model of a fair division problem involves (i) a set of p input goods, $p \geqslant 0$, and a set of q output goods $q \geqslant 0$ (some are privately consumed, some are publicly consumed), (ii) a production set in the space of combinations of inputs and outputs (the resources), and (iii) a finite set of agents endowed with ordinal preferences over combinations of inputs and outputs (decreasing in inputs, increasing in outputs). The problem is to select 'fairly' an efficient production allocation. (We assume away the issue of incentive compatibility: an omniscient arbitrator implements the solution.)

The traditional version of the Fair Division problem (see Thomson and Varian (1985)) corresponds to zero inputs, q private good outputs and a trivial production set (a single vector). For a general production set in the output space, think of the resources as a garden that our agents can plant without effort: they must decide how much of potatoes and carrots to produce *and* how to share them. An important variant is Fair Division when money is available to perform compensatory transfers (one of the q outputs is money, of which there is zero endowment but that can be consumed in negative amounts).

Three particular cases of the general co-operative production model have received considerable attention. The first one has a one input-one (private) output ($p = q = 1$) technology with *de*creasing returns to scale. See the 'tragedy of the commons' stories (Hardin 1968) and the related models of exploitation of exhaustible resources (Gordon 1954, Dasgupta and Heal 1979). The same model appears in the distributive justice literature as a stylized closed economy where agents contribute labour (input) and consume corn (output): see Mirrlees (1974), Cohen (1986), Roemer (1986), Moulin (1990*a*), Moulin and Roemer (1989), Roemer and Silvestre (1988).

The second model has a one input-one (private) output technology exhibiting *in*creasing returns to scale. It is at the heart of the theoretical discussion of regulated monopolies (Sharkey 1982, Baumol, Panzar, and Willig 1982) and of the related coalition production economies (Scarf 1986, Sharkey 1989, Ichiishi and Quinzii 1983, Quinzii 1982, Mas-Colell 1980, Moulin 1987*b*).

The third model is the celebrated provision of a public good problem discussed, among many others, by Foley (1967; 1970) Champsaur (1975), Milleron (1972), Kaneko (1977), Moulin (1987*a*), Mas-Colell and Silvestre (1989) (to mention only some of the literature on normative, first best solutions). Here the input is money (so $p = 1$) and the output is one public good (or several public goods).

This list is not exhaustive. Some important problems of fair division are not included in the general model discussed above: an example is the division of 'items' for which individual preferences are single peaked (goods inducing satiation in preferences), as in a fixed price model where consumption is restricted to a given budget set and has to be rationed: see Sprumont (1991) and Thomson (1990*b*) for a normative discussion. Another example is the provision of a public bad.

3. Equality of (objective) welfare or equality of opportunity?

Most existing solutions to the fair division problems described above fall into one of two (disjoint) categories. The first idea consists of representing ordinal preferences by some 'objective' cardinal utility (as opposed to subjective cardinalization based on the introspective evaluation of utility intensities) and then calling fair an allocation that equalizes objective welfare across agents.

A practical and popular example consists of dividing the resources in such a way that everyone receives the same net benefit, measured in some good taken as numeraire—call that good money. In other words if we ask every agent to name a sum of money that could replace her actual share of the pie without affecting her own welfare, then all agents will give the same answer. Pazner and Schmeidler's (1978) concept of egalitarian equivalence is a more general formulation of the idea of equal objective welfare. They call egalitarian equivalent (in short e.e) an allocation $(z_1, \ldots, z_n)$ (where z_i is agent i's share) if there exists a consumption vector z such that every agent i is indifferent between consuming z_i or z (of course the allocation $z, \ldots, z$ may not be feasible). If we take an arbitrary direction

$$\{\lambda z / \lambda \geqslant 0\}$$

for numeraire, then the equal benefit method described above generalizes.

Thomson's (1989) concept of equivalent opportunity sets allows us to generalize one step further. We fix an increasing sequence of subsets Z_λ, $\lambda \geqslant 0$ within the consumption set (the sequence is common to all agents). The calibration of a utility function for agent i is done as follows

$$u_i(z_i) = \lambda \Leftrightarrow z_i I_i z$$

where z maximizes R_i over Z_λ (here R_i is agent i's preference ordering, and I_i his indifference relation). Given a sequence Z_λ, $\lambda \geqslant 0$, we define the corresponding egalitarian equivalent solution by selecting, for each utility profile, the highest feasible equal utility allocation (for the above utility representation). Thus, everyone's welfare is the highest feasible on the common opportunity set Z_λ. The sequence Z_λ can be chosen fairly arbitrarily, provided it is independent of the preference profile $R_1, \ldots, R_n$.

An example in the Fair Division of an unproduced vector of goods ω, is the egalitarian equivalent solution using the vector ω itself for numeraire:

$$Z_\lambda = \{\lambda.\omega\}$$

(Pazner and Schmeidler (1978)). For another example, consider a one input (x) one output (y) production function f ($y = f(x)$) and construct a e.e. solution with the family:

$$z_\lambda = \{(x, y)/y = \lambda.x\}$$

(where x is input contribution and y is output share). See Moulin (1987*b*; 1990*a*) and Roemer and Silvestre (1988). See also the e.e. solution for the public good provision problem (Mas-Colell (1980), Moulin (1987*a*)).

We now turn to the second category of solutions, conveying the idea of equal opportunity *ex post*. In an e.e. solution, there is a common set of opportunities Z_λ, and every agent is as happy *as if* he was choosing freely from Z_λ. Now we insist that agent i's share be his *actual* best choice from some opportunity set Z (common to all agents), namely

$$z_i \in Z;\ z_i \text{ maximizes } R_i \text{ on } Z \qquad (1)$$

This achieves equality of opportunity *ex post*; in order to ensure efficiency (Pareto optimality of the allocation $(z_1, \ldots, z_n)$) we will now have to make Z depend upon the preference profile (remember that for an e.e. solution, the family of sets Z_λ is independent of the profile). In fact, a given allocation $(z_1, \ldots, z_n)$ satisfies property (1) for some opportunity set Z if and only if it satisfies the following No Envy test:

$$z_i R_i z_j \text{ for all } i, \text{ all } j \qquad (2)$$

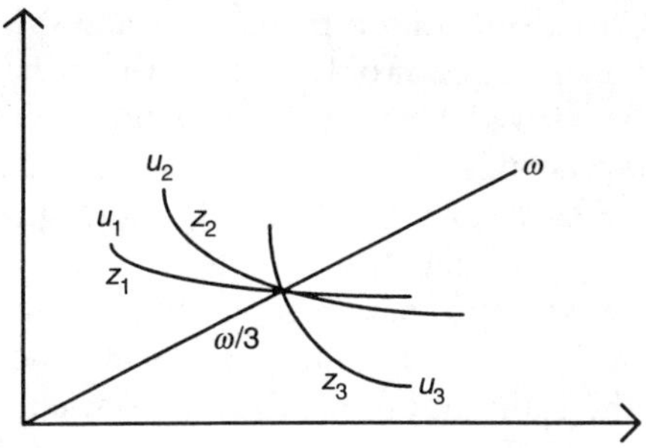

FIG. 8.1

The No Envy test (Foley (1967)) is very appealing in its simplicity. It relies on $n(n-1)$ interpersonal comparisons of shares; this information is presumably easier to elicit (barring strategic misrepresentations) than the information about imaginary allocations in Z_λ required by an egalitarian solution (note, however, that the latter consists of checking only n equalities). Indeed an allocation passing the No Envy test is easily implemented: the arbitrator only has to propose a menu of shares; the distribution of the shares will take place by unanimous consent. Moreover a price decentralization is the easiest way to achieve both No Envy and efficiency: for instance in the Fair Division of the vector ω, a competitive equilibrium allocation, where equal split is the initial endowment, is efficient and passes the No Envy test.

Among economists, the No Envy test has become the dominant interpretation of fairness in distribution problems involving private goods and ordinal preferences (to the extent that the term 'fair' has been used as a synonym of No Envy plus efficiency; this usage is now recognized as inappropriate—see e.g. Thomson (1990*b*)). Furthermore, the interpersonal comparison of shares brings into light a severe difficulty of the egalitarian equivalent solutions: in those, an agent may receive a strictly better share (in physical terms) than another agent's share. Fig. 8.1 illustrates this difficulty by providing a three persons, two goods Fair Division problem where at the e.e. solution taking the vector ω itself for numeraire, agent 2 receives a strictly larger quantity of both goods than agent 1.

Notwithstanding the strength of the arguments for the No Envy test, I wish to argue that the test has some serious flaws, too. The argument is twofold; first an 'internal' criticism based on the documented incompatibility of No Envy and of Pareto optimality (that we retain as the first principle of normative economics); and second an 'external' criticism to the effect that No Envy systematically conflicts with another simple test, the Stand Alone test, to which we feel ready, in some circumstances, to confer ethical pre-eminence over considerations of envy.

The external criticism is the subject of the next section. Let us briefly discuss the internal criticism. If both preferences and the production set are convex, the general distribution problem described in the second paragraph of section 2 can be viewed as an Arrow-Debreu production economy, provided we divide ownership of the firm among the n agents. If we give an equal ($1/n$) share to each one of them, the corresponding competitive equilibrium allocations pass the No Envy test (because every one chooses from the same budget set) and, of course, is efficient as well. It can even be shown that, when we have a continuum of agents and the set of agents' types is connected, these allocations are the only efficient ones generating no envy (see Thomson and Varian (1985) and the references there). See also Zhou (1991) who characterizes the equal income competitive equilibrium outcomes by the two properties of efficiency and strict No Envy (whereby an agent does not envy the average allocation of any coalition of other agents).

Recall that the assumptions of convexity (of preferences and of the technology), are sufficient to guarantee the existence of a competitive equilibrium. It is hard to believe that our search for operational criteria of fairness should be confined to a convex world. But without convexity, the applicability of the No Envy test is seriously limited by two facts. Firstly, if preferences are not convex, it may happen that all efficient allocations generate envy (Varian 1974 gives an example with two agents dividing a vector of two unproduced commodities; see, however, Vohra 1990*b*). Secondly, the same conflict may happen as well if the production set is not convex (Vohra 1990*b* gives a simple example where the two agents have convex preferences and the one input–one output technology has increasing returns).

By contrast the existence of egalitarian equivalent solutions is oblivious to non-convexities (they only require continuity of preferences, without which even Pareto optimality may collapse!). In short, the No Envy test is less robust than egalitarian equivalence.

We now turn to another simple test, challenging the No Envy test even when the latter is compatible with efficiency.

4. The Stand Alone test

Consider an abstract resource allocation problem involving n agents endowed respectively with the preferences $u_1, \ldots, u_n$ (u_i is a utility function representing agent i's preferences R_i; this cardinal notation is used purely as a matter of convenience). A solution must select, for each such configuration of individual preferences, a feasible allocation $(z_1, \ldots, z_n)$ (z_i is agent i's final consumption).

We call this abstract allocation problem a fair division problem when the structure is symmetrical across agents: they all draw a preference within the same domain, and the set of feasible allocations is symmetrical (if z_1, z_2, z_3 is feasible, so is any allocation where the shares are permuted, such z_2, z_3, z_1).

We always assume that a solution respects this symmetry: formally this is the Anonymity condition. It says that only the preferences of the agents, not their names, should matter. For instance if z_1, z_2, z_3 is the allocation selected when preferences are u_1, u_2, u_3 then z_1, z_3, z_2 should be selected when preferences are u_1, u_3, u_2.[2] The second maintained assumption is that of efficiency: our solutions select only Pareto optimal allocations.

The Stand Alone level of a given agent, in a given Fair Division problem, is the utility level that he achieves if he uses the resources all by himself, in the absence of any other agents. To make sense of this definition, remember that we call 'resources' a certain production set (with p input goods and q output goods), and 'using the resources' means the ability to pick freely a net trade in this set (the agent has free access to the technology represented by this production set). Thus the Stand Alone level results when our agent consumes his preferred allocation in the production set. We denote by $sa(u_i)$ this utility level for an agent with utility function u_i.

We say that an (anonymous and efficient) solution S passes the Stand Alone test if all the agents compare their actual utility level and their Stand Alone level in the same way, in other words: for all $u_1, \ldots, u_n$ and for all i, j

$$S_i(u_1, \ldots, u_n) > sa(u_i) \Rightarrow s_j(u_1, \ldots, u_n) \geqslant sa(u_j)$$

This says that the externality imposed by other agents' presence bears uniformly on every agent: either everyone is sorry not to be alone using the resources (in which case the Stand Alone level is used as an upper bound) or everyone is happy to share those resources with others (in which case the Stand Alone level is taken as a lower bound). That both cases could occur is now demonstrated by examples. Those examples also underline the systematic conflict of the No Envy and Stand Alone tests.

Consider the provision of a (single) public good with cost function c. If agent i stands alone, he can achieve the utility

$$sa(u_i) = \max_{z \geqslant 0} u_i(c(z), z) \tag{3}$$

It is well known since Foley (1967) that this level yields a feasible individual rationality constraint, i.e. there exists an (efficient) allocation where each agent gets at least her Stand Alone level (note that the restriction to a single public good is important here).

This lower bound (and its generalization to coalitions) has played a major role in the normative discussion of public goods (see e.g. Milleron 1972,

[2] Actually a weaker definition of Anonymity is enough: if z_1', z_2', z_3' is selected when preferences are u_1, u_3, u_2, then it should be true that $u_1(z_1') = u_1(z_1)$, $u_3(z_2') = u_3(z_3)$, $u_2(z_3') = u_2(z_2)$.

Champsaur 1975, Moulin 1987*a*). See Lemma 6 in section 6 for a discussion of the feasibility of the Stand Alone lower bound in the case of multiple public goods.

We observe next that the Stand Alone lower bound and the No Envy test are incompatible: indeed the latter simply means that everyone pays the same cost share; so when it is efficient to produce a positive level of the public good, an agent who does not care for it will end up below this 'initial' utility $u_i(0, 0)$. Guesnerie and Oddou (1979) show that No Envy and the Stand Alone lower bound may conflict even for non-efficient solutions.

Turn next to the production of a (single) output from a (single) output by a production function f exhibiting increasing returns to scale. The Stand Alone utility

$$sa(u_i) = \max_{x \geqslant 0} u_i(x, f(x)) \tag{4}$$

is, again, a feasible lower bound: as returns increase, the presence of other agents utilizing the technology brings a positive externality. See Lemma 4 in section 6 for a discussion of the feasibility of this bound in the multi-outputs case. The Stand Alone test (and its extension to coalitions) is abundantly studied by the literature on natural monopolies (see e.g. Faulhaber (1975), Sharkey (1982) or Young (1985)). We check its incompatibility with the No Envy test.

Consider a technology producing t units of some indivisible good (cars) at the following costs

$$c(1) = 40,\ c(2) = 70,\ c(3) = 90$$

The three agents want to buy at most one car each, at the following reservation prices

$$u_1 = 45\ u_2 = 35\ u_3 = 25.$$

It is efficient to produce three cars, and under No Envy the three agents must all pay the same price, or 30. But agent 3 then ends up below his Stand Alone level (he would rather not buy the car at that price!). The case against No Envy is very strong in this example: as no one should be forced to trade (which Stand Alone guarantees), the three agents must pay different prices or the cost will not be covered.

Marginal pricing, a two parts tariff solution, or indeed any pricing method offers the same opportunity set to each agent, so that the corresponding solutions must pass the No Envy test; hence they all fail the Stand Alone test.

Consider next the case of a decreasing returns technology. The Stand Alone utility can no longer be guaranteed to every agent; quite the contrary, the vector $(sa(u_1), \ldots, sa(u_n))$ is now on or beyond the feasible utility frontier, so the Stand Alone test becomes an *upper* bound on individual utilities (see Lemma 3 in section 6 for a general statement). Upper bounds are much less common than lower bounds in the distributive justice literature, but they make good sense in the context of common property. Imagine that the technology f represents a lake exploited jointly by n fishermen. They contribute their labour (input) and share the catch (output). The Stand Alone utility (4) is that utility that a given fisherman would enjoy if he had the whole lake for himself; given decreasing returns, it is not feasible to guarantee that level to everyone. So the Stand Alone test tells us to take it as a cap on every agent's gains: everyone should take a share of the burden of decreasing returns. This implies for instance that a fisherman who does not want to fish even if no one else does (because he has a better opportunity usage of his labour), is not entitled to any benefit: his common ownership of the lake with the other agents entitles him to no surplus. By contrast, the privatization solution described in the previous section (giving to each agent an equal share in the ownership of the private firm) gives to everyone a positive quantity of fish for free, plus the opportunity of buying more fish at marginal cost. With that interpretation of common property, everyone is entitled to a share of surplus, even those who are not able to extract any surplus from the technology. In the context of responsibility for one's preferences and of non-marketed goods, I would contend, on the contrary, that the Stand Alone test is compelling; some of Locke's discussion of property rights expresses this very idea.[3]

The mathematical incompatibility of the Stand Alone upper bound and No Envy is a very robust fact (see Moulin 1990*c*). The simplest illustration is an example of Fair Division with money.

Three agents discover an indivisible good (a ticket for a basketball game) and can use money for compensation. They value the ticket respectively at \$30, \$30, and 0 (the ticket has no resale value). Stand Alone precludes giving any compensation to agent 3, who does not like watching basketball in the first place, while No Envy commands to give him at least \$10 . . .

5. The Unanimity test

Consider a solution S for an abstract allocation problem (as defined at the beginning of section 4). Call a profile $(u, u, \ldots, u)$ unanimous if every agent shares the same preferences. Clearly all anonymous and efficient solutions behave in the same way at such a profile: they choose an allocation achieving the highest feasible equal utility vector (that is to say $u(z_i) = u(z_j) = \lambda$ for all i, j, where λ is as high as compatible with the

[3] 'The same law of nature that does by this means give us property does also bound that property, too. "God has given us all things richly", is the voice of reason confirmed by inspiration. But how far has he given it us? To enjoy. As much as any one can make use of to any advantage of life before it spoils, so much he may by his labour fix a property in; whatever is beyond this is more than his share, and belongs to others' (John Locke, *The Second Treatise of Civil Government*, 31).

feasibility constraints). Let us call Unanimity level and denote by $un(u)$ this common utility level. Now the Unanimity test can be defined.

We shall say that an (anonymous and efficient) solution S passes the Unanimity test if all the agents compare their actual utility level and their unanimity level in the same way, in other words: for all $u_i, \ldots, u_n$ and for all i, j:

$$S_i(u_1, \ldots, u_n) > un(u_i) \Rightarrow S_j(u_1, \ldots, u_n) \geqslant un(u_j)$$

The axiom was introduced first in Moulin (1990*b*). Under our assumption that each agent is held responsible for his own preferences, it is natural to regard all agents jointly responsible for the difference in their preferences: the test then says that if agent i benefits from the fact that other agent's preferences are not the same as hers, then no other agent j should suffer for the same reason (if i ends up above her Unanimity level, then j should not end up below his).

It is important to notice that the Unanimity test results in a lower bound on individual utilities if the vector $(un(u_1), \ldots, un(u_n))$ is below the Pareto frontier, and in an upper bound if this vector is above the frontier. We give below some examples of both cases. They will illustrate two important features of the Unanimity test: it is compatible with *either* the No Envy test *or* the Stand Alone test (but not with both, as demonstrated in the previous section).

Start with the traditional Fair Division of unproduced commodities (where no one can receive a negative share of any good—e.g. compensations in cash are not allowed). Say that the vector ω is to be divided and preferences are convex. Then $un(u_i) = u_i(\omega/n)$ and the Unanimity test is the familiar equal split lower bound. It is the oldest axiom of the Fair Division literature (from Steinhaus 1948 to Kuhn 1967 it was the *only* axiom) and still adopted by most authors (from Dworkin 1981 to Thomson and Varian 1985).

In the case of a production technology with decreasing returns, the equal split lower bound generalizes into the following lower bound

$$un(u_i) = \max_{x \leqslant 0} u_i(x, f(nx)/n) \tag{5}$$

In other words each agent can use freely a $1/n$-th reduction of the production set: see Lemma 2 in section 6 for a general statement. The Unanimity test turns this into an individual rationality constraint: I am entitled to the returns that would prevail if everyone else was contributing the same amount of input as me (see Gevers 1986, Moulin 1990*a*, Moulin and Shenker 1991).

The competitive equilibrium solution works by transforming the common ownership of the technology into the private ownership of equal shares of the resources (we initially endow everyone with ω/n in the case of unproduced commodities, or with a $(1/n)$-th share of the firm's profits in the case of a technology). It always passes the Unanimity test, and the No Envy test as well (see section 3 above): therefore those two tests are compatible in those two problems, at least when preferences are convex. To see why the Unanimity and Stand Alone tests are compatible as well, simply observe that the inequality $un(u_i) \leqslant sa(u_i)$ follows from (4), (5) and the decreasing returns assumption. See also an explicit solution passing both tests in section 7.

We now discuss two models where the Unanimity test yields an upper bound on individual utilities. First consider three agents deciding whether or not to buy an indivisible public good with cost 6, when their respective benefits for the good are 3, 3, and 6. The efficient decision is to buy the good, which brings a surplus of $3 + 3 + 6 - 6 = 6$. The Unanimity test implies here the division (1,1,4) of that surplus, much different from a pay-according-to-benefits criterion, which would imply the division (1.5,1.5,3). Indeed agent 1's unanimity level is 1 because three agents with benefits identical to his would buy the good and divide its cost equally; by the same token, agent 3's unanimity level is 4. So the Unanimity test reads:

$$S_1 \leqslant 1 \quad S_2 \leqslant 1 \quad S_3 \leqslant 4$$

By efficiency $S_1 + S_2 + S_3 = 6$ hence all inequalities above are equalities.

Formally, if the cost of producing z units of public good is $c(z)$, then agent i's unanimity level is

$$un(u_i) = \max_{z \geqslant 0} u_i(c(z)/n, z) \tag{6}$$

That the levels $un\,(u_i)$, $i = 1, \ldots, n$ always bring a feasible upper bound is a very general fact (we only need to assume that everyone likes money: see Lemma 7 in section 6). Thus the unanimity test reads

$$S_i(u_1, \ldots, u_n) \leqslant un\,(u_i)$$

The upper bound is automatically satisfied at any allocation where the costs are shared equally (which shows why it is always compatible with No Envy). As our numerical example demonstrates, the unanimity test implies equal cost share if the n maximization problems (6) have a common solution z. Yet (unlike the No Envy test), the Unanimity upper bound is compatible with the Stand Alone lower bound (4) (because $sa(u_i) \leqslant un(u_i)$ is always true).

In the public goods literature, the dominant normative solution is derived from the 'pay according to benefit' idea (the Lindahl equilibrium, for instance, divides costs in proportion to marginal benefits). This approach is challenged by the Unanimity test which, in combination with the Stand Alone test takes us in a radically different route (explored in Moulin 1991*c*). To make this point clear, consider a variant of the numerical example above with the same cost 6 and the benefits (1,3,6). Now agent 1's unanimity level is zero because three agents with benefit 1 would not buy the good; and his stand alone level is zero as well, so agent 1, after all, is not entitled to any benefit at all: he must pay the full extent of his benefit. The remaining cost is now divided as follows

$$c_2 + c_3 = 5,\ 2 \leqslant c_2,\ c_3 \leqslant 3$$

This leaves only a little room for differentiating the costs of agents 2, 3 (if we still insist that costs should increase for agents with higher benefits). But the most radical feature of the Unanimity test in this example is to deprive agent 1 of any share in the surplus. Once again we have to invoke responsibility of one's preferences to justify the outcome: that I derive more benefit than you from this non-rival good is of no moral significance in itself; given that my unanimity level is zero, I would be, as it were, free-riding on other agents' preferences if I were to receive any part of the surplus; this is not fair because they, in turn are paying more because my preferences differ from theirs.

When the resources jointly owned consist of a (private good) production function with increasing returns, the Unanimity test turns into an upper bound as well. The formula for $un(u_i)$ is independent of the nature of the returns: it is always given by (5). When the function f is convex and $f(0) = 0$, those unanimity levels form a feasible upper bound (see Lemma 5 in section 6 for a general statement). Again, the inequality $sa(u_i) \leqslant un(u_i)$ shows that the Unanimity and Stand Alone tests are compatible. Compatibility with No Envy is also easy to check.

The literature has not produced many normative solutions for the common property increasing returns technology problem. The most popular method adapts the privatization idea into the notion of marginal pricing (see e.g. Vohra (1990*a*)). It is rejected by the Stand Alone test (on top of which, it is not always efficient, even when preferences are convex). Another method applies solution concepts from co-operative games to the Stand Alone game (see e.g. Young 1985). It is rejected by the Unanimity test. Section 7 proposes an alternative to those methods, designed specifically to pass both tests.

6. Lower and upper bound interpretations

We discuss first the general principles of highest lower bound and lowest upper bound for an abstract allocation problem; these principles in turn provide new interpretations of the Unanimity and Stand Alone tests. All the results stated in this section are formally proven in Moulin (1990*b*, 1991*b*).

Given a solution S, the lower bound function ϕ_i of agent i associates to each utility u_i his worst conceivable utility level over all possible configurations of other agent's utility functions:

$$\phi_i(u_i) = \min_{u_{-i}} S_i(u_i, u_{-i})$$

The first principle says that an agent's *lower* bound function should be as *high* as is compatible with the same lower bound function for everyone else. Thus we look for the highest feasible individual rationality constraint. This principle is reminiscent of the Lockian idea that individual freedom should be as extensive as allowed by the same freedom for all.

The second principle is new (Moulin (1991*a*; 1991*b*)) and says that an agent's *upper* bound function giving his highest utility level in the best conceivable configuration of the other agent's preferences) should be as *low* as is compatible with the same upper bound function for all.

Think of a solution that has both the highest lower bound function and the lowest upper bound function: then the overall influence of other agents' preferences over a particular agent is minimized; if these two bounds coincide, this influence vanishes altogether. Call a solution fully separable if this property holds. For instance, if the resources consist of a technology with constant returns to scale (CRS), a fully separable solution is to let every agent choose his preferred production plan. Or in traditional Fair Division of unproduced commodities, we divide the cake in equal shares no matter what preferences are. The former yields an efficient allocation (because the technology is CRS) but the latter does not. In all non-trivial fair allocation problems, there exists no efficient, anonymous, and fully separable solution.

So the attempt to minimize the overall influence of other agents on one's final utility is a second-best approach: mathematically, it amounts to seeking a solution with a highest lower bound and a lowest upper bound functions.

Given an abstract fair allocation problem we call feasible lower bound (resp. upper bound) function a real valued function $\phi(u_i)$ (resp. $\psi(u_i)$) such that at any profile $(u_1, \ldots, u_n)$ there exists a Pareto optimal allocation where each agent receives at least $\phi(u_i)$ (resp. at most $\psi(u_i)$). The Unanimity test is deeply related to the notions of feasible lower and upper bounds.

Lemma 1 *Say that in a certain fair division problem, the Unanimity utility* $un(\cdot)$ *is a feasible lower bound (resp. upper bound) function at all profiles* $(u_1, \ldots, u_n)$*: there always exists a Pareto optimal allocation where each agent i receives at least* $un(u_i)$ *(resp. there exists a Pareto optimal allocation where each agent i receives at most* $un(u_i)$*). Then the unanimity utility is* the *highest feasible lower bound function (resp.* the *lowest feasible upper bound function).*

We now interpret the Unanimity and Stand Alone tests in terms of lower and upper bound functions. We start by the co-operative production problem with decreasing returns.

Consider a production set Y in an orthant R_+^{p+q} of privately consumed commodities (with p inputs and q outputs) and a domain D of preferences over R_+^{p+q}. An allocation **z** in Y is a vector of net trades, interpreted as the inputs an agent gives and the outputs he gets in return. We assume throughout that every preference in D is convex and continuous. We also assume monotonicity: each agent prefers to consume more output and to contribute less input.

Lemma 2 *The Unanimity utility of agent i is computed as the Equal Split utility level:*

$$un(u_i) = \max_{z \in Y} u_i(z/n) \tag{7}$$

Moreover if Y is convex, the Equal Split utility yields is a feasible lower bound function, hence (by Lemma 1) the highest feasible lower bound function.

The easy proof does not use any property of monotonicity of preferences: thus it applies to a perfectly general convex set Y of privately consumed items, on which preferences are only restricted by convexity.[4]

Now we assume that Y is closed and comprehensive (that is, if (x, y) is in Y, then any (x', y') with $x' \geqslant x$ and $y' \leqslant y$ is in Y too: producing less output with more input is always possible). We denote by $Y^{\sim}$ the closure of the complement of Y in R_+^{p+q}. In other words $Y^{\sim}$ contains all production plans (x, y) that are either unfeasible or barely feasible (in the sense that they belong to the efficiency frontier of Y).

Lemma 3 *The Stand Alone utility of agent i is given by*

$$sa(u_i) = \max_{z \in Y} u_i(z) \tag{8}$$

Suppose that $Y^{\sim}$ is additive. Then the Stand Alone utility yields a feasible upper bound function. Moreover, if $Y^{\sim}$ contains 0 then it is a minimal feasible upper bound function.

Notice that the additivity assumption on $Y^{\sim}$ is essentially a decreasing returns property. For instance, with one output and p inputs, it amounts to the subadditivity of the production function:

$$f(x + x') \leqslant f(x) + f(x')$$

The additional property that $Y^{\sim}$ contains 0 amounts here to $f(0) = 0$.

Gathering the results of Lemmas 2 and 3 yields a remarkable parallelism of our two tests (Unanimity and Stand Alone) for those production sets Y such that Y is convex, $Y^{\sim}$ is additive, and 0 is in the efficiency frontier of Y.

[4] Moulin (1991*b*) establishes also the converse statement: the Equal Split level is a feasible lower bound function *only if Y* is convex.

Take for instance the one input—one output case ($p = q = 1$): if the production function f is concave and $f(0) = 0$, we obtain the highest lower bound function and a minimal upper bound function:

$$\max_{x \geqslant 0} u_i(x, f(n.x)/n) \leqslant S_i(u_1, \ldots, u_n) \leqslant \max_{x \geqslant 0} u_i(x, f(x)) \quad (9)$$

The same pair of bounds holds with one output and p inputs, provided the production function f is concave, subadditive, and $f(0) = 0$. Similarly with one input and q outputs, if the cost function c is convex, superadditive, and $c(0) = 0$, we get the following pair of the highest lower bound function and a minimal upper bound function:

$$\max_{y \geqslant 0} u_i(c, (n.y)/n, y) \leqslant S_i(u_1, \ldots, u_n) \leqslant \max_{y \geqslant 0} u_i(c(y), y) \quad (10)$$

We turn now to the case of an increasing returns technology.

Lemma 4 *Suppose that Y is additive. Then the Stand Alone utility* ((8)) *yields a feasible lower bound function. Moreover, if Y contains 0, then it yields* a *maximal feasible lower bound function.*

Note that a converse statement of Lemma 4 is proven in Moulin (1991*b*). Also, if we restrict ourselves to those solutions where an agent's utility never goes below his 'initial' level $u_i(0, 0)$ then Stand Alone yields *the* highest feasible lower bound function.

When Y corresponds to a one output—multi output production process, the additivity of Y amounts to a superadditive production function ($f(x + x') \geqslant f(x) + f(x')$), which is the traditional definition of a natural monopoly (see Sharkey (1982)). In that case the Stand Alone utility reads

$$sa(u_i) = \max_{x \in R^q_+} u_i(x, f(x))$$

Lemma 5 *Suppose that $Y^{\sim}$ is convex. Then the unanimity level* ((7)) *is the lowest feasible upper bound function.*

Here the assumption that $Y^{\sim}$ is convex is closely related to a property of increasing returns. For instance with one output ($q = 1$) this says that the production function is convex; or with one input ($p = 1$) it says that the cost function is concave.

Gathering the results of Lemmas 4 and 5, we obtain a pair of tight bounds, the Unanimity upper bound and the Stand Alone lower bound functions, for those production sets Y that are additive, contain 0, and such that $Y^{\sim}$ is convex. For instance with one output, if we have a convex, superadditive production function f with $f(0) = 0$, the two bounds are written as:

$$\max_{x \geqslant 0} u_i(x, f(x)) \leqslant S_i(u_1, \ldots, u_n) \leqslant \max_{x \geqslant 0} u_i(x, f(n.x)/n)$$

And with one input, and a concave subadditive cost function c with $c(0) = 0$, the two bounds are:

$$\max_{y \geqslant 0} u_i(c(y), y) \leqslant S_i(u_1, \ldots, u_n) \leqslant \max_{y \geqslant 0} u_i(c(n.y)/n, y)$$

Finally we turn to the public good provision problem. We consider a model with r public goods and one private input (money), where the technology is described by a cost function c: the cost of producing a given vector z of public goods, $z \in R^r_+$, is $c(z) \geqslant 0$. We assume that individual preferences are continuous, increasing in the public goods and decreasing in monetary contributions.

Lemma 6 *Assume that the cost function satisfies:*

$$\textit{for all } z, z' \in R^r_+: c(z \vee z') \leqslant c(z) + c(z') \tag{11}$$

where $z \vee z'$ is the co-ordinate-wise supremum operation.
Then the Stand Alone utility

$$sa(u_i) = \max_{z \in R^r_+} u_i(c(z), z)$$

is a maximal feasible lower bound function for the public good provision problem.

The straightforward proof is omitted. In fact, if we restrict ourselves to those solutions where an agent's utility is bounded below by the initial level u_i(0, 0, then Stand Alone yields *the* highest feasible lower bound function. Notice that the subadditivity-like condition (11) is automatically satisfied when there is a single public good ($r = 1$).

Lemma 7 *Consider the production of r public goods by an arbitrary cost function c. Then the Unanimity utility:*

$$\max_{z \in R^r_+} u_i(c(z)/n, z)$$

is the lowest feasible upperbound function.

This result is very general and does not depend on any assumption on preferences except that they like money (preferences are decreasing in input contributions but otherwise arbitrary).

Combining Lemmas 6 and 7 we see that if the cost function c satisfies (11), the tightest lower and upper bound functions are derived from Stand Alone and Unanimity respectively

$$\max_{z \geqslant 0} u_i(c(z), z) \leqslant S_i(u_1, \ldots, u_n) \leqslant \max_{z \geqslant 0} u_i(c(z)/n, z)$$

7. An egalitarian-equivalent solution

We construct a solution meeting both the Stand Alone and Unanimity tests. It is inspired by the solution recommended by Pazner and Schmeidler (1978) for the fair division of a vector ω of (unproduced) commodities.

Here is how they define their solution. Find the highest number t, $1/n \leqslant t \leqslant 1$, such that the utility vector $(u_1(t.\omega), u_2(t.\omega), \ldots, u_n(t.\omega))$ is feasible. A corresponding allocation $(z_1, \ldots, z_n)$ (achieving this utility vector) is then necessarily Pareto optimal: it is an egalitarian-equivalent allocation. It is as if every agent was consuming an equal share t of the total resources (but in reality, of course, each agent may be consuming a different vector z_i).

Clearly the above egalitarian-equivalent solution meets the Unanimity (equal split) lower bound and the Stand Alone upper bound: indeed the optimal value of t is between $1/n$ and 1, whether our Fair Division problem allows for monetary compensations or not.

The generalization of the e.e. solution to an arbitrary production set Y in R_+^{p+q} is straightforward. Consider the family of reference sets $t.Y$, $1/n \leqslant t \leqslant 1$. Observe that if Y has decreasing returns (in the sense that $z \in Y$, $O \leqslant \lambda \leqslant 1$ imply $\lambda.z \in Y$) this family is increasing in t:

$$1/n \leqslant t \leqslant t' \leqslant 1 \Rightarrow t.Y \subset t'Y$$

whereas if the set Y has increasing returns (in the sense that $z \sim Y$, 1s imply $\sim.z \sim Y$) then the family is decreasing in t:

$$1/n \leqslant t \leqslant t' \leqslant 1 \Rightarrow t'.Y \subset t.Y$$

In each case we may use the reference sets $t.Y$ to generate a monotone utility path

$$v_i(t) = \max_{z \in t.Y} u_i(z) \tag{12}$$

In the decreasing returns case, the egalitarian-equivalent solution seeks the highest parameter t such that $(v_i(t), \ldots, v_n(t))$ is feasible and picks a corresponding feasible allocation $z_1, \ldots, z_n$.[5]

$$u_i(z_i) = v_i(t) = u_i(t.Y) \text{ for all } i.$$

Assuming now that Y is convex and $Y_i^{\sim}$ is additive, it follows from Lemmas 2 and 3 that the critical value of t must lie between $1/n$ and 1 so that our

[5] Continuity and strict monotonicity of preferences guarantee the existence of such an allocation.

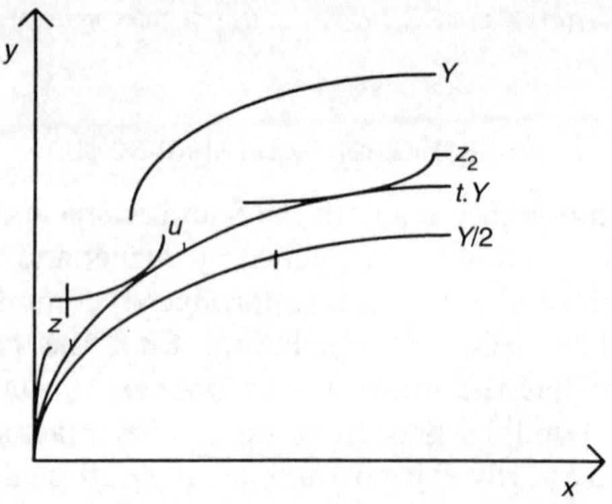

FIG. 8.2

egalitarian equivalent solution is efficient and satisfies both the Unanimity and the Stand Alone tests. See Fig. 8.2.

In the increasing returns case, the egalitarian solution is constructed similarly, with the sole difference that $v_i(t)$ is now decreasing in t, whence we look for the lowest possible parameter such that $(v_1(t), \ldots, v_n(t))$ is feasible. Assuming that Y is additive and $Y\sim$ convex, it follows from Lemma 4 and 5 that the critical value of t lies, again, between $1/n$ and 1. The corresponding solution is efficient and meets the Stand Alone as well as the Unanimity tests.

We turn finally to the provision of a public goods model where the technology is described by a cost function c (see Lemmas 6 and 7). The monotone utility path is generated as follows

$$w_i(t) = \max_{z \geqslant 0} u_i(t.c(z), z) \tag{13}$$

and w_i is a decreasing function of t, $1/n \leqslant t \leqslant 1$.

Given an economy $(u_1, \ldots, u_n; c)$ we look for the lowest possible t such that $(v_1(t), \ldots, v_n(t))$ is a feasible utility vector. By virtue of Lemmas 6 and 7, the critical value of t is between 11n and 1. The egalitarian equivalent solution picks an allocation $(z_1, \ldots, z_n)$ such that

$$u_i(z_i) = w_i(t) \text{ for all } i = 1, \ldots, n.$$

As t is between $1/n$ and 1 the e.e. solution passes the Stand Alone and the Unanimity tests.

Remark

Other egalitarian equivalent solutions for co-operative production problems have been discussed in the literature. They use a different construction of the monotone utility paths (12) (13). For the one input-one (private) output case, see the constant returns equivalent solution in Moulin (1987*b*; 1990*a*) and Roemer and Silvestre (1988). For the provision of a single public good, see the solution using the public good itself as numeraire: Mas-Colell (1980), Moulin (1987*a*). For a general discussion, see Thomson (1989).

8. Concluding comments

The Stand Alone and Unanimity tests emerge as two robust normative requirements (in the sense where No Envy is not robust: see section 3), and are always jointly compatible with full Pareto efficiency, by means of a simple and intuitive egalitarian equivalence construction. In all examples discussed here the two tests complement each other as one yields a lower bound and the other an upper bound on individual utilities (but it is easy to give examples where the two tests are both a lower bound or both an upper bound).[6] Thus they cut a fairly small piece within the Pareto set.

Our two tests bring a critique of most of the familiar (first-best) solutions of the fair division models discussed above. The Stand Alone test rules out any of the non-envious solutions based on a marginal pricing idea: competitive equilibrium from equal split, or, in the case of non-convex productions sets, the marginal pricing concepts (discussed for instance in Ichiishi and Quinzii (1983)). The Unanimity test, on the other hand, rules out the public good provision methods allocating costs in proportion to (marginal) benefits as well as the solutions of the private good production model where we keep the input/output ratio constant across agents or where the constant returns technologies are used to generate an egalitarian equivalent solution.

A number of other normative properties have been discussed in the literature. The most important one is the extension of the Stand Alone lower (resp. upper) bound into a core property (resp. an 'anticore' property: see Moulin (1987*b*)). Due to very severe negative results by Scarf (1986), we cannot hope for a systematically non-empty Stand Alone core (or anticore) when there are at least two outputs or at least two inputs. Nevertheless in the one input-one output model, the Stand Alone core is always non-empty if returns are increasing or if the output is a public good (and the Stand Alone anticore is non-empty if returns are decreasing). It can be shown, then, that there always exists a first-best solution in the Stand Alone core (or anticore) and meeting the Unanimity upper bound (or lower bound). This is a direct application of the fact that an ordinally convex game has a large core (Ichiishi (1988)).

Thus, in the admittedly limited context of a one input-one output process, the Unanimity and (coalitional version of the) Stand Alone ideas still display a remarkable compatibility (one exception is the Fair Division

[6] For instance in the fair division of bads (p inputs and zero output), both tests yield a lower bound. In the provision of a public bad (where each agent wants to contribute more input, but consume less of the public output), both yield an upper bound. When this happens, the Unanimity test always implies the Stand Alone test (in view of Lemma 1).

problem with money, where the Stand Alone anticore and equal split—unanimity—lower bound are not compatible for arbitrary convex preferences: see Moulin 1991*d*).

Other ideas recently discussed in the literature include Resource Monotonicity (originally proposed by Roemer 1986, Thomson 1987) and Population Solidarity (Chun 1986, Tadenuma and Thomson 1989). The former says that when the resources improve (i.e. the vector ω increases, or the production set expands, or the cost function decreases) every agent should benefit from this 'growth' (or at least no one should end up worse off). The latter says that when the population increases, all the previously existing agents experience a change of welfare in the same direction (if one of them benefits, none of the others is hurt).

It turns out that Resource Monotonicity is compatible with the Stand Alone bound only in the simple one input-one output production models (but not in the Fair Division problem with money: see Moulin 1987*a*; 1987*b*; 1991*d*). And Resource Monotonicity is not at all compatible with the Unanimity test (see Moulin and Thomson 1988, Moulin 1990*c*). Population Solidarity, on the other hand, is always compatible with our two tests because it is satisfied by the egalitarian equivalent solutions of section 7.

REFERENCES

Balch, M. S., McFadden, D., and Wu, S. Y. (1974) (eds.), *Essays on Economic Behavior Under Uncertainty* (Amsterdam: North-Holland).

Baumol, W., Panzar, J., and Willig, R. (1982), *Contestable Markets and the Theory of Industry Structure* (New York: Harcourt Brace Jovanovitch).

Champsaur, P. (1975), 'How to Share the Cost of a Public Good?', *International Journal of Game Theory*, 4: 113–29.

Chun, Y. (1986), 'The Solidarity Axiom for Quasilinear Social Choice Problems', *Social Choice and Welfare*, 3: 297–310.

Cohen, G. A. (1986), 'Self Ownership, World Ownership and Equality', *Social Philosophy and Policy*, 3: 77–96.

—— (1990), 'Equality of What? On Welfare, Goods and Capabilities', *Recherches Economiques de Louvain*, 56: 3–4, 357–82.

Dasgupta, P., and Heal, G. (1979), *Economic Theory and Exhaustible Resources* (Cambridge: Cambridge University Press).

Dworkin, R. (1981), 'What is Equality? Part 2: Equality of Resources', *Philosophy and Public Affairs*, 10: 283–345.

Faulhaber, G. (1975), 'Cross Subsidization: Pricing in Public Enterprises', *American Economic Review*, 65: 966–77.

Foley, D. (1967), 'Resource Allocation and the Public Sector', *Yale Economic Essays*, 7/1: 45–98.

—— (1970), 'Lindahl's Solution and the Core of an Economy with Public Good', *Econometrica*, 38: 66–72.

Gevers, L. (1986), 'Walrasian Social Choice: Some Simple Axiomatic Approaches', in Heller (1986).

Gordon, H. S. (1954), 'The Economic Theory of a Common Property Resource: The Fishery', *Journal of Political Economy*, 62: 124–42.

Guesnerie, R., and Oddou, C. (1979), 'On Economic Games Which Are Not Necessarily Superadditive', *Economics Letters*, 3: 301–5.

Hardin, G. (1968), 'The Tragedy of the Commons', *Science*, 162: 1243–8.

Heller, W., *et al.* (1986) (eds.), *Social Choice and Public Decision-Making, Essays in Honor of K. J. Arrow*, i (Cambridge: Cambridge University Press).

Hildenbrand, W., and Mas-Colell, A. (1986) (eds.), *Contributions to Mathematical Economics in Honor of Gerard Debreu* (Amsterdam: North-Holland).

Hurwicz, L., Schmeidler, D., and Sonnenschein, H. (1985) (eds.), *Social Goals and Social Organization* (Cambridge: Cambridge University Press).

Ichiishi, T. (1988), 'Comparative Cooperative Game Theory', mimeo (Ohio State University).

—— and Quinzii, M. (1983), 'Decentralization for the Core of a Production Economy with Increasing Returns', *International Economic Review*, 24: 397–412.

Kaneko, M. (1977), 'The Ratio Equilibrium and a Voting Game in a Public Good Economy', *Journal of Economic Theory*, 16: 2.

Kuhn, H. W. (1967), 'On Games of Fair Division', in Shubik (1967).

Mas-Colell, A. (1980), 'Remarks on the Game Theoretic Analysis of a Simple Distribution of Surplus Problem', *International Journal of Game Theory*, 9: 125–40.

—— and Silvestre, J. (1989), 'Cost Share Equilibria: A Lindahlian Approach, *Journal of Economic Theory*, 47: 239–56.

Milleron, J. C. (1972), 'Theory of Value with Public Goods: A Survey Article', *Journal of Economic Theory*, 5: 419–77.

Mirrlees, J. (1974), 'Notes on Welfare Economics, Information and Uncertainty', in Balch, McFadden, and Wu (1974).

Moulin, H. (1987*a*), 'Egalitarian Equivalent Cost-Sharing of a Public Good', *Econometrica*, 55: 4, 963–77.

—— (1987*b*), 'A Core Selection for Pricing a Single Output Monopoly', *The Rand Journal of Economics*, Autumn 18/3: 397–407.

—— (1990*a*), 'Joint Production with Convex Technology: Comparison of Three Solutions', *Review of Economic Studies*, 57: 439–52.

—— (1990*b*), 'Uniform Preference Externalities: Two Axioms for Fair Allocation', *Journal of Public Economics*, 43: 305–26.

—— (1990*c*), 'Fair Division Under Joint Ownership: Recent Results and Open Problems', *Social Choice and Welfare*, 7/2: 149–170.

—— (1991*a*), 'Welfare Bounds in the Fair Division Problem', *Journal of Economic Theory*, 54/2: 321–37.

—— (1991*b*), 'Welfare Bounds in the Cooperative Production Problem', *Journal of Economic Theory*, 54: 321–37.

—— (1991*c*), 'All Sorry to Disagree: A General Principle for the Provision of Non Rival Goods', *Scandinavian Journal of Economics*.

—— (1991*d*), 'Population Monotonicity in Fair Division with Money', mimeo (Duke University).

—— and Roemer, J. (1989), 'Public Ownership of the External World and Private Ownership of Self', *Journal of Political Economy*, 97/2: 347–67.

Moulin, H., and Shenker, S. (1992), 'Serial Cost Sharing', *Econometrica*, 60/5: 1009–37.

—— and Thomson, W. (1988), 'Can Everyone Benefit from Growth? Two Difficulties', *Journal of Mathematical Economics*, 17: 339–45.

Ostrom, E. (1989), 'Governing the Commons', mimeo (Indiana University).

Pazner, E., and Schmeidler, D. (1978), 'Egalitarian-Equivalent Allocations: A New Concept of Economic Equity', *Quarterly Journal of Economics*, 92: 671–87.

Quinzii, M. (1982), 'An Existence Theorem for the Core of a Productive Economy with Increasing Returns', *Journal of Economic Theory*, 18: 32–50.

Rawls, J. (1971), *A Theory of Justice* (Cambridge, Mass.: Harvard University Press).

Roemer, J. (1986), 'The Mismarriage of Bargaining Theory and Distributive Justice', *Ethics*, 97: 88–110.

—— and Silvestre, J. (1988), 'Public Ownership: Three Proposals for Resource Allocation', mimeo (University of California, Davis).

Scarf, H. (1986), 'Notes on the Core of a Productive Economy', in Hildenbrand and Mas-Colell (1986).

Sharkey, W. (1982), '*The Theory of Natural Monopoly*' (Cambridge: Cambridge University Press).

—— (1989), 'Game Theoretic Modeling of Increasing Returns to Scale, *Games and Economic Behavior*, 1/4: 370–431.

Shubik, M. (1967) (ed.), *Essays in Mathematical Economics in Honor of Oskar Morgenstern* (Princeton: Princeton University Press).

Sprumont, Y. (1991), 'The Division Problem with Single-Peaked Preferences: A Characterization of the Uniform Allocation Rule', *Econometrica*, 59/2: 509–19.

Steinhaus, H. (1948), 'The Problem of Fair Division', *Econometrica*, 16: 101–4.

Tadenuma, K., and Thomson, W. (1993), 'The Fair Allocation of an Indivisible Good When Monetary Compensations are Possible', *Mathematical Social Sciences*, 25: 117–32.

Thomson, W. (1987), 'Monotonic Allocation Mechanisms', mimeo (University of Rochester).

—— (1989), 'Notions of Equal, or Equivalent, Opportunities', mimeo (University of Rochester).

—— (1990*a*), 'Equity Concepts in Economics', mimeo (University of Rochester).

—— (1990*b*), 'Monotonic and Consistent Solutions to the Problem of Fair Division When Preferences are Single-Peaked', mimeo (University of Rochester).

—— and Varian, H. (1985), 'Theories of Justice Based on Symmetry', in Hurwicz, Schmeidler, and Sonnenschein (1985).

Varian, H. (1974), 'Equity, Envy and Efficiency', *Journal of Economic Theory*, 29/2: 217–44.

Vohra, R. (1990*a*), 'On the Inefficiency of Two-Part Tariffs', Review of *Economic Studies*, 57: 415–38.

—— (1990*b*), 'Equity and Efficiency in Non-Convex Economics', mimeo (Brown University).

Young, H. P. (1985*a*), 'Cost Allocation', in Young (1985*b*).

Young, H. P. (1985*b*) (ed.), *Fair Allocation* (Providence, RI: American Mathematical Society).

Zhou, L. (1991), 'Strictly Fair Allocations in Large Exchange Economies', mimeo, (Yale University).

9

On a Mechanism for Implementing Egalitarianism with Responsibility

JOHN E. ROEMER[1]

1. The problem

In modern philosophical theories of egalitarianism, the issue of responsibility plays an important role. A prevalent view is that egalitarians should not recommend complete equality of outcome, or even maximin, but rather that policy which equalizes outcomes in so far as those outcomes are the consequences of traits and environmental factors beyond a person's control, allowing differences in outcomes, however, to the extent that outcomes are the consequences of traits for which persons are deemed responsible. This view is represented most clearly in the work of Arneson (1989), Cohen (1989), and Dworkin (1981).

In Roemer (1993), I propose a way a society can implement the kind of egalitarianism just described, and discuss, for some specific examples, the redistribution of income that would be recommended by a planner for that society. Here, I formulate the social choice problem in a somewhat more abstract way, calculate some examples, and investigate the degree of redistribution that would be implemented by my scheme in comparison to what utilitarianism and a Rawlsian approach would recommend.

A related, abstract approach to egalitarianism, which also highlights the distinction between responsibility and 'talent' (that being a generic term for the traits of a person he is not responsible for—what I call 'circumstances') is undertaken by Fleurbaey (1992).

2. The environment

There is a continuum of agents, characterized by a utility function $u(x, e, a)$, where x is income, e is effort, and a is a vector which specifies the values of an ordered set, N, of traits'. The vector a takes on a finite number of values in the population, $a_1, \ldots, a_t$. The set N is partitioned into a set S

[1] I thank Walter Bossert for a useful discussion we had on this topic.

and its complement; S is the set of traits that society deems persons *not* responsible for. Let a_i^s be the projection of a_i on to the components of the set S: the vectors $a_1^s, \ldots, a_i^s$ may not be all distinct. Let $a_i^s, \ldots, a_r^s$ be the distinct vectors among this set: I shall say there are r types in the population. To simplify notation, let $\alpha_i = a_i^s$, for $i = 1, \ldots, r$. The fraction of type j in the population is p_j. It is convenient to assume that there is a continuum of persons of each type: u is monotone increasing in x and the components of a and monotone decreasing in e.

There is a class of feasible, purely redistributive tax schemes, τ. I will presently assume that this class consists of the linear income tax schemes of the form $d_1 x + d_0$, such that total taxes aggregate to zero. (τ could, in general, contain tax schemes that depend on effort as well as income.) Income for a person of type j is related to his effort according to a monotonic function $x = \varphi^j(e)$.

Typically, given the above information, we would be able to predict an agent's effort choice, facing a given tax policy. But that is not the case here, either because agents do not always optimize, or because the utility functions given above—to be interpreted as the utility functions used by a planner—are not necessarily the utility functions of the agents. In any case, when the agents of type j face a tax scheme τ, there is a distribution of effort responses among the type. Thus, the effort response of agents in type j to tax scheme τ is characterized as a random variable $e = (\tau, \alpha_j)$, distributed according to a probability measure $F^{\tau}_{\alpha_j}$ on some real interval of non-negative numbers. (That is, if Ω is a measurable subset of this interval, then the fraction of type j whose effort ω lies in Ω is $F^{\tau}_{\alpha_j}(\Omega)$.)

Alternatively, we may assume that u is the correct utility function for each agent, that each chooses effort optimally, and that the distribution of effort within a type reflects exactly the differences within the type of values of traits for which persons are held responsible (i.e. traits in $N \backslash S$). For note that e is written as a function of the traits in the set S only. So optimizing persons with different values of their non-S traits, but who are of the same type, will generally choose different efforts.

I am interested in a class of problems in which persons must expend some costly effort to attain a good—e.g. e could measure years of education, x could measure income in a later period, which is monotonically related to e. Education is psychically costly for the individual. A person's choice of e depends on traits beyond his control (his family background, his native intelligence, the degree of discrimination he faces, etc.), but there also may be traits which affect the choice for which society wishes to hold the individual responsible. Thus, we partition the population into a finite number of types, defined by a finite number of values of the vector which records a person's family background, native intelligence, etc. The egalitarian's problem is to choose a tax policy which redistributes income according to the view enunciated in the opening paragraph. *Within* a type, people will generally make different educational choices, and those differences are deemed to be within the control of persons in the type, and not compensable at the bar of egalitarianism. Differences *across* types, however, for the 'same degree' of will power or responsibility exercised, should be grounds for compensation. (I shall describe how to measure that degree presently.)

Finally, the planner assigns one utility function to each type. Since the utility function is defined on the entire vector of traits (S and its complement), the preferences over income x and effort e within a type may differ. In many real-world situations, the planners in fact use the same utility function for all persons in the population (if, for example, they are concerned only with income, or with people having some combination of income and education). I will, henceforth, use the notation $u(x, e, \alpha_j)$ to refer to the planner's assignment of welfare to a person of type j who consumes income x and has expended effort e.

A mechanism is a mapping from environments described as $E = (u, a, p, e, F, T)$ into T. In the definition of the environment, $a = (a_1, \ldots, a_r)$, $p = (p_1, \ldots, p_r)$ is the family of random variables $e(\tau, \alpha_j)$, and F is the family of probability measures $F^{\tau}_{\alpha_j}$.

3. Medical costs and responsibility: an example

The following example is taken from Roemer (1993), to motivate the formal analysis of the rest of the paper.

Suppose society takes the view that a person who contracts lung cancer from smoking should be held in part responsible for the costs of treatment, given the information ubiquitously available to smokers about the risks. Variations in the number of years people smoke are attributable to circumstances, features of the person or the environment beyond her control, and to preferences and choices for which people should be held responsible.[2] Society must first decide what circumstances seem to be important in determining a person's smoking behaviour: it might decide these are a person's occupation, her ethnicity and gender, whether her parents smoked, and her income level. For the purposes at hand, these five characteristics of a person would be considered to be factors that are beyond her control.[3] The next step is to divide the relevant population into types, where each type consists of the subset of the population that have approximately the same values of all five characteristics.

[2] It is important to note that a person's preferences may have been formed in part by circumstance. In this way, my view differs from Dworkin's, for he takes persons to be fully responsible for their choices. For further elaboration of the difference between the position I put forth and Dworkin's, see Roemer (1993).

[3] One might question whether her occupation is beyond her control. For the purpose of analysing smoking behaviour, we might say it is, while we might say it is not if we were trying to explain her income level, because a person arguably should not be held accountable for not considering the effect of her occupational choice on her smoking behaviour, while she might well be held accountable for not considering the effect of that choice on her income.

Now, within each type, there will be a range of smoking behaviour. For instance, the median number of years smoked (by people of age 60, let us say) will vary across type. I will propose that two 60 year olds, each of whom has smoked the median number of years for his type, have exercised a comparable degree of responsibility with respect to smoking behaviour.

Here is the motivation. Within a type, the variation in smoking behaviour is taken to be due to personal (responsible) choice. By definition, society has already accounted for, in the definition of type, all the circumstances affecting smoking behaviour which it takes to be beyond a person's control. Now let us compare two people of different types, both of whom are at the median of their respective type distributions of years of smoking. Although it might not make sense to say they have taken the same degree of responsibility, we can say that, given their type, each has exercised a comparable degree of responsibility—the comparison being to what others in his type have done. According to the egalitarian ethic announced in the introduction, these two people should be equally indemnified by society against the harm they have suffered. Thus, suppose one lung cancer victim is a 60-year-old, white, female college professor, whose parents stopped smoking when she was 7; she smoked the median number of years for her type, which, let us say, is eight years. A second lung cancer victim, also aged 60, is a black, male steelworker, whose parents were both chain smokers. He also happens to be the median smoker of his type, and has smoked for twenty-five years. My egalitarian ethic says both should receive the same degree of social indemnity: if all the medical care costs of the professor are covered by society, then the same should be the case for the steelworker.

(Perhaps providing such complete medical subsidies to the median smokers across types would result in more smoking at the median, and less health as a result. If so, then the policy of complete medical subsidy would not be optimal. The optimal policy is studied in the next section.)

The motivation for saying that two persons, each at the median in his type with respect to years spent smoking, have exercised comparable degrees of responsibility depends on the 'degree of responsibility' being monotonically related (in this case inversely) to years spent smoking. We cannot observe directly the degree of responsibility a person takes, but we may be able to infer that degree from observed behaviour (in this case, years spent smoking). Thus, within a type, it is natural to say that the more a person has smoked, the less responsibly he has behaved (with respect to suffering the possible harm of lung cancer). It may be suggestive to identify the degree of responsibility taken with the degree of will power exercised. Thus, in this example, there is a monotonic relationship between (unobservable) will power and (observable) years spent smoking.

It is not hard to extend this principle to people who are not 'median' smokers. The median number of years smoked by people of a given type is the number such that exactly 50 per cent of the population have smoked that number of years or fewer. Now replace 50 per cent by any percentage, say p. I will say that two people, of different types, have exercised a comparable degree of responsibility if each is at the pth percentile of his type-distribution, for some p.

4. An egalitarian mechanism

My intent is to design a mechanism that equalizes utility (as the planner measures it) across types, for those who have taken comparable degrees of responsibility, but allows utility to differ within type according to how persons have exercised different degrees of responsibility.

After the example of the previous section, I propose to identify two persons of types i and j as having exercised the same degree of responsibility if their efforts lie at the same percentile of their respective type distributions $F^{\tau}_{\alpha_1}$ and $F^{\tau}_{\alpha_j}$. This presupposes, then, a monotonic relationship between unobservable will power exercised, and observable effort. Thus we can define r functions $\omega^j\pi$ by

$$\int_0^{\omega^j(\pi)} dF^{\tau}_{\alpha_j}(\omega) = \pi \text{ for } j = 1, \dots, r. \tag{4.1}$$

(More precisely, I should write $\omega^j(\pi; \tau)$, but I suppress τ.) Thus the fraction of type j persons who have expended effort $\omega \leqslant \omega^j(\pi)$ is exactly π.

It is now convenient to introduce the functions

$$\hat{e}(\tau; \alpha_j; \pi) = \varpi^j(\pi) \tag{4.2a}$$

$$\hat{x}(\tau; \alpha_j; \pi) = \varphi^j(\hat{e}(\tau; \alpha_j; \pi)) \tag{4.2b}$$

We think of two agents who have the same value of π as having exercised comparable degrees of responsibility. I shall also refer, for short, to π as a person's 'responsibility'.

Let us now suppose that the measures $F^{\tau}_{\alpha_j}$ can be represented by density functions $f^{\tau}_{\alpha_j}(\omega)$ and also that the functions $\omega^j(\pi)$ are differentiable. Then, differentiating (4.1) w.r.t. π gives:

$$f^{\tau}_{\alpha_j}(\omega^j(\pi)) \frac{d\omega^j(\pi)}{d\pi} = 1 \tag{4.3}$$

Let us define the indirect utility function $v^j(\tau, \pi)$ as the utility of a person with responsibility π of type j facing tax scheme τ. To be more explicit, suppose II is a function only of income, and we may therefore write $\pi(x)$ as the tax paid by a person who 'earns' x. Then

$$v^j(\tau, \pi) = u(\hat{x}(\tau; \alpha_j; \pi) - \tau(\hat{x}(\tau; \alpha_j; \pi)), \hat{e}(\tau; \alpha_j, \pi), \alpha_j). \tag{4.4}$$

Facing τ, the frequency of those in the population who exercise responsibility π is $\sum_i P_i f^{\tau}_{\alpha_j}(\omega^i(\pi))$. That is, we have

$$\sum_i P_i \int_0^1 f^{\tau}_{\alpha_j}(\omega^i(\pi))\, d\omega^i(\pi) = 1.$$

Ideally, what the responsibility-sensitive egalitarian would like to do is choose that τ that equalizes (more precisely, maxi-mins) utility across types j for each value of π. Obviously, this cannot be done: a continuum of maximizations cannot be simultaneously performed. What I propose is to choose that τ which maximizes a weighted average of the minimum utilities across types, where the weight assigned to a given π is its frequency in the entire population.

We are, so to speak, interested in choosing τ to make

$$\mathop{Min}_j v^j(\pi, \tau)$$

as big as possible for each π, an impossible task: we implement this by maximizing an average of the

$$\mathop{Min}_j v^j(\pi, \tau)$$

where the net weight assigned to responsibility π persons is their population frequency. Let $N(\pi, \tau)$ be the fraction of the population, at tax scheme τ, who have taken responsibility less than or equal to π. N is the C.D.F. of a probability measure on [0,1]. Let $n^{\tau}(\pi)$ be its density; then $n^{\tau}(\pi)$ is the frequency of people in the population of responsibility π. Thus, the above proposal implies that the planner chooses π to

$$\mathop{Sup}_{\tau} \int_0^1 \mathop{Min}_i v^i(\pi, \tau)\, n^{\tau}(\pi)\, d\pi$$

But $N(\pi, \tau) = \sum_j P_j F^{\tau}_{\alpha_j}(\omega^i(\pi))$. Hence, by differentiating,

$$n^{\tau}(\pi) = \sum_j P_i f^{\tau}_{\alpha_j} \frac{d\omega^j(\pi)}{d\pi}$$

Substituting from (4.3), we have $n^{\tau}(\pi) = 1$. This is the sensible result that the population frequency of persons is the same at every degree of responsibility. Hence, our recommended choice of tax scheme is

$$\mathop{Sup}_{\tau} \int_0^1 \mathop{Min}_j v^j(\pi, \tau)\, n^{\tau}(\pi)\, d\pi \tag{4.5}$$

Note that the integral and Min operators do not commute in (4.5).

$$\mathop{Min}_j v^j(\pi, \tau)$$

is the function which, for each value of π, takes on the minimum of $v^j(\pi, \tau)$ across j.

Let us call this mechanism Φ^E.

It will be instructive to compare Φ^E to utilitarianism and Rawlsianism. The utilitarian chooses that tax policy which maximizes average utility in the population. Thus, she solves

$$\underset{\tau}{Sup} \sum_j \int_0^1 P_j f_{\alpha_j}^{\tau}(w)\, u(x(\tau;\alpha_j,\omega) - \tau(x), e(\tau;\alpha_j,\omega)\alpha_j)\, d\omega$$

Although responsibility is not relevant for the utilitarian, we may nevertheless reparametrize by π, and the above expression can be written

$$\underset{\tau}{Sup} \int_0^1 \sum P_j f_{\alpha_j}^{\tau}(\omega^j(\pi)) \frac{d\omega^j(\pi)}{d\pi} v^j(\pi,\tau)\, d\pi$$

which, by (4.3), equals

$$\underset{\tau}{Sup} \int_0^1 \sum P_j v^j(\pi,\tau)\, d\pi \tag{4.6}$$

Thus we say

$$\Phi^u(E) = Arg\, \underset{\tau}{Sup} \int_0^1 \sum P_j v^j(\pi,\tau)\, d\pi \tag{4.6a}$$

Finally, the Rawlsian also pays no attention to responsibility, but chooses that π that maximizes the minimum utility in the population. (Alternatively, to be more faithful to Rawls, we should now think of the function v as being an index of primary goods.) Then

$$\Phi^R(E) = Arg\, \underset{\tau}{Sup}\, \underset{\pi, j}{Min}\, v^j(\pi,\tau)$$

We thus have three mechanisms defined by expressions (4.5), (4.6*a*), and (4.7).

In section 6, 1 shall calculate the action of the three mechanisms for an example. But before that, we briefly study feasible linear tax schemes.

5. Feasible linear tax schemes

Let T be the set of tax schemes of the form $d_1x + d_0$ which are purely redistributive: that is, total taxes aggregate to zero. This means that

$$\sum P_j \int_0^1 (d_1 x(\omega;\alpha_j,\tau) + d_0) f_{\alpha_j}^{\tau}(\omega)\, d\omega = 0 \tag{5.1}$$

where $x(\omega; a_j, \tau)$ is the output produced by type i at tax rate τ who expends effort ω. Here τ can be identified as the ordered pair (d_1, d_0) with $0 \leqslant d_1 \leqslant 1$. We can reparametrize by π, as usual, and (5.1) becomes

$$d_1 \int_0^1 \sum P_j \hat{x}(\tau;\alpha_j,\pi)\, d\pi + d_0 = 0$$

or

$$d_0 = - d_1 \int_0^1 \sum p_j \hat{x}(\tau; \alpha_j, \pi)\, d\pi \quad (5.2)$$

Thus the set of feasible tax schemes T can be identified by the single parameter $d_1 \in [0, 1]$, where d_0 is given by (5.2). I shall, from now on, refer to the generic tax scheme as d_1.

6. An example

Let $u(x, e, a)$, $u(x, e, e) = x - e^2/2a$, and $\varphi^j(e) = \delta e$ for all j, where $\delta > 0$ and $a \in \Re_{++}$. Think of e as years of education, x as income in a later period, and a as native intelligence. Thus, more intelligent people find education less costly. In the population, a takes on values $0 < a_1 < a_2 < \ldots < a_r$ with frequencies p_j. People are viewed as not responsible for the value of a—so in this case there are r types, and $a_j = \alpha_j$.

Were an agent of type j an optimizer with utility function u, she would, facing the linear tax scheme d_1, solve the problem

$$\underset{e}{Max}(1 - d_1)\delta e - \frac{e^2}{2a_j}$$

yielding $e = \delta a_j(1 - d_j)$. We shall assume, however, that, among those of type j, actual educational levels achieved are given by the random variable

$$e(d_1; a_j)(\omega) = \delta a_j \omega (1 - d_1), \quad (6.1)$$

where ω is uniformly distributed on [0,1]. In terms of our previous notation, $F_{a_j}^{d_1}$ is the uniform distribution on [0,1] for all (aj, d_1). This yields the very simple formulae

$$\omega^j(\pi) = \pi$$

and so we may write

$$\hat{e}(d_1; a_j, \pi) = \delta a_j \pi (1 - d_1) \quad (6.2)$$

The interpretation of (6.1) may be that will power is required to undertake the amount of education that, rationally, one should. Most people, because they are myopic or suffer from weakness of will, only undertake a fraction of the education that they should. The Φ^E planner is an egalitarian who wishes to compensate persons for their differential native intelligence, that being beyond their control, but not for their weakness of will.

From (6.2), it follows that

$$\hat{x}(d_1; a_j, \pi) = \delta^2 a_j \pi (1 - d_1) \quad (6.3)$$

and from (5.2),

$$d_0 = - \sum_i P_j d_1 (1 - d_1) \delta^2 a_j \int_0^1 \pi\, d\pi$$

or,

$$d_0 = d_1(1-d_1)\delta^2 \frac{\overline{a}}{2} \tag{6.4}$$

where

$$\overline{a} \equiv \sum P_j a_j$$

By plugging into the utility function, we have

$$v^j(d_1, \pi) = \delta^2 a_j \pi (1-d_1)^2 - d_0 - \tfrac{1}{2}\delta^2 a_j \pi (1-d_1)^2 \tag{6.5}$$

To find

$$Arg \underset{j}{Min}\ v^j(d_1, \pi),$$

we examine the coefficient of a_j in (6.5), which is

$$\delta^2 \pi (1-d_1)^2 - \tfrac{1}{2}\delta^2 \pi^2 (1-d_1)^2,$$

which has the same sign as $1 - 1/2\pi$ and hence is positive for all $\pi \in [0, 1]$. It follows that $\forall \pi\ 1 = Arg \underset{j}{Min}\ v^j(d_1, \pi)$, and so (4.5) is written:

$$\underset{d_1}{Sup}\left[\delta^2 a_1 (1-d_1)^2 \int_0^1 \left(\pi - \frac{1}{2}\pi^2\right) d\pi - d_0\right],$$

or, using (6.4) and integrating:

$$\underset{d_1}{Sup}\left[\frac{\delta^2 a_1 (1-d_1)^2}{3} + \frac{d_1(1-d_1)\delta^2 \overline{a}}{2}\right] \tag{6.6}$$

We can factor out δ^2 from (6.6), and expand, and we have

$$\Phi^E(\text{E}) = Arg \underset{d_1}{Sup}\left[2a_1 - d_1(4a_1 - 3\overline{a}) + d_1^2(2a_1 - 3\overline{a})\right]. \tag{6.7}$$

Since $a_1 = \min aj$, we have $2a_1 - 3\overline{a} < 0$ and it follows that the function in brackets in (6.7) is concave in d_1. Hence setting its derivative w.r.t. d_1 equal to zero yields

$$\tilde{d}_1 = \frac{4a_1 - 3\overline{a}}{4a_1 - 6\overline{a}},$$

which is the required tax rate if $\tilde{d} \in [0, 1]$. Noting the denominator of $\tilde{d}_1$ is negative, but the numerator can be either positive or negative or zero, we have

$$\Phi^E(E) = \left[\begin{array}{l} 0 \text{ if } \dfrac{a_1}{\overline{a}} \geqslant \dfrac{3}{4} \\ \dfrac{3\overline{a} - 4a_1}{6\overline{a} - 4a_1} \text{ if } \dfrac{a_1}{\overline{a}} \leqslant \dfrac{3}{4} \end{array}\right. \tag{6.8}$$

In sum, the egalitarian mechanism Φ^E does not redistribute at all if the variance among the $\{aj\}$ is sufficiently small ($a_1/\bar{a} > 3/4$), but does tax, up to a maximum tax rate of $d_1 = 1/2$ as $a_1/\bar{a}$ approaches zero.

Next we calculate Φ^u. From (4.6*a*), we have

$$\Phi^u(\mathrm{E}) = Arg\ \underset{d_1}{Sup} \sum_j \int_0^1 \sum p_j \left(\delta^2 a_j \pi (1-d_1)^2 - d_0 - \frac{1}{2}\delta^2 a_j \pi^2 (1-d_1)^2 \right) d\pi, \quad (6.9)$$

which can be reduced to

$$\Phi^u(\mathrm{E}) = Arg\ \underset{d_1}{Sup}\left[2(1-d_1)^2 + 3d_1(1-d_1)\right]$$

which in turn implies $\Phi^u(\mathrm{E}) = 0$. There is no taxation under the utilitarian scheme.

Finally, by applying (4.7) and (6.5), the Rawlsian mechanism is given by

$$\Phi^R(\mathrm{E}) = Arg\ \underset{d_1}{Sup}\ \underset{j,\pi}{Min}\left[\delta^2 a_j \pi (1-d_1)^2 - d_0 - \frac{1}{2}\delta^2 a_j \pi^2 (1\ d_1)^2\right] =$$

$$= Arg\ \underset{d_1}{Sup}\underset{\pi}{Min}\ \delta^2 a_1 \pi (1-d_1)^2 \left(1 - \frac{1}{2}\pi\right) + d_1(1-d_1)\delta^2 \frac{\bar{a}}{2} = Arg\ \underset{d_1}{Sup}\ d_1(1-d_1)\delta^2 \frac{\bar{a}}{2} = \frac{1}{2}$$

In sum, we have

$$0 = \Phi^u(\mathrm{E}) \leqslant \Phi^E(\mathrm{E}) \leqslant \Phi^R(\mathrm{E}) = \frac{1}{2} \quad (6.10)$$

Since we can say, for linear tax schemes, that the degree of redistribution is measured by the size of d_1, it follows from (6.9) that Φ^E redistributes no more than Φ^R and no less than Φ^u. Furthermore, (6.8) shows that the inequalities in (6.10) are tight: there are non-degenerate environments E such that $\Phi^E = \Phi^u$, and, there is a sequence of non-degenerate environments E^k such that

$$lim \mid \Phi^E(\mathrm{E}^k) - \Phi^R(\mathrm{E}^k) \mid = 0.$$

In words, Φ^E may prescribe any tax rate between what a Rawlsian and a utilitarian would recommend.

7. More on the relationship of Φ^E to Φ^R and Φ^u

In the example of section 6, we found that Φ^E always redistributed less than Φ^R, and this seems to be a reasonable result, as *E*-egalitarians hold persons responsible for more than *R*-egalitarians do. It is therefore somewhat surprising that this relationship between Φ^E and Φ^R does not hold universally. It is also the case that the utilitarian mechanism may redistribute more than the *E*-mechanism. In this section, examples are constructed to demonstrate these claims.

The first example shows that Φ^R can redistribute less than Φ^E does on some environments. Let there be one type, let $u(x, e) = x - 1/2e^2$, let $x = e$ (i.e., $\varphi(e) = e$), and let the tax schemes be linear. The random factor shall be written $\omega(\pi, d_1)$; let

$$\hat{e}(d_1, \pi) = \omega(\pi, d_1)(1 - d_1) \tag{7.1}$$

An optimizer with this utility function would choose effort equal to $1 - d_1$

I specify, for values $\hat{d}$, δ, and ε small positive numbers to be chosen presently, the following:

$$\left.\begin{aligned} &\text{For } d_1 < \hat{d}\text{: } \omega(\pi, d_1) = \begin{cases} 1 & \text{for } 0 < \pi < 1 - \varepsilon \\ 1 + \delta & \text{for } 1 - \varepsilon < \pi < 1 \end{cases} \\ &\text{For } d_1 > \hat{d}\text{: } \omega(\pi, d_1) = \begin{cases} 1 & \text{for } 0 < \pi < 1 - \varepsilon \\ 1 + \delta & \text{for } 1 - \varepsilon < \pi < 1 \\ 1 & \text{for } \pi = 1 \end{cases} \end{aligned}\right] \tag{7.2}$$

From (5.2) we have

$$d_0 = -d_1 \int_0^1 (1 - d_1)\omega(\pi, d_1)\, d\pi$$

It follows from (7.2) that, for all d_1,

$$d_0 = -d_1(1 - d_1) \int_0^1 \omega(\pi, d_1)\, d\pi = d_1(1 - d_1) = 1 + \varepsilon\delta \tag{7.3}$$

Thus we may write the indirect utility as:

$$v(\pi, d_1) = (1 - d_1)^2(\omega(\pi, d_1) - \tfrac{1}{2}\omega(\pi, d_1)^2) + d_1(1 - d_1)(1 + \varepsilon\delta). \tag{7.4}$$

Since there is only one type, we have, by (4.5),

$$\Phi^E = \mathop{Arg\ Sup}_{d_1} \int_0^1 v(\pi, d_1)\, d\pi$$

$$\Phi_E = \mathop{Arg\ Sup}_{d_1} \left[(1 - d_1)^2 M(d_1) + d_1(1 - d_1)(1 + \varepsilon\delta)\right] \tag{7.5}$$

where

$$M(d_1) := \int_0^1 \left(\omega(\pi, d_1) - \frac{1}{2}\omega(\pi, d_1)^2\right) d\pi.$$

It is easily computed that:

$$\forall d_1\ M \equiv M(d_1) = \frac{1}{2} - \frac{1}{2}\varepsilon\delta^2,$$

and so

$$\Phi^E = Arg \underset{d_1}{Sup} \left[(1-d_1)^2 \left(\tfrac{1}{2} - \tfrac{1}{2}\varepsilon\delta^2 \right) + d_1(1-d_1)(1+\varepsilon\delta) \right]. \quad (7.6)$$

It follows that the coefficient d_1^2 in (7.6) is negative, and so the maximand in (7.6) is a concave function of d_1, whose supremum may be found by equating the first derivative to zero; thus

$$\Phi^E = Max\left(0, \frac{(1+\varepsilon\delta) - 2M}{2((1+\varepsilon\delta) - M)}\right) \quad (7.7)$$

But $1 + \varepsilon\delta > 2M$, and so

$$\Phi^E = \frac{1+\varepsilon\delta - 2M}{2(1+\varepsilon\delta - M)} = \frac{\varepsilon\delta + \varepsilon\delta^2}{1 + 2\varepsilon\delta + \varepsilon\delta^2}. \quad (7.7')$$

We next compute

$$\Phi^E = Arg \underset{d_1}{Sup} \underset{\pi}{Min}\, v(\pi, d_1).$$

Note that the function $\omega - \frac{1}{2}\omega^2$ has its maximum at $\omega = 1$ and is symmetric about $\omega = 1$; thus

$$\underset{\pi}{Min}\, v(\pi, d_1) = \begin{cases} (1-d_2)^2(1+\delta) - \frac{1}{2}(1+\delta)^2 + d_1(1-d_1)(1+\varepsilon\delta) \text{ for } d_1 \leqslant \hat{d} \\ -\frac{1}{2}(1-d_1)^2 + d_1(1-d_1)(1+\varepsilon\delta) \text{ for } d_1 > \hat{d} \end{cases}$$

For δ close to zero,

$$\underset{d_1}{Max} \underset{\pi}{Min}\, v(\pi, d_1)$$

is therefore achieved for $d_1 \leqslant \hat{d}$; in fact:

$$\Phi^R = Arg \underset{d_1 \leqslant \hat{d}}{Sup} \left[(1-d_1)^2 \left((1+\delta) - \tfrac{1}{2}(1+\delta)^2 \right) + d_1(1-d_1)(1+\varepsilon\delta) \right]. \quad (7.8)$$

For small δ, the maximand in (7.8) is a concave function of d_1; in particular, it is increasing at $d_1 = 0$. Therefore, for d sufficiently close to zero, it follows that

$$\Phi^R = \hat{d} \quad (7.9)$$

Since $\hat{d}$ may be chosen arbitrarily close to zero, it follows that ε, δ, and $\hat{d}$ may be chosen so that $\Phi^E > \Phi^R$ (check (7.7′) and (7.9)). The only restriction on ε is that it be positive and less than unity.

There might be two objections to the robustness of this example: first, that $\omega(\pi, d_1)$ is not continuous, and second, that the Rawlsian mechanism is driven by the behaviour of a set of agents of zero measure. Reconsideration of the argument, however, will convince the reader that both of these characteristics can be relaxed without destroying the result.

The intuition behind the above example is as follows. The Rawlsian mechanism pays attention to the worst-off person. If the tax rate is too high (larger than $\hat{d}$), then that person is he for whom $\pi = 1$. Only by keeping d small (less than $\hat{d}$) can we prevent anyone from being as badly off as that person. The *E*-mechanism, however, pays no attention to the fate of that person, as it looks at average fates, and that person has very small measure (in fact, measure zero in the example).

What is the class of problems for which $\Phi^E \leqslant \Phi^R$? The next result gives a partial answer.

PROPOSITION. *Suppose there exist functions $M_j(\pi)$ for all types j, and twice differentiable functions $\varphi_1(d)$ and $\varphi_2(d)$ such that:*

1. $v^j(\pi_1, d_1) = \varphi_1(d) M_j + \varphi_2(d)$,
2. $v^j(\pi, d)$ *is strictly concave in d for all* π,
3. $\varphi_1 \geqslant \varphi'_2 \leqslant 0$.

Then $\Phi^E \leqslant \Phi^R$.

Proof

1. Suppose $F(\alpha, d) \equiv \varphi_1(d)\alpha + \varphi_2(d)$ is strictly concave in d, and let the solution of the equation

$$\varphi_1'(d)\alpha + \varphi_2'(d) = 0$$

define a function $\hat{d}(\alpha)$. By the implicit function theorem, we may calculate that

$$\hat{d}'(\alpha) = \frac{-\varphi_1'(\hat{d}(\alpha))}{\alpha\varphi_1''(\hat{d}(\alpha)) + \varphi_2''(\hat{d}(\alpha))}.$$

The denominator is strictly negative and the numerator is non-negative, so $\hat{d}(\alpha) \leqslant 0$.

2. Now consider the function $v^j(\pi, d)$. By assumption 2, $\underset{d}{Max}\, v^j(\pi, d)$ is achieved where

$$\varphi'_1(d) M_j(\pi) + \varphi'_2(d) = 0 \tag{7.10}$$

or at $d = 0$ or 1; call the solution of (7.10) $d(\pi)$. By step 1, $d(\pi)$ is a (weakly) decreasing function of $M_j(\pi)$.

3. $$\Phi^E = \underset{d}{Arg\, Sup} \int_0^1 \underset{j}{Max}\, v^j(\pi, d)\, dpi.$$

Since $\varphi_1 \geqslant 0$, it follows that

$$\underset{j}{Arg\, Min}\, v^j(\pi, d)$$

is achieved at j such that $M_j(\pi) \leqslant M_i(\pi)$, for all i.

Let $j^*(\pi)$ be the smallest index j satisfying this inequality. Thus

$$\Phi^E = \underset{d}{Arg\ Sup} \int_0^1 v^{j^*(\pi)}(\pi, d)\, d\pi = \underset{d}{Arg\ Sup}\left[\varphi_1(d)\int_0^1 M_{j^*(\pi)}(\pi)\, d\pi + \varphi_2(d)\right]$$

4. $$\Phi^R = \underset{d}{Arg\ Sup}\ \underset{\pi, j}{Min}\ v^{j(\pi, d)} = \underset{d}{Arg\ Sup}\ \underset{\pi}{Min}\, v^{j^*(\pi)}(\pi, d)$$

$$= \underset{d}{Arg\ Sup}\ \underset{\pi}{Min}\left[\varphi_1(d) M_{j^*(\pi)} + \varphi_2 d\right]$$

But the minimum over π of the expression in square brackets is achieved at $\pi^* = \underset{\pi}{Arg\ Min}\ M_{j^*(\pi)}(\pi)$, and so

$$\Phi^R = \underset{d}{Arg\ Sup}\left[\varphi_1(d) M_{j^*(\pi^*)}(\pi^*) + \varphi_2(d)\right].$$

5. Now apply the conclusion of step 1 to the last lines of steps 3 and 4; we have

$$\Phi^R = \hat{d}\left(M_{j^*(\pi^*)}(\pi^*)\right) \text{ and } \Phi^E = \hat{d}\left(\int_0^1 M_{j^*(\pi)}(\pi)\, d\pi\right)$$

Since $\hat{d}'(\alpha) \leqslant 0$, it follows that $\Phi^R \geqslant \Phi^E$.

Proposition 1 covers a fairly broad class of cases. For example, it covers the example of section 6.

We next proceed to show that the utilitarian mechanism can redistribute more than the *E*-mechanism. Let there be two types. The utility functions are $u(x, e, 1) = x - \frac{1}{2}e^2$ and $u(x, e, 2) = k(x^2 - \frac{1}{2}e^2)$. Let $e(d_1; \pi, 1) = 1 - d_1$ for all π, and $e(d_2; \pi, 2) = R(1 - d_1)$. The fraction of type 1 in the population is p_i. Choose $(k, R, p_1) = (.05, 5, .9)$.

With these data, we have $v^1(d_1) = \frac{1}{2}(1 - d_1)^2 + d_1(1 - d_1)(p_1 + p_2 R)$ and $v^2(d_1) = k(R(1 - d_1)^2 - (R(1 - d_1))^2 + d_1(1 - d_1)(p_1 + p_2 R))$. Note that, since effort is the same for all members of each type, at any tax rate, the *E*-mechanism collapses to the Rawlsian mechanism. Fig. 9.1 plots $v_1(d_1)$ and $v_2(d_2)$ (the convex function is v^2). The Rawlsian tax rate occurs where the two curves intersect, at $d_1^R = .039$. On the other hand, the utilitarian tax, which maximizes $p_1 v_1 + p_2 v_2$ is $d_1^u = .077$. Thus, the utilitarian scheme redistributes more than the Rawlsian scheme, and hence, than the *E*-scheme.

8. Summary

The philosophy motivating the *E*-mechanism is equality of opportunity. A person's opportunities are influenced by her circumstances, aspects of her environment and self over which she has no control. The goal is to compensate people, as fully as possible, for the effects differences in their circumstances have on outcomes, but to allow difference in outcomes

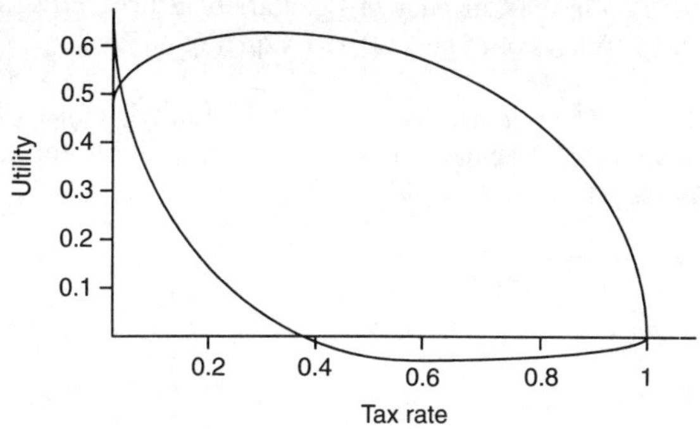

FIG. 9.1.

between persons in so far as they are the consequence of choices that are *not* accounted for by circumstances. In the language used here, the goal is to equalize outcomes (as measured by the planner) at the highest possible level for all persons who have acted with a comparable degree of responsibility, regardless of their circumstances—and to do this for every degree of responsibility. This is impossible, for it would involve solving a continuum of maxi-min problems simultaneously. Call the subset of the population at a given degree of responsibility a tranche. The solution proposed is to give equal weight to the maxi-min problem for each tranche. Thus, the *E*-mechanism is a kind of combination of utilitarianism and Rawlsianism. When looking at a tranche, it is Rawlsian; among tranches, it is utilitarian, in giving equal consideration to each.

We have seen that the distributional behaviour of the *E*-mechanism is complex. Although, intuitively, it might appear that it would redistribute more than utilitarianism and less than Rawlsianism, neither of these inequalities holds universally.

The *E*-mechanism makes no attempt to reward persons who have taken greater responsibility than others. Its motto is 'equal outcomes for all those in a given tranche', not 'better treatment for those who have behaved more responsibly than others'. The result may be, in many cases, that those who have exerted more effort will end up better off than others of their type who have exerted less will at the policy recommended by the *E*-mechanism. A thorough study of this issue has yet to be done.

REFERENCES

Arneson, R. (1989), 'Equality of Opportunity for Welfare', *Philosophical Studies*, 56: 77–93.

Cohen, G. A. (1989), 'On the Currency of Egalitarian Justice', *Ethics*, 99: 906–44.

Dworkin, R. (1981), 'What is Equality? Part 1 Equality of Welfare', *Philosophy and Public Affairs*, 10: 185–246.

Fleurbaey, M. (1992), 'The Requisites of Equal Opportunity', mimeo (INSEE, Paris).

Roemer, J. E. (1993), 'A Pragmatic Theory of Responsibility for the Egalitarian Planner', *Philosophy and Public Affairs*, 22: 146–66.

10

Free-Riding Versus Rent-Sharing: Should Even David Gauthier Support an Unconditional Basic Income?[1]

PHILIPPE VAN PARIJS

1. Basic income as free-riding

Some years ago, I spent a few months with my family in a house we were sharing with my father-in-law. Very soon, one feature of our daily routine started disturbing me greatly. I noticed that my father-in-law was quite sensitive to the floor getting dirty, far more sensitive at any rate that I was myself. As soon as dust started covering the lounge floor, he would take out the vacuum cleaner and deal with it, long before I would start thinking it was necessary. The result, of course, was that the floor was tidied up for me beyond my wishes, without my doing anything for it. This bothered me because I could not help feeling it was unfair. True, I did manage to convince myself that I was not *exploiting* my father-in-law, because, even though I derived a benefit from his work, and one that was not meant as a gift, I did not do so by exercising any power over him.[2] But I had to concede that this semantic response did not settle the ethical issue, and that such a situation, if continued—and taken in isolation from other aspects of the interaction—was *unfair*. This I found particularly annoying because of a puzzling connection with an idea which I was beginning to explore at the time and to which I soon became committed to the point of spending a considerable amount of time advocating it in all sorts of circles.

This is the idea of a basic income, or citizenship income, or universal grant, i.e. the idea of an income granted unconditionally to every citizen, of a specific form of guaranteed minimum income that differs from the

[1] This chapter is based on my contribution to the Summer School 'Ethics and Economics' organized by the International School for Economic Research (Siena, July 1991). I am grateful to Christian Arnsperger, Sam Bowles, Ronald Dworkin, Marc Fleurbaey, Hervé Moulin, Robert Nozick, Amartya Sen, Bernard Stainier, Bob Sugden, and particularly David Gauthier, for fruitful discussions in connection with it.

[2] The underlying analysis of exploitation in terms of work, benefit, and power is spelled out in Van Parijs (1993: ch. 5).

guaranteed minimum incomes that exist in advanced welfare states in two main ways: (1) there is no means test: it is given *ex ante* to all; (2) there is no willingness-to-work test: it is given to housewives, students, and tramps as well as to workers, pensioners, and the involuntarily unemployed. In the course of advocating this idea and thinking about it, I soon became persuaded that the ethical issue it raised was both more important and more difficult than I first thought. More important because the real stumbling-block that prevents a reform of advanced European welfare states in that direction lies in moral resistance more than in economic misgivings; more difficult because some of the ethical objections raised are serious ones, which need to be taken seriously and handled carefully.

One serious objection consists in criticizing the introduction of a basic income—in particular, at the highest feasible level—on the grounds that it illiberally discriminates in favour of leisure lovers at the expense of income lovers. Another serious objection consists in criticizing the idea of a basic income on the ground that it is too gross, too undifferentiated, and does not give what justice requires be given to the handicapped. I have dealt with these two objections elsewhere,[3] and shall leave them aside in the present discussion, in order to concentrate on a third, equally threatening objection, which will take us back to my father-in-law.

Suppose a basic income is introduced: some (the Lazies) find it sufficient to live from and do not work; others (the Crazies) do not find it sufficient, therefore decide to work and are taxed so as to finance everyone's basic income. The objection I want to consider now is not that there exists some asymmetry or discrimination in the treatment of Lazies and Crazies, but that the Lazies are living off the Crazies' work, that they are exploiting them (if one is willing to extend the concept of exploitation to cases where someone is deriving a benefit from someone else's work by virtue of an externality—not of power) or, as I shall here prefer to say, that they are free-riding on them. Whichever of these terms is used to describe this situation, it seems that the latter should definitely be viewed as unfair, at least by someone—like myself—who has conceded that it would be wrong for my father-in-law to do all the cleaning. For there is a close analogy between the two situations. Just as I can only get all the cleaning done without doing any work because my father-in-law cares more about cleanliness than I do, Lazies can only get some income without doing any work because Crazies care more about income than they do.

In both cases the options open to the beneficiaries and the providers of the free ride may be identical and no coercive power needs to be involved. The Lazies can tell the Crazies: 'Don't complain, if you prefer our lifestyle, just choose it!', just as I can tell my father-in-law: 'I did not ask you to do all that cleaning, this is your choice'. Yet it is obvious to me that it would

[3] See chs. 4 and 3 of Van Parijs (1995), which are substantially revised and expanded versions of van Parijs (1991) and Van Parijs (1990).

be unfair to let my father-in-law do all the cleaning, and that a fair solution, though it may not involve him and me doing the same amount of cleaning, will definitely require my doing some of it. If this is the case, given the strength of the analogy, it seems to follow that I have to concede that the Lazies exploit the Crazies, that they take unfair advantage of the Crazies' work just as I would do with my father-in-law's work if I were to let him do all the work. Fairness, it seems, must require the Lazies to do some work if they are to get some income. Hence, an unconditional basic income cannot possibly be just.

Or can it? I consider elsewhere various relevant conceptions of fairness which have been appealed to, more or less explicitly, to condemn exploitation in the context of the radical critique of capitalist relationships, and I argue that either (as with the notion of a right to the full fruit of one's labour) they do not make sense, or (as with the notion that underlies John Roemer's game-theoretical or property-relations concept of exploitation) they are perfectly consistent with an unconditional basic income (Van Parijs 1995: ch. 5). Here, I shall focus on another, quite different conception of fairness, the one formulated by David Gauthier under the name of equal relative benefit and precisely used by him to articulate his condemnation of free-riding. I shall concede—in part against Gauthier himself—that his criterion does provide an attractive criterion for allocating burdens in the presence of externalities such as the one illustrated by my father-in-law example. But I am not thereby forced to concede, I shall argue, that an unconditional basic income is unfair. Indeed, Gauthier's own treatment of factor rents indicates how the legitimacy of an unconditional basic income can be vindicated, consistently with the adoption of his proposal as a criterion of fair co-operation.

2. Equal relative benefit

Let me first briefly state Gauthier's criterion, using his own example of two partners who have an interest in co-operating by pooling their capital because of increasing returns to scale on investment (Gauthier 1986: 140–1, 152–3). Each of the partners makes a claim equal to the return on the total investment minus what is required to induce the willing co-operation of the other partner, i.e. what the other partner would get if she invested her capital separately. This claim minus the return she could obtain herself separately represents, for each partner, her maximum gain from co-operation. This amounts to letting each partner claim the whole surplus from co-operation, and it is therefore obvious that, when such claims are made by both partners, there is no way in which they can be satisfied simultaneously. What constitutes a fair solution to this conflict? Gauthier's proposal amounts to requiring that the partners should gain from co-operation in proportion to the maximum gains implied by these claims. One partner's relative benefit is the ratio between the welfare she gains from the cooperative deal that is actually made (relative to the absence of co-operation) and the maximum welfare she could gain from co-operation (relative to the same baseline) without making the other co-operator worse off than the latter would be in the absence of co-operation. Proportionality between gains and claims can therefore also be expressed as equality of relative benefits.

I hasten to add two important qualifications to this brief account. Firstly, this criterion does not exhaust Gauthier's theory of economic justice: in the absence of externalities and rents, a perfect market realizes what justice requires, providing it operates on the background of a distribution of endowments that respects the Lockian proviso. It is only when externalities and/or rents are present that Gauthier's criterion for the fair distribution of the co-operative surplus comes in. Secondly, for the criterion of equal relative benefit to be applicable, the good that is produced by co-operation (here a monetary return) must be divisible at will. Otherwise equality of relative benefits is generally unachievable. If the good is not divisible at will, the criterion should be replaced by the more general criterion of maximin relative benefit.[4] But this complication I shall ignore in the present discussion (as Gauthier does most of the time). I shall concentrate on the simpler case where divisibility can be assumed and where Gauthier's proposal therefore comes down to demanding straight proportionality between actual and maximal gains from co-operation.

How is this proposal to be justified? Gauthier's own main (and official) justification consists in arguing that this criterion provides a sensible solution to the rational bargaining problem. This claim is probably the aspect of Gauthier's work that has attracted most attention, especially on the part of economists. But in the present context I shall not discuss it at all, if only because I do not share Gauthier's meta-ethics—in particular, his conception of the connection between morality and self-interest—and therefore fail to attach any special significance to the validity or otherwise of this aspect of his theory.[5] There is, however, a different sort of justification to which Gauthier occasionally appeals (or indulges in) and which, being a reflective equilibrium theorist, I find far more relevant. It consists in showing that the proposed criterion encapsulates some intuitively appealing notions and manages to accommodate our well-considered judgements about particular situations, whether real or fictional.

Thus, in Gauthier's investment example, application of the criterion attractively justifies at the same time (1) a distribution of the total return from the joint investment in proportion to the share of each partner in total

[4] See Gauthier (1986: 140). Gauthier's preference for a maximin formulation over strict equality has nothing to do with efficiency considerations, since we are here concerned with *relative* benefits, and not, as in Rawls's difference principle, with absolute amounts.

[5] For a general discussion of Gauthier's approach, which I find, on the whole, persuasive, see Barry (1988, 1989).

investment, and (2) an equal sharing of the surplus from co-operation between the two partners. Feature (1) expresses 'the reasonable insistence that overall returns be proportionate to (differing) overall contributions', while feature (2) fits in with the 'egalitarian view of co-operation' which Gauthier says is implicit in his whole analysis: 'The co-operative surplus is in the fullest sense the joint product of the co-operators. No one may reasonably or fairly expect more, and no one should reasonably or fairly accept less, than an equal share of the co-operative surplus' (Gauthier 1986: 153). If these results hold generally, Gauthier's approach can plausibly be viewed and defended as a sophisticated version of the principle 'To each according to her contribution', and as directly implying, therefore, that it would be unfair to give anything to those who contribute nothing.

Let us be careful, however. For whether (1) and (2) are features of Gauthier's solution crucially depends on some specific assumptions he brings into his example. One of these is that 'utilities are linear with monetary values', i.e. that each increase of a given size in either partner's income boosts her welfare at a constant rate—though possibly at a rate that is not the same for both partners. Why does this assumption matter? I have mentioned earlier that the maximum gain, for each partner, consists in appropriating the whole surplus. Under the linearity assumption just stated, it directly follows that each should be given an equal share in the surplus if relative benefits are to be equalized. But suppose I face a decreasing marginal utility of income, whereas your utility gains are a linear function of your monetary gains. I shall then reach any given ratio of actual to maximum gain in welfare terms with a smaller ratio in monetary terms (since the last pennies matter less to me than the first ones). Equal relative benefit will therefore require that a greater proportion of the co-operative surplus (not of the overall return), expressed in monetary terms, be allocated to you than to me. This holds not just if we have both contributed the same investment, but irrespective of the amount contributed.

Thus, in the absence of a linear relationship between utilities and monetary values, Gauthier's criterion does not require feature (2), i.e. an equal distribution of the surplus. Since the surplus is a component of the overall return, its distribution being affected by individual utility functions will obviously prevent any neat match between contributions and returns, as implied by feature (1). But even if there were a linear relationship between income and utility, the distribution of the return on the joint investment in proportion to the investment of each partner requires, in Gauthier's example, an additional specific assumption, namely that the returns to scale (which create the co-operative surplus) increase in linear fashion. If instead they increased, in the relevant range, at a decreasing rate, the non-cooperative pay-off of the partner who contributes less to the joint investment would differ more from that of the partner who contributes more than is assumed by Gauthier. Consequently, the compensation for this forgone pay-off that is incorporated in each partner's return (along with the relative-benefit equalizing share in the co-operative surplus) will differ more from one partner to the other—too much, therefore, for the total return to be proportional to the unequal contributions, despite the equal share in the surplus.

This twofold qualification may prompt the following weakening of the claim that Gauthier's approach offers a sophisticated version of the principle 'To each according to her contribution'. Though the criterion of equal relative (net) benefits does not generally require proportionality between (gross) benefits and contributions, it does require that the latter should be a positive function of the former. Even this would be misleading, however. For suppose that you and I are involved in a co-operative venture to which we allocate our equal time and equal woodwork skills. According to Gauthier's criterion (and assuming linearity between income and utility), we should get equal shares in the co-operative surplus and also, one might think, equal overall returns. But suppose I also have a talent for singing that you do not possess and that therefore my next best option is not far worse for me than participation in our common venture, whereas you have no similarly attractive option to fall back on. Then my relative benefit from the egalitarian distribution of (gross) returns that is being contemplated is very small compared to yours. Equal relative benefit will require that I should be given more, despite our strictly equal contribution to the total product. This does not show that Gauthier's criterion implies no positive relationship between contribution and reward, but only that the reason why it does has nothing to do with contribution as such and reflects instead the fact that a greater contribution (for example, a greater share in investment) generally goes hand in hand with a greater return from an alternative use. The positive relationship between contribution and return is simply a consequence of the fact that the opportunity cost of each factor must be fully compensated. This ties in perfectly with Gauthier's treatment of market rewards, for at equilibrium, in a perfect market, the full compensation of opportunity costs is achieved and exhausts the whole product, leaving no 'surplus from co-operation' to be shared.

3. The fair way with free-riding

We are thus very far from a simple criterion of distribution in proportion to contributions. But this does not prevent Gauthier's criterion from being appealing enough in those situations—of market failure—to which they are precisely intended to apply. Let us check its plausibility by examining how it works in my initial father-in-law example, slightly simplified. For this purpose, let me quote Gauthier's most explicit formulation of his principle and put in brackets what I believe to be the most sensible application to the particular example:

In the non-cooperative outcome, which serves as the initial position, the good [i.e. the cleaning] is not produced. Each person claims the maximum level of the good that can be produced without cost to himself, and that leaves every other person at least as well off as if the good were not produced at all [my father-in-law determines the level of cleaning he would do if I did the amount of cleaning that would leave me indifferent between doing it myself and living in a dirty house; I determine the amount of cleaning I would do—if any—if he did the amount of cleaning that would leave him indifferent between doing it all himself and living in a dirty house]. The actual level at which the persons then agree to produce the good, and the actual division of costs among them, is determined by applying . . . maximin relative benefit. For each possible level and division of costs [for example, we share equally the small amount of cleaning I would do if he did nothing], the net gain of each person [for each of us, the positive difference between our welfare under this arrangement and our welfare if no cleaning was done] is measured as a proportion of the gain he would receive from his claim [i.e. for me as a proportion of what I would gain from some higher level of cleanliness with my father-in-law doing all the work; for him, as a proportion of what he would gain from a situation in which I would do all, rather than half of what I am prepared to do, with him doing some more], and the level and distribution maximizing the minimum proportionate gain is selected [i.e. given that amounts of work are divisible, an arrangement which equalizes our actual gains from it as a proportion of what we would respectively gain under the cleaning arrangement that suits us best without making the other person worse off]. (Gauthier 1986: 271–2).

In this sort of situation, Gauthier's criterion of fair co-operation seems to provide a sensible, non-arbitrary intermediate point between two unacceptable extreme solutions. One of these condones the situation that arises spontaneously in the absence of any agreement: owing to the externality involved, I get away with enjoying a clean house while doing no cleaning at all. The other extreme solution expresses in simple-minded fashion the notion that identical benefits should be matched by equal contributions: it consists in dividing equally between us the amount of work required to achieve the level of cleanliness my father-in-law deems appropriate. The attractive intermediate solution demands proportionality between the welfare gains people actually get as a result of the activity concerned and the maximum welfare gains they could get out of it consistently with the other party involved not being made worse off than if none of the activity had been performed. Under this third solution, providing I care to any extent for the good that is being produced, I shall no longer be able to enjoy it without contributing, because doing so would enable me to get a higher relative benefit (I get close to my maximal claim) than my father-in-law (who does not get his maximal claim, since I care about the good and hence would be willing to contribute to it, thereby reducing how much he would need to perform for a given level of cleanliness). Thus, free-riding is banned. On the other hand, those who care little about a particular good will not be asked to contribute much towards it. If cleanliness is not among my priorities, any significant contribution demanded of me will soon drive my actual gain from the co-operative arrangement into negative figures. So, even though, for the same reason, my maximal gain will also be low, my contribution will have to remain small if my ratio of actual to maximal gain is not to fall below my father-in-law's.

Whether or not this criterion can be justified as the outcome of rational bargaining and however tricky its application may be,[6] it seems to provide us with an ethically attractive criterion of fairness in the presence of externalities. It plausibly tells us which arrangements—in terms of both level and distribution—are unfair and hence who, if anyone, is taking unfair advantage of someone else's work. But then, because of the analogy sketched earlier, it also presents a major challenge to the legitimacy of the institutionalization of an unconditional basic income—an obvious recipe for free-riding on an unprecedented scale. Surely, those who get an income without work only because they care less about income than others do, are getting a free ride at the workers' expense, just as those who enjoy the cleanliness without doing any cleaning only because they care less about cleanliness than others do, are getting a free ride at the cleaners' expense. And if one wants no one to take unfair advantage of others' work, one will have either to equalize (or maximin) relative benefit, which will involve requiring all to contribute at least somewhat towards the product to be distributed, or more simply to get rid of the externality, in this case artificially created through the transfer system.

4. Gauthier's response

Before examining how this argument can be tackled, let me briefly mention David Gauthier's reaction to it.[7] Even though the conclusion is right, Gauthier argues, the point of departure of the argument is in his view fundamentally misguided, because it rests on a misapplication of his criterion due to an overstretching of its scope. I failed to see that when offering to my father-in-law to contribute to the cleaning, I was only being nice to him, and by no means correcting a situation that should be judged unfair according to Gauthier's criterion. Why not? Simply because there is in this case no co-operative surplus to be shared and hence no point in talking about the fair distribution of the co-operative surplus. There can only be a co-operative surplus if the *status quo* can be Pareto improved. By construction, there is nothing for me to gain from a deal with my father-in-law, and it was therefore for the wrong reason that I found his

[6] True, in order to apply the criterion, one does not need to assume that welfare can be measured so as to allow for interpersonal comparisons in absolute terms. But one does need to assume that each co-operator's utility can be measured on an interval scale—otherwise ratios would not make sense—and that reliable information can be obtained about their preferences, in particular about how much they really care for the good that is being produced.

[7] In his immediate public response to the version of this argument presented in Siena, and in subsequent conversations.

criterion attractive in this case. Once the scope of the equal-relative benefit criterion is properly circumscribed, Gauthier's approach does not condemn but condones free-riding in this case. This does not mean, of course, that basic-income-enjoying Lazies are safe. For in the basic income case, it is the Crazies who have nothing to gain from a deal with the Lazies (relative to the pre-transfer *status quo*). It is, therefore, straightforward that there should be no compulsory transfer from the Crazies to the Lazies. The analogy with the father-in-law example is not only misguided. It is also superfluous.

Part of my reply to this response consists in defending Gauthier against himself. When enjoying the cleanliness of the house without doing any work myself, I may or may not be a 'parasite', i.e. someone who 'in obtaining a benefit displaces part or all of the cost on to some other person', depending on whether the cleaning is needed because of dust entering through the window or because of crumbs I drop on the floor. But I am uncontroversially a free-rider, i.e. someone who 'obtains a benefit without paying all or part of its cost' (Gauthier 1986: 96). Now Gauthier claims to show that 'in satisfying the conditions of practical rationality, co-operation ensures the elimination of the free-ridership and parasitism endemic to our natural condition, so that we may identify justice with the rational disposition to co-operative behaviour', since 'justice is the disposition not to take advantage of one's fellows, not to seek free goods or to impose uncompensated costs, provided that one supposes others similarly disposed' (Gauthier 1986: 113). Thus, the sort of (free-riding) behaviour illustrated by my father-in-law example is clearly meant to be ruled out by the practical rationality that must govern co-operation. What does this practical rationality require? Precisely the satisfaction of the criterion of equal-relative benefits:

> The moral significance of externalities is found in the possibility that one person may take advantage of another, either as a free-rider, obtaining some benefit cost free as a spin-off from the others' activities, or as a parasite, transferring the cost of some benefit to the other. Co-operation, to avoid this possibility, must ensure that the ratio between the benefit the co-operator receives and the contribution she makes is, so far as possible, constant, the same for all. (Gauthier 1986: 151–2)

These passages are unequivocal: Gauthier's criterion is meant to realize justice by putting an end to the free-riding and parasitism generated by externalities, and it must therefore apply in the way I sketched to the example I described. On the other hand, these passages, and the application to my example they warrant, are of course at odds with Gauthier's general view that morality flows out of self-interest. His present position, as I understand it, is therefore that they should be rephrased, or qualified, so as to be made consistent with this view. I have already mentioned that I do not care much for the rooting of morality in self-interest and am far more concerned with the fit between moral principles and considered judgements.

TABLE 10.1. Gauthier on free-riding

	A		B	
	Father-in-law	*me*	*Father-in-law*	*me*
For a given level of cleanliness				
total cost	10		10	
gross benefit	11	8	9	8
maximum claim	9[= 11 – (10 – 8)]	8[= 8 – (10 – 10)]	7[= 9 – (10 – 8)]	7[= 8 – (10 – 9)]
total gross benefit	19[= 11 + 8]		17[= 9 + 8]	
total surplus	9[= 19 – 10]		7[= 17 – 10]	
Under the equal relative benefit rule				
cost borne	6.2	3.8	5.5	4.5
net benefit	4.8[= 11 – 6.2]	4.2[= 8 – 3.8]	3.5[= 9 – 5.5]	3.5[= 8 – 4.5]
relative benefit	0.53[= 4.8/9]	0.53[4.2/8]	0.5[= 3.5/7]	0.5[= 3.5/7]
share of surplus	0.53[= 4.8/9]	0.47[= 4.2/9]	0.5[= 3.5/7]	0.5[= 3.5/7]
According to Gauthier's justice				
cost borne	10	0	5.5	4.5
net benefit	1[= 11 – 10]	8[= 8 – 0]	3.5[= 9 – 5.5]	3.5[= 8 – 4.5]
relative benefit	0.11[= 1/9]	1[= 8/8]	0.5[= 3.5/7]	0.5[= 3.5/7]
share of surplus	0.11[= 1/9]	0.89[= 8/9]	0.5[= 3.5/7]	0.5[= 3.5/7]

Hence, it will come as no surprise that I believe on the contrary that such a move should be resisted, and that Gauthier should strive for consistency by sticking to the impulse that led to the passages I just quoted and giving up instead the demand that fair co-operation should not worsen the fate of those who would get a free ride in the absence of an explicit deal—together with the conception of morality that underlies it.

To encourage Gauthier further in this (for him, no doubt, unattractive) direction, let me develop somewhat the implications of the position he holds in the example I gave.[8] Suppose, for the sake of the argument, that costs and benefits can be measured in units of welfare that are homogeneous across individuals. The total cost of achieving some given level of cleanliness is 10 units. In situation *A*, the utility derived from that level is 11 for my father-in-law, and 8 for myself. In situation *B*, the utility I derive from the same level of cleanliness is unchanged at 8 units, but the utility derived by my father-in-law is somewhat lower than in the first situation, say 9 units (see Table 10.1). In situation *A*, which corresponds to my initial formulation of the example, it is in my father-in-law's interest to do the cleaning, even on his own, and he does it. I just let him do it, and enjoy the cleanliness he produces. The distribution of costs is 10 to 0, and I cash in 8/9 of the

[8] I owe this development to a conversation with Hervé Moulin.

surplus. Nothing wrong with this according to Gauthier, accurately construed by himself. In situation *B*, however, it is only in my father-in-law's interest to do the cleaning if I co-operate. Hence, the equal-relative benefit criterion applies. Strangely enough, whereas in situation *A* there was nothing wrong with my getting away with a 0 to 10 distribution of burdens, in situation *B*, even a 4 to 6 distribution is unfair. (As shown in Table 10.1, equal-relative benefit requires a 4.5 to 5.5 distribution.) When doing 40 per cent of the job in situation *B*, not only do I work far more than when doing nothing in situation *A*, but I appropriate a smaller relative share of the surplus (less than 60 per cent instead of nearly 90 per cent), derive a welfare gain that is half as big (4 units instead of 8), and leave to my father-in-law a welfare gain that is three times as big (3 units instead of 1). And yet this is, according to Gauthier, when I am treating my father-in-law unfairly, whereas my free-riding in situation *A* is perfectly all right. Surely, there must be something badly wrong with Gauthier's interpretation of his own approach, if the latter is to provide us with a sensible criterion of fairness in the presence of externalities.

The line taken in the previous section therefore seems to me far more satisfactory. And if it is, the challenge described there sticks: I cannot consistently feel compelled to condemn free-riding in my father-in-law example, it seems, while declaring that basic income recipients can legitimately get away with doing no work. Such a charge of inconsistency I cannot discard or ignore as easily as I could have done with the short-cut version of the same objection suggested by Gauthier. Jumping to the conclusion by invoking the principle 'No co-operation, no income' smacks too much of question-begging for me to feel forced to take the challenge seriously. But a serious challenge there certainly is.

5. Factor rent as supplier surplus

How can I hope to meet it? Perhaps by drawing on resources provided by Gauthier himself in another, seldom scrutinized corner of his stimulating book: his discussion of factor rents. While Gauthier grants people the full right to what they produce on their own and requires co-operative ventures to be governed by the criterion just presented, he gives a special status to factor rent. While 'each person's right to his basic endowment is a right to the exclusive use of that endowment in market and co-operative interaction', the latter 'does not entail a right to receive factor rent'. For since the taxing of factor rents does not, by the latter's definition (to which I shall return shortly), affect anyone's willingness to supply the factor he controls, 'each person's exclusive use of his capacities in market interaction is left untouched if rent is confiscated'. Nor is 'the right to use one's capacities as one sees fit in co-operation with others' violated when someone is denied the factor rent that arises in society, which 'may be considered as a single co-operative venture'. For such rent 'arises only in social interaction', and hence all factor providers can legitimately expect is 'to share, with others, in the surplus represented by such rent. In so far as this surplus takes the form of a single, transferable good [thus making the substitution of maximin for strict equality unnecessary], *each member of society is entitled to an equal portion of it*. Inequalities from factor rent are excluded if we apply the criterion of minimax relative concession [or, equivalently, maximin relative benefit] to the overall terms of social co-operation' (Gauthier 1986: 273–4, my emphasis).

At first sight, this amounts to a plain, unambiguous and rather unexpected assertion of the legitimacy of a substantial unconditional basic income. Gauthier (1986: 274), however, immediately 'warn[s] against an overly egalitarian application of this result': 'In practice', he writes, 'the equal distribution of factor rent might have little effect on inequalities of wealth.' In order to assess such claims, let us first have a closer look at Gauthier's notion of factor rent, or rather at the family of rent notions he appeals to in his discussion.

'Rent is by definition a return over and above the cost of supply' (Gauthier 1986: 98). It consists, in other words, in a supplier surplus. But what is the cost of supply? A restrictive interpretation of this cost leads to a fairly broad conception of rent as

(SS1) the part of a factor's payment that exceeds what 'is needed to induce her to bring her factors to the market' (ibid. 98), i.e. as the payment received by the provider of a factor in addition to what is needed to offset the loss of welfare incurred as a result of putting the factor to its current productive use rather than withdrawing from the market altogether. It will no doubt be pointed out that the relevant counterfactual remains grossly underspecified (withdrawing with how high a monetary income, and with what non-market possibilities?). But this need not retain us for the moment because there is another, less problematic, and far more generous interpretation of the cost of supply, matched by a correspondingly narrow notion of factor rent as

(SS2) the 'payment for [a person's] services over and above the cost to him, including the opportunity cost, of supplying those services' (ibid. 272), where the opportunity cost is given by the income (and other advantages) associated to the next best option. On this interpretation, the rent incorporated in Roberto Baggio's record-breaking contract with Juventus, for example, is only the comparatively small difference with either the fee Fiorentina was willing to pay to keep him or the fee some other club was offering, whichever was higher.[9] This gives us a clear definition of the supplier surplus as the difference between actual payment and inclusive opportunity cost that should satisfy the economist. The notion of factor

[9] See Harsanyi's (1987: 346–7) relevant discussion of the arbitrariness of what is taken as the 'opportunity cost'.

rent, of course, has shrunk significantly in the process—though not quite enough if one heeds some further characterizations offered by Gauthier.

To start with, he also characterizes by factor rent as

(RP) the part of the remuneration of a factor that can be taxed away without 'affecting the preferential ordering of alternative courses of action' (ibid. 273).

But this only coincides with the previous definition (SS2) if this preferential ordering is determined abstracting from strategic considerations.[10] The reservation pay (the pay required to attract the factor) can exceed the opportunity cost (and hence the pay required to compensate the factor owner for forgoing her next best option) because the factor owner can credibly threaten to withhold the factor. In that case, taking the whole of the supplier surplus away will not affect, by definition, what can be called the *intrinsic* 'preferential ordering of alternative courses of action', but it will modify the preferential ordering *all things considered*, and hence also actual behaviour. According to this plausible interpretation, the definition of factor rent as the difference between actual pay and reservation pay (RP) is obviously narrower than the narrower supplier surplus definition. But this is not all: Gauthier is even more restrictive when characterizing factor rent as

(EP1) 'the difference between the least amount that would induce [a person] to [perform] as well as he does and his actual remuneration' (ibid. 273). For in this case, it is not just the part of the supplier surplus whose taxation would lead to a different allocation that drops out of the rent, but also the part whose taxation would lead to a lesser level of effort in the current allocation. And this part, as efficiency wage theorists have been at pains to argue, is by no means insignificant. More restrictively still, Gauthier further characterizes factor rent as

(EP2) the part of a factor's payment that 'may be redistributed without affecting the efficiency of the market' (ibid. 262), or as the part of the remuneration of a factor that can be taxed away without this 'lead[ing] to any form of inefficiency' (ibid. 273). For part of some supplier surplus, as Gauthier himself points out, though not required to attract her factor to its current use or to elicit her current level of effort, may provide the 'jackpot needed to encourage [other people in the same occupation] to perfect themselves' and thereby constitute a 'condition necessary to induce widespread effort' (ibid. 274). According to the conception of factor rent to which we are thus led, one may wonder whether there can ever be any factor rent at all. For however high a fee Baggio gets from Juventus, no part of it constitutes factor rent if a reduction in the fee would reduce, however little,

[10] Gauthier (1986: 273) ignores this distinction and conflates the opportunity cost definition (SS2) and the reservation wage definition when he states that 'if, as a result of anticipated taxation on remuneration from playing hockey, [some hockey player] were to choose an alternative career, then that taxation would necessarily affect his opportunity cost and so would not be levied only on rent'.

his regularity at training sessions or his stamina on the pitch—or that of any other soccer player who is trying to emulate him. One may no doubt raise doubts about the underlying conception of efficiency, which does not seem to make any room, for example, for the possibility of inefficiency through excessive effort.[11] But the proposed definition of factor rent is uncontroversially restrictive enough to alleviate any fear one might have that the taxation of rent recommended by Gauthier would gravely impair efficiency by taxing too much away from factor owners,[12] and to justify fully Gauthier's warning against rushing into egalitarian conclusions.

6. Factor rent as return on scarcity

Although this sequence of five increasingly restrictive characterizations of factor rent may have a strong claim to fit and organize many of Gauthier's formulations, it may well have missed his central intuition, as expressed in the statement with which he starts the discussion of this whole issue: 'Rent is determined by factor scarcity' (ibid. 272). This suggests, at first sight, a fairly narrow definition of factor rent as monopoly rent, i.e. as

(MR) 'the premium certain factor services command [. . .] because there is no alternative to meet the demand' (ibid. 272).

This interpretation is supported by Gauthier's (1986: 276) insistence, against Nozick and other libertarians, that it would be illegitimate for basket ball star Wilt Chamberlain 'to extract rent from his unique talents'. Clearly there can be a supplier surplus (SS1 or SS2) without there being a monopoly rent. For while there are cases, such as Roberto Baggio's or Wilt Chamberlain's, where the supplier gets more than his opportunity cost because (his employer believes) no one else can do what he does, there are other cases where one supplier of some service gets a surplus while another with the same pay does not, simply because she is keener to do the job (whether owing to her enjoying it more or to having worse alternatives) and benefits from the fact that the wage rate is uniform. Furthermore, if the actual payment ever exceeds not just the opportunity cost, but also the reservation pay (RP) or the efficiency pay (EP1 or EP2), there is no reason why this should necessarily be due to a monopoly position. It could simply stem, for example, from managerial sloppiness. Hence, this new notion of factor rent is not strictly broader than any of the previous five notions. Strictly speaking, it is not strictly narrower than any of them either, since there can conceivably be a monopoly rent without a supplier surplus even in the broader sense (Baggio might get what he does because of his unique talent, but hate so much this only job he can do that what he gets just compensates him for not staying at home), and hence also without factor

[11] On this possibility, see e.g. Suzumura's (1987) illuminating formal analysis.

[12] Such fear is expressed by Harsanyi (1987: 347) with the less restrictive definition SS2 in mind.

rent in any of the other four senses.[13] It is quite natural, however, to combine this monopoly condition with the surplus condition, as Gauthier (1986: 272) actually does in the passage a truncated version of which I used above:

(MR*) 'the premium certain factor services command, over and above the full cost of supply, because there is no alternative to meet the demand', thus providing an alternative way of strengthening the supplier surplus definition.

There is, however, another—related but far broader—notion of rent which Gauthier must have in mind in the crucial passage in which he spells out his argument for the equal distribution of rents among all members of society. '[Hockey player] Wayne Gretzky's talents command factor rent because they are scarce, but their scarcity is not a characteristic inherent in his talents, but a function of the conditions of supply, and so of the relations between his talents and those of others, and a function also of the conditions of demand, and so of the relations between his talents and the interest of others in attending hockey games' (ibid.: 274). The criterion he is proposing, Gauthier (1986: 276) further stresses in his discussion with Nozick, 'does interfere with a particular liberty—specifically, the freedom to collect factor rent. But this is no part of the freedom of a solitary being; the surplus represented by rent arises only through social interaction. And so it is not a necessary part of market freedom conceived as an extension of the natural freedom enjoyed by Robinson Crusoe.' Factor rent, thus conceived, is not specifically related to monopoly situations, or absolute scarcity, but turns out to be, far more broadly, (SR) the payment a factor owes to its relative scarcity, i.e. the part of a factor's remuneration which it can fetch because of social interaction, and hence over and above what it would provide its owner in a Robinson Crusoe world. Clearly, even if a factor's payment does not exceed its efficiency pay in either sense, its reservation pay or its next best option, and even if the factor owner enjoys nothing like a monopolistic situation, there can still be a very large rent in this last sense. Indeed, this notion is even broader than the broader supplier surplus definition (SS1), since the part of a factor's payment that exceeds what 'is needed to induce her to bring her factors to the market' only includes the net gains over a Robinson Crusoe situation that are due to market interaction, not those deriving from non-market economic co-operation. A summary of the relations between the eight notions of factor rent I have distinguished is provided in Fig. 10.1.

It is clearly this broad notion of factor rent which is on Gauthier's mind when he challenges the legitimacy of its appropriation by talent owners: 'The recipient of rent benefits from the scarcity of the factors she controls—a scarcity which is of course entirely accidental from her standpoint, since it depends, not on the intrinsic nature of the factors, but on the relation

[13] The logical independence of scarcity-based and surplus-based notions of rent is pointed out by Cohen (1990: section 10).

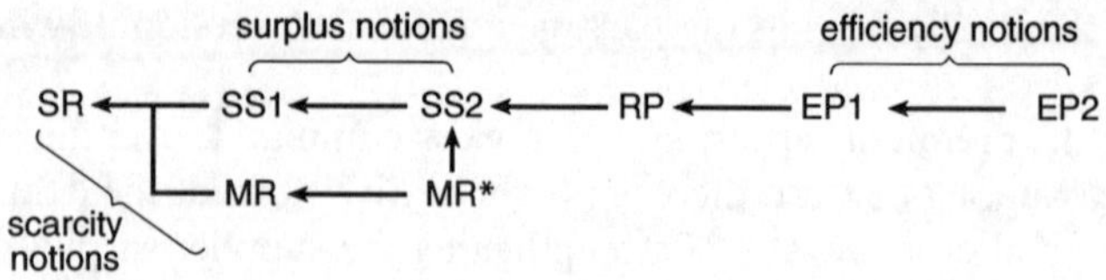

FIG. 10.1

between them and the factors controlled by others' (ibid. 98). And if it is, he is not protected against 'overly egalitarian' implications by the availability of a family of narrower definitions, since it is the broad definition that is ethically relevant. By the same token, of course, nothing that has been said so far is left to alleviate Harsanyi's (1987) fear that Gauthier's radical rent confiscation programme would wreck the economy. But to go a long way towards alleviating such fear, it is sufficient to substitute maximin for strict equality, and go for sustainable yield maximization rather than for confiscatory taxation. Once this obvious move is taken on board, the question arises whether there is still any significant difference left between Gauthier and Rawls.

7. Gauthier and Rawls reconciled?

True, Gauthier can still make a meaningful distinction between what a person owes to her talent and what a person owes to the scarcity of her talent. It is only the latter that can legitimately be redistributed. This is why he can consistently reject the Difference Principle in so far as it 'licenses those with lesser talents to take advantage of those naturally more fortunate, requiring the latter to use their abilities, not primarily for their own well-being, but to minimise the minimum level of well-being' (Gauthier 1986: 252). For Rawls, 'morality demands the giving of free rides; no other interpretation can be put on the insistence that talents be treated as a common asset' (Gauthier 1986: 219 20).

However, in an implicit reply to a partly similar criticism by Nozick (1974: 228), Rawls (1990: section 21.3) corrects this interpretation:

> Note that what is regarded as a common asset is the distribution of native endowments and not our native endowments. It is not as if society owned individuals' endowments taken separately, looking at individuals one by one. To the contrary, the question of the ownership of our endowments does not arise; and should it arise, it is persons themselves who own their endowments . . . What is to be regarded as a common asset, then, is the distribution of native endowments, that is, the differences among persons. These differences consist not only in the variation of talents of the

same kind (variation in strength and imagination, and so on) but in the variety of talents of different kinds. This variety can be regarded as a common asset because it makes possible numerous complementarities between talents when organised in appropriate ways to take advantage of these differences. Consider how these talents are organised and coordinated in games and in performances of musical compositions. The latter is illustrated by the analogy of the orchestra. Variations of talent of the same kind (as in degrees of strength and endurance) also allow for mutually beneficial complementarities, as economists have long known and formulated in the principle of comparative advantage.

Thus, Rawls can concede that what people can produce with their own talents without relying in any way on social co-operation must remain theirs. Only the rest, namely the benefits of social co-operation, is strictly speaking, and consistently with Rawls's (1971: 4) original formulation of the scope of his principles of justice, governed by the Difference Principle. But given how little someone could achieve on her own, under current conditions, with a fair share of external resources, this is hardly a concession at all for practical purposes. Associated with the constraint imposed by the first principle (in particular the prohibition of forced employment), Rawls's maximin criterion is most likely to operate in such a manner that even the most talented people will be left with far more than they would get in the absence of social co-operation.

In this light, the contrast between Gauthier and Rawls loses much of its sharpness. True, the aspects of social interaction to which Gauthier and Rawls draw attention are not strictly equivalent: co-operation between diverse talents in one case, interaction of supply and demand in the other. But the outcome is hardly different. For allowing for the redistribution of factor rent in a broad sense that covers all benefits people owe to the scarcity of their talents amounts to imposing as the sole constraint on redistribution the need to compensate people for what they could achieve in the absence of social interaction with a fair share of external resources. Assuming that fairness requires a thin spreading of external resources,[14] this cannot amount to much under contemporary conditions. With each participant in social interaction claiming the whole of the co-operative surplus, the criterion of equal-relative benefit will give them an equal share in it (or one that deviates from equality only because of variations in preferences, not in contributions). Once efficiency considerations have prompted the substitution of maximin for strict equality, this cannot lead to a distribution very different from the one that is justified by the Difference Principle, as clarified above by Rawls himself. Thus, contrary to what Gauthier (1986: 252) asserts, Rawls does not hold, after all, 'a very different view of what justice requires', at least in a society such as ours in which most of the benefits people derive from their talents are the product of the interaction of supply and demand.

14 See Gauthier's (1986: 262, 300–2) treatment of the right to bequeath, which is only justified, in his view, if (and to the extent that) it contributes to overall efficiency.

For in such a context, Gauthier must share the position he ascribes to Rawls and contrasts with his own:

The person who takes advantage of her fellows is not the less talented individual who benefits from the maximin principle, but the more talented individual who uses her talents solely for her own benefit. For she diverts to her exclusive use an undue proportion of the total assets of society. She robs her fellows of what is rightfully theirs [namely, the factor rent which more talented individuals are in a better position to extract]. (Gauthier 1986: 52).

8. Basic income and Gauthier's justice

This pulling together of Gauthier and Rawls is important for my purposes because it links up this discussion of Gauthier's challenge to the more straightforward ethical argument for basic income I have developed elsewhere (Van Parijs 1995). For I there use a version of the Difference Principle, duly corrected along Dworkinian lines, to formulate my 'real-libertarian' justification of basic income, my liberal defence of Malibu surfers against the harsh treatment to which Rawls says they should be subjected. However, by bullying Gauthier towards both Rawls and basic income, I may well have been far too rash and overlooked some crucial differences.[15]

Firstly, what leads Rawls to the position just described, according to Gauthier (1986: 252), is his rejection of the supposition (to which Gauthier is committed) 'that each person's characteristics, in enabling him to make a certain contribution to the social product, also provide him with a claim to a certain share of that product'. This suggests that we have been far too generous in indiscriminately distributing the social surplus in maximin fashion. It is true that Gauthier sometimes simply says that 'no person may claim a co-operative surplus if he would not be a participant in the interactions required to provide it' (Gauthier 1986: 143) or that 'each claims as much of the social surplus as it is possible for him to receive, but only

[15] One potential difference, which I shall leave aside, relates to what is to be done with the rent that has been collected. In a passage in which he indicates that Rawls's view may not be that different from his own, Gauthier (1986: 277) argues that from Rawls's first principle of justice 'the right to one's basic endowment would seem to follow, and so the entitlement to payment for opportunity costs in return for the provision of factor services' and that 'Rawls implicitly distinguishes factor rent from payment for factor services, agreeing with [Gauthier's] view that each person is entitled to the latter, but supposing that the former, *instead of being divided equally among all co-operators. is to be used to the benefit of the least disadvantaged*' (my emphasis). But this difference vanishes if Rawls's Difference Principle is tidied up along Dworkinian lines, as I have argued (in Van Parijs 1995: sect. 4.6) it needs to be in order to deal adequately with the Crazy–Lazy challenge. For this leads us to the adoption of a principle of maximin distribution of external resources received, including the rent people receive as part of their wage. On the background of predictable tax rates and a ban on involuntary *em*ployment, an *equal* distribution of the part of the rent that is collected is required to guarantee that none of the workers gets a lesser share in the rent than some of the non-workers, and hence that the maximin principle is satisfied (see Van Parijs 1995; ch. 4).

for those co-operative interactions in which he participates. Thus no contribution yields no claim; some contribution yields full claim.' (Gauthier 1986: 154). And such formulations may encourage us to give all members of society, who all participate in the complex interaction of supply and demand that generates the scarcity of some talents, the same title to the benefits of social co-operation. But elsewhere Gauthier (1986: 134) is more explicit:

> In a situation involving more than two persons, each person may not always claim all of the co-operative surplus that he might receive, but only that part of the surplus to the production of which he would contribute. Each person's claim is bounded by the extent of his participation in co-operative interaction. For if someone were to press a claim to what would be brought about by the co-operative interaction of others, then those others would prefer to exclude him from agreement.

Clearly, if such a criterion made sense, it would impose a far tighter link between contribution and share in the overall surplus than is implied (for purely instrumental reasons) by Rawls's approach. But it does not.

To see why, just imagine a situation in which returns to scale are such that *A*, *B*, and *C* (with equivalent endowments) produce 1 unit if one of them works on her own (surplus = 0), 7 units if two of them co-operate (surplus = 5), and 9 units if the three of them work together (surplus = 6). Gauthier's proposal implies that none of the three (interchangeable) co-operators can legitimately claim more than her marginal contribution to the surplus (which is 1 unit). But this would leave half of the total surplus unclaimed. Gauthier's formulation can no doubt be altered to cope better with this particular case. (Shapley values and related notions may provide a way out.) But any such attempt is bound to hit eventually against the general fact that when the product is the outcome of a complex interaction between natural resources, inherited technology, the legal and customary framework, and particular capital and labour inputs, it is hopeless to try to parcel out the product according to contributions. In particular, it is very difficult to see how anything along these lines would provide Gauthier with the required conceptual resources for excluding any member of a society from claiming a share in what would otherwise be appropriated as factor rent. My claim is that once unease has been conceded about the libertarian endorsement of all (coercion-free) factor rent, one finds oneself on a steep slope, along which it is all too easy to slip all the way to the neighbourhood of Rawls, Sen, or Dworkin, where large material claims can be made simply by virtue of being a member of society, rather than a contributor. For factor rent, in the broad sense to which we have seen that Gauthier's rationale for egalitarian redistribution applies, does not only cover the advantages some derive from the unequal scarcity of native internal endowments, but also those derived from the unequal availability of opportunities—a source of unfairness which Gauthier (1986: 263–5) is particularly concerned to reduce as much as possible. These advantages in turn derive not only from gender- or race-based differences in educational opportunities (the sort of case Gauthier has primarily in mind), but are even more directly illustrated by the existence of involuntary unemployment.[16] Thus the room for justice-based, contribution-insensitive redistribution is very large indeed, limited only by the (practically negligible) constraint that everyone should get at least as much as what she would get as a Robinson Crusoe with a share of natural and other inherited resources that leaves 'enough and as good' for everyone else.[17] Thus, I am not denying that there remains, in principle, a difference between a 'mutual benefit' approach and an 'equal concern' approach, and that the latter can provide support for an unconditional income in a more straightforward, less clumsy way. What I am saying is that a 'mutual benefit' approach that wants to deny factor owners the right to appropriate factor rent in the appropriate sense will barely make less room than the 'equal concern' approach for material claims which, for all practical purposes, are grounded on nothing but membership in the community.[18]

There is, however, another point on which Gauthier, even reconstructed backward from what he says on factor rents, does clash in a practically significant way with Rawls, Sen, Dworkin, Ackerman, and other left liberals. The consistent treatment of factor rent forces Gauthier to erode considerably the market advantages yielded by native or socially generated

[16] The associated employment rents play a key role in the argument of Van Parijs (1991). Note that there is an employment rent when there is excess demand *for jobs* (given the going wage and current working conditions), i.e. an excess supply of labour, whereas there is a factor rent when there is excess demand *for labour* (or other factors) at some reference level of pay (given by the Robinson Crusoe opportunity cost). Yet employment rent can be viewed as a part of factor rent: the part of someone's pay that exceeds what is required to find someone else to fill her particular job is bound to be included in the part of that person's pay that is required to make her better off under social co-operation than in isolation (or, put differently, less of a pay cut is needed to clear the market than to make the worker as badly off as she would be in isolation).

[17] As we have seen in the previous section, there is a similar limit in (recently clarified) Rawls, but not in Dworkin or Sen.

[18] Admittedly, this interpretation is blatantly at odds with some of Gauthier's explicit statements, for example with his discussion of the plight of Sam MacGee, who has discovered a vein of gold but lacks the necessary cash to register his claim. Banker Grasp is the only person in town who can provide it. According to Gauthier (1986: 153–4), the co- operative surplus should in this case be split equally between Sam and Grasp—whereas if there had been a competitive capital market, Sam could have kept the whole of the surplus to himself, paying Grasp no more than the going rate of interest, equal to Grasp's opportunity cost of lending to Sam. Thus, in a situation of capital shortage, it would be unfair both for Sam to pay Grasp no more than the latter's opportunity cost and for Grasp to appropriate as factor rent all benefits deriving from the registration of the claim that are not needed to match Sam's opportunity cost. But why should this rent be divided just between Sam and Grasp? Under equal division between them, Grasp would still be appropriating as factor rent something that is due, not just to Sam's discovery, but to the 'conditions of demand and supply', to the complex 'social interaction' which makes the registration of Sam's claim on the vein of gold as valuable as it is, and thereby makes the demand for Grasp's scarce factor as pressing as it is. Why should Sam and Grasp be allowed to share the surplus among themselves, whereas Wilt Chamberlain has to share the whole of his potential factor rent with all those who take part in the social interaction that generates demand for his services?

talents, and hence to reduce the disadvantages generated by the lack of such talents. But it provides no reason for redistributing anything to the handicapped in excess of what follows from the equal distribution of factor rent. On Gauthier's account, however reconstructed, the blind or paraplegic can claim no specific compensation for their handicap. Rawls makes some room for such claims, even though they are not firmly rooted in the Difference Principle, or in either of his principles of justice.[19] Dworkin, Sen, Ackerman, and others emphatically recognize such claims, on the ground that people's internal endowments, the talents they owe to their birth or social origin, are, to use Dworkin's phrase, part of their 'circumstances', and that justice therefore requires that the less well endowed be compensated. A mutual benefit conception of justice, however massaged, cannot possibly accommodate such a requirement, and this is no small part of the reason why I find such a conception unacceptable. But this remaining crucial difference is one that should make Gauthier's approach more and not less favourable to a substantial uniform basic income, as it implies that no resources need to be set aside for targeted transfers to the less well endowed.[20]

Let us return, in this light, to the version of the challenge that Gauthier himself endorses, i.e. to the claim that, on a mutual benefit conception of justice, there can be no unconditional basic income because those who make no contribution have no claim on any part of the social product. The response that flows from the previous discussion is that, once the relevant notions of factor rent and contribution are suitably clarified, it appears that the part of the social product that—on Gauthier's own account—must be distributed equally (or in maximin fashion) among all contributors is very considerable, while the conditions required for qualifying as a contributor are very weak. Hence, for all practical purposes, Gauthier's own approach seems to offer resources for the justification of an unconditional basic income that are hardly less potent than what can be expected from an equal concern approach, indeed in some respects more potent since it does not require any special provision to be made for the poorly talented or the handicapped.

But what about the other version of the challenge, the one based on the attraction of Gauthier's criterion of maximin relative benefit in situations in which externalities provide opportunities for free-riding? Gauthier himself, as we have seen, dismisses it because it is inconsistent with his mutual benefit conception of justice. But as I do not share the latter, I do not have this option and must find some way of reconciling the condemnation of benefits without work in my father-in-law example with the acceptance of income

[19] See Rawls (1990). Redistribution to (some of) the handicapped is justified by the need to enable them to exercise their moral powers, not by egalitarian or maximin considerations.

[20] I discuss at length the challenge that arises from the need for such transfers in Van Parijs (1995; ch. 3).

without work that follows from the endorsement of an unconditional basic income. The key component of the answer, it seems to me, must lie in a distinction between, on the one hand, the 'basic structure', the institutional framework that determines the co-operators' legitimate endowments, and, on the other, the co-operative ventures conducted within this framework. A just distribution of factor rents (in the broadest sense) is an important component of the basic structure. As we have seen, even Gauthier finds unacceptable that those rents should be appropriated by whomever the operation of the market happens to give them to—as libertarians would have it. But whether or not he does, my considered moral judgement is certainly that such appropriation would be unacceptable and that the endowment of each member of the community (whatever the latter's boundaries may be) should include an equal (or maximin) share in the value of these rents. Under certain conditions, this provides the basis for the justification of an unconditional basic income as a central component of the institutional framework. But, on the background of this framework, nothing prevents us from using Gauthier's criterion for expressing the demands of distributive justice in the presence of externalities. When receiving one's basic income (pitched at an appropriate level), one is not taking unfair advantage of others, because one is getting a share that is no larger than what others get of what is there for all to share. When receiving in addition the benefit of a public good which some others are producing, one may well be taking unfair advantage of others. Gauthier's attractive criterion of maximin relative benefit tells us—arguably—when exactly this is the case.[21]

REFERENCES

Barry, B. (1989), *Theories of Justice* (Hemel Hempstead: Harvester-Wheatsheaf).
—— (1995), *Justice as Impartiality* (Oxford: Oxford University Press).
Cohen, G. A. (1990), 'More on Self Ownership: The Bisection Proposal, Rawls and Gauthier', mimeo (Oxford: All Souls College).
Carling, A. (1992), *Social Division* (London: Verso).
Gauthier, D. (1986), *Morals by Agreement* (Oxford: Oxford University Press).
Harsanyi, J. C. (1987), Review of Gauthier (1986), *Economics and Philosophy*, 5: 339–51.
Mack, E. (1992), 'Gauthier on Rights and Economic Rents', *Social Philosophy and Policy*, 9: 171–200.
Nozick, R. (1974), *Anarchy, State and Utopia* (Oxford: Basil Blackwell).

[21] For a sophisticated and subtle analysis of public goods in a household context, see Carling (1992: part v). For a critical analysis of Gauthier's notion of rent which is largely parallel to the one proposed here while leading in the opposite direction, see Mack (1992).

Rawls, J. (1990), *Justice as Fairness. A Restatement* (Harvard University: unpublished lecture notes).

Suzumura, K. (1987), 'Equity and Incentives: Homans' Theory of Distributive Justice Reconsidered' (Hitotsubashi University, Institute of Economic Research: working paper).

Van Parijs, P. (1990), 'Equal Endowments as Undominated Diversity', *Recherches Economiques de Louvain*, 56: 327–56.

—— (1991), 'Why Surfers Should be Fed. The Liberal Case for an Unconditional Basic Income', *Philosophy and Public Affairs*, 20: 101–31.

—— (1992), 'Basic Income Capitalism', *Ethics*, 102: 448–64.

—— (1993), *Marxism Recycled* (Cambridge: Cambridge University Press).

—— (1995), *Real Freedom for All: What (if anything) Can Justify Capitalism?* (Oxford: Oxford University Press).

IV

THE ETHICAL DIMENSION OF RATIONAL DECISIONS

11

Social Preferences, Equity, and Non-Expected Utility Theory[1]

FRANCESCO FARINA

1. Introduction

This chapter enquires into the kind of behavioural pattern to be followed by an ethical decision-maker so as to make a concern for equity influence social preferences. Following Harsanyi's 'constructivistic' model of social choice, the 'veil of ignorance' assumption is adopted. Each individual evaluates the possible outcomes of random prospects by assigning an 'equal probability' to the event of being placed in the objective position (a given state of the world x, with $x = 1, \ldots, h$) and in the subjective position i (with $i = 1, \ldots, n$) of everyone else. This corresponds to introducing a decision-maker who overcomes possible conflicts between self-interested individuals. Social preferences are then determined by means of interpersonal utility comparisons employing a uniform conversion index between each individual's own and other individuals' utility units. With reference to the *ex ante* approach to social welfare, expectational utility functions will be interpreted as mathematical instruments by which the ethical decision-maker expresses social preferences. The utility differences resulting from interpersonal comparisons will then be deemed not as measurements of pleasure but as the determinants of judgements of social welfare.

The usual social choice foundations in the theory of individual decision under uncertainty will be maintained: in expressing social preferences by means of interpersonal utility comparisons the ethical decision-maker is supposed to be bound to the same behavioural patterns as observed by the pursuit of purely personal objectives in individual choice between lotteries. Therefore, the aim of the chapter is to select a notion of equity—to be implemented in the ethical decision-maker's social judgements—which is consistent with the behavioural patterns of individual decision-making. The

[1] I wish to thank John Broome, Frank Hahn, Philippe Mongin, Robert Sugden, and Stefano Vannucci for comments and suggestions on a previous version of this chapter. Financial support by MURST (the Italian Ministry of University and of Scientific and Technological Research) is gratefully acknowledged.

method consists in applying in the ordering of social situations the behaviour predicted by the so-called Non-Expected Utility Theory (see Machina (1983), Tversky and Kahneman (1986), Sugden (1986), and Gul (1991)) originated by observed violations of the axioms of Bayesian rationality. This non-conventional experimental evidence, in so far as it challenges the descriptive and predictive validity of the traditional approach to individual decision between lotteries—Expected Utility Theory—will be employed to suggest new foundations for renovating the link between decision theory under uncertainty and social choice.

In section 2, the two dimensions of the aggregation of utility indexes—across states of the world and across individuals—are indicated as the analytical framework in which conditions for equity-concerned social preferences have to be verified. It is shown that the axioms of Expected Utility Theory (thereafter, EUT) allow the ethical decision-maker to determine social preferences by means of all functional forms which comply with the 'separability' condition. In section 3, following critiques about using the von Neumann—Morgenstern (thereafter, vN–M) utility representations, Harsanyi's notion of 'equal treatment' social preferences is put in question. In the successive sections, behavioural foundations for equity-concerned social preferences are searched in Non-Expected Utility Theory (thereafter, NEUT). In section 4, the moral principle of equality in distribution, which can be considered as an 'extreme' notion of equity, is excluded because a concern for equality in social choice contradicts the Pareto principle. In section 5, the possibility that NEUT evaluations of random prospects might influence the determination of social preferences is maintained. In section 6, the derivation of an 'inequality averse' decision-maker from the 'common consequence effect' observed violations of the independence axiom proves to be unsatisfactory. In section 7, behavioural foundations for an 'inequality averse' decision-maker are found in Disappointment Theory. The application of this NEUT approach to individual decision under uncertainty in the determination of equity-concerned social preferences allows a concern for equity to be implemented by means of an utility function modified by a measure of the degree of equity in each location—named the 'equity function'. With the assumption of 'inequality aversion', the notion of equity applies to the whole interpersonal distribution, since the decision-maker manipulates the individual utilities by means of strictly concave transformations. Instead, with the 'equity function', an 'individualistic' notion of equity is implemented by the ethical decision-maker.

2. The link between decision theory and social choice

In Table 11.1 two situations are considered, each one formed by a couple of random prospects, where utility indexes have been attributed to the positions occupied by the generic individuals i and j, from arbitrarily displayed possible outcomes relative to the states of the world x and y.

TABLE 11.1

		x	y			x	y
	i	u_{ix}	u_{iy}		i	v_{ix}	v_{iy}
A				B			
	j	u_{jx}	u_{jy}		j	v_{jx}	v_{jy}

With reference to the two states of the world of situation A, the sum of the individuals' expected utility values (multiplied by the respective probabilities) gives the total utility of the random prospects:

$$U_i = p u_{ix} + (1 - p)\, u_{iy} \quad \text{and} \quad U_j = p u_{jx} + (1 - p)\, u_{jy}.$$

Two interpersonal distributions correspond to the same individual utilities, one for each state of the world. From these, the social preference is set up by means of interpersonal utility comparisons. The same, of course, applies to situation B.

A connection between these two dimensions—states of the world and individuals—can be established. Each row represents an individual lottery where personal preferences multiplied by the respective probabilities express total utility; similarly, the very same utility values can be aggregated in each column as indexes belonging to a certain social situation. In EUT—the conventional approach to decision theory under uncertainty—the (strong) independence axiom requires that the 'separability' condition across states of the world is respected. This condition implies that the total utility of a lottery has to be determined by the summation of utility indexes which depend on the possible outcomes (one for each state of the world) on which personal preferences have been expressed.

If the view is taken that social preferences must be bound to the same behavioural patterns of individual decisions under uncertainty, the connection between intrapersonal aggregation (across states of the world) and interpersonal aggregation (across individuals) of the utility values has an important consequence: the 'separability' condition has to be met also in the dimension of individuals. Therefore, the aggregation across individuals in each state of the world has to follow the rule by which an individual determines the total utility of a lottery: just as in each expectational utility function total utility must result from the sum of the utilities each of which is determined *only* by the respective possible outcome in its own state of the world, in each interpersonal distribution the same holds for possible outcomes in each individual location. Under the assumption that individuals agree on assigning identical probabilities to each possible outcome, the 'separability' condition amounts to stating that the Pareto principle has to be respected, since it implies that the evaluation of each individual's possible outcomes has to be independent of any individual's possible outcomes.[2] Given an appropriately complete description of the states of the world (each row in Table 11.1), each individual's welfare maximization will then be independent of any other's welfare maximization.

If the 'separability' condition applies both in the dimension of states of nature and in the dimension of individuals (that is, if the ordering has 'cross-cutting separability'), the 'additive separability' of utility indexes—i.e. the property of any ordering which can be represented by a summation of utilities and where each row and column are separable—will result.[3] I will now investigate to what extent this connection between aggregation across states of the world and aggregation across individuals impinges upon the functional form by which social preferences have to be expressed. In fact, the question might be posed whether the aggregation rule across individuals should be a linear combination just because the 'separability' condition in the aggregation across states of the world happens to be satisfied by the linear combination of the utility indexes (multiplied by the respective probabilities) resulting from each state of the world.

The expectational utility functions determined by individuals behaving according to the EUT axioms will be now examined.

Following an approach previously put forward by Marshack, Machina (see Machina (1987: 98–101)) has sketched the set of all probability distributions over the wealth levels $x_1 < x_2 < x_3$ by the points in the unit triangle (see Fig. 11.1). In the (p_1, p_3) plane (with $p_2 = 1 - p_1 - p_3$) the indifference curves are parallel straight lines which are the loci of solutions of the prospect:

$$V(p) = p_1 U(x) + (1 - p_1 - p_3)\, U(x) + p_3 U(x)$$

(total utility will obviously be constant along an indifference curve).

North-east movements along such loci, which preserve the mean but augment the probability of the best and worst outcomes (p_1 and P_3 increase at the expense of p_2), are considered 'mean preserving spreads'. Whenever the attitude towards risk deviates from neutrality, the shape of the indifference curves will be different from the lines corresponding to the 'isoexpected value loci', i.e. loci where probability distributions have the same mean. For a 'risk averse' individual who feels worse off because of mean preserving spreads, the indifference curves will be steeper than these loci (the bold lines in Fig. 11.1); whereas for a 'risk lover' these lines would be flatter than the 'isoexpected value loci'.

[2] Broome demonstrated that—due to diversity in the probabilities expressed by the individuals—the Pareto principle can collide with the coherence of individual preferences. He claims that in order to overpass the conflict with coherence the Pareto principle has to be related to good rather than preferences. He then substitutes the Pareto principle with the 'principle of personal good' (see Broome (1991: chs. 7 and 8)).

[3] For a formal demonstration of the 'separability' theorems, see Broome (1991: appendix to ch. 4), following Debreu (1959) and Gorman (1968).

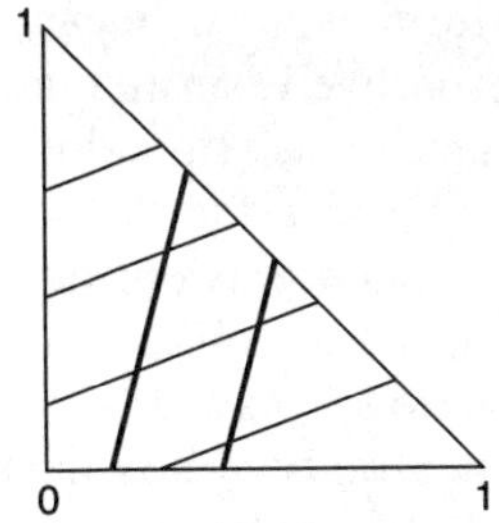

FIG. 11.1.

Strictly concave or strictly convex functions, respectively expressing a 'risk averse' and a 'risk lover' individual, reflect indifference curves which are respectively steeper and flatter than isoexpected lines; yet, they still comply with the independence axiom of EUT, because they are linear and parallel and exhibit a uniform direction of preference. I will briefly dwell upon a 'risk averse' individual and illustrate how he complies with the independence axiom of EUT when deciding on random prospects. Suppose this individual has to choose between two lotteries in each situation below.

TABLE 11.2

I	$A: p\lambda_x + (1-p)\,G^*$	*II*	$B: p\lambda_x + (1-p)\,g^*$
	$C: pG + (1-p)\,G^*$		$D: pG + (1-p)\,g^*$

In the two couples of lotteries shown in Table 11.2, where λ_x denotes the prospect which yields x with certainty, G involves outcomes in turn higher and lower than x, and G^* stochastically dominates g^*. If λ_x is preferred to G and A is chosen in the first situation, according to the independence axiom, C should be chosen in the second. These preferences indicate that the independence axiom is respected by individuals whose indifference curves are particularly steep due to risk aversion (see Fig. 11.1).

By recalling what is implied by EUT about attitudes towards risk, it was shown that the ethical decision-maker is allowed different functional forms for the aggregation of individual utilities. From the assumption that the ordering of social situations must be founded in Bayesian rationality it follows that EUT legitimizes all functional forms which comply with the 'separability' condition and not solely the linear combination. Let us apply these functions to interpersonal distributions.

It is well known that the evaluation of inequality in welfare economics can be formally treated similarly to the attitude to risk in individual choice between lotteries (see Atkinson 1970). The attitude towards inequality determines the form of aggregation of the utility indexes across individuals just as the attitude towards risk does with the aggregation across states of the world: whether the form will be linear, strictly concave, or strictly convex, is conditional, respectively, on the decision-maker's attitude being neutral, averse, or favourable to risk (in individual decisions) and inequality (in social choice). Therefore, once the ordering and continuity conditions are met, the (strong) independence axiom puts the 'separability' restriction on the functional form, but the correspondence between risk and inequality allows a variety of aggregation rules.

Depending on whether neutrality or non-neutrality towards the dispersion of expected utility values holds, different orderings among prospects might result. In order to determine the moral preferences, the ethical decision-maker can use functions f_i, by which the individual utilities derived from each individual's income x are evaluated:

$$V = f_1\,[u_1(x)] + \ldots + f_n\,[u_n(x)]$$

Just as in the case of attitudes towards risk in individual choice between lotteries, the ethical decision-maker might be 'neutral' with respect to inequality, so that f_i will be linear functions, but also, say, 'inequality averse', so that f_i will be strictly concave functions.

A linear function causes each possible outcome to transfer its utility value to the social welfare. A strictly concave function, instead, changes the weight of the utility values: the higher the possible outcomes are relative to a position, the less they count in the determination of total utility. In Table 11.3, the expected utility indexes of Table 1 are replaced by money values which determine individual utilities.

TABLE 11.3

	A		*B*	
	i	*j*	*i*	*j*
x	90	20	40	60
y	25	10	25	10

Since in the state of the world y the possible outcomes expressed in utility values are the same for each individual in both situations *A* and *B*, by virtue of the independence axiom the ethical decision-maker can ignore that state. His social judgement will be based on the interpersonal utility comparisons represented by the following utility differences:

$$[U(90) - U(40)] \quad \text{and} \quad [U(60) - U(20)]$$

If the ethical decision-maker adopts a linear functional form, situation *A* will be socially preferred by the utilitarian ordering. If he decides that an 'inequality averse' aggregation rule has to be applied, by using a strictly concave transformation f (for simplicity, all the functions f_i are assumed to be equal), the following expression might be obtained:

$$f[U(90)] - f[U(40)] < f[U(60)] - f[U(20)]$$

Just opposite as in the previous case, situation B will be socially preferred. When the ethical decision-maker follows the EUT axioms which apply in individual decision-making under uncertainty, this behavioural pattern does not bind him to a particular functional form in the aggregation of the individual utilities. Similarly to the individual who calculates the total utility of a lottery, the ethical decision-maker must satisfy the 'separability' condition in the evaluation of the individual positions. However, this requirement does not imply the obligation to aggregate individual utilities exclusively on the basis of the specific attitude towards inequality corresponding to the attitude towards risk—e.g. risk neutrality—followed by the individuals in the aggregation across the states of the world.

Therefore, the answer to the question posed above is that the EUT axioms do not impose linearity as the aggregation rule across individuals but allow all functional forms that abide by the 'separability' condition. Even when it is agreed that both personal and social preferences must comply with the EUT axioms, it does not follow that, for social choice to be consistent, linearity must be the sole possible aggregation rule of individual utilities. Depending on the ethical decision-maker's risk neutrality or risk aversion, social preferences will implement, respectively, the utilitarian moral principle of 'equal treatment' or the moral principle of a concern for equity in the form of 'inequality aversion'.

3. The 'impartial' decision-maker

The conclusion reached in the previous section is in contrast with Harsanyi's tenet about the foundations in rational choice theory of the utilitarian social choice. The rationale that an ethical decision-maker has necessarily to behave according to the utilitarian moral principle of 'impartiality' is derived from the extension to the aggregation of the individual utilities of the same rule which, in individual decisions under uncertainty, EUT imposes for the determination of the total utility of lotteries. In other words, the connection between the two dimensions of states of the world and individuals is interpreted by Harsanyi as if it would impose that the linearity of the 'impartial' decision-maker's social preferences must be inferred from the linearity of personal preferences. In this section, the rationale proposed by Harsanyi for the determination of his linear social welfare function (SWF) will be critically discussed.

Although recently more sophisticated axiomatizations of utilitarianism have been put forward (see Fishburn 1988), Harsanyi's representation is the most articulated in so far as the ethical dimension of the utilitarian approach to social choice is concerned. From the assumption that social choice—just as with individual choice between random prospects—must be rooted in rational decision theory, Harsanyi moves on to demonstrate that a linear SWF will result. The ethical decision-maker will be indifferent towards two distributions yielding the same total utility, whatever the dispersion of the utility indexes among individuals.

Harsanyi's rationale for social choice implies that Bayesian rationality definitely consists of compliance with the vN–M axioms—that is, choice of vN–M representations—by the ethical decision-maker: since 'inequality neutrality' in social choice is equivalent to 'risk neutrality' in decision theory under uncertainty, the ethical decision-maker must be indifferent towards whatever inequality appears in the interpersonal distribution corresponding to the maximum average utility for society. This rationale, which forces the interpretation of individual behaviour predicted by EUT to dictate linearity in the determination of the social welfare function, will be now questioned by examining the Impartial Observer model.[4]

As is well known, the Impartial Observer corresponds to a decision-maker whose ethical behaviour consists of the principle of 'universalizability' (see Hare 1961: 29–31), i.e. all individuals must benefit from the social welfare function to the same extent. If the ethical decision-maker's interpersonal utility comparisons comply with the axioms underlying the so-called 'Addition Theorem', considering that he uses a common utility unit, in his social preferences the conditions of 'impartiality' and 'impersonality', respectively, must hold.[5]

The 'impartiality' condition represents the axioms leading to additive functional form: once equal scales for two individuals, say (A, B), and two

[4] A primitive version of the Impartial Observer model was elaborated by Harsanyi (1953). The model has successively been developed in Harsanyi (1955) and (1979).

[5] Harsanyi's social choice derives from the integration of two analytical schemes:
(i) The 'equal probability' model, according to which everybody can win the 'prize' of being any individual in society. This condition is expressed by the theorem following the axioms stating that both the personal and the moral preferences abide by the EUT axioms and that the Pareto principle is respected. In fact, the Addition Theorem, which states the linearity of the social welfare function:

$$W_i(A) = \sum_{i=1}^{n} a\,U(A), \text{ with } a > 0; \text{ and } i = 1, \ldots, n;$$

(ii) The 'symmetry' axiom, which means that the interpersonal utility comparisons are performed by a single individual j, the ethical decision-maker, who has an equal probability to be put in the place of each individual i. This axiom states that every utility function must have the same weight. Once $a_1, \ldots, a_n = a$, by choosing $a = 1/n$, the social welfare function:

$$W_i(A) = \frac{1}{n} \sum_{i=1}^{n} U(A)$$

is obtained.

states of the world (x, y) have been decided and conventional values have been chosen for the 'extreme' situations 0 and 1, the determination of vN–M utility indexes allows that—due to cardinality and unit comparability—the intensity of preferences will order the situations (A, x), (A, y), (B, x), (B, y): the social judgement consists of deciding whether—by moving from the state of the world x to the state of the world y—the utility difference for A is higher, equal, or lower than the utility difference for B. The 'impersonality' condition is represented by the 'symmetry' axiom. Once the interpersonal utility comparisons determined by individuals are expressed by means of a common utility unit, their moral preferences can be modelled as the single-profile Impartial Observer's social preferences: in the construction of the social welfare function each individual's utility function will be given the same weight a. In fact, the 'similarity postulate',[6] which allows a single ethical decision-maker to decide on social situations, corresponds to the assumption that an Impartial Observer adds up the individual utility functions by using a uniform a weight.

As for the first condition, according to the 'veil of ignorance' consisting in the 'equal probability' of being put in the place of anyone else, each individual acts as an ethical decision-maker. The interpersonal aggregation of the utilities relative to each state of the world $U(x) = u_1(x) + \cdots + u_n(x)$ for the n individuals must reproduce the same rule of the intrapersonal aggregation of the utility values (multiplied by the respective probabilities) in relation to the h states of the world of a lottery:

$$U_i(x_1, \ldots, x_h) = p_1 u_i(x_1) + \ldots + p_h u_i(x_h) \text{ with } \sum p_i = 1.$$

In Harsanyi's words, 'social choice among alternative social situations would be a choice among alternative risk prospects' (see Harsanyi (1977*a*: 50), so that 'all interpersonal utility comparisons could be reduced to intrapersonal utility comparisons' (see Harsanyi 1977*a*: 58).

It is the second condition, however, that is the critical one. It must be recalled that the Addition Theorem does not include 'symmetry' but the a weights can be different and even change depending on the chosen profile.[7] The further 'symmetry' axiom entails that uniform a weights are applied to the pre-determinate utility indexes. Only when this axiom is

[6] In Harsanyi's own words, 'given the basic similarity in human nature (i.e., in the fundamental psychological laws governing human behavior and human attitudes), it is reasonable to assume that different people will show very *similar* psychological reactions to any given objective situation, and will derive much the *same* utility or disutility from it—*once proper allowances have been made for any empirically observed differences* in their biological make-ups, in their social positions' (Harsanyi 1979: 301).

[7] The Addition Theorem 'deals only with single-profile exercises and does not claim that the constants a (. . .) will remain the same when the individual utility functions change (i.e. when a *family* L_i of each other as under the utilitarian formula (indeed for the axioms specified they can even be negative), but it does not even require that the set of a_i will be invariant with respect to changes in individual utility characteristics (as opposed to representational change *within* a given positive affine family)' (Sen 1986: 1124).

added, is the utilitarian condition of 'equal treatment' of all individuals established.[8] As it was observed, 'an axiomatic justification of utilitarianism would have more content to it if it started off at a place somewhat more distant from the ultimate destination' (see Sen 1977*a*: 279).

This separation between the first three postulates (from which the Addition Theorem is derived) and the 'symmetry' axiom puts at risk the foundation of the moral principle of 'equal treatment' in decision theory under uncertainty. If the vN–M functions are mere cardinal representations of preferences, although the assignment of the *a* uniform weights is conditional on a chosen profile which consists of vN–M representations, no moral principle can be found in the linearity of Harsanyi's social preferences.[9] On the other hand, if individual utilities are to be taken as quantities of 'pleasure', as Harsanyi sometimes appears to think, the implementation of a moral principle is certainly involved in the social judgements stemming from the ethical decision-maker's interpersonal utility comparisons. In this case, the choice of the utility function by which personal preferences are expressed turns out to be decisive also for the determination of social preferences. Therefore, if social preferences must be linear in order to convey the moral principle of 'equal treatment', a reason should have been provided by Harsanyi to justify the selection of the linear vN–M representations as the functional form by which personal preferences have to be expressed.

To this extent, it can be observed that the individual behaviour leading to the linear social welfare function could be modelled in away different from the one chosen by Harsanyi. Even though they satisfy the EUT axioms, personal preferences might not—or not all of them—be vN–M utility functions. In this case, the Impartial Observer's moral preferences stemming from the interpersonal utility comparisons will not comply with the EUT axioms (see Weimark 1991: 297–313). Hence, the determination of social preferences consisting of the utilitarian ordering will vanish and only an ordinal representation of social situations will be feasible. In addition, whichever utility function represents the personal preferences, utility representations of the social preferences different from the vN–M ones could also be preferred by the Impartial Observer and again the utilitarian ordering of social situations will not ensue.[10]

[8] Mongin has recently demonstrated that, due to its mismatch with the 'symmetry' axiom, Harsanyi's single-profile approach needs additional hypotheses in order to circumvent Arrow's Impossibility Theorem (see Mongin 1991: 17).

[9] Following Sen (1977*a*), Weimark (1991) elaborates a similar critique of Harsanyi's Addition Theorem as a 'representation theorem'. In particular, see Weimark (1991: 312).

[10] According to Sen, the use of the von Neumann–Morgenstern functions in the determination of social preferences is a quite arbitrary choice: '*individual* utilities need not always have cardinal representations and need not be cardinally comparable between persons. . . . When people talk about social welfare being a non-linear function of individual welfares, they *in fact* typically refer to representations other than those emanating from the von Neumann–Morgenstern system' (Sen 1977*b*: 298–9).

Yet, Harsanyi maintains that the vN–M utility functions are the sole correct representations of social preferences: 'If the decision maker follows the rationality postulates of Bayesian theory, then he *must* measure the utility of a lottery ticket by its expected utility (assuming that all utilities are expressed in von Neumann–Morgenstern utility units)' (see Harsanyi 1976: 74). This proposition can be put in terms of the 'additive separability' condition: due to the 'separability' both of rows and columns in Table 11.1, since personal preferences are expressed by vN–M representations, the ethical decision-maker must adopt a linear combination as the functional form of the social welfare function. Even if 'additive separability' were a necessary condition for the social welfare orderings, from the EUT axioms it does not follow that this condition dictates that the social welfare function be linear. As it was shown above, the EUT axioms do not oblige individuals to adopt linearity in deciding between random prospects, so that all functional forms which comply with the 'separability' condition are admissible in deciding between interpersonal distributions of individual utilities.

Therefore, the argumentation cited above is beyond the point. As it was observed before, the real problem is the functional form of the individuals' expectational utility functions, and no justification is given by Harsanyi for the linear form by which personal preferences are expressed. Since the use of vN–M representations for the determination of the personal preferences is only assumed, Harsanyi's social preferences rely completely on the arbitrary choice of these linear utility functions. Thus, the Impartial Observer model does not succeed in providing a clear demonstration that from the EUT axioms a linear social welfare function will result.

Harsanyi's ambition to affirm linear combination as the sole coherent aggregation rule of individual utilities and 'equal treatment' as the moral principle to be adopted by the ethical decision-maker is thus questionable. In fact, the requirement that both individual and social preferences comply with the EUT axioms leads only to respecting the 'separability' condition both in the dimension of states of the world and in the dimension of individuals. Nothing is said about which particular function complying with 'separability' has to be used. Unless it is assumed that the utilitarian decision-maker wants the social welfare function to be linear just because the moral principle of 'impartiality' has been chosen, a theoretical foundation in decision theory under uncertainty should be given for the use of vN–M utility functions, in order for this stricture to be added to the aggregation process of individual utilities.

Since there is no Bayesian rationality axiom by which an ethical decision-maker could be forced to the linear combination of the individual utilities, the possibility of 'inequality averse' social preferences has to be investigated. In order to pursue a concern for equity in social choice on the individual behavioural patterns which have been studied in decision theory under uncertainty, the next sections will focus on NEUT. It will be assessed under what conditions observed deviations of individual decision-makers under uncertainty from the behaviour predicted by EUT allow a concern of equity to be inserted in social choice. I will begin by demonstrating that the NEUT approach shows that the sole constraint imposed by the connection between aggregation across states of the world and aggregation across individuals is by respecting the 'separability' condition in the aggregation of the individual utilities.

4. The separability condition and social choice

The experiments put forward by NEUT demonstrate that individual behaviour with regard to lotteries tends to contradict the 'separability' condition. I will start from the extreme case of 'complementarity' among expected values, which will be transferred from the dimension of states of the world to the dimension of individuals.

After the well-known 'Allais Paradox' (see Allais 1953; see also Machina 1987: 98–9), a large number of experiments conducted by the NEUT theorists has shown that the violation of the independence axiom can be caused by the presence of the special feature of certainty of a positive outcome in one of the random prospects of the decisional scheme. The behavioural pattern predicted by NEUT will be extended to social choice. It will be shown that the violation of the independence axiom, which in individual decision-making under uncertainty is caused by the special value given to *certainty*, in social choice is caused by the special value given to *equality*.

Let us clarify why the Allais Paradox is an extreme form of deviation from the prediction of the independence axiom in individual decisions between lotteries. Kahneman and Tversky (see Kahneman and Tversky 1979: 265–7) proposed an experiment composed of the following two situations. In the first situation, the first prospect (A) gives 2,400 Israeli shekels with certainty while the second one (B) gives 2,500 with probability 0.33, 2,400 with probability 0.66 and nothing with probability 0.01. In the second situation, the first prospect (C) gives 2,400 with probability 0.34 and nothing with probability 0.66, while the second one (D) gives 2,500 with probability 0.33 and nothing with probability 0.67. Since the disequalities:

$$u(2{,}400) > 0.33\, u(2{,}500) + 0.66\, u(2{,}400)$$

and

$$0.34\, u(2{,}400) > 0.33\, u(2{,}500)$$

relative to the first situation (only the sign will change with reference to the second situation) turn out to be the same in both situations, if $A < B$—by virtue of the independence axiom—necessarily $C < D$. Yet, since evidence shows that individuals tend to prefer A in situation I, but keep choosing D

in situation II, the independence axiom is violated due to preference reversal.

The peculiarity of the Allais Paradox does not lie only in the circumstance that the decision to be made by the individual between lotteries depends both on what happens in each single consequence *and* on a judgement of 'complementarity' among possible outcomes stemming from an overall evaluation of all the prospect. In fact, it is a peculiar overall evaluation, because the certainty of a positive outcome results. In the example above, the change in behaviour which contradicts the independence axiom would arise once a 'complementarity' link among the utility indexes of lottery *A* is established. The individual is supposed to take into account the certainty of a positive utility in lottery *A* because from the overall evaluation of all possible outcomes the reduction to zero of the risk inherent in this lottery ensues. Thus, in choosing between the two lotteries in situation I the individual modifies his own attitude to risk—with respect to situation II—towards one of greater aversion.

It might be asked whether individual behaviour based on 'complementarity' observed in the NEUT experiments could be extended from individual to social choice, that is, from the dimension of states of the world to the dimension of individuals. Table 11.4 presents equally probable money values (for individuals *i* and *j*, in the states of the world *x* and *y*) from which interpersonal distributions of utility indexes are determined.

Unlike the Allais Paradox, the absence of 'separability' here concerns one of the two interpersonal distributions: the same 'extreme' kind of 'complementarity' appearing in the Allais Paradox as *certainty* turns up in situation *A* as equality.

TABLE 11.4

	A		*B*	
	i	*j*	*i*	*j*
x	90	90	90	20
y	20	20	20	90

Suppose that in Table 11.4 the 'separability' condition were respected in the determination of social preferences, and that linearity applies in both the interpersonal distributions of situation *A* and of situation *B*.[11] Obviously, the calculation of the total utility for each situation shows that they are equal:

$$\tfrac{1}{2}[u(90) + u(90)] + \tfrac{1}{2}[u(20) + u(20)] = \tfrac{1}{2}[u(90) + u(20)] + \tfrac{1}{2}[u(20) + u(90)].$$

[11] An analysis of equality under uncertainty as a case of absence of 'separability' among possible outcomes has been elaborated by Broome (1991: 185–92). Table 11.4 and the following discussion are drawn on Broome's presentation of the subject.

Since the individual utilities add up to the same total utility, social welfare will be maximized indifferently by socially preferring any of them. Moreover, both the prospects *A* and *B* give to each individual equal chances of getting 90 and 20, so that by the Pareto principle *A* and *B* are equally good for each individual.

Suppose now that the ethical decision-maker comes to the conclusion that social welfare is higher in situation *A*, because there it is evenly distributed though unevenly in situation *B*: instead of being indifferent between the two situations, he then prefers *A* to *B*. The reason for this choice is 'complementarity', which does not appear in an intrapersonal distribution, that is, in the aggregation of utility values across states of the world, but in an interpersonal distribution. In fact, when *A* is chosen in Table 11.4 the overall evaluation and the consequent violation of the 'separability' condition concerns—instead of lottery *A* of the Allais Paradox—the interpersonal distribution of situation *A*'s state of the world *x*. However, if the ethical decision-maker ranks a situation which is characterized by equality higher than the other situation showing the same total utility, the evaluation of each individual's possible outcomes is not independent of another individual's possible outcome, and the Pareto principle is not respected.

This social preference, which contradicts Bayesian rationality, shows that equality is a peculiar feature of interpersonal distributions which can be considered only by means of an overall evaluation of the interpersonal distributions. Given the existence of this peculiar feature, the utility attributed to each expected value also depends on the expected values attributed to *all* other individuals. The violation of the Pareto principle derives from the tendency to assign a special value to this extreme feature of interpersonal distributions which is equality.

Therefore, the representation in social choice of a social situation similar to the extreme case of 'complementarity' in individual choice casts light on the existence of a problem. While in the Allais Paradox the presence of certainty in possible outcomes leads to the violation of the independence axiom, although, after the NEUT experiments, reasons for this violation in individual decisions can be found, in the 'equality example' the feature of equality in the distribution of individual utilities leads the ethical decision-maker to renege on the Pareto principle, and for a social choice based on this premiss reasons are actually hard to find. The fact is that the conflict between individualism and equality is far from being solved. Equality is an 'extreme' concern for equity, the implementation of which implies that the evaluation of each individual's possible outcomes is made conditional on another individual's possible outcomes, so to violate the Pareto principle. If no overriding reason is given for equity to be considered in this 'extreme' version, the principle of individualism would not be renounced. In the latter case, although the ordering of social situations by no means may depend on assigning a special value to equality, a social choice can be envisaged such that at the same time it does not conflate with the Pareto principle and contemplates a concern for equity.

5. The Non-Expected Utility Theorem approach to social choice

While in the previous section the extension to social choice of the violation of the independence axiom was embedded in the interpersonal distributions of the 'equality example', in this section the application of the Allais Paradox case of 'complementarity' to social choice will be embedded in the intrapersonal distributions of the framework sketched in Table 11.5. In each situation (I and II), the choice is made between two prospects (*A* and *B*, *C* and *D*, respectively) composed of the utility indexes expected by the individuals *i* and *j* and related to the equally probable social states *x* and *y*. The same utility numbers used by Diamond (see Diamond 1967: 765–6) to criticize Harsanyi's social choice have been used.[12] However, Diamond's example is limited to the choice defined in situation I; since the distribution relative to state *x* does not alter from one prospect to another, state *y* should be the only one to influence that choice. In the scheme with four prospects shown in Table 11.5, the same argument has to be applied to situation II.

TABLE 11.5

	x	*y*		*x*	*y*
	IA			*IIC*	
i	1	1	*i*	0	0
j	0	0	*j*	1	1
	IB			*IID*	
i	1	0	*i*	0	1
j	0	1	*j*	1	0

According to EUT, in the case of 'risk neutrality' the overall utilities expressed from each of the two prospects turn out to be equal:

$$1/2[U(1) + U(0)] = 1/2[U(0) + U(1)].$$

Thus, just as with the lotteries, one might see no difference between *A* and *B* and between *C* and *D*. However, if one prefers *B* in situation I, for the choice to remain consistent with the independence axiom one should then choose *C* in situation II. The reason lies in the circumstance that in state *y* prospects *B* and *C* have equal indexes (whereas in state *x*, *A* and *B*, and *C* and *D* respectively present equal interpersonal distributions of utility

[12] The assumption of interpersonal comparability, however, differs in the two determination processes of social welfare. In the Diamond example, 'full comparability' (i.e. the individual utility levels, and then also 'origins') is required, whereas in Harsanyi's social choice only 'unit comparability' is needed (see Sen 1970: 144–5).

values). On the contrary, Diamond would suggest that, although *B* is preferred to *A*, *D* should be preferred to *C*. The rationale has to be trace to 'complementarity' between possible outcomes: from an overall evaluation of the possible outcomes of position *j* in *A* and position *i* in *C* the certainty of starvation follows. Thus, Bayesian rationality, which imposes that *C* be preferred in situation II, is in contrast with moral behaviour, which forces an ethical decision-maker to prefer *D* to *C*.

In the prospects sketched in Table 11.5, 'complementarity' does not occur across individuals—as in the 'equality example'—but in one of the intrapersonal distributions. While the ordering of the interpersonal distributions is not in question, the fairness of the risk distribution process in the intrapersonal distributions is under scrutiny. The special feature connecting the expected values by which 'complementarity' is established is the unfairness of the risk allocation between individuals. An ethical decision-maker should be led to a negative overall evaluation of the lottery of individual *j* because 'complementarity' among possible outcomes makes lottery *A* a 'no chance' lottery.

Both in the Allais Paradox related to individual decision and in Diamond's example related to social choice, the decision-maker's change in risk attitude is due to a special interaction between the evaluation of each single possible outcome and that of all other expected values. The Allais Paradox deals with the certainty of 'no risk' included in lottery *A* (the rationale proposed by Kahneman and Tversky for evidence showing the violation of the independence axiom is that—from situation II to situation I—the subject's behaviour changes towards 'risk aversion'). Similarly, the Diamond example deals with the certainty of 'no chance' for the individual who will occupy position *j*: the rationale for the violation of the independence axiom is that an ethical decision-maker would condemn social situations implying this kind of lottery because of the unfairness—for individual *j* with respect to individual *i*—of the process of interpersonal allocation of risk. This is the moral motivation for the social preference which conforms to Bayesian rationality to be rejected by the ethical decision-maker. Every social judgement based on an uneven distribution of risk between the two individuals should be dismissed. It is important to add that, unlike the previous 'equality example', this violation of the 'separability' condition due to the certainty of unfairness leads to a social choice which does not contradict the Pareto principle.

Following Harsanyi, it might be objected that if social choice has to be rooted in rational choice a social judgement in terms of unfairness cannot be a substitute for Bayesian rationality. In other words, the 'separability' condition should be respected not only in the dimension of individuals, in order for social choice to comply with the Pareto principle, but also in the dimension of states of the world. In his appraisal of Diamond's example, Harsanyi maintains that the denial of rationality constraints in the field of social issues involving moral judgements is not well founded.[13] While Diamond suggests that a judgement conflicting with Bayesian rationality can be put forward in the case of social situations, Harsanyi argues it should not make a difference from the decision theory viewpoint whether an 'extremely high risk for one individual' occurs in relation to a natural situation or to a social situation.

Therefore, Harsanyi points to the homogeneity among all natural and social situations. An ethical decision-maker cannot decide that the independence axiom should not be satisfied whenever social and not natural factors originate an uneven distribution of risk among individuals. The rationale of this theoretical position can be traced back to Samuelson, whose justification for the universal validity of the independence axiom is that the possible outcomes of a prospect must be evaluated separately from one another: 'if one comes, the other cannot' (see Samuelson 1952: 672, and also von Neumann and Morgenstern 1953: 17–18). Moreover, Savage (see Savage 1954: 100–4) has observed that the states of the world which give the same possible outcomes in their respective locations should be ignored by rational individuals, and this amounts to saying that no form of 'complementarity' can be established.

However, it has to be stressed that Diamond's judgement in terms of unfairness is by no means the sole possible foundation for orderings of social situations different from the utilitarian one, and compatible with individualism, to be determined by an ethical decision-maker. In fact, individuals behavioural patterns observed in the NEUT experiments tend to diverge significantly from the individual behaviour predicted by the EUT axioms. Hence, Harsanyi's remark according to which no special exemption should be devised for social situations can be answered by pointing to the pervasiveness of situations in which the individual tends to violate the independence axiom. Yet, he should not be considered irrational. If one agrees that 'conventional expected utility theory . . . represents an unnecessary restrictive notion of rationality' (see Loomes and Sugden 1982: 820), he should also advocate that an 'enlarged' notion of rationality is needed for social judgements.

In the remainder of this chapter, the Non-Expected Utility approach to the determination of social preferences will be conceived as the approach by which social choice is founded in individual decision-making under uncertainty characterized by 'complementarity' among the possible outcomes of a random prospect. In other words, it might well happen that 'separability' is not required for aggregation across states of the world even though it has

[13] 'Diamond's suggestion that economic and social privileges allocated by government policies with random components are morally more acceptable than social and economic privileges allocated by the accidents of birth and of personal life history—i.e., the suggestion that the first kind of personal "luck" is morally superior to the second kind—is wholly without merit. Therefore, his claim that social choices are not subject to the sure-thing principle falls to the ground' (Harsanyi 1976: 71). See also Harsanyi (1977*b*) and the rejoinder by Sen (1977*b*).

to be respected in aggregation across individuals, due to the Pareto principle. To this extent, I will continue my attempt to extend non-conventional behaviour observed in NEUT to determining the ordering of social situations by examining different cases of 'complementarity' among expected values observed in non-conventional analyses of individual decisions between lotteries as they impinge on the determination of social preferences.

6. The 'inequality averse' decision-maker

Among the experimental evidence presented by NEUT about deviations from Bayesian rationality in individual decision theory, cases of violation of the independence axiom have been attributed to 'risk aversion'. The link between 'inequality aversion' and 'risk aversion' mentioned above will be used here to show that lack of 'separability' among possible outcomes might induce such an utility evaluation of the prospects that an ordering of social situations different from the utilitarian one may result.

I will submit an analysis of 'inequality averse' social preferences along the lines of the 'enlarged' notion of rationality pointed out by NEUT following empirical evidence called the 'common consequence effect' (see Machina 1987: 100–1). As was suggested above, the aim is to examine whether a description of equity-concerned social preferences can be constructed by extending to the ordering of interpersonal distributions experimental evidence which challenges the validity of EUT in individual choice between random prospects. Looking back at Table 11.2, the preference ordering between A and B, and between C and D should not depend on the value g^*, since the probability of G^* and g^* being drawn is identical for both couples of random prospects. Yet deviations from the behaviour predicted by EUT have been observed. It will now be shown that, when C is preferred to D in situation II, a tendency to preference reversal in favour of B in situation I can occur, so that the independence axiom is violated.

This non-conventional behaviour predicted by EUT was denominated the 'common consequence effect' because it has to be traced back to 'complementarity' among possible outcomes of the states of the world. In this case 'complementarity' is brought about by the 'stochastic dominance' due to G^*. According to Machina's Hypothesis II (see Machina 1983: 232–9), there seems to be a tendency for 'risk aversion' to increase as individuals move from stochastically dominated to stochastically dominating distributions. Since G^* stochastically dominates g^*, the degree of local 'risk aversion' might be different between the first and the second situation, so that the independence axiom is violated: once $C < D$ results from 'risk neutrality' in situation II, $A < B$ is caused by the 'higher' risk aversion characterizing situation I.

Diagrammatically, the consequent violation of the independence axiom can be sketched in the Marshak–Machina triangle shown in Fig. 11.1: the

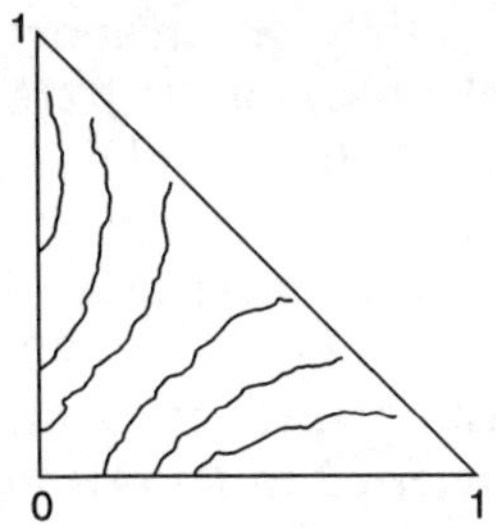

FIG. 11.2

indifference curves will no longer be parallel—as in the orthodox case of Fig. 11.1—but upward sloping (movements north and west being preferred as $x_1 < x_2 < x_3$) and will tend to fan out (see Fig. 11.2).

Let us now extend this case of preference reversal to social choice. In Table 11.6, I consider random prospects composed of money values from which the utility indexes (expected by two individuals *i* and *j* in two equally probable states of the world *x* and *y*) are determined. In each situation, the pair of prospects presents a common consequence in one of the two states of the world. The values expected by the two individuals are identical in both pairs of prospects in relation to the social state *y*. In this regard, there is no difference between *A* and *B*, or *C* and *D*. Yet it is apparent that each pair of prospects stochastically dominates the other because the common consequence of situation I has to be preferred to the common consequence of situation II.

TABLE 11.6

	x	y		x	y
	IA			IIC	
u_i	90	50	u_i	90	25
u_j	20	30	u_j	20	10
	IB			IID	
u_i	40	50	u_i	40	25
u_j	60	30	u_j	60	10

Once the ethical decision-maker imagines that he has a fifty-fifty probability of becoming any of the two individuals, his social judgements result from interpersonal comparisons like the following one referring to situation I: should the equal probability of being individual *i*, with expected utility varying from *U*(90) to *U*(50) or individual *j* with expected utility varying from *U*(20) to *U*(30) be preferred to the equal probability of being individual *i* with expected utility which varies from *U*(40) to *U*(50) or individual *j* with expected utility which varies from *U*(60) to *U*(30)? According to the EUT axioms, the ethical decision-maker should prefer the interpersonal distribution with the highest total utility. In situation I, the choice will fall on the highest between the total utility of A: $1/2[U(90) + U(20)] + 1/2[U(50) + U(30)]$ and the total utility of B: $1/2[U(40) + U(60)] + 1/2[U(50) + U(30)]$. Thus, A should be socially preferred to B. The same should occur in situation II: C should be socially preferred to D.

However, if the 'common consequence effect', consisting of preference reversal in situation I with respect to situation II, is applied to social preferences, when C is preferred to D, B is preferred to A. The deviation from the social choice predicted by the independence axiom can be interpreted in the following way. In situation I, a case of 'complementarity' among consequences occurs: the utility evaluation of each possible outcome in state x does not depend just on the money value in that position but is conditional on the money values in state y, which represents the common consequence. Preference reversal in situation I is then due to the dependence of the evaluation of each outcome of the state x on state y's values (50 and 30) which are much 'higher' than those appearing in situation II (25 and 10). Think of a decision-maker in situation I, who is determining the utility evaluation of the 0.5 probability of getting in state x the values 90 and 20 as individual i and j, respectively: this evaluation will be influenced by the fact that the values 50 and 30 appear in the other state y, while in situation II the much 'lower' values 25 and 10 are expected.

Therefore, in the first situation, due to an improvement in the common consequence with respect to the other situation, the random prospects stochastically dominate those displayed in the second. This improvement brings about a change in behaviour which can be thought of as an increase in 'inequality aversion' in an evaluation of utility differences between the two individuals. This change might be expressed as a non-linear utility evaluation which takes into account the less uneven distribution of the state x's values in prospect B with respect to prospect A and then makes the total utility greater than in prospect B. On the other hand, in the second situation, in which the common consequence in state y makes the prospects 'worse' (in the sense of 'stochastic dominance') with respect to the first situation, the much wider dispersion—in state x—of the values of prospect C with respect to prospect D is not taken into account because of the linear utility evaluation, so that C is preferred to D. Briefly speaking, in situation I the 'highest' possible outcomes of the common consequence (state y) cause the ethical decision-maker to be 'inequality averse', whereas in situation II the values of state y are much 'lower', so that 'inequality neutrality' prevails. Therefore, due to the change to 'inequality aversion' in moving from one situation to another, the 'common consequence effect' generates a social choice which does not conform with the behaviour predicted by EUT.

However, since preference reversal is a consequence of the divergence of a situation relatively to another one, the change to 'inequality aversion' occurs in only one of the two situations. The linear utility evaluation of situation II—from which *C* preferred to *D* follows—therefore means that the concern for equity is missing just in the most unequal situation (the one characterized by 'stochastically dominated' prospects). In decision theory under uncertainty, *mutatis mutandis*, there would be an obvious explanation for this apparent paradox. Were the ethical decision-maker a gambler choosing between lotteries, it would be plausible to reduce 'risk aversion' and choose the most unequal distribution only relatively to the situation with the 'stochastically dominated' prospects. Although this behaviour is doubtlessly in conflict with Bayesian rationality, none the less it has its own logic: it can be compared to the behaviour of the gambler who, having lost small sums in each previous game, tries to recuperate his losses in the last game by betting on the most risky option. In more general terms, such behaviour can be related to the psychological attitude that combines a propensity to risk in the domain of losses and an aversion to risk in the domain of gains that was formalized in Prospect Theory.[14]

This explanation, although plausible in cases of individual decisions between lotteries, does not work in the case of social choice. Once transferred to social preferences, it turns out to be counter-intuitive: it amounts to assuming that, when the common consequence for each individual is 'higher', the ethical decision-maker takes a 'inequality averse' attitude and when each individual's prospect is 'worsened' by the common consequence he feels indifference towards inequality in the interpersonal distribution of the utility values. Since the extension to social choice of the behaviour compatible with the NEUT 'common consequence effect' cannot make the decision-maker's social preferences coherently 'inequality averse', this kind of preference reversal cannot be presented as a foundation in non-conventional decision theory for a tendency to choose the most equitable distribution.

A different approach should then be pursued in order to consider the concern for equity which causes the ethical decision-maker to avoid too unequal a distribution of the utilities among individuals no matter what the social situation, that is, not only when preference reversal occurs. Indeed the 'inequality averse' attitude in *both* situations might find its behavioural foundations in decision theory under uncertainty. In fact, a tendency towards 'risk aversion' in *both* situations—so that the independence axiom is not violated: if $D > C$, then $B > A$ is implied—is consistent both with the EUT axioms and the NEUT 'common consequence effect' (see Sugden (1986: 8). Diagrammatically, this corresponds to the bold lines steeper than the indifference curves in the Marshak–Machina triangle of Fig. 11.1, with the upper extremes of each line being *D* and *B*. Thus EUT is compatible

[14] 'The aggravation one experiences in losing a sum of money appears to be greater than the pleasure of gaining the same amount' (Kahneman and Tversky (1979: 279)).

with the above-mentioned choice forecasted by the NEUT 'common consequence effect'.[15] From the extension of this case to social choice the 'inequality averse' decision-maker in *both* situations of Table 11.6 follows: he will decide in favour of B in situation I *and* in favour of D in situation II.[16]

An 'inequality averse' social choice in *both* situations, unlike 'common consequence effect' preference reversal, does not rely on 'complementarity' among the states of the world. According to the discussion in section 2, concerning the functional forms compatible with the conventional approach to decision theory, the ethical decision-maker can be supposed to determine the social preferences by means of strictly concave functions. If a strictly concave transformation is applied to the interpersonal distributions, social preferences will stem from the attribution of higher importance to the less favourable positions in the determination of social welfare.

Let us suppose that in Table 11.6, by applying 'inequality aversion' in *both* situations, the ethical decision-maker modifies the utilities of state x (the common consequence of state y can in fact be eliminated, being irrelevant to the decision) by a strictly concave transformation f. This type of transformation expresses the decision-maker's 'inequality aversion' because it causes the contribution of individual utility to overall utility to be in an inverse proportion to the value attributed to each outcome. In consequence, the interpersonal distribution in which individual utilities are allocated in the less unequal way will be chosen by the 'inequality averse' decision-maker. In both situations depicted in Table 11.4, a disequality between the two total utility might then result:

$$\tfrac{1}{2}[f[U(90)] + f[U(20)]] < \tfrac{1}{2}[f[U(40)] + f[U(60)]].$$

Therefore, the most equitable distribution should always turn out to be the socially preferred one: $B > A$ and $D > C$.

However, the problem with this equity-concerned social preference is that no significant evidence of this behaviour has been provided yet by the NEUT experiments. In fact, experimental evidence of the 'common consequence effect' shows an overwhelming tendency to preference reversal, that is, to a change towards 'risk aversion' only in one situation. Therefore, 'inequality averse' social preferences in all social situations cannot find their behavioural foundation in the 'common consequence effect'.

[15] I owe this remark to Robert Sugden.

[16] Since this choice is compatible both with EUT and NEUT, one might conclude that the case of preference reversal towards 'risk aversion' represents the only difference. Instead, once applied to social choice, NEUT excludes the case of the decision-maker who is 'inequality-oriented' however 'low' or 'high' are the money values of the common consequence. While in EUT the independence axiom dictates both that $D > C$ entails $B > A$, and that $B > A$ entails $D > C$, the 'common consequence effect' simply forecasts that when $D > C$, then $B > A$, and *not* also that when $B > A$ then $D > C$. Hence, it can be said that the case for an 'inequality lover' decision-maker—which corresponds to $B > A$ and then $D > C$—is excluded.

The attempt to found a strictly concave social choice on the 'inequality averse' behaviour of the ethical decision-maker has thus not succeeded. In section 3, it was demonstrated that the EUT axioms do not provide a sufficient analytical basis to support Harsanyi's advocation of linearity as the aggregation rule to be adopted by an ethical decision-maker who wants to implement the moral principle of 'impartiality'. Similarly, in this section, it was demonstrated that the non-conventional behaviour predicted by NEUT does not lead to strict concavity as the aggregation rule to be adopted by an ethical decision-maker implementing the moral principle of a concern for equity in the form of 'inequality aversion'.

7. The 'individualistic' notion of equity

I will now turn to another line of research in NEUT which shares the absence of 'separability' among possible outcomes of the states of the world with the approach followed in the previous section. A utility function 'modified' by a concern for equity will be described, where deviations from linearity across states of the world do not depend on the 'complementarity' between an expected value and the common consequence's one (as in the previous section) but are specific to single utility values. Hence, a different approach to equity-concerned social preferences is introduced, where the concern for equity is not considered in relation to *whole* interpersonal distributions—as in the 'equality example' and in the case of the 'inequality averse' decision-maker—but in relation to *each* location which individuals might occupy by chance. It will be shown that the concern for equity implemented by the 'modified' utility function represents an 'individualistic' notion of equity.[17]

The NEUT research line which inspires the proposed conception of equity is the one represented by Regret Theory (see Loomes and Sugden 1982), and Disappointment Theory (see Loomes and Sugden 1986), the predictions of which have been confirmed by experimental evidence. The main feature of this approach is that, in the maximization of the expected utility, the individual is supposed to anticipate those feelings which he might experience in case a specific outcome materialises *ex post*.[18] The utility function is then modified in order to take into account the psychological expression of regret or disappointment which is associated with that consequence. Formally, the utility evaluation of the possible outcomes will not solely consist of the (probability-weighted) average of the utilities but also of an analytical expression of regret aversion or disappointment aversion.

[17] The view according to which distributive issues should be considered from the perspective of the individual and the need for an 'individualistic' approach to an equity-concerned ordering of social states have been put forward by Broome (1991: ch. 9).

[18] 'To assume that people maximise expected modified utility is to generalise Bernoulli's theory in a very natural way, since the individual who *does* experience rejoicing and regret can be expected to try to anticipate those feelings and take them into account when making a decision under uncertainty' (Loomes and Sugden 1982: 809).

Let us compare the two hypotheses—regret aversion and disappointment aversion—which have been put forward by this NEUT research line in order to explain a deviation from the (probability-weighted) average of the utilities. In the first case, the deviation is attributed to a failure in participating in that lottery to which the outcome actually drawn belongs, so that the feeling of regret follows. In the second case, the deviation is attributed to the possibility that the outcome actually drawn belongs to a state of the world which is not the one with the preferred outcome, so that the feeling of disappointment follows. Therefore, while in the regret case 'what might have been' belongs to a different lottery in the same state of the world, in the disappointment case 'what might have been' belongs to the same lottery but in a different state of the world (see Loomes and Sugden 1986: 281).

Hereafter the attempt will be made to suggest an application of this non-conventional approach to utility evaluations in the determination of social judgements. The insertion of a concern for equity in the evaluation of the positions by which interpersonal distributions are composed should be specified by a function similar to a utility function which includes 'disappointment aversion'.[19]

The reason why a concern for equity is better modelled by making reference to a function which includes disappointment aversion rather than regret aversion is that the feeling of regret is the result of a consequence desired in a given state of the world that has been 'drawn' in a lottery that the individual has not chosen.[20] Since the ethical decision-maker formulates social judgements by taking into account all prospects, no feeling of regret can be reproduced in his utility evaluation. On the contrary, in the disappointment case, the decision-maker might consider unfavourably—

[19] In Disappointment Theory, the following representation of a utility function with 'disappointment aversion' has been proposed by Gul (1991):

$$V(p) = \hat{O}(a) \sum_{u(x) > V(p)} U(x_i)\, p_i/a + (1 - \hat{O}(a)) \sum_{U(x) < V(p)} U(x_i)\, p_i/(1 - a)$$

where $a = \Sigma P_i$ for $U(x_i) > V(p)$, $\hat{O}(a) = a/[1 + (1 - a)\delta]$ and $\delta \in (-1, \infty)$.

In this function, both disappointment and elation are incorporated, with disappointment occurring when $\delta > 0$. However, since the model makes a decomposition of the utility of a lottery by means of the weights $\hat{O}(a)$ and $(1 - \hat{O}(a))$, disappointment ends up to count more than elation (see Gul 1991: 670–6). Differently from the 'common consequence effect' type of violation of the independence axiom, the indifference curves in the Marshak–Machina triangle, although not parallel, still preserve the linear form. By fanning out (in the bottom half) and fanning in (in the top half), they eventually intersect outside the triangle in two points. Some features of expected utility theory are then retained.

[20] 'Suppose you consider betting £5 on a 50-1 outsider in the Grand National. You decide not to bet, but the horse wins. You cannot feel *disappointment* since, not having bet, you had no expectation of winning. But you may feel *regret* when you reflect on the fact that, *had you chosen differently*, you would now be £250 better off. Regret, then, is a route by which the utility you derive from a particular consequence of one action may be influenced by a consequence of a *different* action' (see Sugden 1986: 16).

relatively to the individual who has got a certain random prospect by chance—the comparison between an outcome and a 'might have been' which is related to outcomes of the other states of the world of the random prospect. The Disappointment Theory thus allows us to think of an ethical decision-maker whose social judgements do not comply with the 'separability' condition across states of the world. 'Separability' across individuals is instead warranted: the Pareto principle, according to which the evaluation of one individual's possible outcome cannot be made dependent on the evaluation of another individual's possible outcome, is not violated.

To represent a concern for equity in the determination of social preferences similar to individual utility evaluation influenced by disappointment in NEUT allows the proper characterization of an ethical decision-maker. In considering each individual independently from each other, he can be supposed to take into account the decrease in utility which would be felt *ex post* by that individual due to the 'complementarity' among possible outcomes of alternative states of the world. This dependence might be expressed by an indicator—derived from the other expected values of the individual's prospect—from which the ethical decision-maker gets the judgement relative to the degree of equity of each location.

A utility function modified by a concern for equity might then be conceived, in which a measure of the degree of equity belonging to a random prospect that an individual might have by chance induces a decrease of the utility evaluation relatively to particularly 'low' possible outcomes. The proposed assumption is that the ethical decision-maker foresees the sense of loss in personal dignity that might arise *ex post* in the individual who encounters consequences which fall short of a certain threshold—for instance, one-half of the average value of the utility distribution—and then corrects by a negative value the utility evaluation relative to that consequence. Hence, in each position in Fig. 11.3 with a money value inferior to one-half of the average value—indicated as $u^*(x)$—the utility evaluation will also include a negative judgement on the degree of equity. Let us name 'equity function' the following utility function 'modified' by the consideration of a concern for equity:

$$V(p_1, \ldots, p_n) = \sum p_i \, [u_i + E[u(x) - u^*(x)]\,]$$

where the term $E(\cdot)$ brings about the possible reduction which the 'inequality averse' judgement of the ethical decision-maker can cause to the utility relative to a specific outcome.

A local utility function might be constructed, according to the approach proposed by Machina.[21] Starting from a linear function, if a given

[21] 'Even though an individual with a smooth preference functional will not necessarily satisfy the independence axiom and possess no "global" von Neumann–Morgenstern utility function, we see that there will exist a "local utility function" ' (Machina 1983: 221. See also Machina 1982: 293–5).

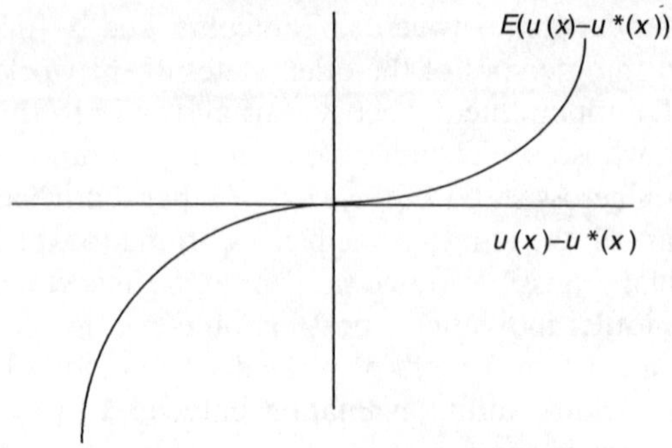

FIG. 11.3

consequence of a prospect is expected with certainty, it will be at the inflexion point of the local utility function. Under the hypothesis that $0 < E[u(x) - u^*(x)] < 1$ for all $u(x) - u^*(x)$, the term $E(\cdot)$—as represented in Fig. 11.3—will be concave if the ethical decision-maker expresses a negative judgement on the degree of equity of a consequence—i.e. if $u(x) - u^*(x)$ is negative—and will instead be convex in the opposite case (see Sugden 1986: 11–16).

In each prospect of individual utilities, the ethical decision-maker determines the value of $E(\cdot)$ for each value lower than the $u^*(x)$ threshold. Since the term $E(\cdot)$ expressing the decision-maker's concern for equity provokes a deviation from linearity in the dimension of states of the world, even though the utility of each position is considered individually (that is, independently of any relationship with the other individual utilities), a substantial diversity of the ordering of social situations with respect to the one resulting from the conventional approach to decision theory results.

The step further in the consideration of a concern for equity which the 'equity function' allows is substantial. The 'inequality averse' decision-maker in the previous section who aggregated the individual utilities by strictly concave functions tends to determine equity-concerned social preferences in which, the lower individual utilities are, the more they count in social welfare. Thus the concern for equity was implemented by considering equity as a feature belonging to society: the strictly concave transformations were overimposed by the ethical decision-maker on the individual utility functions, so that the social judgements influenced by 'inequality aversion' referred the concern for equity to interpersonal distributions as a *whole*. Instead, the ethical decision-maker who expresses social judgements by means of the 'equity function' takes into account the degree of equity of *each* location, so that a concern for equity is embedded in each utility evaluation. It can then be said that an 'individualistic' notion of equity is implemented.

8. Conclusions

Following the proposed application of non-conventional individual choice under uncertainty to the determination of equity-concerned social preferences, some final remarks can be made. I will comment on the three analytical forms by which, in this chapter, attempts to consider a concern for equity in social choice were made.

Equality in distribution

The 'equality example' introduced a concern for equity in social choice by employing the NEUT behaviour in individual decisions under uncertainty. An Allais Paradox-like type of 'complementarity' in the dimension of states of the world characterized by the extreme feature of certainty of a positive outcome has been extended to social choice as 'complementarity' in the dimension of individuals characterized by equality in the interpersonal distribution. In the 'equality example', the compatibility between this extreme concern for equity and Bayesian rationality was not fulfilled due to the absence of 'separability' between the individual utilities of the interpersonal distributions. The 'separability' condition as for interpersonal distributions needs be met because it corresponds to the Pareto principle. Therefore, unless individualism is abandoned, the concern for equity cannot be represented by this extreme version of equity and no special value should be given in social choice to the feature of equality among individuals as for the utility distribution.

Inequality aversion

The NEUT approach to social choice was then introduced, in which 'complementarity' between states of the world was regarded as impinging on the ordering of social states, so that social preferences are determined by a non-linear aggregation of individual utilities. According to the 'common consequence effect' type of violation of the independence axiom, each value of the common consequence makes in one situation the prospects of the individuals 'stochastically dominant' with respect to those of the other situation. As in Diamond's example, 'complementarity' occurs in the dimension of states of the world but the independence axiom's violation—instead of being due to the unfairness attributed to risk allocation among individuals—derives from stochastic dominance created by 'better' common consequence in one situation (with respect to that of the other situation). This induces the decision-maker to preference reversal, that is, to become 'inequality averse'. However, the result that the most equitable interpersonal distribution turns out as the socially preferred one proves to be unsatisfactory, because it does occur in the 'low inequality' case but it does not in the 'high inequality' one. In other words, preference reversal does not establish a general tendency in the ethical decision-maker to equity-oriented social preferences. Therefore, this attempt to obtain equity-oriented social preferences by employing individual behaviour predicted by NEUT—where 'separability' is violated only in the dimension of states of the world, so that the Pareto principle is respected—cannot be relied upon because the moral principle of concern for equity gets a counter-intuitive implementation.

In order to determine equity-concerned social preferences, the hypothesis of a moral attitude of the decision-maker towards 'inequality aversion' might be substituted to preference reversal. Since the utility evaluation of the random prospects displaying the expected values of the individuals satisfies the 'separability' condition, social choice happens to be compatible not only with one of the individual behaviours predicted by NEUT but also with the EUT axioms. A formal representation of a concern for equity as 'inequality aversion' is the transformation of individual utility functions by means of strictly concave functions. Yet, 'risk averse' behaviour without preference reversal is not confirmed by experiments.

However, on the theoretical ground one must take into account that the utilitarian approach to social choice proposed by Harsanyi considers illegitimate this move. In the Impartial Observer model, the rationale by which the ethical decision-maker—from the vN–M representation of personal preferences—should derive linear combination as the functional form of the aggregation of individual utilities, is centred on the 'principle of acceptance'.[22] The Impartial Observer must be sympathetic with individuals' psychology without retaining—in evaluating the individuals' random prospects—his own attitude towards the dispersion of utility values. Would the decision-maker's attitude towards inequality influence the social preferences, the social choice would be biased.

In Harsanyi's opinion, 'the utility of any possible money income is measured by the decision maker's von Neumann–Morgenstern utility function, which already makes appropriate allowance for his attitude toward risk' (see Harsanyi 1976: 73). 'It is quite *unnecessary* and, indeed, it is *morally inadmissible*, to make the social welfare function itself non-linear in the individual utilities—just as it is unnecessary and inadmissible to make the utility of a lottery ticket non-linear in the possible utility outcomes' (see Harsanyi 1976: 77). Since in the Impartial Observer model the individuals' attitude towards the risk inherent to the allocation of money values inside the prospects was already expressed in the personal preferences, any further evaluation of the same risk by an ethical decision-maker would be 'double-counting'. Since the individuals' attitude—vN–M representations of personal implicit in the preferences—is 'inequality neutrality', social preferences

[22] 'The interests of each individual must be defined fundamentally in terms of his *own* personal preferences and not in terms of what somebody else thinks is "good for him" ' (Harsanyi 1977*a*: 52).

should not be biased by the aggregation of the individual utility functions which an 'inequality averse' Impartial Observer performs by means of strictly concave transformations.

It has also been observed that the identification of interpersonal distributions with the (probability weighted) intrapersonal sum of utility indexes across states of the world suggests that a correspondence should be preserved between the two aggregation rules. The value attributed to the utility values in weighing across the dimension of individuals, i.e. in the evaluation of social welfare, should not diverge from the quantities which express preferences in weighing across the dimension of states of the world, i.e. in the evaluation of random prospects.[23] This argument gives support to Harsanyi's theoretical position to the extent that 'equal treatment'—the utilitarian decision-maker's moral principle which combines with the linearity of the social welfare function—is the sole moral principle which fits with the functional form expressing the individuals' personal preferences.

However, section 3 stressed that Harsanyi does not succeed in bridging the gap between the rationality requirement that the Impartial Observer has to comply with the EUT axioms and the utilitarian tenet that linear combination is the only possible aggregation rule of individual utilities. If analytical reasons were given for the linearity of personal preferences, the 'additive separability' condition might offer a reason for the 'impartial' decision-maker to adopt linear combination as the aggregation rule of individual utilities. In fact, this condition could be used to extend linear combination from the addition of possible outcomes across states of the world to the addition of the individual utilities, as the above-mentioned argument suggests. Yet a reason for linearity as the sole aggregation rule to be used by the ethical decision-maker was not provided, as linearity is just an assumption deriving from the arbitrary choice of vN–M representations for the personal preferences.

Therefore, in so far as equity is conceived as a feature belonging to society as a *whole*, no moral principle—'equal treatment' or 'inequality aversion'—stands out as the sole one an ethical decision-maker should consider: to different attitudes towards inequality will correspond different functional forms to aggregate the individual utilities, and eventually different moral principles will be implemented in the ordering of social situations.

The equity function

The connection between decision theory under uncertainty and social choice has finally been pursued by formalizing the concern for equity similarly to

[23] 'The very same functions [in the Addition Theorem] give the weights in weighing across two different dimensions. This very much strengthens the claim that they determine the meaning of quantities, of good. A distinction between quantities of good and how much those quantities count now seems very empty' (Broome 1991: 217).

the NEUT research line relative to utility functions characterized by 'disappointment aversion'. The 'modified' utility function—named the 'equity function'—was presented, by which the ethical decision-maker avoids social situations in which individual dignity is not respected in single locations. The ethical decision-maker selects the sum of individual utilities modified by the evaluation of the degree of equity in each location as the interpersonal distribution to be socially preferred.

In the analytical expression of a concern for equity as previously discussed, the decision-maker manipulated the individual utility functions by transforming them by means of strictly concave functions. The ordering of social situations then derives from a judgement in terms of 'inequality aversion' concerning the whole interpersonal distributions. Although strictly concave transformations allow one individual's welfare to be determined independently from other individuals' welfare, his welfare is considered directly as part of a more or less equitable interpersonal distribution in the ethical decision-maker's social choice.

On the contrary, with the 'equity function' individual utilities are formed by utility evaluations of each location depending on a measure of the degree of equity. Thus, the notion of equity incorporated in the ethical decision-maker's social preferences is not related to the society as a whole but is truly 'individualistic'.

I conclude by arguing that equity-concerned social judgements stemming from a functional form where equity applies to the individual's locations should be clearly distinguished from equity-concerned social judgements stemming from a functional form where equity applies to the society as a whole. Public policies might be plagued by less inefficiencies were they pursued by referring a concern for equity to individual welfare instead of conceiving equity as a property of the whole interpersonal distribution.

REFERENCES

Allais, M. (1953), 'Le Comportement de l'homme rationnel devant le risque: Critique des postulates et axiomes de l'Ecole Americaine', *Econometrica*, 21: 503–46.

Atkinson, A. B. (1970), 'On the Measurement of Inequality', *Journal of Economic Theory*, 2: 244–63.

Broome, J. (1991), *Weighing Goods: Equality, Uncertainty and Time* (Oxford: Basil Blackwell).

Debreu, G. (1959), 'Topological Methods in Cardinal Utility', in K. Arrow, S. Karlin, and P. Suppes (eds.), *Mathematical Methods in the Social Sciences* (Stanford, Calif.: Stanford University Press).

Diamond, P. A. (1967), 'Cardinal Welfare, Individualistic Ethics and Interpersonal Comparisons of Utility: Comment', *Journal of Political Economy*, 75: 765–6.

Fishburn, P. C. (1988), *Nonlinear Preference and Utility Theory* (Brighton: Wheatsheaf).
Gorman, W. M. (1968), 'The Structure of Utility Functions', *Review of Economic Studies*, 35: 367–90.
Gul, F. (1991), 'A Theory of Disappointment Aversion', *Econometrica*, 59: 667–86.
Hare, R. M. (1961), *The Language of Morals* (Oxford: Clarendon Press; 1st edn., 1952).
Harsanyi, J. C. (1953), 'Cardinal Utility in Welfare Economics and in Risk-taking', *Journal of Political Economy*, 61: 434–5.
—— (1955), 'Cardinal Welfare, Individualistic Ethics and Interpersonal Comparison of Utility', *Journal of Political Economy*, 63: 309–21.
—— (1976), 'Nonlinear Social Welfare Functions: Do Welfare Economics have a Special Exemption from Bayesian Rationality?', in J. C. Harsanyi (ed.), *Essays on Ethics, Social Behavior and Scientific Explanation* (Dordrecht: Reidel).
—— (1977*a*), *Rational Behavior and Bargaining Equilibrium in Games and Social Situations* (Cambridge: Cambridge University Press).
—— (1977*b*) 'Nonlinear Social Welfare Functions: A Rejoinder to Professor Sen', in R. Butts and J. Hintikka (eds.), *Foundational Problems in the Special Sciences* (Dordercht: Reidel).
—— (1979), 'Bayesian Decision Theory, Rule Utilitarianism and Arrow's Impossibility Theorem', *Theory and Decision*, 12: 289–317.
Kahneman, D., and Tversky, A. (1979), 'Prospect Theory: An Analysis of Decision Under Risk', *Econometrica*, 47: 263–91.
Loomes, G., and Sugden, R. (1982), 'Regret Theory: An Alternative Theory of Rational Choice under Uncertainty', *Economic Journal*, 92: 805–24.
—— and—— (1986), 'Disappointment and Dynamic Consistency in Choice under Uncertainty', *Review of Economic Studies*, 53: 271–82.
Machina, M. (1982), 'Expected Utility Analysis without the Independence Axiom', *Econometrica*, 50: 277–323.
—— (1983), 'Generalized Expected Utility Analysis and the Nature of Observed Violations of the Independence Axiom', in B. P. Stigum and F. Westop (eds.), *Foundations of Utility and Risk Theory with Applications* (Dordrecht: Reidel).
—— (1987), 'Choice Under Uncertainty: Problems Solved and Unsolved', *Journal of Economic Perspectives*, 1: 124–54.
Mongin, P. (1991), 'Harsanyi's Aggregation Theorem: Multi-Profile Version and Unsettled Questions' (CORE Discussion Paper No. 9136, Université Catholique de Louvain).
Samuelson, P. A. (1952), 'Probability, Utility and the Independence Axiom', *Econometrica*, 20: 670–8.
Savage, L. J. (1954), *The Foundations of Statistics* (New York: Wiley).
Sen, A. (1970), *Collective Choice and Social Welfare* (San Francisco: Holden-Day).
—— (1977*a*), 'Welfare Inequalities and Rawlsian axiomatics', *Theory and Decision*, 7 (1976); reprinted in R. Butts and J. Hintikka (eds.), *Foundational Problems in the Special Sciences* (Dordrecht: Reidel).
—— (1977*b*), 'Non-linear Social Welfare Functions: A Reply to Professor Harsanyi', in R. Butts and J. Hintikka (eds.), *Foundational Problems in the Special Sciences* (Dordrecht: Reidel).
—— (1986), 'Social Choice Theory', in K. J. Arrow and M. D. Intrilligator (eds.), *Handbook of Mathematical Economics*, iii (Amsterdam: Elsevier).

Sugden, R. (1986), 'New Developments in the Theory of Choice Under Uncertainty', *Bulletin of Economic Research*, 3: 1–24.

Tversky, A., and Kahneman, D. (1986), *Rational Choice and the Framing of Decisions, Journal of Business*, 59: 251–78.

Von Neumann, J., and Morgenstern, O. (3rd edn., 1953), *Theory of Games and Economic Behaviour* (Princeton: Princeton University Press).

Weimark, J. A. (1991), 'A Reconsideration of the Harsanyi–Sen Debate on Utilitarianism', in J. Elster and J. E. Roemer (eds.), *Interpersonal Comparisons of Well-Being* (Cambridge: Cambridge University Press).

12

Commitment and Choice: An Essay on the Rationality of Plans[1]

DAVID GAUTHIER

1

Human beings are planning animals. In his recent book, *Intentions, Plans, and Practical Reason*, Michael Bratman (1987: 2–3) explains plans as arising from 'two very general needs. . . . we need ways for deliberation and rational reflection to influence action beyond the present; and we need sources of support for co-ordination, both intrapersonal and interpersonal. Our capacities as planners help us meet these needs.' Another recent writer, Allan Gibbard (1990: 57) relates plans to the human capacity to be moved by words. 'Humans plan together; they make agreements, they exhort. Their language facilitates both complex co-ordination among individuals and complex individual plans—and if words lacked all power to move us, none of this would be possible.' Gibbard speaks of this motivation as normative—'motivation of a particular, linguistically infused kind . . . that evolved because of the advantages of coordination and planning through language' (Gibbard 1990: 57).

1.1

Plans enter into our motivation. How do they do this? We might first suggest that the adoption of a plan provides an agent with reasons that bear on his subsequent decisions—that an action would conform with an adopted plan provides a reason for its performance, that an action would conflict with such a plan provides a reason against its performance. As a

[1] This chapter offers a preliminary account of part of a theory of rational commitment. Discussion at the 'Ethics and Economics' workshop, at a meeting of the Society for Ethical and Legal Philosophy, and at a meeting of the faculty colloquium in my Department, has been especially valuable in helping me to identify many of the problems and issues that must be resolved, as I seek to build from this essay to the full theory.

first approximation, this is I think correct, but only because it leaves unresolved all controversial issues about the way in which plans govern one's actions.

From the standpoint of the economist, it is natural to think of a person's reasons for acting as determined by his preferences over the expected outcomes of his possible actions. I shall refine this standpoint presently, but again as a first approximation, and taken very loosely and blandly, I think it correct. Suppose then that we ask how the view that plans provide reasons for subsequent actions relates to the thesis that these reasons are determined by the agent's preferences. We might initially suppose that a plan provides reasons by inducing preferences favouring the outcomes of actions conforming to the plan over the outcomes of actions conflicting with the plan.

There is a problem with this suggestion, which Bratman identifies as the bootstrapping problem (see Bratman 1987: 24 ff.). Most of us do not plan merely for the joy of planning. And most of us do not execute our plans because of a direct desire to follow them. Planning is instrumental to the attainment of our objectives, not an objective itself. We plan to avoid deliberating from scratch on each occasion of choice. And we plan to ensure the effective co-ordination of our actions, both for the efficient realization of our own varied objectives, and for the fuller realization of those objectives through interaction with others. We plan on the basis of our existing preferences for outcomes; in planning, we schedule our actions so that they may best bring about those outcomes that we prefer. We do not, or at least need not, acquire new preferences as a result of planning. It would therefore seem that typically our reasons for acting should be unaffected by the adoption of a plan.

To suppose otherwise would be to give undue weight to the outcome of the plan in relation to other outcomes we might bring about. Suppose that on the basis of my existing preferences, I plan to spend tomorrow morning working in my office and tomorrow afternoon running various errands. Then I learn that one of my colleagues, with whom I need to discuss certain matters, will be at her office adjacent to mine in the afternoon but not in the morning. It is not urgent that I talk with her tomorrow, but it would be convenient, and I now have a slight preference, *ceteris paribus*, for running errands in the morning and being in my office in the afternoon. However, if in adopting my plan I have acquired a preference for carrying it out, then this may mean that my overall preference is still to be in my office in the morning and run errands in the afternoon. My plan has, as it were, acquired a weight of its own in the preferences that enter into my subsequent choices. And this seems wrong, given that I am not a plan-fetishist, and take planning to have a purely instrumental role in my activities. Bratman's remedy, with which I am in substantial agreement, is to treat plans as constraining the range of actions available for choice (see Bratman 1987: 32 ff.). This constraint is not inflexible; he recognizes that circumstances may justify reconsideration, in which actions compatible with a plan are not privileged over those incompatible. But as long as an agent, having adopted a plan, does not reconsider, he restricts subsequent deliberation to those of his possible actions compatible with the plan. In deliberating among those actions the agent considers his preferences for their possible outcomes; to this extent his reasons for acting remain as before. But he does not consider his preferences for the possible outcomes of actions incompatible with the plan, and so in the context of his plan not all of his preferences give rise to reasons relevant to his deliberation. Thus having adopted the plan of being in my office tomorrow morning and running errands in the afternoon, in my subsequent deliberation I consider only options compatible with this plan. However, when I learn that my colleague will be in her office only in the afternoon, I reconsider my plan, and in reconsidering it not only do I no longer restrict consideration to those actions compatible with it, but I give no additional weight to those actions, or to their outcomes, because they fit my initial plan, but rather evaluate all available actions in relation to my current direct preferences for their outcomes.

1.2

Now it is of course necessary to lay down conditions for rational reconsideration. Presumably—and again I am following Bratman (1987: 67)—these conditions will typically involve awareness of changes, whether in the circumstances in which I am acting, the possible outcomes I might realize, or the preferences I seek to fulfil. An irresolute planner is one who reconsiders without such awareness; irresolution undermines the effective realization of the benefits that planning affords, whether in avoiding repeatedly deliberating from scratch, or in bringing about intrapersonal and interpersonal co-ordination. But what changes justify reconsideration? Or to put matters the other way round, what limits an agent's *commitment* to his plan?

To approach this question, let us return to considering reasons for acting. A person's reasons for acting are a function of his preferences over the expected outcomes of his possible actions. But not all of these reasons are on a par. One might suppose in the light of what I have said so far that we might classify reasons as preference based or plan based. A reason for an action is directly preference based when it favours that action in the light of a preference for its outcome or one of its possible outcomes. I shall say more about such reasons shortly. Among the actions open to an agent may be the adoption of a plan; an agent may therefore have a directly preference-based reason for doing so. Also among the actions open to an agent may be the reconsideration of a plan, and again an agent may have a directly preference-based reason for doing so. A reason for an action is plan based when it favours that action as compatible with the agent's plans. An agent will take himself to have such a reason whenever he has adopted and not reconsidered a plan, and we might suppose that his reason is genuine just in case he had adequate preference-based reasons for adopting and not reconsidering the plan.

But this supposition would be in several ways too restrictive. First of all, it ignores the possibility that a plan may be embedded in a further plan or in a policy; a fuller treatment than I can offer here would set out the somewhat involved but, I think, in principle unproblematic reformulation of the view required to accommodate it. Second, an agent may have a genuine plan-based reason for an action even though he lacked adequate directly preference-based reasons for adopting the plan; I shall show this in a moment.

Third, and most important, an agent may have a genuine plan-based reason for an action even though his directly preference-based reasons favour reconsidering the plan; this I shall also show. Indeed, I shall claim that an agent may have such a reason even though he *knows* his preference-based reasons favour reconsideration. This is the principal thesis I want to defend, and it will lead me to oppose a central thesis of the prevailing orthodoxy about economic rationality. For I want to argue that an agent's commitment to a plan may rationally *override* preference-based reasons that in themselves would adequately support an action incompatible with the plan. Or in other words, rational commitment to a plan may require counter-preferential choice. I shall return to this claim shortly, since it is central to my account of rational planning.

That one may have not only a plan-based reason, but sufficient plan-based reasons to restrict one's choice to actions compatible with a mistakenly chosen plan, may initially appear implausible, but in fact is quite straightforward. Clearly one's reasons for acting must be related to what one has previously done, in so far as what one has done affects both what one is now in a position to do and what one's pay-offs from one's possible actions will be. Now suppose that an agent has adopted an ill-considered plan. Even if she has not begun to implement it, and even if, were she to reconsider, she would do best to adopt an alternative plan, she may lack adequate preference-based reasons for reconsidering it, since the expected cost of reconsideration may outweigh any expected increase in benefits from an alternative plan. And of course if she has begun to implement her plan, then it may be the case that not only does she lack adequate reason to reconsider it, but that, if she were to reconsider it, she would have adequate preference-based reasons to reaffirm it. For example, suppose I have adopted a plan that involves meeting you in my office tomorrow, and in the light of my plan have arranged the meeting with you. Even if I now realize that it was foolish of me to adopt such a plan, and that in particular I should have done better not to arrange the meeting, it may well be the case that, given the costs of failing to show up, I do best now to reaffirm the plan.

Reconsideration raises a more complex problem. For it may be the case not only that, were I to reconsider my plan, I would abandon or alter it, but also that I have sufficient preference-based reasons to reconsider my plan, and yet I am quite reasonably unaware of this. And if this is the case, then it seems that I may reasonably take myself to have adequate plan-based reasons to restrict my deliberations to actions compatible with my plan, although I do not really have such reasons. But can this be right? If my unawareness is reasonable, then it is reasonable of me to ignore actions incompatible with my plan, and so surely I have genuine plan-based reasons to ignore them.

Without pursuing the matter in detail, I want to endorse this last suggestion. If I have adopted a plan and am reasonably not reconsidering it, then I have plan-based reasons for restricting my deliberation to actions compatible with my plan. In discussing reasons for acting, we should distinguish the subjective perspective of the agent from an ideal, objective perspective, and we should further distinguish between reasonable and unreasonable subjective perspectives. The agent's subjective perspective reflects his beliefs—about circumstances, possible actions, possible outcomes, and their probabilities in relation to his possible actions. I suggest that the agent's subjective perspective determines what he takes to be reasons for acting, and that if his perspective is itself reasonable, then it determines what are his reasons for acting. The objective perspective reflects the agent's actual circumstances, possible actions, and their outcomes; it determines what the agent's reasons would be, were he to be fully and truly informed on these matters. Henceforth I shall ignore problems created by this multiplicity of perspectives, except where they are directly relevant to my argument.

2

In section 3 I shall argue that an agent may have a genuine plan- based reason for an action even though he knows that his directly preference-based reasons favour reconsidering the plan. I shall attempt to show that a full appreciation of the role that plans play in deliberation requires revisions in the orthodox view of economic rationality. But, before I do this, it may be useful to rehearse certain crucial features of the orthodox view, as they bear on planning. I have said that from the standpoint of the economist, a person's reasons for acting are determined by his preferences over the expected outcomes of his possible actions. But the economist has a more precise view of this, which may be expressed in the thesis that human beings are maximizing animals. An agent's reasons for an action are adequate just in case he prefers the expected outcome of that action no less than the expected outcome of any of its alternatives. The expected outcome of an action is the probability-weighted sum of the possible outcomes of the action. On the usual account, which I shall not question, an agent's preferences over outcomes may be represented by an interval measure such that his preference for the expected outcome of an action is represented by the sum of his probability-weighted preferences for its possible outcomes. This interval measure, termed utility, then provides a perspicuous representation of the agent's reasons for acting. Each possible action may be associated with a number, representing the expected utility of its outcome, such that the larger the number, the more preferred the outcome. An agent has adequate preference-based reasons for an action if the expected utility of its outcome is at least as great as the expected utility of the outcome of any alternative action. This is the upshot of the thesis that human beings are maximizing animals.

2.1

How does this thesis apply to rational planning? Two possibilities may suggest themselves. The first is to suppose that an agent has adequate reasons for adopting a plan if at the time of adoption the expected utility of (the outcome of) carrying it out is at least as great as the expected utility of carrying out any alternative plan, and that an agent has adequate reasons for conforming to an adopted plan if at the time of execution the expected utility of (the outcome of) conforming to it is at least as great as the expected utility of any non-conforming behaviour. On this view an agent may have adequate reasons for adopting a plan despite the fact that he neither will have nor expects that he will have adequate reasons for conforming to it. To illustrate this, consider the familiar example of Ulysses and the Sirens, interpreting it in such a way that the effect of the Sirens is not to make Ulysses incapable of exercising his reason, but rather to alter his desires so that his preferred outcome is to approach them. Given this interpretation, and given also the orthodox view of rationality, it is rational for Ulysses to steer for the Sirens, once he has heard them singing. Suppose then that Ulysses embarks on his voyage past the rocks of the Sirens with the plan of sailing straight to Ithaca; given his preferences at the time of embarkation, he believes that carrying out this plan will afford him greater utility than carrying out any alternative. But when he hears the Sirens singing his preferences will change, and he will then lack adequate reasons for conforming to his plan, since he will expect greater utility from not conforming to it, and remaining with the Sirens, than from sailing straight home. And since the effects of the Sirens are well known, Ulysses believes on embarkation that his preferences will change, so that he does not expect that, on hearing them sing, he will have adequate reasons to conform to his plan.

This view insulates an agent's reasons for adopting a plan from his reasons for executing or conforming to it. He considers it rational to adopt a plan if it best meets his current preferences, whether or not executing it will best meet his preferences as they will be at the time that he puts it into effect. In discussions of dynamic choice, such an agent is characterized as myopic. As has frequently been noted, if Ulysses is myopic, he will fail dismally to fulfil his initial preferences, since he will take no forethought for what he will judge himself to have reason to do when he hears the Sirens; adopting the plan of sailing straight home to Ithaca, he will in fact, when he hears the Sirens sing, steer towards them.

Consider then a second view. Aware that he will conform to a plan only if, at the time that conformity is called for, he prefers the outcome of executing it to that of any alternative behaviour, an agent rejects a plan as infeasible if it would require him at any point to choose an action whose outcome he anticipates he would then disprefer to that of some alternative. Thus an agent has adequate reasons for adopting a plan if he considers it feasible, and if at the time of adoption the expected utility of (the outcome of) carrying it out is at least as great as the expected utility of carrying out any alternative feasible plan. Instead of insulating his reasons for adopting a plan from his reasons for executing or conforming to it, an agent seeks to ensure that any plan he adopts is such that he expects to have adequate reasons for executing it. Thus Ulysses, aware of the effect of hearing the Sirens sing, embarks on his voyage with the plan of sailing straight to Ithaca, and of stopping up the ears of his sailors and binding himself to the mast when he nears the Sirens, so that he will be unable to deviate, and his crew will have no reason to deviate, from his present course. Given his current preferences, he has adequate reason to execute that part of his plan that requires constraining his crew and himself, so that, when his preferences are changed, he will be unable to act on his new preferences and deviate from his plan. In contrast with the myopic Ulysses of the preceding paragraphs, this Ulysses is identified by students of dynamic choice as sophisticated. And his sophistication is expressed by his ability to plan effectively so that he fulfils his initial preferences, those he has at the time of planning, albeit at the cost of being bound to the mast—a cost to which I shall return.

Both myopic and sophisticated Ulysses take their reasons for acting from their preferences over outcomes. And both do so in a maximizing way; each chooses to act in a way that he believes will maximize his expected utility. But in so choosing, myopic Ulysses in effect assumes—even if in some sense he knows otherwise—that he will continue to take his reasons for acting from his present preferences, whereas sophisticated Ulysses recognizes that in future he will take his reasons for acting from the preferences he will then have. Neither gives his future preferences weight in his present deliberation—that is, neither takes them as reasons for acting, but sophisticated

Ulysses recognizes, as his myopic counterpart does not, the impact his future preferences will have as providing future reasons for acting.

2.2

I have illustrated the difference between myopic and sophisticated choice in terms of a situation in which the agent's preferences change. But we may also consider situations involving no such change. Suppose that M. Leblanc supplies widgets which Mme Lenoir consumes in large quantities. Knowing that her business is important to Leblanc, Mme Lenoir tells him that she will purchase her widgets elsewhere unless Leblanc discounts the unit price to her by 10 per cent. Suppose that she knows that if she takes her business elsewhere, she will have to pay more than Leblanc's present price for widgets—say 5 per cent more. But she believes, let us suppose reasonably, that he will very likely give in to her demand, but that he would very likely refuse to give her a larger discount. So she calculates that demanding a 10 per cent discount is her best course of action as it minimizes her expected layout for widgets (which we may assume is in this case to maximize her expected utility).

So far, so good. But what if Mme Lenoir demands a 10 per cent discount and Leblanc resists? At that point it will be costly to her to make good her threat to take her business elsewhere. Let us suppose that there are no compensating advantages to making her threat good, such as significant reputation effects. Now if she is a myopic chooser, this will be of no concern to her in making her demand. She will not look beyond the expected pay-offs from her present options; in particular, she will not consider whether they conditionally commit her to actions that she would not have adequate reason to perform. She will simply go ahead and demand her discount. But if she is a sophisticated chooser, and looks ahead, then she will realize that she will not have adequate reason to carry out her threat should Leblanc refuse her demand. Her reasons for making the demand are not reasons for carrying out the threat it contains—not because her preferences change but because the expected outcome of making the demand bears quite differently on her preferences than the expected outcome of carrying out the threat. As a sophisticated chooser she recognizes that planning to take her business elsewhere should her demand for a discount be refused is an infeasible course of action. She may of course make the demand anyway, but if she does, the threat implicit in her demand is simply a bluff. Ulysses could *say* to his mariners, 'We'll ignore the Sirens and sail straight home to Ithaca', but if he is sophisticated and not myopic, his saying this, in the absence of effective precautions against changing course, would be mere bluff; he would know that they would not do it. Similarly Mme Lenoir could say, 'If you don't discount the unit price by 10 per cent I'll take my business elsewhere', but unless she has some way of making it impossible for herself not to carry out her threat, or some way of changing the pay-offs if she is faced with the option of carrying it out, then what she says is mere bluff; she knows she will not take her business elsewhere.

Now in this example it may seem grandiose to speak of a plan. But the essential feature of a plan, as I understand it, is to predetermine future choices, or at least to constrain the range within which future choices are made. And this is what Mme Lenoir purports to do, in a very minimal way. She purports to predetermine the choice she will make if she finds herself facing Leblanc's refusal to discount his price on widgets. But as a sophisticated chooser she *cannot* do this; she can not predetermine a choice that she knows she will lack adequate reason to make. She can only purport to adopt a minimal plan that she recognizes to be infeasible. As a myopic chooser she can adopt the plan, but of course she will not actually make the choice she believes herself to have predetermined, should she face Leblanc's refusal to discount his price. In this situation, as with Ulysses, the myopic chooser's planning is ineffective.

Reflecting on the differences between our two examples, we might introduce a new character, the semi-sophisticated chooser, who looks ahead, but only in terms of his present preferences. Semi-sophisticated Ulysses would behave like myopic Ulysses, since he would consider sailing straight home to Ithaca feasible given his present preferences, whereas the semi-sophisticated widget purchaser could only bluff, since she would consider taking her business elsewhere infeasible given her present preferences. But semi-sophisticated choice offers nothing of interest to detain us; my concern is to develop a very different alternative.

2.3

Both the myopic and sophisticated interpretations of maximizing choice in dynamic contexts assume that directly maximizing considerations are to be brought to bear on each particular choice. Each choice is to reflect directly the agent's preference-based reasons at the time of choice. A rational agent is never supposed to choose an action—including adopting a plan—if at the time of choice he supposes that some alternative would afford him greater expected utility. This requirement enters in a twofold way into the deliberation of the sophisticated chooser, leading him first to rule out plans as infeasible if they would require him to make choices that, he believes, would at the time of choosing afford him a lesser expectation of utility than some alternative of which he would expect to be aware, and then to select among the remaining feasible plans in a directly utility-maximizing way. It enters only into the direct choices of the myopic chooser, and its failure to affect his deliberation in ruling out plans that he will not choose to execute as infeasible is the source of the ineffectiveness that we have noted in his planning.

This requirement is related to the separability condition discussed by McClennen in *Rationality and Dynamic Choice*. This condition, as he formulates it, assumes that plans are fully determinate; as he says, 'A plan for a decision problem T . . . consists of a complete specification of what choice is to be made at each choice node in T reachable as a result of the implementation of the earlier portions of the plan' (McClennen 1990: 101). Some of these choice nodes may, of course, not be fully determined by the implementation of the plan, but may also depend on probabilistically determined or chance events; for McClennen, a plan must specify a choice for every such node. I have characterized a plan much more loosely, requiring neither that it specify a choice for every possible contingency nor that it specify a unique choice for any contingency, but only that it specify that a choice be made from a proper subset of options for at least some contingency.

Given McClennen's conception of a plan, he then specifies separability as requiring that 'How one is prepared to evaluate the options still available [whether permitted by the plan or not] at some point [i.e. choice node] within the context of . . . choices and chance events already executed . . . should be independent of that context' (McClennen 1990: 123). Now the requirement I have introduced is weaker; it does not require an agent to deliberate as if he had not adopted a plan, which is the real effect of McClennen's separability condition. But what it does require is that if an agent at any time becomes aware of an option—a possible action—that would afford him, at that time, an expected utility greater than that of any option permitted by his plan, then he will have adequate reason to reconsider, and indeed to abandon or modify his plan, and to choose an action with expected utility as great as that of any alternative of which he is aware. The requirement that directly maximizing considerations are to be brought to bear on each particular choice does rule out deliberately counter-preferential choice.

Of course, if an agent does not become aware of a superior option, then he may in fact choose counter-preferentially, but unwittingly. And this does not violate the requirement that directly maximizing considerations are to be brought to bear on each particular choice. Suppose as before that I plan to spend tomorrow morning working in my office and tomorrow afternoon running various errands. And suppose again that one of my colleagues, with whom I need to discuss certain matters, will be at her office adjacent to mine in the afternoon but not in the morning. Suppose further that were I to reconsider my plan, and in so doing to check my colleague's schedule, I would reschedule my own activities. Nevertheless I need have no reason to reconsider my plan, and, if I do not do so, then I will not entertain actions incompatible with it. I will not deliberate as if I had not adopted the plan.

And I will choose to act in a way that in fact does not maximize my expected utility—but of course I will not be, and will have no reason to be, aware of this. I will choose counter-preferentially, but not deliberately or knowingly so. If by chance I were to learn of my colleague's schedule, then I would be aware of an option that would afford me a greater utility than I could expect following my plan, and I would then have adequate reason to reconsider and modify my plan to incorporate this option.

2.4

The idea that directly maximizing considerations are to be brought to bear on each particular choice is related not only to the separability condition on dynamic choice but also to the game-theoretic requirement that equilibria be subgame perfect. In interaction we suppose that each person seeks to maximize his expected utility given the actions of the others, since otherwise he would fail to fulfil his preferences to the fullest extent possible. If each person is successful, then the outcome must be in equilibrium; that is, each person's action must afford him as great a utility as possible given the actions of all of the others. Now in a dynamic context the requirement of subgame perfection extends this demand for equilibrium to each possible interaction node, even those that in fact will not be reached by agents who choose rationally; at each possible point, the actions that would be selected by all of those interacting must be in equilibrium. If we think of an equilibrium outcome as brought about by a set of mutual best responses, then we may say that at each possible point in interaction, the actions that would be chosen by the agents were they to find themselves at that point must be mutual best responses.

I noted at the outset that plans have a role in interpersonal co-ordination. Indeed, we may think of agents as jointly adopting a plan that predetermines actions, or at least restricts choices, for each. Now if we suppose that the agents are sophisticated, so that they consider a plan infeasible if it would require any non-maximizing behaviour, then we may suppose that a joint plan must be, in so far as the agents can determine, subgame perfect; each choice that an agent makes or would make must be, so far as the agent is aware, a best response to the choices being made by the others. Of course, on my account of plans, subgame imperfections may arise quite acceptably when the agents have no reason to be aware of better responses to their expectations of their fellows' behaviour than what their plan permits. They may have no reason to engage in the reconsideration that would bring such better options to light. But the deliberate execution of an option believed to be inferior in terms of the agent's preference-based reasons for acting must be ruled out, and with it the execution of any known inferior responses to the expected behaviour of one's fellows.

3

I want now to introduce my challenge to the view that directly maximizing considerations are to be brought to bear on each particular choice. I want to challenge both the demand for dynamic separability and for subgame perfection in equilibria. The view that requires these is incompatible with the degree of commitment to a plan that makes planning maximally efficacious in co-ordinating one's own actions, and in co-ordinating one's actions with those of others, so that one may best realize one's objectives.

3.1

Let us return to Ulysses. When he hears the Sirens sing his preferences change—he becomes, we might say, a different person, and to keep this difference before us, I shall distinguish prior Ulysses, the man who sets sail for Ithaca, and posterior Ulysses, the man who hears the Sirens sing. If Ulysses is myopic, then posterior Ulysses does just fine; hearing the Sirens, he steers towards them. (Of course, he may not continue to do just fine, but that is another story.) Prior Ulysses, however, ends up in what for him is the worst possible situation. If Ulysses is sophisticated, then prior Ulysses does better, in binding himself to the mast and so preventing his posterior self from approaching the Sirens, and posterior Ulysses of course does worse. From the planning perspective, which is my interest, it is the gain to the planner, prior Ulysses, that counts. But note that, for all his sophistication, prior Ulysses must still face being bound to the mast. He would do better still if he formed the same plan as his myopic self, but *resolutely* carried it out. However it is posterior Ulysses who must carry the plan out, and he may seem to have neither desire nor reason to do so. But is this really so? Even posterior Ulysses can recognize some advantage in carrying out the plan of his prior self and sailing straight on to Ithaca if, as we may plausibly suppose, he prefers doing that to spending his time bound to the mast. Both prior and posterior Ulysses benefit if prior forms the plan of sailing straight home to Ithaca and posterior executes it despite the Sirens' song, rather than if prior, believing that posterior will not execute this plan voluntarily, arranges that he—and so also posterior—be bound to the mast while in the vicinity of the Sirens.

This is old news. And in using the term 'resolute' my intention is to refer to the approach to dynamic choice developed by E. F. McClennen. For McClennen proposes to reject the separability condition, and so the requirement that one deliberates without regard to the context in which one has adopted, and perhaps begun to execute, a plan. McClennen notes that the myopic chooser fails to achieve dynamic consistency; what he adopts is one thing, what he executes quite possibly another. The sophisticated chooser achieves dynamic consistency by constraining his choice among plans in the light of his expectations as to how he will choose among later options; or, as McClennen puts it, 'by regimenting *ex ante* evaluation [of plans] to projected *ex post* independently determined choice [i.e. independently of the plan]' (McClennen 1990: 160). 'The resolute chooser, in contrast, achieves dynamic consistency by regimenting *ex post* choice to his *ex ante* evaluation of plans' (McClennen 1990: 161). But he achieves dynamic consistency 'at the price of a disparity between how the agent would evaluate the *ex post* options were he faced with making the *ex post* choice *de novo* and how he would evaluate them as continuations of plans already evaluated' (McClennen 1990: 161)—or, we might say, already adopted.

The orthodox consider this price unacceptable. But why? Certainly one would not want to propose that a rational planner be inflexibly resolute. I have insisted from the outset that adopting a plan must leave open the possibility of reasonable reconsideration. And certainly it will typically be appropriate to reconsider when one has reason to believe or to suspect that executing a plan would deprive one of the opportunity to bring about a preferred outcome. But must it always be appropriate so to reconsider? Bringing prior and posterior Ulysses back together again, suppose that Ulysses does not consider it appropriate to reconsider his plan of sailing straight to Ithaca even when the Sirens sing to him. Suppose he considers himself committed to his plan despite his changed preferences. Then he can adopt and execute such a plan, and in doing so he will be better off in terms of both his preferences at embarkation, and his preferences on hearing the Sirens, than if he considered it appropriate to reconsider, and would do so given the opportunity. For then, being sophisticated, he would deprive himself of the opportunity by having himself bound to the mast. Ulysses pays a cost for his willingness to reconsider, and he pays this cost both in terms of his original preferences, and in terms of his Siren-induced preferences. Since this cost can be avoided, is it not rational for him to accept standards of reconsideration that enable him to avoid it? Is not the supposed requirement that directly maximizing considerations are to be brought to bear on each particular choice pragmatically unacceptable?

To be sure, it would not be rational for him to accept standards of reconsideration, if the benefits they made possible were offset by increased costs in other circumstances. But without offering a comprehensive treatment, I shall suggest how standards of reconsideration may be specified to permit advantageous planning, without requiring an agent to forgo opportunities that it would be to his overall benefit to seize, or to open himself to exploitation by others who, it might be feared, could prey on his willingness to abide resolutely by his plans.

Reflection on the situations of both Ulysses and Mme Lenoir should enable us to see why a resolute planner adopts and executes plans even though they require him to forgo options that, were they to be presented to him outside the context of his plan, would be adequately supported by his directly preference-based reasons for acting. Why does he take himself to have a plan-based reason for forgoing these options, and indeed one sufficient to override his directly preference-based reasons favouring them? Since his preference-based reasons fully reflect his concern with the possible outcomes of his options, his plan-based reason must be independent of those outcomes, and so of the actual effects of his choice. But it may relate to expectations, whether of other agents or of his prior self, regarding his choice. That prior Ulysses expects his posterior self to have a plan-based reason for sailing straight home to Ithaca sufficient to override his preference-based reasons for approaching the Sirens, gives prior Ulysses reason not to arrange to be bound to the mast—and this benefits his posterior self. That M. Leblanc expects Mme Lenoir to have a plan-based reason for taking her business elsewhere should he not discount his price on widgets despite her preference-based reasons for continuing to give him her business, gives him a reason to agree to reduce his price—and this benefits her. In both cases the agent adopts a plan, not to benefit from executing its last stage, but to benefit from the expectation that he will, or would, execute it.

3.2

Standards for reconsideration should support this expectation. Prior Ulysses must suppose his posterior self will not consider it rational to reconsider on hearing the Sirens, and Leblanc, the widget manufacturer, must suppose that Mme Lenoir would not consider it rational to reconsider were he to refuse her demand. What standards for reconsideration will support resoluteness in these contexts without imposing a costly inflexibility?

Consider first Ulysses. At the time at which he must sail on in the face of his preference-based reasons for changing course, he can see himself as better off than he could have expected to be were he to choose strictly on the basis of his preferences. For if he were, and knew himself to be, someone who reconsidered his plans whenever following them would require overriding his preference-based reasons, then he would have himself bound to the mast. In other words, posterior Ulysses can say to himself as he sails straight for Ithaca, 'I'm better off doing this—despite my preference for approaching the Sirens—than I would have been, had I not been prepared to let my plan override that preference'.

Posterior Ulysses thus relates his situation to what he believes it would have been, were his prior self a sophisticated chooser who considered a plan feasible only if he would not expect it to require him deliberately to forgo an option better supported by his preference-based reasons than any option it allowed. As a resolute chooser, his prior self adopted a plan that committed him to forgoing such an option, in the expectation that the plan would prove more beneficial than any alternative available to a sophisticated chooser. So long as he has no reason to doubt the correctness of this expectation, he has no reason to reconsider.

The benefit that Ulysses receives from not reconsidering his plan is one that frequently arises in situations that require interpersonal co-ordination. Consider an example. Paola is willing to confer some benefit on Lorenzo now, provided she believes that, as a result of benefiting him, he will at some later time confer a reciprocal benefit on her. Even though benefiting Lorenzo may be in itself a cost to Paola, she expects on balance to gain, preferring the outcome of exchanging benefits to the outcome of no exchange. Similarly, we may suppose, Lorenzo also prefers the outcome of exchanging benefits to no exchange. Nevertheless, when the time comes for him to reciprocate, he may have insufficient preference-based reasons to do so since he has already gained his benefit. His choice is between conferring a benefit on Paola and conferring no benefit, and it is possible that in the absence of any expectation of influencing her further behaviour (or that of anyone else) by what he does, he prefers the outcome of not benefiting her. Taken in themselves, his directly preference-based reasons then support not reciprocating. If Paola expects these reasons to be decisive, then she will have no reason to benefit him.

But if Lorenzo plans to reciprocate, and Paola may expect him not to reconsider on the basis of his preference-based reasons, then she will also expect to gain from benefiting him, and will do so. And even though he then reciprocates, he will end up with an outcome that he prefers to what he would have expected, had his view of feasible planning been that of a sophisticated chooser. Like posterior Ulysses he can say to himself, 'I'm better off doing this despite the cost of benefiting Paola than I would have been, had I not been prepared to let my plan override that cost'. In this case, it would of course be more natural to think of Lorenzo as offering Paola the assurance that he would reciprocate, rather than of him forming a plan to reciprocate, but, for him sincerely to assure her, he must be committed to making good on the assurance, and this is in effect to predetermine his future choice in the way that I characterize as resolutely adopting a plan.

3.3

I have quoted McClennen as describing the resolute chooser as one who 'achieves dynamic consistency by regimenting *ex post* choice to his *ex ante* evaluation of plans' (McClennen 1990: 161). But this is not quite what is achieved by the condition on reconsideration that I have proposed. To see this, consider a variant on the story of Ulysses. Suppose that prior Ulysses plans to sail straight home to Ithaca, but posterior Ulysses, hearing the

Sirens, finds not only that he prefers approaching them, but that he would rather be bound to the mast than deliberately refuse to approach them. He rejects the expectation of his prior self that he would prefer the outcome of the resolute plan to what he could have expected were that prior self a sophisticated chooser. And so he does not simply accept his prior self's evaluation of plans but finds that he has reason to reconsider. *Ex post* choice is not regimented to the *ex ante* evaluation of plans, but rather *ex post* choice is constrained by the *ex ante* evaluation of plans, as long as, but only as long as, no reason to question the benefits of the plan presents itself.

McClennen would not, I think, disagree with what I have just said. For he does not suppose that resolute choice is always feasible, and he would allow that it is infeasible for Ulysses to be resolute if his posterior self has nothing to gain from it (see McClennen 1990: 21 ff.). I shall return to McClennen's discussion of feasibility later. But I propose to use 'resolute' somewhat differently than he does, so that when I speak of a resolute planner, I shall intend someone whose commitment to a plan extends to her willingness to execute counter-preferential choices required by the plan as long as, but only as long as, she believes herself better off making these choices than she could have expected to be, had she adopted a plan that did not require them.

Thus I recognize a significant asymmetry between sophisticated and resolute planning. The sophisticated planner is in effect at the mercy of his future selves. He can adopt only those plans that he will have directly preference-based reasons to carry out, no matter how advantageous, either at the time of adoption or overall, other plans might be. But the resolute planner, as I conceive her, does not put her future selves at her mercy. She can not impose plans on them simply because they are advantageous at the time of adoption. The plan must continue to be advantageous, in the sense that following it must make her future selves better off, or at least no worse off, than they would have expected to be had she been a sophisticated chooser. When they allow their plan-based reason to override their preference-based reasons, they must see a benefit in so doing—not of course a benefit in consequential terms, but in, we might say, counterfactual terms. They must see themselves as better off than they would expect to be, were they not plan-based reasoners. Lorenzo sees himself as better off benefiting Paola than he would expect to be, had he been unable to give her a genuine assurance.

3.4

What I have said about rational reconsideration should accommodate Ulysses and Lorenzo. But now consider Mme Lenoir's efforts to get M. Leblanc to discount his price on widgets. She plans to take her business elsewhere should he refuse; this plan, she reasons, affords her the expectation of a more favourable outcome than any alternative that would be feasible for a sophisticated chooser. But suppose that Leblanc does indeed refuse to discount his price. Unlike Ulysses, Mme Lenoir may not say to herself, as she takes her business elsewhere, 'I'm better off doing this—despite my preference for dealing with M. Leblanc—than I would have been, had I not been prepared to let my plan override those preferences'. She expected to be better off because she expected M. Leblanc to capitulate to her threat. But his refusal leaves her worse off, should she continue with her plan, than had she not adopted it in the first place. And so, it seems, she does indeed have reason to reconsider. But if she does, then, since her situation is exactly what she envisaged, in adopting her plan, that it would be should he refuse, she can not have intended, knowingly and seriously, to take her business elsewhere in the first place. She did not predetermine her choice, but only pretended to do so; her 'plan' was mere bluff.

Mme Lenoir, like Lorenzo, adopts a plan that may require her to override her preference-based reasons for acting. But Lorenzo expects and hopes to be in the position in which his plan will require this; he expects and hopes that Paola will benefit him. Mme Lenoir on the other hand neither expects nor hopes to be in the position in which her plan would require her to override her preferences; she hopes and expects that M. Lenoir will accept her demand for a discount. Whereas Lorenzo's plan succeeds if he finds himself required to override his preferences, Mme Lenoir's plan fails if she finds herself required to override hers. And if it is rational not to reconsider a successful plan, but to reconsider a failed one, then it is rational for Lorenzo not to reconsider, but rational for Mme Lenoir to reconsider. But her plan can be genuine only if it is not rational for her to reconsider.

The difference between the two types of plans that I have been discussing may be perspicuously represented by the usual tree-structure diagrams. Lorenzo's situation has the structure shown in Fig. 12.1. Lorenzo is better off if he reaches his choice node whatever he then chooses, than if he does

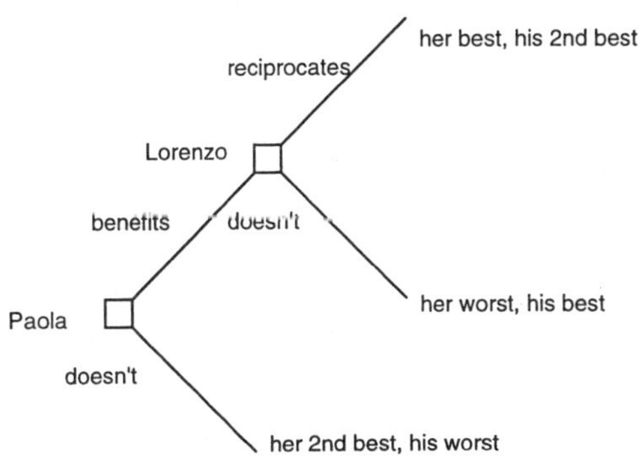

FIG. 12.1 *Lorenzo and Paola*

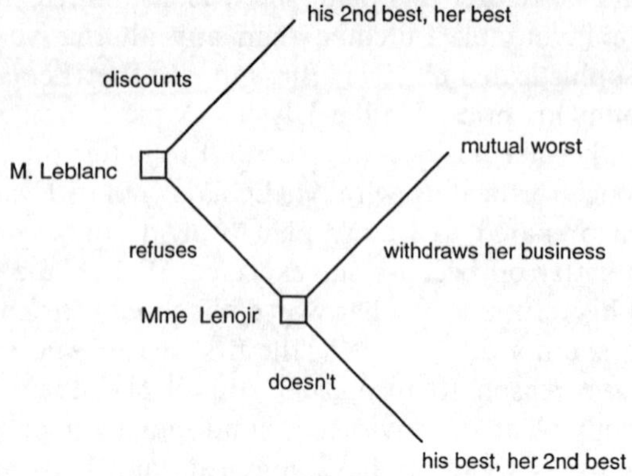

FIG. 12.2 *Mme Lenoir and M. Leblanc*

not. To reach it, he must induce in Paola the expectation that he will choose to reciprocate, which is therefore what he plans to do.

Contrast Mme Lenoir's situation as shown in Fig. 12.2. Mme Lenoir is worse off if she reaches her choice node than if she does not, whatever she then chooses. To avoid it, she must induce in M. Leblanc the expectation that she would choose to withdraw her business, which is therefore what she plans to do. But whereas Lorenzo can appeal to counterfactual benefit in support of his refusal to reconsider his plan and his consequent decision to reciprocate, Mme Lenoir can not.

We might identify a plan similar to Lorenzo's as offering an assurance, in contrast to a plan similar to Mme Lenoir's which contains a threat. (The two correspond to the 'pure promise' and 'pure threat' distinguished by Daniel Klein in formalizing the pioneering work on commitment by Thomas Schelling. See Klein (1991) and Schelling (1960: chs, 2, 5, 7). And we might suppose that I have offered an account of the rationality of honouring assurances, but not of carrying out threats. However, assurances need not be as straightforward as Lorenzo's. Consider the situation, shown in Fig. 12.3.

The parenthesized numbers represent utilities, with Pauline's appearing first. In this situation chance determines whether reciprocating yields a net benefit or a net cost to Lawrence, in comparison with the outcome if neither helps the other. And chance determines this, I have supposed, in such a way that the estimated probability that reciprocating yields him a net benefit is 0.8; the probabilities of the alternative chance results are shown in the figure. Lawrence's initial expectation favours reciprocation; he determines this by calculating its probability-weighted pay-off, which is $(0.8 \times 8) + (0.2 \times 0)$, or 6.4, and comparing it with the pay-off if Pauline does not help him, 5. So assuring her that he will return her help seems on the face of it

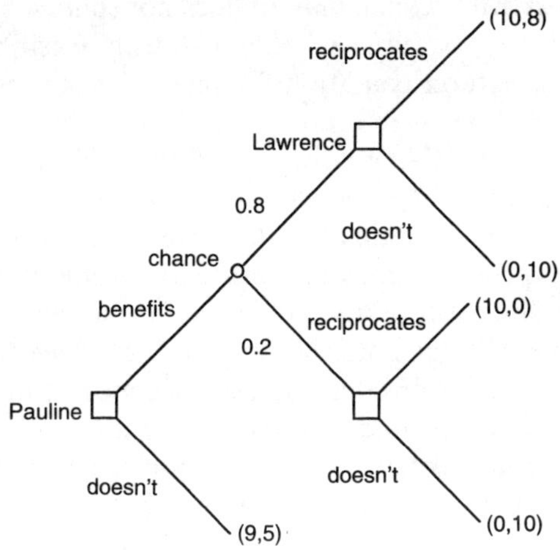

FIG. 12.3 *Laurence and Pauline*

rational. But suppose that he plans to reciprocate but finds himself unlucky; if he carries through with his plan, he will end up with 0. Then he would clearly have been better off not to have planned to reciprocate, and if it is rational for him to reconsider a plan when carrying it out would leave him worse off than had he not made it, or had he made only a plan that would not override his directly preference-based reasons for acting, then he will conclude that he should not honour his assurance. On this account of rational reconsideration, the only plan he could rationally and sincerely adopt would be conditional, calling for him to reciprocate if but only if chance is favourable, so that reciprocating leaves him better off than had Pauline not benefited him. But such an assurance will not suffice to elicit her benefit. For if she calculates her probability weighted pay-off of benefiting Lawrence, given only such a conditional assurance, she finds it to be $(0.8 \times 10) + (0.2 \times 0)$, or 8, which is less than her pay-off if she does not benefit him, 9. Only an unconditional assurance would elicit her help, by giving her an expected pay-off of 10.

3.5

Offering an unconditional assurance is risky for Lawrence. Similarly, threatening to take her business elsewhere is risky for Mme Lenoir. But it does not seem irrational for Lawrence and Mme Lenoir to run these risks. One might then suppose that, contrary to what I have argued, one should simply regiment *ex post* choice to one's *ex ante* evaluation of plans, to use the language of McClennen's characterization of resolute choice. But as I have already noted, McClennen himself does not endorse this regimentation in an unqualified way, or suppose it unqualifiedly feasible, and he appeals to the idea that 'a natural condition for the self being resolute is precisely its becoming aware that there are benefits to both the present self and the future self that will have to be forgone if the self cannot act resolutely' (McClennen 1990: 212). McClennen speaks of this as intrapersonal optimality. But intrapersonal optimality does not seem to be what is at issue. Any plan that uniquely maximizes *ex ante* expectation of benefit is intrapersonally optimal—since it is best for the agent at the time of adoption it can not be Pareto inferior to any alternative. But there need be nothing in such a plan for the later self. Consider Ulysses once more. Since the plan to sail straight home to Ithaca is uniquely best for his prior self, it is intrapersonally optimal, but if his posterior self would prefer being bound to the mast to sailing on (as in the variant of the example that I discussed in 3.3 above), then there is nothing for him in the plan. If there must be 'benefits to both the present self and the future self that will have to be forgone if the self cannot act resolutely', then the plan must be a Pareto improvement on any plan feasible for a sophisticated chooser; it is necessary, but not sufficient, for it to be intrapersonally optimal.

Must we then conclude that Lorenzo, but not Mme Lenoir or Lawrence, can be rationally resolute? Or is it possible that they too may have plans that are Pareto improvements on any alternatives feasible for sophisticated choosers? Suppose that Mme Lenoir's demand for a discount is part of a larger-scale plan, or policy, that she has adopted. I shall not attempt to spell out precisely what this policy might be, but we may assume that in demanding a discount on widgets from M. Leblanc she is simply acting as her policy requires. Now if M. Leblanc were to refuse her demand she need not believe that, should she take her business elsewhere, she would be worse off than if she had not adopted and followed her general policy. She may have received past benefits from her policy that she could not have expected had she not been prepared to carry out the threats that it required her to make, and she may expect future benefits from being prepared to carry out threats in other situations—even though, in the present situation, carrying out her threat is sheer cost, since she does not anticipate any beneficial reputation effects. In this broader context, Mme Lenoir's policy, or general plan, may well be a Pareto improvement on any plan that would be available to her were she sophisticated rather than resolute—a Pareto improvement in that in every choice situation she may reasonably expect that she is or will be better off in virtue of her policy than she would expect to be from any alternative policy. She can not gain the benefit of successful threats without paying the cost of unsuccessful ones, but she need never be in a situation in which the costs outweigh the benefits.

Lawrence, similarly, may have a policy of offering assurances, even in risky situations, that pays him better than any alternative that would not require him to keep a particular assurance if it turns out that he would have been better off not to have made it. He can not gain the benefits from risky assurances without paying the costs when chance goes against him, but if his policy is sound he will always find that the benefits have outweighed, or may be expected to outweigh, the costs.

3.6

A resolute planner does not flinch from overriding her directly preference-based reasons for acting, if her plan requires it and she has no reason to reconsider that plan. I have argued that she has reason to reconsider only if circumstances suggest that, should she continue to execute her plan, she will do worse in terms of fulfilling her current preferences than she would have expected, had she not adopted a plan that required overriding choices. But reason to reconsider need not be reason to abandon her plan. Reconsideration may lead her to recognize that her plan is itself required by some higher-order plan, or policy, that she has no reason to reconsider.

A resolute planner compares her situation with what she would expect, were she a sophisticated planner. She asks herself, 'Could a sophisticated planner expect to do as well?' She is, and remains, resolute only when her answer to that question is negative. When, but only when, she believes that a sophisticated planner would not have done as well, she considers the limitations of sophisticated planning pragmatically unacceptable, and the commitments of resolute planning adequately defended.

Resolute planning requires the rejection of separability as a condition on dynamic choice; in the context of a plan, it may be rational to choose what it would be irrational to choose otherwise. It requires the rejection of subgame perfection as a condition on interaction; maximally effective co-ordination is achieved by agents whose plans are best responses to those of their fellows. Thus even in a one-shot Prisoner's Dilemma, resolute choosers who can exchange credible assurances will plan to co-operate—and the credibility of their assurances will of course be in part dependent on their resoluteness.

What resolute choice reintroduces into the theory of rational planning is the capacity for genuine commitment. I have spoken throughout of an agent's commitment to his plan, but myopic choosers lack any conception of commitment, and sophisticated choosers recognize their inability to commit themselves to act in ways that they may come to recognize as inadequately supported by their directly preference-based reasons. Unable effectively to commit themselves, myopic and sophisticated choosers fail to fulfil their preferences in contexts in which those preferences change, or in which they must co-ordinate with others, as effectively as resolute choosers.

4

I want now to consider several objections to and proposed modifications of the view of rational planning that I have been developing. It might first be claimed that it is impossible for an agent to choose contrary to her conscious considered preferences. Lawrence can not choose to reciprocate Pauline's help, if all things considered he disprefers the outcome of reciprocating to that of not doing so. This claim of impossibility may, it seems to me, be offered on three quite distinct grounds.

The first is psychological. An agent can not choose just anything, even within her physical capacities. I am physically capable of jumping out of the window of my tenth-storey office, but I am psychologically incapable of choosing to do so. And so, it is urged, I am also incapable of choosing an action if I knowingly prefer the outcome of some alternative. Now it seems to me on the contrary that we—all of us—are psychologically perfectly capable of making the various choices and carrying out the various actions that I have been discussing in this paper. But it would be futile to argue or debate this matter in the present context. If the question of choosing against one's direct preferences is a psychological issue, then it must be settled in one of two ways. It may involve an appeal to theory; our best explanatory account of choice behaviour may require interpreting some choices as counter-preferential, or conversely may forbid interpreting any choices in this way. Or our best explanatory account may leave the matter open, while specifying an operational test for counter-preferential choice; then the question is settled by employing the test. These matters we must leave to psychologists. Planning on the basis of resolute choice, as I have characterized it, may not fit our best psychological theories, but so far as I am aware there is no present reason to suppose this.

The second is conceptual. Economists link choice and preference so that an agent's preferences are revealed by her choices. There is no conceptual room, it may be insisted, for commitments that override her directly preference-based grounds for choice. But conceptual arguments of this kind are unconvincing. Of course there must be some link between choice and preference, but such a link is present in my account; particular choices are subsumed into plans that are directed to the fullest possible realization of one's preferred outcomes. To decide whether there is conceptual room for choice to override preference in the way I have supposed is really to decide whether the best explanatory and justificatory accounts of our choice behaviour require such room whether we understand an agent's behaviour better if we interpret her as choosing on the basis of plan-based as well as directly preference-based considerations. To assume from the outset that she can have only one kind of reason for choice is not to acknowledge an independently given conceptual requirement on our understanding of choice behaviour but to impose a conceptual strait-jacket that may prove to distort our understanding.

But, it may be insisted, even if it is both psychologically and conceptually possible for an agent to commit herself so that her plan overrides her preference-based reasons for acting, it is irrational for her to do so; it is impossible for a rational agent to choose counter-preferentially. This claim begs the question, and simply ignores the rationale that I have offered for such choice. Resolute Ulysses does better than sophisticated Ulysses, in terms of both his initial and his Siren-induced preferences. Lorenzo expects to do better if he makes and is willing to carry out a plans that involves counter-preferential choice—to do better in terms of his preferences as he views them both when he adopts the plan and when he executes the plan. And the same is true of Mme Lenoir and Lawrence if we suppose their particular plans embedded in overarching policies.

5

More interesting and important than these objections are what I think of as modifications. These are intended to accommodate plans that on the face of it would require agents to override their preference-based reasons for acting, within the orthodox conception of directly preference-based maximizing rationality. Again I shall examine three possibilities, which I shall label rational irrationality, endogenous preference formation, and moral preference.

5.1

The idea behind rational irrationality is straightforward. It is irrational, its proponent claims, actually to choose in the face of one's directly preference-based reasons. However, it is in some circumstances rational to bring it about that one so chooses. If Lorenzo were rational he would not choose to reciprocate Paola's benefit. Paola, expecting Lorenzo to choose rationally, would then not benefit him. Lorenzo, realizing this, seeks to induce in Paola the expectation that he will choose irrationally to reciprocate, and his best way of doing this may be actually to make himself irrational in the appropriate way—to induce himself to choose to reciprocate, or perhaps to believe that, having formed his plan to reciprocate, he has no further choice to make.

I do not reject the idea of rational irrationality out of hand, but it seems to me utterly inapplicable to the commitments we undertake in planning. There are circumstances in which an agent may rationally choose to put her subsequent behaviour beyond her reasoned control—to make herself impervious to the force, or at least to the normal force, of her reasons for acting. But in committing herself to execute her plan an agent does not put her subsequent choices beyond her reasoned control. She does, of course, bring other reasons to bear on those choices—plan-based reasons. And plan-based reasons do not bear on her choices in the way that preference-based reasons do; her plan provides in effect a filter through which her preferences must pass for them to bear on her subsequent choices. But the filter is itself subject to her reasoned control; as I have insisted, the rational planner has standards for the rational reconsideration of her plans.

Consider—once more—Ulysses. Suppose that on embarkation he expects that his future self would prefer being bound to the mast to voluntarily sailing past the Sirens. In this variant of the situation, if prior Ulysses were to adopt the plan of sailing straight to Ithaca, his posterior self would, on my account, have reason to reconsider—carrying out the plan would not leave him better off than he would have been had his prior self had him bound to the mast. In this case prior Ulysses might, as an alternative to having himself bound, seek to induce his future self into an irrational conformity with the plan of sailing straight to Ithaca. If he had a drug of the type that Schelling and Parfit introduce into their discussions of rational irrationality (see Parfit 1984: 12–13)—one that causes brief temporary irrationality—he might arrange to drink it as his ship approached the Sirens' rocks. Then as he heard them singing he might say, 'I adore the Sirens! I long for them! It kills me to ignore them! So I'll sail straight on.' This would indeed be rationally induced irrationality. But it has nothing to do with resolute planning.

5.2

McClennen, whose pioneering defence of resolute choice has strongly influenced my own thinking, nevertheless conceives it in a way that I think concedes too much to the orthodox. Despite his rejection of separability, he supposes that directly maximizing considerations are to be brought to bear on each particular choice. Thus he insists that the resolute chooser does not in fact override his preference-based reasons for acting, but rather revises 'the preferences he would ordinarily have in the context of certain choice situations', and does this 'from a sense of what would better serve the maximisation of whatever previously specified preferences for outcomes he brings to that kind of decision situation' (McClennen 1990: 214). And so he claims that 'a full argument for the feasibility of resolute choice must make appeal to what can be termed a theory of *endogenous preference changes*. The resolute agent can be interpreted as altering his given preferences in certain situations', and this interpretation is 'to be explained by reference to his commitment to act so as to maximise with respect to his preferences' (McClennen 1990: 215). We might think of the resolute chooser as altering his preferences so that, if he acts to maximize the fulfilment of his altered preferences in his actual choice situation, he will succeed overall in maximizing the fulfilment of his antecedent preferences, although I should note that this is now my formulation and not McClennen's.

But I do not find that endogenous preference change offers a perspicuous interpretation of the behaviour of the rational and resolute planner. I have in the past argued that endogenously formed preferences are simply an explanatory fifth wheel, that they do no useful work. They are thought to be necessary only because of what I consider the mistaken dogma that directly maximizing considerations are to be brought to bear on each particular choice without regard to its context. Although McClennen emphasizes the relevance of context, he nevertheless leaves this dogma intact, and so must make the agent's preferences context dependent. I have argued instead that we should make the agent's reasons context dependent, without supposing any change in his preferences. We can perfectly well understand the particular choices that an agent makes in the course of executing a plan by reference to the maximizing objective of the plan, provided the plan continues to meet that objective throughout its execution. And this objective relates to the agent's exogenously given preferences—given at least for the purposes of his deliberations—and not to any endogenously formed preferences.

But endogenously formed preferences are not merely useless. I argued in 1.1 above that to suppose that plans give rise to preferences is to provide the opportunity for improper and irrational bootstrapping. Suppose that in adopting a plan I come to have a preference for executing it—a preference that carries weight in relation to my other preferences, and that gives me a preference-based reason to act in ways needed to carry the plan through even though, apart from these plan-induced preferences, I would not have adequate preference-based reasons so to act. Then, as I argued, these preferences may lead me to carry out my plan even when the original preferences on which it was originally based have changed, so that in their terms I would do better to abandon the plan. Although these new preferences were formed so that I might better fulfil my original preferences, they have acquired a life of their own, so to speak.

It may of course be replied that these endogenously formed preferences should not be given a life of their own, and that they should remain dependent for their force on the continuation of the original preferences—or, in cases of preference change such as that of Ulysses, dependent on the emergence of the anticipated preferences. But this reply simply reveals the unsatisfactoriness of postulating them. The role they play is quite different from that of the agent's exogenously given preferences, which provide the basis for his planning, and is not adequately represented either by bestowing on them an independent role as preferences, or by making them simply dependent for their force on the agent's given preferences. The distinction between preference-based and plan-based reasons provides, it seems to me, a much more perspicuous interpretation of the agent's choices in the context of planning.

5.3

A third modification invokes ideas of morality. I have included the giving of assurances—as well as the issuing of threats—under the rubric of resolute planning, and one might then suggest that in giving an assurance, one invokes a moral reason, or moral preference, for carrying out the assured action, and this typically outweighs, or should outweigh, whatever contrary reasons one may have. In assuring Paola that he will reciprocate Lorenzo morally binds himself, and if she believes that he takes his obligations seriously, then she will expect him to reciprocate and so will find it advantageous to help him. More generally, it may be urged that the commitment required for effective interpersonal co-ordination depends on an antecedent moral framework. Without this framework agents would be able to carry out plans only if their objectives in planning translated directly into preferences for the outcomes of the actions required by the plan. What morality provides is a set of antecedent preferences that support resolution, commitment, and obligation. Rather than having a plan-based reason for restricting her deliberations to actions compatible with her plan, an agent has a moral reason for maintaining whatever commitments she has undertaken in her plan. And this moral reason either outweighs or overrides the other reasons that reflect her non-moral preferences.

Now I do not want to deny that moral considerations do enter into the honouring of assurances. But no appeal to an antecedent morality is needed to understand Lorenzo's interest in being able to offer Paola an assurance—even if he can do this effectively only if he is genuinely willing to honour the assurance. Resolute planning benefits Lorenzo, or any planner, in realizing his objectives. These objectives may be self-directed or other-directed, prudent or moral or neither; they reflect whatever concerns the planner may happen to have. Each of us needs to be able to co-ordinate his own activities, and to co-ordinate his activities with those of others. Planning enables us to do this, and resolute planning enables us to do this more effectively.

Of course each of us benefits not only from being a resolute planner but also from being able to count on the resoluteness of others. And it is therefore easy to understand how conventions develop, not only for honouring assurances but more generally for adhering to plans adopted to facilitate interpersonal co-ordination. Mutual respect for these conventions takes on moral significance. Resolute planning requires resistance to the direct appeal of preference—resistance, we might say, to temptation—and we may well develop and appeal to our moral feelings to strengthen this resistance. Rather than supposing that effective planning requires an antecedent moral framework, I suggest that our need for planning is one of the factors that brings such a framework into existence. We need to be able to commit ourselves to actions that are not supported by directly preference-based reasons, and we treat our plan-based commitments as moral. We disapprove of our fellows if they fail to honour the commitments that they undertake in co-ordinating their activities with our own, and we feel guilt if we ourselves fail. But these moral attitudes are not simply a given part of our nature to which we can conveniently appeal in order better to co-ordinate with our fellows. Rather their deep rationale—or at least a major part of it—is found in their co-ordinative role.

6

Effective planning requires commitments to choices that are not directly supported by preferences for their outcomes. Taking this as a starting-point leads us to a better understanding of both rationality and morality, as having a pragmatic foundation in the temporal and interpersonal relations that give shape and substance to the lives of human beings as planning animals.

REFERENCES

Bratman, M. E. (1987), *Intention, Plans, and Practical Reason* (Cambridge, Mass.: Harvard University Press).

Gibbard, A. (1990), *Wise Choices, Apt Feelings: A Theory of Normative Judgement* (Cambridge, Mass.: Harvard University Press).

Klein, D. B. (1991), 'A Game-Theoretic Rendering of Promises and Threats', *Irvine Economics Paper*, 90-97-21.

McClennen, E. F. (1990), *Rationality and Dynamic Choice: Foundational Explorations* (Cambridge: Cambridge University Press).

Parfit, D. (1984), *Reasons and Persons* (Oxford: Clarendon Press).

Schelling, T. C. (1960), *A Strategy of Conflict* (Cambridge, Mass.: Harvard University Press).

13

Rational Co-ordination[1]

ROBERT SUGDEN

Suppose that two people, who are unable to communicate with one another, are each asked to write down either 'heads' or 'tails'. If they both write down the same word, they will both win a prize; if they write down different words, they will win nothing. This is an example of a tacit co-ordination game—a class of game discovered by Thomas Schelling (1960: 53–8). People often seem to be remarkably successful at co-ordinating their actions in games of this kind, even when they are playing them for the first time. In this paper, I ask *how* people achieve this success. Is co-ordination the by-product of some kind of non-rational behaviour? Or is it reached by some process of reasoning, and if so, what kind of reasoning is involved? I shall suggest that co-ordination is indeed the product of reasoning, but reasoning of a kind that is not compatible with the conception of rationality that is conventionally used in economics and decision theory. The reasoning involved has some affinity with some familiar forms of moral reasoning. If I am right; then the project of explaining behaviour in tacit co-ordination games may throw light on the relationship between moral reasoning and rational choice.

1 Tacit co-ordination games

Following Schelling, I shall define a tacit co-ordination game (for short, a co-ordination game) as a non-cooperative game in which, whatever combination of strategies is chosen, every player receives the same utility as every other. Thus, the players may be said to have common interests. For simplicity, I shall consider only games with two players. I shall consider only games in which each player makes only one choice between alternative strategies, and in which the two players make their choices simultaneously. The strategic structure of such games can be fully described using the

[1] This chapter was written as part of the Foundations of Rational Choice Theory project, which is supported by the Economic and Social Research Council of the UK (award number R 000 23 2269). The ideas contained in it developed out of discussions with Michael Bacharach, Robin Cubitt, Marco Mariotti, Judith Mehta, Martin Hollis, and Chris Starmer.

normal form of the game. And I shall consider only one-shot games—that is, games that are played once and only once. The question of how co-ordination might be achieved in repeated games is very interesting (see e.g. Sugden 1986, Crawford and Haller 1990), but it is not my concern here. Throughout this chapter, I shall assume that the player's preferences satisfy the axioms of expected utility theory, so that pay-offs can be described using von Neumann–Morgenstern utility indices.

The co-ordination game described in the first paragraph of this paper may be described by the matrix shown in Table 13.1. (In assigning the particular utility indices shown in this table, I am assuming only that each player

TABLE 13.1. Heads and Tails

		Player B	
		heads	*tails*
Player A	*heads*	1,1	0,0
	tails	0,0	1,1

prefers winning the prize to not winning it: no significance attaches to interpersonal comparisons of von Neumann–Morgenstern utility indices.) Using this example, I wish to draw a distinction between the strategic structure of a game and its labelling.

In conventional game theory, solution concepts are defined so that they operate on games that have been described in particular ways. The description of a game that is relevant for the operation of a particular solution concept is the game's strategic structure: any other features of the game are matters of labelling. For simultaneous-move non-cooperative games, the relevant description is usually taken to be the normal form: two games which have a common normal form are treated as identical. For such games, then, the strategic structure is given by the normal form. Game theorists often attach labels to strategies, but these are not part of the strategic structure. Sometimes, labels (such as 'left' and 'right', 'top' and 'bottom') are used merely for the convenience of the game theorist, and are not supposed even to be known to the players themselves. Other labels (such as 'co-operate' and 'defect' in the Prisoner's Dilemma, 'enter' and 'stay out' in the Chain Store Game) refer to features of the game which would presumably be known to the players; but, even so, the analysis of the game is quite independent of these labels. It is of no significance, then, that the classic Prisoner's Dilemma is played between prisoners: any conclusion that can be drawn about the game between the prisoners (for example, that confessing is the dominant strategy for each prisoner, and therefore the uniquely rational choice) would apply to any game with the same strategic structure.

In Heads and Tails, the strategic structure is given by the 2 × 2 matrix of strategies and pay-offs. The words 'heads' and 'tails' which are attached to the strategies are merely labels, and have no strategic significance—even if they are common knowledge between the players. From the viewpoint of conventional analysis, it would make no difference if 'red' and 'green' were substituted for 'heads' and 'tails'. Similarly, it would make no difference if 'heads' and 'tails' were transposed for one player but not for the other (so that the game became one in which the players would be rewarded if their answers were different.)

Even if the labels 'heads' and 'tails' are removed from Table 13.1, the matrix display is in itself a form of labelling. A 2 × 2 matrix has rows and columns: so one player is implicitly the 'row player' and the other is the 'column player'. Of two rows, one is above the other: so the row player's strategies are implicitly labelled 'top' and 'bottom'. Similarly, the column player's strategies are implicitly labelled 'left' and 'right'. These features of the game, like the explicit labels, are generally taken to be outside its strategic structure. If, for example, we redrew the matrix so that the 'tails' row was placed above the 'heads' row, this would make no difference to the analysis of the game.

We may wonder whether it is conceptually possible to remove *all* labelling from a game. In the case of Heads and Tails, the strategic structure is symmetrical between the two players, and, for each player, it is symmetrical between the two strategies. The strategic structure is fully described as follows: 'Each player has to choose one of two strategies. For each strategy which one player might choose, the outcome is either that each player receives a utility of 1 or that each receives a utility of 0; which of these is the case depends on which strategy the other chooses.' Now suppose we tell a player that this is the game he is playing, and tell him to choose one of the two strategies open to him. This would be a meaningless instruction: there is no way that the player could identify one strategy rather than the other as the one he had chosen. It is not merely that he is indifferent between the two strategies, as he might be between two cans of baked beans in a supermarket. If the strategies are not distinguished in *any* way, he cannot even pick at random. If the instruction to choose one of the two strategies is to be meaningful, it must be presented in the form: 'Choose this, or choose that'. And by distinguishing between 'this' and 'that', we have introduced labels.

For a game with the symmetry properties of Heads and Tails, then, it is impossible to remove all labelling. The most we can do is to ensure that labels are private knowledge for individual players: each player knows a set of labels which allow him to distinguish between strategies in the game, but neither player knows anything about the other player's labels. (Crawford and Haller 1990: 573–4, appeal to a similar idea, which they refer to as the lack of a 'common language'.)

To see how this is possible, imagine the following set-up. An experimenter takes four sheets of paper, writes 'heads' on two of them and 'tails' on the other two. She then seals the four messages in identical envelopes. One pair of envelopes, containing one 'heads' message and one 'tails' message, are put in a bag which is then shaken up. The other pair of envelopes are put in another bag, which is also shaken up. Two players are placed in separate rooms. Each is given one of the bags and asked to take out both envelopes and then choose one of them. They will each win a prize if and only if the two envelopes chosen contain the same message. All of this set-up is common knowledge between the players. In this version of Heads and Tails, each player is able to label the two strategies open to her: for example, she might notice the order in which she draws the envelopes out of the bag, and describe her problem to herself as that of choosing between the first envelope and the second envelope. In thinking about the choice problem faced by the other player, she might use the same labels: he too has a first envelope and a second envelope. But whichever envelope ('first' or 'second') she chooses, and whichever one ('first' or 'second') the other player chooses, the probability that the two envelopes contain the same message is 0.5. The labels, then, carry no useful information. If labels are private knowledge, they may help a player to describe a game to herself, but they cannot help her to decide which strategy will give the highest expected utility. Such labels, we may say, have no strategic significance.

If we are to pursue the project of conventional game theory, in which all that matters is the strategic structure of a game, we cannot quite eliminate labelling altogether. But we can say that a game is fully described by its strategic structure and by a system of labelling which is private knowledge. The conventional position, I take it, is that this is the only information that is relevant for the deliberations of rational players. On this view, rational players of Heads and Tails would have a 0.5 probability of co-ordinating their strategies.

But ordinary players of Heads and Tails, with common knowledge of a system of labelling, are able to do much better than this. Schelling (1960: 54–8) reports an informal experiment in which people were asked how they would choose if they were playing Heads and Tails. Out of forty-two people, thirty-six (i.e. 86 per cent) said they would choose 'heads'. (As I shall explain later, I and two colleagues have replicated this result in a more formal experimental setting.) If two people were chosen at random from Schelling's group and asked to play Heads and Tails, they would have a 0.76 chance of co-ordinating. How is it that ordinary players are more successful than they would have been, had they acted on the prescriptions of game theory? Presumably they make some use of the labels 'heads' and 'tails', but how do they do this?

The usual answer is that, of the two labels 'heads' and 'tails', 'heads' is more prominent or more salient: in some way, it sticks out. ('Prominent' is

Schelling's term; 'salience' is used by Lewis (1969: 24–36).) Heads and Tails is a game with two pure-strategy Nash equilibria. The (heads, heads) equilibrium is associated with salient strategies, and so sticks out too. It is a focal point—that is, it provides a point on which mutual expectations can 'focus' (Schelling 1960: 57). But, of course, these are no more than suggestive metaphors. How can these metaphors be used to explain how people co-ordinate their actions?

2. Primary salience and the iteration of best replies

Suppose that each person in a large sample is asked to name either 'heads' or 'tails'. No explanation is given for setting this apparently pointless task, and no incentives are offered. Have we any reason to expect that the responses would be random? Surely not. We might expect that a person will give the answer that first comes to mind, or that seems most natural or obvious. I shall use the term 'primary salience' for this notion of 'coming to mind'; it is to be understood as a psychological phenomenon, independent of conscious reasoning. Presumably, primary salience will in part be determined by a person's experiences and culture. If, for example, 'Heinz' comes to mind when I am asked to name a manufacturer of baked beans, that may be a tribute to the success of certain advertising campaigns; if 'John Major' comes to mind when I am asked to name a politician, that may be because I read British newspapers. So we might expect that, for people with some common cultural background, there would be some correlation between what has primary salience for one person and what has primary salience for another. It need not be surprising if 86 per cent of people say 'heads' when asked simply to name either 'heads' or 'tails'.

Now consider two people playing Heads and Tails. Suppose they both act without any thought about the strategic structure of the game, simply choosing the first strategies that come to mind. Perhaps 'heads' is primarily salient for 86 per cent of the population. Then these two non-rational players would act just like the players in Schelling's experiments, and they would have a 0.76 chance of co-ordinating. Alternatively, we might suppose the players to be experts in game theory. Each player begins by analysing Heads and Tails using the principles of classical game theory, treating the labels as irrelevant. Each deduces that he has no reason to choose one strategy rather than the other: as a rational person, he must be indifferent between them. (As an expected utility maximizer, he must also be indifferent between these pure strategies and all mixed strategies.) But he has to choose something, so he chooses the first strategy that comes to mind. If both players choose in this way, they may have a high probability of co-ordinating.

Thus, it might be possible to explain co-ordination in terms of primary salience. Either players are non-rational, and choose those strategies that are primarily salient; or they are unable to find any rational grounds for choice, and fall back on primary salience. Co-ordination, then, might be achieved as a fortunate by-product of non-rational (but not necessarily irrational) behaviour.

If some degree of co-ordination can be achieved non-rationally, this opens the way for some more sophisticated modes of reasoning. Suppose I am playing Heads and Tails against you, and I expect you to choose the strategy that has primary salience for you. Then, as a rational person, I should choose the strategy which maximizes my expected utility given my beliefs about what has primary prominence for you. If, as a result of reading Schelling, I believe that 'heads' is more likely to have primary prominence for you than 'tails', then I should choose 'heads'—even if 'tails' happens to be the strategy that first comes to mind for me. I shall say that a strategy has second-order salience for a player to the extent that he expects it to have primary salience for the other. Further levels of sophistication are possible. For example, I may expect you to expect me to choose the strategy that has primary salience for me. Then I will look for a strategy that has third-order salience—that is, which I expect that you will expect that I will find primarily salient. And so on.

If we were to take the limit of *n*th-order salience as *n* tends to infinity, we would have a theory with some similarities to Harsanyi's 'tracing procedure' (Harsanyi 1975; Harsanyi and Selten 1988), to Skyrms's (1989) model of 'Bayesian deliberation', and to a model which has been sketched by Binmore (1988: 20–8). Roughly speaking, these theories begin by postulating some prior probability distribution over each player's strategies, working out best replies to these probability distributions, revising these probabilities according to the principle that best replies are more likely to be chosen than other strategies, and iterating this procedure until it converges on an equilibrium. A theory of *n*th-order salience uses primary salience to fix the prior probability distributions and then iterates best replies.

Lewis (1969) presents a brief analysis of 'co-ordination by salience' in which players are apparently motivated by a mixture of primary-and higher-order salience. He defines a salient equilibrium as 'one that stands out from the rest by its uniqueness in some conspicuous respect', and then adds the gloss that such an equilibrium must be unique 'in some way the subjects will notice, expect each other to notice, and so on'. Then, he suggests:

> The subjects might all tend to pick the salient as a last resort, when they have no stronger ground for choice. Or they might expect each other to have that tendency, and act accordingly; or they might expect each other to have that tendency and act accordingly, and act accordingly; and so on. Or—more likely—there might be a mixture of these. Their first-and higher-order expectations of a tendency to pick the salient as a last resort would be a system of concordant expectations capable of producing coordination at the salient equilibrium. (Lewis 1969: 35–6)

This account seems to merge together two different concepts of salience. It may be plausible to suppose that a person who has no other grounds for choice will be likely to choose an option which sticks out from the rest by its uniqueness in some conspicuous respect; but it is not clear why there needs to be a common recognition of its uniqueness. Why is it not enough that the option sticks out for the person concerned? Suppose, for example, that I am asked just to name any British town or city; no explanation or incentive is offered. Since I have no reason to name any one town rather than any other, I may name the first one that comes to mind. This might be Middlesbrough—the town where I was brought up. I would not expect many other people to give this answer (except in Middlesbrough). But I am not trying to give the same answer as anybody else: I am just saying what comes to mind for me. *For me*, Middlesbrough is unique among British towns in a conspicuous respect: it has primary salience for me.

Secondary (and higher-order) salience is a more public matter. Suppose that I am trying to predict how another British person, unknown to me, would respond to the instruction, 'Just name a town'. Generalizing from my own response, I might predict that the other person would name *her* home town. Thus, I might maximize the probability of making a successful prediction by naming the largest British city, London. If I reason like this, London has secondary salience for me. Notice that secondary salience, unlike primary salience, is not something given, which we simply recognize: it is the product of a process of reasoning. To decide that London has secondary salience, I have to make psychological hypotheses about the properties which have primary salience for other people; I need some knowledge about the statistical distribution of those properties in the relevant population; and I need to use both in combination to solve a maximization problem.

Although Lewis's analysis is not spelled out in detail—his discussion of salience is incidental to the main arguments of his book—it seems to involve the iteration of best replies from a set of prior probabilities which are determined by primary salience. Schelling (1960: 94) sees a similar theory at work in Keynes's famous discussion of the newspaper competition in which competitors have to choose the six prettiest faces from a set of 100, the winner being the entrant whose choices are closest to the average of those of all entrants. According to Keynes, a sophisticated competitor will not choose the faces he thinks prettiest, or even those that he expects most entrants to find prettiest:

> We have reached the third degree where we devote our intelligences to anticipating what average opinion expects the average opinion to be. And there are some, I believe, who practise the fourth, fifth and higher degrees. (Keynes 1936: 156)

In Keynes's account, people's personal judgements about prettiness are playing the same role as primary salience in Lewis's theory of co-ordination.

Given the rules of the competition, the fact that a face is pretty provides no direct reason for choosing it. But Keynes seems to be supposing that, in the absence of any better reasons, a competitor would choose the prettiest faces. This provides a set of prior probabilities from which a rational competitor can iterate best replies.

3. Schelling's theory

Schelling does not endorse Keynes's analysis of the newspaper competition. Although, according to Schelling, both writers are dealing with exactly the same kind of co-ordination problem, Keynes's 'conception of the solution is *not* the same' as his own (1960: 94, italics in original). Schelling rejects the idea that salience is ultimately grounded on hypotheses about how people would act if they had no rational grounds for choosing one option rather than another. Exactly what Schelling *does* have in mind is not entirely clear, but the passage to which his discussion of Keynes is attached offers some hints. Schelling considers a co-ordination game in which the instruction is 'Write down a positive number':

> most people, just asked to pick a number, will pick numbers like 3, 7, 13, 100, and 1. But when asked to pick the same number the others will pick when the others are equally interested in picking the same number, the motivation is different. The predominant choice is the number 1. And there seems to be good logic in this: there is no unique 'favoured number'; the variety of candidates like 3, 7, and so forth is embarrassingly large, and there is no good way of picking the 'most favourite' or most conspicuous. If one then asks what number, among all positive numbers, is most clearly unique, or *what rule of selection would lead to unambiguous results*, one may be struck by the fact that the universe of all positive numbers has a 'first' or 'smallest' number. (Schelling 1960: 94; italics in original)

In the language of this paper, Schelling is saying that if players of the Name a Number game were motivated by primary salience, they would be unlikely to co-ordinate: there are too many different numbers which have primary salience for different people. Schelling suggests that intelligent players will look for a 'rule of selection' that would work better than primary salience.

Roughly, then, the idea seems to be that intelligent players will look for a rule which, if followed by both of them, would be particularly successful in bringing about co-ordination. Having found such a rule, each follows it, in the expectation that the other will do the same. For Schelling, I suggest, an equilibrium is salient if it is reached when both players follow such a rule.

Schelling does not formulate this concept of salience precisely, and it is far from easy to do so. Nevertheless, I shall suggest, Schelling's approach captures the essence of the kind of reasoning we employ to identify focal points; Lewis's approach does not.

Consider, for example, the co-ordination game shown in Table 13.2. Suppose the labels are private knowledge, so that the players cannot co-ordinate by using, for example, the special significance of the central cell in a 3 x 3 matrix. In this game, I suggest, intelligent players would recognize the salience of 'bottom' and 'right', and the associated outcome (9, 9). There are three Nash equilibria, or three ways in which the players might be rewarded for co-ordinating their strategies: one gives (9, 9) and the other two give (10, 10). In this set (9, 9) clearly stands out. The property in virtue of which it stands out is an undesirable one: it stands out because it is worse than the other two, while the other two are exactly as good as one another. Nevertheless, 'Choose the worst equilibrium' is a rule of selection which, if followed by both players, would give unambiguous results. In contrast, 'Choose the best equilibrium' would not tell either player how to discriminate between the two strategies that are compatible with (10, 10) outcomes, and so would give only a 0.5 probability of co-ordination. (Since the labelling is private knowledge, *every* rule which tells the players to try to achieve a (10, 10) outcome has the same 0.5 probability of success. Each player might use his own labels to discriminate between the two strategies, but since these labels are unknown to the other player, this cannot help them to co-ordinate.)

TABLE 13.2. An undesirable focal point

		Player B		
		left	*centre*	*right*
	top	10, 10	0, 0	0, 0
Player A	*middle*	0, 0	10, 10	0, 0
	bottom	0, 0	0, 0	9, 9

Now compare the implications of Lewis's analysis for this game. It is hard to see how (9, 9) could have primary salience—how this could be said to stand out in a way that would make 'bottom' or 'right' particularly likely to be chosen by a player who had 'no stronger ground for choice'. In the absence of any other reasons for discriminating between 'top', 'middle', and 'bottom', the fact that 'top' and 'middle' give the possibility of a pay-off of 10 while 'bottom' gives only the possibility of 9 would seem to be a reason for *not* choosing 'bottom'. If this is right—if there is a reason for not choosing 'bottom'—then primary salience should be relevant only in determining *A*'s choice between 'top' and 'middle'. It might reasonably be objected, however, that the previous argument involves an appeal to a principle of insufficient reason. Someone who was sceptical of this principle might argue that *A* really has no grounds for choosing between his three strategies. Then we would need to ask whether the property that leads 'bottom' to stand out—the property of being worst—is the sort of property that would make an option more likely to be chosen. The claim that it is such a property does not seem particularly plausible. But if 'bottom' and 'right' do not have primary salience, they cannot have higher orders of salience either. Lewis's theory, then, seems to provide no reason for players to co-ordinate on (9, 9).

In arguing against Keynes's analysis of salience—which is also Lewis's analysis—Schelling appeals to evidence about how people play Name a Number. The implication is that he has carried out some informal investigations into this issue; but if he has, he does not report them. It is useful, therefore, to report some of the results of an experiment which I have carried out with Judith Mehta and Chris Starmer. We recruited 178 subjects who were divided at random into two groups. Each group was given the same set of twenty questions (or instructions), each of which had no right or wrong answer. One of these questions—and a typical example—was Schelling's 'Write down any positive number'. In one of the groups, the motivated group, subjects were formed into random and anonymous pairs. Each subject was paid according to the number of questions on which his answer was exactly the same as that of the other member of the pair. (The rate of payment was £0.62 per player per question on which co-ordination was achieved.) In the other group, the unmotivated group, subjects were simply told to answer the questions however they liked, and that any payment they received for taking part in the experiment would be entirely independent of their answers. (The only condition we imposed was that every question had to be answered in some way.) The point of having an unmotivated group was to enable us to find out which answers had primary salience.

The responses to 'Write down any positive number' were almost exactly as Schelling would have predicted. In the unmotivated group, the most common response was 7, given by 11.4 per cent of subjects. This was followed by 2 (10.2 per cent), 10 (5.7 per cent); 1 was only the fourth most common response (4.5 per cent). In the motivated group, in contrast, 1 was by far the most common response, given by 40.00 per cent of subjects. (It was followed by 7 (14.4 per cent), 10 (13.3 per cent), and 2 (11.1 per cent).) This suggests that 1 is not an especially salient number in the primary sense, but that it nevertheless has some property which makes it a focal point for players who are consciously playing a co-ordination game.

We found similar contrasts between the two groups for several other questions. Perhaps the most striking contrast was for the instruction 'Write down any day of the year'. The eighty-eight members of the unmotivated group gave seventy-five different responses. (Many of them named their own birthdays.) The most common response, 25 December, was given by only five subjects (5.7 per cent); only one subject named 1 January; and only one subject named the current date (10 December). In the motivated group, however, the three most common responses were 25 December (44.4 per cent), 10 December (18.9 per cent), and 1 January (8.9 per cent). It is easy to see how each of these three dates is conspicuous in some public respect. For each of them, there is an obvious 'rule of selection' which, if followed by both players, would ensure a very high probability of co-ordination.

4. Gauthier's and Bacharach's theories of salience

It is one thing to have intuitions about the determinants of salience, and quite another to construct a formal theory of salience based on Schelling's approach. Two people who have been brave enough to try are Gauthier (1975) and Bacharach (1991).

Gauthier defines 'the salient outcome' in a co-ordination game as 'that which is apprehended as standing out from the others'. This notion of 'apprehension' seems to involve some element of common knowledge, so that each player can expect that the salient outcome stands out for the other player, and so on; but 'the apprehension of salience is itself not, or at least not only, a rational apprehension' (Gauthier 1975: 211). Gauthier bypasses some difficult problems by simply assuming that—at least in the co-ordination problems he discusses—a uniquely salient outcome exists, and is commonly known to exist. But this still leaves the problem of explaining why rational players choose the strategies that lead to the salient outcome.

Gauthier's solution rests on what he calls the Principle of Co-ordination. This principle is defined for non-cooperative games in general, and not only for co-ordination games. Gauthier defines a 'best equilibrium' as a Nash equilibrium which is weakly preferred by all players to all other Nash equilibria. The Principle of Co-ordination is:

> In a situation with one and only one outcome which is both [Pareto] optimal and a best equilibrium, if each person takes every person to be rational and to share a common conception of the situation, it is rational for each person to perform that action which has the best equilibrium as one of its possible outcomes. (Gauthier 1975: 201)

If we confine our attention to two-player co-ordination games, as I have defined them, and assume that the structure of the relevant game is common knowledge, we may write the principle more simply as:

> *The Principle of Co-ordination*. If one outcome is preferred to every other by both players, it is rational for each player to perform the action which has that outcome as one of its possible outcomes.

As it stands, this principle provides no guidance for the players of games like Heads and Tails, in which two or more outcomes are indifferent to one another but preferred to all others. But, Gauthier argues, the players of such games can use their common apprehension of salience to redescribe the game in a form to which the Principle of Co-ordination *does* apply. Discussing a problem with a similar structure to Heads and Tails, but in which the problem is to choose one of two stations in London as a meeting place, he says:

You and I want to meet in London. We want, then, one meeting place. Our problem is that we have two equally good meeting places. What we need is a way to restructure our conception of the situation so that we are left with but one. We must restrict the possible actions we consider, in such a way that we convert our representation of the situation into one with but one best equilibrium. . . . We effect the necessary restriction by singling out some characteristic of some one equilibrium outcome. (Gauthier 1975: 210–11)

Gauthier starts from the idea that a given strategic situation may be described in many different ways, all of which are, on the face of things, equally valid. In Gauthier's co-ordination problem, which we may call Station Rendezvous, the players know that they must go to a London railway terminus which has services to Leicester. (The story refers to long-gone days.) Each player might be said to face a choice between 'St Pancras station' and 'Marylebone station'; but we might equally well say that each player has to choose between 'the Midland Railway terminus' and 'the Great Central Railway terminus'. We might even say that 'choosing the Midland railway terminus' and 'choosing St Pancras' are different options, even though St Pancras *is* the Midland Railway terminus: an act must be chosen under some description. Now suppose that St Pancras is salient in the set (St Pancras, Marylebone): both players apprehend St Pancras as standing out in some way, can expect the other to apprehend this, and so on. (Gauthier suggests that it is common knowledge that more people travel to St Pancras than to Marylebone.) Then, according to Gauthier, the game can be described as one in which each player chooses between 'seeking the salient outcome' and 'ignoring the salient outcome'. 'Seeking the salient outcome' is the act of 'going to St Pancras' under a different description. 'Ignoring the salient outcome' is the act of 'choosing at random between St Pancras and Marylebone' under a different description.

Gauthier claims that rational players would use the descriptions 'seek salience' and 'ignore salience' rather than 'St Pancras' and 'Marylebone'. This claim, I think, depends on an extension of the Principle of Co-ordination.

To see how Gauthier's argument works, consider how it might be applied to Heads and Tails. (Alternatively, substitute 'St Pancras' and Marylebone' for 'heads' and 'tails'.) Assuming that 'heads' is salient, that game may be redescribed in the form shown in Table 13.3. (If either player chooses at random, the probability of coordination is 0.5, and so each player's expected utility is 0.5.) In Heads and Tails Redescribed, the Principle of Co-ordination tells each player to choose 'seek salience'. Thus, the common pay-off for rational players of Heads and Tails Redescribed would be 1. In the original game of Heads and Tails, in contrast, the players seem to have good reason to attach a probability of less than 1 to the prospect of their co-ordinating. So they could expect to do better by playing Heads and Tails Redescribed than by playing the original game. Gauthier seems to be thinking of the players' decision problem as having two stages. In the first stage, each player chooses a set of descriptions, and thus conceptualizes the situation as a particular game; in the second stage, each player plays the game that he has chosen to use as a description of the situation. The first stage of this process is itself a kind of co-ordination game, in which the players have a common interest in their choosing descriptions which will lead them to have a high probability of co-ordinating in the second stage. Applying the Principle of Co-ordination at the first stage, we might say that it is rational for each player to choose the description which, if chosen by both players, would give the highest expectation of utility in the second stage. If we may assume that Heads and Tails Redescribed is the only description under which each player has an expected utility of 1, then, on Gauthier's analysis, it is rational for the players to describe the game in this way.

TABLE 13.3. Heads and Tails Redescribed

		Player B	
		seek salience	*ignore salience*
Player A	*seek salience*	1,1	0.5, 0.5
	ignore salience	0.5, 0.5	0.5, 0.5

Bacharach (1991) presents a similar line of argument in a much more formal way. Like Gauthier, Bacharach takes a player's options to be 'acts under descriptions'. Bacharach sees a co-ordination game as having a first stage in which the players conceptualize their situation. Unlike Gauthier, however, Bacharach sees this stage as involving entirely involuntary mental processes. In Bacharach's theory, the way people conceive their options is taken to be beyond their conscious control: particular descriptions either come to mind or remain unimagined. A single act may come to mind under several descriptions. ('Go to the Midland Railway terminus' and 'Go to the station on the west side of St Pancras Road' are different descriptions of the same act.) Conversely, a single description may cover several acts. (Consider: 'Go to a London railway terminus'.) *All* the act-descriptions that come to mind for a player are treated as options that he might choose. In the second stage of a co-ordination game, the players make rational choices among these options. At this stage, Bacharach invokes a version of the Principle of Co-ordination.

The general drift of Bacharach's theory can be seen in his analysis of Station Rendezvous. Bacharach models the descriptions of options in terms of 'predicates' which belong to 'families'. (For example, 'red', 'green', 'blue', and so on are predicates which belong to the family of 'colours'.) A particular family of predicates either comes to mind (in which case, all its members come to mind) or remains unthought of (in which case, none of its members comes to mind). In Station Rendezvous, Bacharach assumes that the family of names which refers to stations with Leicester services—the 'base class' of predicates—will come to mind for any normal player, and that it is common knowledge that this family will come to mind. This is the family (St Pancras, Marylebone). He also assumes that a predicate which applies only to one of the stations, and which is the only member of its family, will come to mind in a similar way. Following Gauthier's version of the story (Bacharach's is slightly different), we may take this predicate to be 'most popular among travellers to and from Leicester'. (We might wonder why 'not the most popular' is not another predicate in the same family. This is an awkwardness in Bacharach's argument, which would be overcome if there were more than two stations to choose between.)

These predicates are taken to be the only ones that come to mind. This gives each player four options: (1) 'Go to a station with Leicester services' (i.e. pick at random from the set (St Pancras, Marylebone), (2) 'Go to a station called "St Pancras" ', (3) 'Go to a station called "Marylebone" ', and (4) 'Go to a station which has the property of being most popular'. Bacharach argues that there are no rational grounds for discriminating between (2) and (3): these are symmetrical options (each being identified by a member of the same family of predicates). Thus neither (2) nor (3) can be 'endorsed' as the one that should rationally be chosen. If both players choose (1), their common expected utility is 0.5; if both players choose (4), their common expected utility is 1. Bacharach's form of the Principle of Co-ordination then tells us that (1) cannot be endorsed as the rational choice. By elimination, the rationally endorsed option is (4), which is the act of going to St Pancras, but under a different description.

Gauthier's and Bacharach's analyses of salience may both be viewed as attempts to formalize Schelling's idea that the players of a co-ordination game look for the 'rule of selection' which, if followed by both of them, would give the best results for both of them. Gauthier proposes a two-stage process. The players first look for the description of the game which, if recognized by both, would be best for both. Then, having settled on a particular description of the game, they look for the combination of strategies within that game which, if played by both, would give the best results for both. Bacharach's concept of an 'option' seems to correspond closely with Schelling's concept of a 'rule of selection'. (In the case of

Station Rendezvous, for example, the options 'Pick one of the two stations at random' and 'Choose the most popular station' might naturally be called rules of selection.) Bacharach suggests that rational players will look for the combination of options which, if chosen by both, would be best for both.

It is central to Schelling's, Gauthier's, and Bacharach's analyses of co-ordination games that the players do not act as maximizing individuals. Instead, each player conceives of the two of them as comprising a kind of team, the actions of whose members are to be planned so that they fit together. Each looks at the game as if from the viewpoint of a team manager, looking for the combination of actions by the team members which will give the best results. This mode of reasoning may be called joint maximization, in contrast to the individual maximizing of conventional rational choice theory.

5. Is joint maximization rational?

To dramatize the idea of joint maximization, consider the following variant of Heads and Tails. *A* and *B*, the actors who independently have to choose whether to name 'heads' or 'tails', are employees in a firm that is owned by *C*. If *A* and *B* both choose 'heads', or if they both choose 'tails', the firm earns one unit of profit; otherwise it earns nothing. The employees' own interests are not involved. Then the game may be described as in Table 13.4: the single number shown in each cell of this matrix is the pay-off to the firm. Suppose that *C* can rely on *A* and *B* to follow any instructions she gives them. Knowing that they are about to play this game, what instructions should she give them?

TABLE 13.4. Heads and tails as a team game

		Agent B	
		heads	tails
Agent A	heads	1	0
	tails	0	1

In this case, of course, the answer is obvious: she should *either* instruct them both to choose 'heads', *or* instruct them both to choose 'tails'. (Either instruction is as good as the other.) But consider the mode of reasoning that *C* is using. She asks herself what set of instructions, if followed by both players, would lead to the best outcome for the firm (or, equivalently, for her). She is solving a single maximization problem (what combination of actions by *A* and *B* would be best for the firm?), and she is treating *A* and *B* merely as the agents by which the maximizing solution is brought about. It would be no different if *A* was her left hand and *B* was her right hand.

The problem of giving instructions to one's agents has a trivial solution if the agents are to play a co-ordination game and if all the details of that game are known in advance. But imagine that all the details are not known. Suppose it is known that *A* and *B* will have to play *some* co-ordination game, but that is all. The nature of the game will not become known until *A*, *B*, and *C* are out of communication with one another. Thus, if *C* is to give instructions to her agents, these instructions must take the form of general rules, applicable to wide classes of co-ordination games. An example of such an instruction might be: 'If it is common knowledge between you that one outcome is better than any other, choose the strategies that lead to that outcome.' This is the Principle of Co-ordination. Another example might be: 'If it is common knowledge that two or more outcomes are "best" (i.e. these outcomes are equally as good as one another and better than all other outcomes), and if one of the best outcomes stands out from the others by virtue of some feature that you are each likely to recognize as particularly conspicuous, then choose the strategies that lead to that outcome.' Agents who followed this instruction would probably co-ordinate on 'heads' in Heads and Tails, on the number 1 in Name a Number, and so on.

In the analysis proposed by Schelling, Gauthier, and Bacharach, players of co-ordination games whose own interests are at stake act as if they were the agents of a single principal, whose interests coincided with their own. Each player considers the game as if from the viewpoint of the principal; he asks himself what instructions the principal would choose to give the two players; and then he acts as if following those instructions.

The difficulty with this approach is to explain *why* rational individuals act in this way. Suppose a player knows that a certain rule, if followed by both players, would lead to the best possible outcome. How does that imply that *he* should follow that rule? This difficulty emerges most starkly when we try to justify the Principle of Co-ordination. Consider the game of Black, Red, and White, shown in Table 13.5. Each player knows that (10,10) is the best outcome for both of them, and that this outcome will be reached if and only if they both choose 'red'. The Principle of Co-ordination tells each of them that he should therefore choose 'red'. But what is the status of this 'therefore'? How does the fact that they both want it to be the case that they both choose 'red' provide a reason for either of them, as a rational individual, to choose 'red'?

TABLE 13.5. Black, Red, and White

		Player B		
		black	red	white
	black	9, 9	0, 0	9, 9
Player A	red	0, 0	10, 10	0, 0
	white	9, 9	0, 0	9, 9

As many writers have pointed out, the Principle of Co-ordination can *not* be derived from the conventional theory of rational choice (see e.g. Hodgson 1967, Regan 1980, and Hurley 1989). In the conventional theory, each individual maximizes his expected utility, given his beliefs about what other individuals will do. It is rational for *A* to play 'red' in Black, Red, and White if and only if he attaches a sufficiently high probability—to be precise, a probability of at least 9/19—to the event that *B* plays 'red'. But if *A* knows that *B* is rational, he knows that she will choose whichever strategy is rational for her. So if *A* is to justify attaching a positive probability to *B*'s playing 'red', he must satisfy himself that this is a strategy that she can rationally choose. But it is rational for her to choose 'red' if and only if she attaches a probability of at least 9/19 to the event that *A* plays 'red'. Clearly, this line of analysis leads to an infinite regress. The most we can say is that *A*'s playing 'red' is rationalizable in the sense of Bernheim (1984) and Pearce (1984): the claim that it is rational for *A* to play 'red' can be supported by an infinitely long, internally consistent but ungrounded chain of reasons. But *A*'s playing 'black' and *A*'s playing 'white' are rationalizable in exactly the same sense.

Notice that this problem does not arise for Lewis's theory of salience. Lewis allows the chain of expectations to be grounded on propositions about primary salience—about how people would choose in the absence of adequate reasons. Could a similar manœuvre be used to support the Principle of Co-ordination? I think not. Consider Black, Red, and White. Notice that if *A* were to attach equal probabilities to each of the strategies that *B* might play, he would not choose 'red'. So we cannot justify the choice of 'red' by an appeal to the Principle of Insufficient Reason. More intuitively, we might say that 'red' does not seem an obviously more attractive strategy than 'black' or 'white' for a player who does not already accept the rationality of the Principle of Co-ordination.

How, then, might the Principle of Co-ordination be justified? Bacharach and Gauthier both seem to see this principle as one which, if not actually derivable from the conventional theory of rational choice, is at least a natural addition to that theory. Bacharach (1991) is hopeful that the principle might eventually be justified in conventional terms, perhaps in a 'trembling hand' model. Gauthier characterizes the conventional theory of rationality as 'act-consequentialism'. He claims that the Principle of Co-ordination 'completes' and is 'consonant with the spirit of act-consequentialism:

> What distinguishes the . . . act-consequentialist, is, first, that he attends to, and only to, the consequences of particular actions, and second, that he is concerned with the maximisation of utility. The coordination principle satisfies these two requirements. (Gauthier 1975: 206)

It is certainly true that the Principle of Co-ordination recommends acts on the grounds that they lead to the maximization of utility. But *to whom* are the acts being recommended? *Whose* utility is being maximized? The conventional theory of rational choice treats the individual as the unit of agency. Recommendations are addressed separately to each individual: an act is recommended to a person on the grounds that, if *he* performs it, *his* ends will be advanced. But the Principle of Co-ordination does not work like this.

Consider the position of someone who is playing Black, Red, and White as *A*. Appealing to the Principle of Co-ordination, we recommend her to choose 'red'. But suppose she asks us to show her that it is in her interest to choose this strategy. We can show that it is in *A*'s interest to choose 'red' if *B* can be expected to choose 'red' too. But what reason does *A* have to expect this? It would be circular for us to appeal to the Principle of Co-ordination at this point, since the validity of that principle is precisely what is at issue. Nor would we make any progress by pointing out that it is in *B*'s interest to choose 'red' if he can expect *A* to choose 'red': that is just another step in an infinite regress.

If *A* insists on being shown that it is in her interest to choose 'red' before accepting that this is what it is rational for her to do, and if she supposes that *B* is thinking in a similar way, then we cannot show her that she should choose 'red'. What we *can* say is something like the following: 'Think of yourself and *B* together. It is in both your interests that you both choose "red".' Paradoxically, if *A* and *B* both accept that this provides them each with a sufficient reason to choose 'red', then each person's choosing 'red' *will* in fact be in his or her individual interest. Perhaps this is what Gauthier has in mind when he says that the Principle of Co-ordination is consonant with the spirit of act-consequentialism. In other words: two players who act on the Principle of Co-ordination will achieve the ends that, had they been act-consequentialists, they would have tried to achieve. But it is only because they are *not* act-consequentialists that they are able to act on the Principle of Co-ordination.

I began this chapter by asking how people achieve success when playing co-ordination games. If the argument of this chapter is correct, this success depends on the players' ability to think of their relationship to one another in a way that is foreign to the conventional theory of rational choice. As in the Kantian tradition of moral reasoning, each player follows principles that he can will to be rules for all players. But although each player is motivated by something beyond his individual objectives, each achieves success as measured by those objectives. Co-ordination problems seem to call for something more than instrumental rationality but something less than morality.

REFERENCES

Bacharach, M. (1991), 'Games with Context-sensitive Strategy Spaces', paper presented at International Conference on Game Theory, Florence, June 1991.

Bernheim, B. D. (1984), 'Rationalisable Strategic Behaviour', *Econometrica*, 52: 1007–28.

Binmore, K. (1988), 'Modeling Rational Players: Part II', *Economics and Philosophy*, 4: 9–55.

Crawford, V. P., and Haller, H. (1990), 'Learning How to Cooperate: Optimal Play in Repeated Coordination Games', *Econometrica*, 58: 571–95.

Gauthier, D. (1975), 'Coordination', *Dialogue*, 14: 195–221.

Harsanyi, J. C. (1975), 'The Tracing Procedure: A Bayesian Approach to Defining a Solution Concept for N-Person Non-cooperative Games', *International Journal of Game Theory*, 4: 61–94.

—— and Selten, R. (1988), *A Several Theory of Equilibrium Selection in Games* (Cambridge, Mass.: MIT Press).

Hodgson, D. H. (1967), *Consequences of Utilitarianism* (Oxford: Clarendon Press).

Hurley, S. L. (1989), *Natural Reasons* (Oxford: Oxford University Press).

Keynes, J. M. (1936), *The General Theory of Employment Interest and Money* (London: Macmillan).

Lewis, D. (1969), *Convention: A Philosophical Study* (Cambridge, Mass.: Harvard University Press).

Pearce, D. G. (1984), 'Rationalisable Strategic Behaviour and the Problem of Perfection', *Econometrica*, 52: 1029–50.

Regan, D. (1980), *Utilitarianism and Cooperation* (Oxford: Clarendon Press).

Schelling, T. C. (1960), *The Strategy of Conflict* (Cambridge, Mass.: Harvard University Press).

Skyrms, B. (1989), 'Correlated Equilibria and the Dynamics of Rational Deliberation', *Erkenntnis*, 31: 347–64.

Sugden, R. (1986), *The Economics of Rights: Co-operation and Welfare* (Oxford: Basil Blackwell).

V

STRATEGIC INTERACTION AND MORAL ANALYSIS

14

An Evolutionary Dynamic Approach to Altruism[1]

PIER LUIGI SACCO
AND
STEFANO ZAMAGNI

> A man who is a mathematician and nothing but a mathematician may live a stunted life, but he does not do any harm. An economist who is nothing but an economist is a danger to his neighbours. Economics is not a thing in itself; it is a study of one aspect of the life of man in society . . . Modern economics is subject to a real danger of Machiavellism—the treatment of social problems as matters of technique, not as facets of the general search for the Good Life.
>
> (Hicks 1941)

1. Introduction

A social convention is, according to the classical definition of Lewis (1969), a state of things which is customary, expected, and self-enforcing. In game-theoretic terms (as pointed out, for example, by Ullman-Margalit 1977), these requirements can be translated into the familiar Nash equilibrium conditions. Very recently, Sugden (1989) has pointed out that historically relevant social conventions need not only be self-enforcing *vis-à-vis* themselves but also against the possible 'invasion' of 'rival' conventions, i.e. against the possibility that a relatively small number of players act as 'deviants'. This additional feature amounts to a refinement of Nash equilibrium known as evolutionary stability (see e.g. van Damme 1987). This characterization of social conventions clearly stresses their stability, i.e. the fact that, once the social convention has been established, its destruction requires the successful co-ordination of a relatively large number of players. Unfortunately, as is well known, it is often the case that social conventions do not correspond to socially desirable outcomes; this can be due to the fact that:

[1] Financial support by MURST is gratefully acknowledged.

(*a*) there exist many possible social conventions, but for some reason the 'wrong' one has become salient. One such example is the so-called co-ordination failure: workers co-ordinate on an inefficiently low level of activity despite the fact that a uniformly higher level of activity would make them all better off (see e.g. Cooper and John (1988));

(*b*) the only feasible social convention is Pareto inferior to some other, non-implementable outcome. The most famous example in this respect is the Prisoner's Dilemma game; another well-known situation is the so-called Tragedy of the Commons (see e.g. Hardin 1968 but also Bromley 1991).

Even when socially preferable conventions other than the ruling one exist, the transition from the latter to the former is problematic for the reasons hinted at above. To explain the transition between social conventions one has therefore to invoke some additional feature that forces the economy away from the original situation. Boyer and Orlean (1992) provide an example of transition between conventions based on a certain pattern of localization of strategic interaction between players. More examples based on different factors may be devised; in this paper, we are particularly interested in one of them, namely altruistic behaviour.

To understand how the emergence of altruistic behaviour may cause the transition between different social conventions or even the emergence of a desirable convention when there is none, consider, as a simple example, the specification of the standard Prisoner's Dilemma game shown in Table 14.1 where $\zeta, \psi, \lambda > 0$, $\psi > \zeta$.

TABLE 14.1

	C	D
C	(ζ, ζ)	$(\zeta - \psi, \zeta + \lambda)$
D	$(\zeta + \lambda, \zeta - \psi)$	$(0, 0)$

As can be easily checked (*D, D*) is the only Nash equilibrium here, and hence the only enforceable social convention. If on the other hand at least one player (say, the row player) is altruistic in the sense that her target pay-off function is a weighted average of her own and the opponent's pay-off, it turns out that co-operation is a dominant strategy for her provided that ω, i.e. the weight assigned to the opponent's pay-off, is large enough. More precisely, if $\zeta + \lambda > \psi$, it is required that $\omega > \lambda/(\lambda + \psi)$, whereas if $\zeta + \lambda < \psi$, it is required that $\omega > (\psi - \zeta)/(\lambda + \psi)$.

If on the other hand *both* players are altruistic, mutual co-operation may become the only enforceable social convention. It might be objected that the emergence of mutual co-operation as a social convention requires a relatively high degree of altruism. It can indeed be shown that, when $\zeta + \lambda < \psi$, even for lower degrees of (row player's) altruism (namely, for

$\lambda/(\lambda + \psi) < \omega < (\psi - \zeta)/(\lambda + \psi)$) the original Prisoner's Dilemma can be transformed into a so-called assurance game in which free-riding is not the most attractive option for the altruistic player (who now ranks outcomes as follows: $(C, C) \succ (D,C) \succ (D,D) \succ (C,D)$; see e.g. Sen (1967)). The pay-off matrix then becomes (with the row player as the altruist) that shown in Table 14.2.

TABLE 14.2

	C	*D*
C	(ζ, ζ)	$(\zeta - \psi + (\lambda + \psi)\omega, \zeta + \lambda)$
D	$(\zeta + \lambda - (\lambda + \psi)\omega, \zeta - \psi)$	$(0, 0)$

In this case, the altruistic player has no longer a dominant strategy; it is often suggested (see e.g. Elster 1984) that defection is the rational strategy for her to play. However, as argued by Collard (1978), the row player's assurance about the opponent's choice of (co-operative) strategy need not be complete in order for her to choose to behave co-operatively. The altruistic player will indeed co-operate as long as her subjective estimate p of the probability that the opponent will co-operate is large enough;[2] it is easily checked that, the larger the player's altruism, the less assurance she requires to justify her own co-operation.[3] If on the other hand *both* players are sufficiently altruistic (i.e. $\omega > \lambda/(\lambda + \psi)$), the co-operative outcome is again self-enforcing, i.e. mutual co-operation is a (stable) social convention. In conclusion, some (possibly relatively small) degree of altruism may upset the non-cooperative social convention; if moreover a large enough number of players behave (possibly just moderately) altruistically, an efficient, co-operative social convention could be eventually brought about.

Analogous arguments might be constructed for other games in which players' self-interest causes the emergence of inefficient social conventions, as in the well-known Centipede game. These results suggest that altruism is not easily dismissible as an instance of irrational decision-making and that, consequently, it might be an important motivating factor for players at least in certain situations. This possibility is somewhat backed by the available experimental evidence that shows that co-operative behaviour tends to be observed more often than it should be on the basis of the standard model of self-interested players and that co-operation is typically the 'default' initial choice (see e.g. Roth (1991)), as well as by the evidence that shows that equity considerations play a substantial role in individual bargaining decisions (see Ochs and Roth 1989). In fact, recent experimental results by

[2] Specifically, the altruistic player will co-operate if $p > (\psi - \zeta(\lambda + \psi)\omega)/(\psi - \zeta - \lambda)$; recall that the restrictions $\psi > \lambda + \zeta$ and $\omega > \lambda/(\lambda + \psi)$ are needed here.

[3] At $\omega = (\psi - \zeta)/(\lambda + \psi)$ she will co-operate even if she believes that the opponent will certainly defect.

Frank, Gilovich, and Regan (1993) suggest that subjects which have been exposed to micro-economics courses based on the notion of rational choice as self-interested maximizing behaviour tend to co-operate significantly less frequently than subjects who have not. This seems to indicate that the standard paradigm of self-interest may have a self-fulfilling nature: the exposed subjects are brought to perceive self-interest as a normative characterization of rational behaviour and to act accordingly. Thus, rather paradoxically, one could conclude that the take-over of the self-interest paradigm outside the narrow community of economists might induce an inefficient social convention at which co-operative deals become harder to enforce than it might otherwise be.[4]

Once made clear that altruism may play an important role in the solution of some well-known social dilemmas and that self-interest may work in the opposite direction, one has to explain why self-interest has traditionally become the dominant behavioural assumption on which the theory of rational decision-making has been built. It is indeed true that a vast literature on altruism has developed nowadays (as a mere but representative example see Bernheim and Stark (1988), Stark (1989)). But what about the main message conveyed by such literature?

Some traits that are common to the various authors may be identified:

(i) altruism is represented as a pre-existing, fixed 'stock';
(ii) the analysis focuses on the allocative effects of the fixed stock;
(iii) it turns out that if the level of altruism falls below a certain threshold, negative welfare effects emerge, in that, in order to prevent systematic exploitation, the altruist must undertake inefficient courses of action (the so-called altruist's moral hazard);
(iv) if the level of altruism falls above the threshold, welfare effects are instead positive;
(v) on the other hand, given that high levels of altruism are not practically reachable, self-interested behaviour seems preferable: the welfare losses the economy must bear before a large enough stock of altruism is built are likely to be too large.

In conclusion, the main message of this literature seems to be that, all things considered, altruism is irrelevant and/or wasteful! It is our opinion that this conclusion heavily depends on an incorrect conceptualization of altruism and more specifically of its role in the complex motivational system that lies behind individual decisions. A first, peripheral remark is that altruism cannot be understood as a stock that is worn out by use, as it is the case with any scarce resource. Altruism is not a resource, it is a virtue. As a consequence, as Aristotle put it, its stock is likely to be increased by

[4] Lattimore (1992) examines the results of a standard ultimatum bargaining game involving economists who behave according to the familiar self-interest paradigm and non-economists who value attitudes such as fairness and altruism. The (relatively) surprising finding is that economists make smaller expected monetary gains than non-economists.

frequent use, rather than worn out. More importantly, the standard approach to altruism is flawed by a basic methodological error. It is assumed that the preference orderings of players do not change as the process of choice unfolds, i.e. it is implicitely postulated that behaviour and experience do not feed back on players' preference judgements. Now, while this assumption is certainly reasonable in comparative static analyses, it is much too restrictive when it comes to dynamics. A player's degree of altruism at a certain time is likely to be affected by his past history of choices and experiences; this in turn implies that his original preference judgements may be reshaped several times and in several different ways. A second, related point is that 'altruism' is a far too vague notion that calls for further qualification; in fact, one can consistently define several different *types* of altruism, all of them having peculiar allocative consequences. Therefore, once it is admitted that there are important feedbacks from the dynamic choice process to individual judgements, it must be recognized that such judgements may evolve towards, or away from, different sorts of altruism, and that the actual law of motion may in principle heavily depend on the type of altruism that is currently actualized in the player's preference judgements.

In conclusion, a proper dynamical analysis of the allocative consequences of altruism must focus not only on the actual level of altruism that characterizes the economy, but also on the type(s), keeping in mind that the time evolution of the stock(s) of altruism crucially depends on the distribution of the various types across the population. The dynamical mechanism just outlined lends itself quite naturally to an evolutionary dynamic treatment; in this perspective, the diffusion and the eventual take-over of a certain type of altruistic norm of behaviour (or of a certain distribution of types of altruism across the population) may be seen as the emergence of a social convention in the sense of Lewis and Sugden.[5] In this framework one can also easily model 'altruistically driven' phenomena of transition between conventions, by studying if and how the appearance of some 'new' sort of altruism upsets the existing social convention laying the foundations of a new, different one, with the corresponding bearings in terms of social welfare.

The remainder of this chapter is organized as follows. In section 2 we review some recent and some less recent literature on altruism and selfishness to elucidate the current state of the debate. In sections 3 and 4 we discuss in greater detail the issue of the relevance of altruistic motivations, as opposed to self-interest, in a well-grounded theory of rational choice. Section 5 discusses the basic characteristics of our evolutionary approach. Sections 6 and 7 describe the reference model we use for our formal analysis.

[5] The need to model social conventions as the outcomes of density-dependent dynamical evolutionary processes has already been pointed out by Bicchieri (1990).

Section 8 discusses the dynamical structure of the model. Section 9 describes our results. Section 10 provides a short summary of our main findings.

2. A brief review of new and old literature

The approach to rational choice that identifies self-interest as the sole motivating force behind individual decisions is still the dominant one in the current literature. Several justifications have been given for this choice. As Tullock (1976) puts it, 'As a result of empirical research . . . the average human being is about 95 per cent selfish in the narrow sense of the term'. On the other hand, Downs (1956: 29), observes that 'In reality, men are not always selfish, even in politics . . . In every field, no account of human behaviour is complete without mention of such altruism . . . Nevertheless, general theories of social action always rely heavily on the self-interest axiom'. Stigler (1981) explains economic behaviour as almost entirely self-interested. He contends that deviations from narrow self-interest are generally confined to one's 'family, plus a close circle of associates'. Mueller (1986: 14), argues that 'the only assumption essential to a descriptive and predictive science of human behaviour is egoism'.

Sen's 1977 celebrated paper (on 'Rational Fools') is the first major theoretical attack against the self-interest assumption. Sen argued that sympathy for other people and commitment to a principle produce two key departures from self-interest and that commitment which involves counter-preferential choice 'drives a wedge between personal choice and personal welfare' while 'much of traditional economic theory relies on the identity of the two' (p. 328). In 1978, Collard's 'Altruism and Economy' supported the thesis that 'human beings are not entirely selfish, even in their economic dealings' (p. 3). Hirschman's 'Against Parsimony' in 1984 criticized the parsimonious postulate of a 'self-interested, isolated individual' and argued for a new focus on changes in values (rather than 'wanton' tastes) and on non-instrumental action. Very recently, Kirzner (1990) has made the fine point that 'Self-interest is indeed a central element, but this self-interest must . . . be understood with a certain subtlety. Properly understood, self-interest does not exclude altruistic motivation; it depends on purposefulness, but not on any selfishness of purpose. The point to be stressed is that it is one's *own* purposes which inspire one's actions and excite one's alertness. One's purposes may be altruistic or otherwise' (p. 39). In other words, it is, necessarily, the agent who makes the agent's choices, but the interests pursued need not be those of the agent. Thus, the familiar suggestion that every action is necessarily self-interested ('I am pursuing *my* concern that others should be able to . . .') misses the point since it confuses the concept of choice as purposeful action with the concept of choice as self-interested action—a purpose is not the same thing as personal interest. As a general point, Frank (1988) argues that there is no need for economics to assume exclusive rationality, understood as complete freedom from emotion and passion. The validity of economics is therefore not threatened by pervasive real-world examples of passionate behaviour. Building on earlier work of Schelling and others, Frank shows how the practice of moral behaviour may not only be good for society, but it may also be materially beneficial to the practising individuals themselves.

In a recent work, Sen (1987) marks the current state of the debate with the following, sweeping judgement: 'Universal selfishness as *actuality* may well be false, but universal selfishness as a requirement of *rationality* is patently absurd' (p. 16).

Neither one should think that the tension between self-interest and altruism as motivating forces behind rational choice was not felt by the founding fathers of the modern orthodoxy. Steedman (1989) has a most illuminating discussion of Wicksteed's thought centred on the relations between rational choice theory, as commonly understood in economics, and a broader conception of the individual in society, who might have altruistic purposes, social and ethical ideals. Steedman's paper provokes important reflection on the relations between rationality and altruism: altruistic conduct, when it occurs, is fully consistent with rational economic conduct. Wicksteed (1933) pointed out that 'The economic relation does not exclude from my mind every one but me, it potentially includes every one but you' (p. 174). To stress this point Wicksteed introduced the term 'non-tuism' to mean that, in an economic relation, *A*'s lack of concern for the purposes of *B* (and vice versa) by no means entails that *A* acts for selfish motives. 'The specific characteristic of an economic relation is not its "egoism" but its non-tuism' (p. 180). It follows from the above characterization of the nature of the economic relation that 'The proposal to exclude "benevolent" or "altruistic" motives from consideration in the study of Economics is . . . wholly irrelevant and beside the mark' (p. 179).

In fact, by further widening our historical perspective, we discover that, even apart from the classical references to Mandeville and Smith, the issue of the role of altruism vs. selfishness in the working of complex economies and societies is far from being a recent discovery. Throughout history, economic philosophers were fascinated by the phenomenon that general welfare develops from egoism of merchants. It seems that the earliest writer who noticed this point was Anonymous Jamblichi, a Sophist and apparently an expert in economic ethics, who wrote around 450 BC. He compared the wealth of the Greek city-states—the *poleis*—which did not have much gold, with the general Persian poverty that existed despite the immeasurable treasure in gold possessed by the Great King. Anonymous Jamblichi solved this paradox by stating that it is the merchants' activity that caused Greek wealth. In turn, this activity of the Greek merchants was made possible by the manifold relations of trust and credit that existed as a legal framework both within and between the numerous city states in the Greek *koiné*. Thus, resulting from the egoism of the many, a general system of welfare developed (see Fikentscher (1988)).

The Roman philosopher Seneca, in his *De Beneficiis*, says that a merchant selling corn does no benefit even if, in reality, he saves an individual or a whole city. Not one of those who profit by his action is obliged to him, because he did not mean to help them, but had in mind his own interest (Seneca, VI. 14. 4). The sentence with which Seneca explains that whatever is done to make a profit is no benefit has a Smithian flavour: he brings advantage to other people in order to have his own ('ad alienum commodum pro suo veniunt', IV. 13. 3). Therefore, merchants produce a 'good' result without having this purpose.

Much before the celebrated Mandeville's 'Fable of the Bees', in 1564 the German scholar Leonhard Fronsberger from Ulm published an essay, *Vom Lob deβ Eigen Nutzen* (*The praise of self-interest*), in which he explained that farmers, merchants, and artisans are busy only in pursuit of their self-interest and in so doing create public order and well-being in the general interest (see Schultze 1987).

Although very brief and of course quite incomplete, our survey demonstrates that the issue of the relevance of altruism in the motivational system of rational decision-makers is far from being a marginal or ephemeral one; indeed, it may be regarded as one of the few issues that permeate the whole Western intellectual history. Its somewhat marginal role in the research agenda of economists looks therefore suspect and calls for a deep rethinking. To this purpose we devote the next two sections.

3. The selfishness assumption: ethical status and factual relevance

The claim that self-interest alone motivates economic behaviour must be either tautological, and as such deprived of any cognitive content, for if self-interest can encompass any motive altruism becomes a kind of sophisticated self-interest, or factually false, if self-interest means behaviour that consciously intends only self as the beneficiary (i.e. all behaviour is instrumental to one's self-interest and all actions are commensurate in terms of their impact on one's own welfare). It is therefore important to distinguish the two interpretations of the self-interest paradigm. The present section is devoted to the latter (the behavioural one) whereas the next is devoted to the former (the all-encompassing one).

The presumption that selfishness is a morally 'neutral' assumption, as Collard (1978) argues, is based on the view that, on a continuous scale ranging from envy, malevolence, or hatred to sympathy, benevolence, or love, self-interest lies in the middle. This position is, however, not defendable. Indeed, Collard seems here to confuse the notion of self-interest with its degree.

On the other hand, the fact that I neither hate nor love other people does surely imply that I am indifferent towards them, but it does not imply that

I am selfish—as suggested by Collard—since I might even hate myself. At times, the hatred-to-love feelings may represent the motivation for either egoism or altruism; but they do not lie on the same scale as egoism and altruism.

The point made here is not to deny the possibility or even the likelihood of man being selfish and therefore the legitimacy of a theory based on this assumption. What is argued rather is that the self-interest assumption is a non-neutral one on ethical grounds. The simplest way to see the point is the following. Start with the standard theory of rationality as utility maximization and add the assumption of self-interested behaviour. Next notice that it is part of the meaning of the term 'rational' that a rational individual does not intentionally choose what is worse irrespective of the objective pursued by the individual. So rational *and* self-interested people never intentionally choose what is worse for themselves. Moreover, since, according to the theory of rationality, intentional choice follows preference, rational and self-interested individuals never prefer what is worse for themselves to what is better. Finally, add a moral principle of minimal benevolence—a non-controversial one indeed—according to which, other things being equal, it is a morally good thing if people are better off. Then it is, *ceteris paribus*, a morally good thing to satisfy an individual's preferences. As it can be seen, the self-interest assumption transforms rationality—which is not by itself a moral notion—into an ethically laden concept. For this reason, we believe it is safe to claim for the altruistic assumption as much attention as that paid to its opposite—egoism.

It is of course beyond doubt that self-interest is an important motivator of individual choices and that not all individuals are concerned with the welfare of others. Indeed, self-interest explains *most* of human interaction in some contexts, typically in market-mediated transactions, and it plays *some* role in almost every context. We aim, however, at making thinking about self-interest more subtle: when people think about what they want, they think about more than just their narrow self-interest. Moral principles and the interests of others do have a weight in the definition of self-interest. Consequently, one can argue that people often take account of other individuals' interests when they decide what constitutes a 'benefit' they want to maximize; this extended set of motivations is of course perfectly consistent in principle with the idea that individuals choose rationally. What is in doubt is whether the standard approach to rational choice is able to capture the actual complexity of individual motivations.

It is a fact that people do co-operate more than the self-interest model (useful though it is) seems to predict. In their already cited paper, Frank, Gilovich, and Regan (1993) shed light on one reason for this. Imagine a world in which people move from one Prisoner's Dilemma to the next (as happens in real-life situations). If people can choose their partners freely, and if honest types can spot each other in advance, co-operators will be able to interact selectively with each other—and will therefore do better than cheats; this argument presents interesting analogies with the 'secret handshake' effect pointed out by Robson (1990) in an evolutionary game-theoretic context. Experiments have shown that people are surprisingly good at telling co-operators and cheats apart, even on the basis of what seems to be limited information. One can therefore argue that, on broad evolutionary grounds, narrowly self-interested behaviour might ultimately be self-defeating.

The possibility that narrowly self-interested behaviour may be 'selected away' from a population of rational decision-makers at least under certain circumstances is an intriguing one—and is certainly at odds with most of the received wisdom about the relative survival possibilities of egoistically vs. altruistically motivated economic agents. One important avenue for future research would be to spell out the conditions under which self-interested and altruistic behaviours can coexist as opposed to those under which self-interest is likely to undermine altruism altogether.

In fact, it is hard to deny that a complex society is not likely to survive if *all* its members are governed by exclusively selfish motives. Although a counterfactual test of this statement is hard to implement or even to conceive, the available indirect experimental evidence tends to support it. For example, Dawes, van de Kraagt, and Orbell (1988) have conducted a series of experiments over a decade, the results of which warrant the conclusion that the co-operation rate, in situations involving social dilemmas, can be enhanced in the absence of egoistic incentives.

To understand why these results do support our statement one must keep in mind that complex societies *cannot* survive without a certain amount of co-operation; see e.g. Argyle (1991). This of course does not rule out the possibility that there can be vital, complex societies that are characterized by an inefficiently low level of co-operation. A viable, complex economic system must balance between institutions that assume self-interest and those that assume the existence of broader sets of motivations. At the moment, institutions geared to self-interest probably have far more weight in liberal democracies than is likely to be compatible with the long-term public good. (This is possibly a consequence of the self-interest bias that has characterized most of modern and contemporary thought about the structure and evolution of modern industrialized societies.) Therefore, it makes sense to try to redress this imbalance by revitalizing or creating institutions that foster a commitment to the common good. Yet efforts at revitalization will not be undertaken if it is common knowledge that such efforts will not work because of a widespread conviction that the only way to achieve efficiency is the promotion of selfish motives. In order to be able to design and implement institutions which rely on mixed sets of motives (selfish plus altruistic) it is necessary to acknowledge more fully the relevance and the potential of altruistic motivations and to give them a less marginal status in analytical and policy investigations.

4. Why should not altruism be encompassed by the self-interest paradigm?

We describe individuals as 'altruistic' when they feel and act as if the long-term welfare of others is taken as an end in itself; i.e. it is of relevance independently of its effects on their own welfare. If my concern with the welfare of others is merely an instrumental means for promoting my longer-term selfish ends and ceases once these selfish ends can be more easily pursued in some other way, I am an enlightened self-interested subject rather than an altruist subject.

One must distinguish between degrees and varieties of altruism. Every act falls somewhere on a line between extreme selfishness and extreme altruism, depending on the relative weight we give to our own interests and to the interests of others. Following Jencks (1979), we will distinguish 'complete' altruism (counting our own good as neither more nor less important than anyone else's); 'partial' altruism (taking some account of the interests of others), and 'extreme' altruism (weighting other people's individual interests more heavily than our own). Jencks also distinguishes three sources of altruism: empathy, community, and morality.

(i) Empathic altruism derives from the fact that we 'identify' with people outside ourselves. We incorporate their interests into our subjective welfare function, so that their interests become our own.
(ii) Communitarian altruism involves identification with a collectivity rather than with specific individuals (group identity as solidarity).
(iii) Moralistic altruism involves the incorporation of external moral ideals into our sense of 'self'.

These three varieties of altruism can lead to quite different forms of behaviour. For instance, empathy usually induces us to promote the interests of some specific individual, whereas communitarian altruism tends to focus on larger groups, possibly imposing pain and sacrifices on individual subjects if this can help to promote the interest of the community. Therefore, these two forms of altruism can lead to conflicting prescriptions. Many moral dilemmas involve precisely such conflicts between varieties of altruism, rather than just conflicts between selfishness and altruism.

According to the tautological formulation of the self-interest paradigm, the above listed types of altruism can all be encompassed by the standard approach to rational choice once one properly specifies the subject's utility function. For example, consider an empathic altruist who cares about the well-being of another subject; call the two A and B, respectively. If we assume that the relative weights assigned by A to her own and to B's well-beings are given by $1 - \omega$ and ω, respectively, we can write a 'motivation function' for A

$$M_A = (1 - \omega)\, U_A + \omega\, U_B$$

where U_A and U_B are the utilities of the two subjects. At this point, one could claim that the assumption that *A* maximizes M_A correctly describes the motivations that lie behind *A*'s choices. This claim, however, seems to miss the fundamental difference between the demand of consistency of choice and that of self-interest. Indeed, the former is a procedural demand without any substantive content as to what is being pursued, whereas the latter is a particularly substantive command as to what is being pursued without necessarily inducing a rigid procedural structure (see Sen 1987). Therefore, the encompassing of altruism by the standard approach to rational choice would imply the recognition of the impossibility of an empirically based micro-economics, a consequence that very few economists would be willing to endorse (see Broome 1978).

The 'reductionist' strategy just described need not be attacked on purely methodological grounds only. In the motivation function approach to altruism, the altruist subject *A* regards the utility of *B* as instrumental; therefore, *A* will behave altruistically only to the point where *her* marginal benefit is equal to *her* marginal cost. From *A*'s point of view, *B*'s utility is something like a consumption good among others, apart from the obvious positive externality effect. The existence of a positive externality, however, gives rise to the well-known free-riding problems. This implication seems to be markedly at odds with the large available evidence on individual donors contributing to large charities, which have only a marginal impact on the total income of the charity but a substantial opportunity cost; as a consequence, even putting methodological perplexities apart, this approach is only able to explain a small part of observed altruism (see Sugden 1982).

Another, more subtle encompassing strategy makes reference to the sociobiological literature. Becker (1976) and Tullock (1978), among others, borrow the inclusive fitness hypothesis that has been made popular by the work of Wilson (1975) and Dawkins (1976). According to this assumption, the natural selection process does not elicit the maximization of the genes' own fitness but rather the maximization of the fitness of duplicate genes which happen to be carried by kin-related organisms. As a consequence, the mutual aid phenomena that are so commonly observed in nature are prompted by genetic programming aimed at increasing the probability of survival of the corresponding genes. In this perspective, altruism may be once again encompassed by a suitably expanded notion of self-interest.

The sociobiological framework allows for the modelling of the pursuit of beneficience and of the adherence to sub-optimal choice principles as an expanded set of tastes. This is the case because, as argued for example by Becker, the utility function of the agent also includes the utility functions of other individuals. In this light, altruism, loyalty, and trust are not really far-sighted strategies of self-interest, say, à la Axelrod (1984). Rather, they are tastes in themselves. It is important to stress that this reference to sociobiological categories does not mean that Becker makes a case for biological reductionism; indeed, he imports only the superficial make-up of the inclusive fitness hypothesis, not its biological content; more specifically, Becker explains the allocation of endowments between self-interest and other-interest by means of the standard individual utility maximization procedure rather than by means of the maximization of a genetic fitness criterion.

Hirschleifer (1977*a*; 1977*b*; 1982 (1987)) also regards altruism and loyalty as tastes, i.e. not as merely contingent outcomes of educated self-interested calculations. However, he regards such tastes as genetically guided: 'Economic man's behaviour is constrained by *inbuilt* emotions and tastes. While these no doubt contain accidental elements, they are not completely arbitrary. What tastes sweet to us is mainly what serves our own interest and our "irrational" or "unselfish" drives have largely met the evolutionary test of enabling us the better to compete via group membership' (Hirschleifer 1982 (1987): 263).[6]

Frank (1988) also seems to regard 'unselfish' tastes as being genetically programmed. Frank blends standard analytical tools with a Darwinian selection mechanism in order to explain the prominence of 'irrational' sentiments. He treats analytically the tastes for conscience, revenge, and altruism as part of a continuous utility function.

Whether such tastes are chosen for their own sake à la Becker or as a consequence of specific genetical programming à la Hirschleifer and Frank, one cannot help noting that sociobiologically based explanations of altruism provide at best a partial picture of the phenomenon; in particular, none of these authors seems to be willing to embrace a fully reductionist position. On the other hand, the link between natural selection at the genetic level and economic selection at the behavioural level still remains obscure at the current state of knowledge. In lack of a general explanatory principle that is able to connect and elucidate the interplay of the various selection mechanisms, it is hard to claim that sociobiological ideas may provide the basis for an all-encompassing theory of rational choice.

In order to provide a fully convincing account of altruism as a motivating force behind individual rational choice, it is therefore necessary to embed altruistic concerns in a more fully specified theory of extended rationality. The remaining sections of this paper are aimed at moving some steps in this direction.

5. An alternative evolutionary approach to altruism

The fact that evolutionary explanations of altruism based on the sociobiological principle of inclusive fitness maximization at the genetic level do not

[6] The competition via group membership advanced by Hirschleifer amounts to the advocacy of evolution via group selection, as opposed to via individual selection. Group selection is opposed by ultra-Darwinists like Dawkins but has found some credit in the more recent literature; see e.g. Eshel (1972).

provide us with a well-founded theory of extended rationality does not rule out the possibility of building an alternative evolutionary approach based on different principles. The recent developments of the debate around the sociobiological paradigm seem to hint that, after all, radical genetic reductionism is a somewhat far fetched position as far as the explanation of human conduct is concerned (see e.g. Gallino 1980). As extensively argued, for example, by Harris (1989), genetic factors are only able to account for a narrow minority of human customs and behaviours, the majority of which seem instead to be the outcome of a much more teleologically oriented process of cultural evolution whose action is often not traceable to any specific characteristic of the genetic substratum.

It seems therefore reasonable, as a first approximation, to study the evolutionary mechanisms that account for the selection of behaviours abstracting from the action of genetic factors. Unlike natural selection, cultural selection is dominated by the transmission of individual experiences from one generation to another; culture itself is after all nothing but a sophisticated mechanism aimed at the storing of past experiences and at the selective prompting of new ones.

The long-term dynamics of cultural evolution processes is very complicated and requires a unified approach which melts together the insights coming from the various social sciences such as economics, sociology, anthropology, social psychology, history, and so on. It is not excluded that in the future the need of such a widening of perspective will be acknowledged in order to arrive at a truly satisfactory approach to rational choice. For the moment, we confine ourselves to a much less ambitious objective and limit our attention to the short (–medium)-term dynamics of cultural evolution. We will assume that, in the short-term perspective we focus on, the evolution of behaviours is essentially driven by the imitation of relatively more rewarding behaviours. We do not mean to deny that learning can occur through much more complex modes including structural inference, active research, or sophisticated adaptive rules (see e.g. Selten 1991 for a comprehensive survey on this topic); our aim, however, is to make the model as simple as possible in order to elucidate its basic features especially as far as the modelling of altruistic behaviour is concerned; for a general discussion of the methodological issues raised by this model see Sacco (1993).

We have so far criticized the existing approaches to the modelling of altruistic behaviour by arguing that (*a*) they fail to account for the dynamic, history-dependent feedback effects from experience to tastes through which altruism is reinforced within, or wiped out from, the individual's motivational system; (*b*) there exist different varieties of altruism which can induce quite different behaviours as well as quite different 'motivational dynamics' in the above specified sense. We will argue that these two crucial features may be captured by means of a simple dynamic model of cultural evolution. Instead of trying to build a general theory, we will concentrate on a specific example, a contribution game with two donors and one receiver. We will distinguish the various sorts of altruism in terms of the respective preference orderings on the outcomes of the game and will show under what conditions they are selected (or selected away) when matched to different types of altruism (or of egoism). We will moreover be able to extract a few stylized facts which are likely to be exportable to some degree to a more general context. It is important, however, to stress that we mean this exercise as a preliminary step that calls for extensive further exploration in later work.

It is worth remarking that the taxonomy of altruist types we introduce below is not Jencks's taxonomy discussed in section 4. The relationship between our and Jencks's taxonomy is not immediate because the two sit at different levels of specificity; Jencks classifies altruism according to its possible motivations, whereas our classification criterion is based on the preference orderings that are induced by the various types. As a consequence, each of our altruist types may in principle be compatible with more different motivations in the sense of Jencks.

Our taxonomy is meant as an original contribution that partly draws on the previous literature and has been designed for the specific model we have in mind, although its validity is probably not limited to this narrow context.

6. The contribution game and player types

In this section we introduce the following contribution game: two parties (*I* and *II*) have to decide whether to contribute a sum of money to a third party (*P*) who is in a state of need. To simplify matters, we assume that, in order to survive, *P* needs to receive one dollar; *I* and *II* have to decide whether to contribute one dollar, half a dollar, or nothing. The 'pay-off' the contributors get depends on the amounts they contribute (respectively) and on the total amount collected by *P*. Given our assumptions, the outcome space for the contribution game contains nine elements; we index the outcome space by means of couples (., .), where the first entry indicates *I*'s contribution whereas the second indicates *II*'s contribution.

In order to classify various possible types of players, the first basic distinction to be introduced is between altruists and egoists. In the present context, altruistic players are those whose 'pay-off' depends not only on the amount contributed but also on the amount collected by *P*. Egoists, on the other hand, do not care for *P*'s well-being; their main concern is to minimize their expenditure. Within the class of altruistic players, various types of altruism are characterized by the corresponding preference orderings $\succ$ over the outcome space. In particular, we distinguish four different types of altruists.[7] Take for example the point of view of player *I*. We say that *I* is a Subsidiary Altruist (SA) if

[7] Miller (1989) considers as a special instance of a contribution game the case concerning the institution of a welfare state. The basic question he raises is: 'What must be true of people's

$$\left(0, \frac{1}{2}\right) > \mathrm{I}\left(\frac{1}{2}, 0\right)$$

$$(0, 1) > \mathrm{I}\left(\frac{1}{2}, \frac{1}{2}\right) > \mathrm{I}(1, 0)$$

$$(1, 0) > \mathrm{I}(0, 0)$$

$$\left(\frac{1}{2}, 0\right) > \mathrm{I}(0, 0)$$

(Here and in the following, we will restrict ourselves to strict subsets of possible outcome comparisons, i.e. those which characterize specifically the particular type of player we are considering.)

In other words, a Subsidiary Altruist is an individual *I* who cares for *P*'s well-being but prefers that, if possible, the contribution rests on the shoulders of the other player, *II*. On the other hand, if *I* knew that *II* is not willing to contribute, she would contribute something rather than nothing.

I is said to be a Reciprocal Altruist (RA) if

$$(0, 0) > \mathrm{I}\left(\frac{1}{2}, 0\right) > \mathrm{I}(1, 0)$$

$$\left(\frac{1}{2}, \frac{1}{2}\right) > \mathrm{I}(0, 0)$$

$$\left(\frac{1}{2}, \frac{1}{2}\right) > \mathrm{I}(0, 1)$$

A Reciprocal Altruist is thus an individual whose aspiration is that of having himself and the other player both contributing the same amount. If *I* now knew that *II* is not going to contribute, he would contribute nothing. On the other hand, *I* would prefer to contribute something if he knew that *II* is going to contribute something. In other words, a Reciprocal Altruist is someone who wants the responsibility for contribution to be equally divided among all subjects; if this is not the case, he prefers giving up contributing rather than carrying the burden of contribution alone.[8]

We say that *I* is a Kantian Altruist (KA) if

$$\left(\frac{1}{2}, 0\right) > \mathrm{I}(0, 0)$$

$$\left(\frac{1}{2}, 0\right) > \mathrm{I}(1, 0)$$

altruistic concern for others if they would prefer to see a welfare state in existence rather than relying on private charitable schemes?' (p. 100).

[8] Trivers (1971) calls 'reciprocal altruism' an ongoing pattern of interaction in which I help you, then you help me and so on. Reciprocal Altruism is a matter of 'enlightened self-interest' in the sense clarified by Axelrod (1984). It is interesting to note that Reciprocal Altruism seems to depend on trust and that trust in turn probably depends, at least to some extent, on empathy.

$$\left(\frac{1}{2}, \frac{1}{2}\right) > \text{I}(0, 1)$$

A Kantian Altruist is someone who is ready to contribute independently of the other player's decision. On the other hand, if *I* knew that *II* is not going to contribute, she would contribute one-half rather than one, i.e. she would contribute her part of an equal sharing of the burden of contribution, in spite of the fact that this contribution alone is not enough to warrant *P*'s well-being. Moreover, *I* prefers a situation where both players contribute something rather than a situation where all the burden is on the shoulders of the other player.[9]

Finally, *I* is a Superkantian Altruist (SKA) if

$$(1, 0) > \text{I}\left(\frac{1}{2}, 0\right) > \text{I}(0, 0)$$

$$\left(\frac{1}{2}, \frac{1}{2}\right) > \text{I}(0, 1)$$

The main feature that distinguishes a Superkantian Altruist from a Kantian Altruist is that, if she knew that the other player is not going to contribute, she would be ready to carry all the burden of contribution alone rather than merely her part of an equal sharing of the burden. In other words, whereas a KA is mainly concerned with the fulfilment of her moral duty to contribute, a SKA's main concern is *P*'s actual well-being.

Coming to egoist types of players, we say that *I* is a Pure Egoist (PE) if

$$(0, 1) > \text{I}\left(\frac{1}{2}, 1\right) > \text{I}(1, 1)$$

$$\left(0, \frac{1}{2}\right) > \text{I}\left(\frac{1}{2}, \frac{1}{2}\right) > \text{I}\left(1, \frac{1}{2}\right)$$

$$(0, 0) > \text{I}\left(\frac{1}{2}, 0\right) > \text{I}(1, 0)$$

In other words, a Pure Egoist is someone who is neither concerned with *P*'s well-being nor is willing to contribute anything for any reason.

Alternatively, we say that *I* is an Egoist with Regret (ER) if

$$(0, 1) > \text{I}\left(\frac{1}{2}, 1\right) > \text{I}(1, 1)$$

9 Laffont (1975) introduces and formalizes the notion of Kantian behaviour in a model with externalities and public goods. He shows that efficiency will result if everybody acts as a Kantian. The Kantian contribution is defined as the maximum amount that each individual would perceive as morally right to contribute in each group to which he belongs. Sugden (1984), building upon Laffont, presents a theory based on a notion of reciprocity and Kantian behaviour. Other related works are those of Collard (1978; 1991).

$$\left(0, \frac{1}{2}\right) >_I \left(\frac{1}{2}, \frac{1}{2}\right) >_I \left(1, \frac{1}{2}\right)$$

$$(0, 0) >_I \left(\frac{1}{2}, 0\right) >_I (1, 0)$$

$$(0, 0) >_I \left(0, \frac{1}{2}\right) >_I (0, 1)$$

That is, an Egoist with Regret is someone who is not interested in *P*'s well-being but nevertheless is disturbed by the fact that someone else is willing to contribute, the more so the higher the amount of the contribution. Notice that this does not imply any evidence of concern for *P*'s well-being: *I*'s 'pay-off' is higher the less *P* receives; moreover, she will not contribute anything anyway.

The discussion above is illustrated in Fig. 14.1. In order to proceed with the formal analysis, however, we have to introduce some more structure. In order to make 'pay-offs' of the various types of players commensurable, we

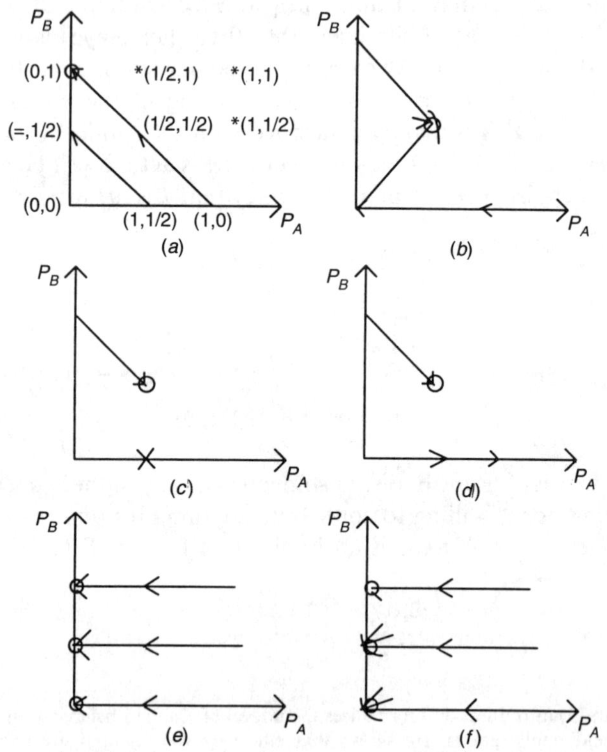

FIG. 14.1. *Preference orderings for player types. (a) SA; (b) RA; (c) KA; (d) SKA; (e) PE; (f) ER*

will identify for each a 'bliss outcome' (not necessarily unique) to which we will assign a 'pay-off' levels equal to one. As to outcomes which are less preferred w.r.t. the bliss one, we will assign 'pay-off' levels equal to $\frac{1}{2}$, 0, $-\frac{1}{2}$, or -1, according to cases, thus completing the preference orderings introduced above and choosing a specific numerical representation. There are of course many possible completions and numerical representations that are compatible with the preference judgements listed above; the one chosen does not seem to entail, however, a relevant loss of generality in any specific sense.

To avoid unnecessary complications, we assume that players' (negative) 'pay-offs' at outcomes in which there is overcontribution are the same irrespective of the specific type. Indicating the 'pay-off' function for I as $\pi(.,.)$, we therefore postulate that:

$$\pi(1, 1) = -1 \quad \pi\left(1, \frac{1}{2}\right) = -1 \quad \pi\left(\frac{1}{2}, 1\right) = \frac{1}{2}$$

The numerical representation of players' preferences on the remaining six outcomes, according to the respective types, are as follows:
(*a*) Subsidiary Altruist:

$$\pi_{SA}(0, 1) = 1 \quad \pi_{SA}\left(0, \frac{1}{2}\right) = \frac{1}{2} \quad \pi_{SA}(0, 0) = -1$$

$$\pi_{SA}\left(\frac{1}{2}, 0\right) = 0 \quad \pi_{SA}\left(\frac{1}{2}, \frac{1}{2}\right) = \frac{1}{2} \quad \pi_{SA}(1, 0) = 0$$

(*b*) Reciprocal Altruist:

$$\pi_{RA}(0, 1) = -\frac{1}{2} \quad \pi_{RA}\left(0, \frac{1}{2}\right) = 0 \quad \pi_{RA}(0, 0) = \frac{1}{2}$$

$$\pi_{RA}\left(\frac{1}{2}, 0\right) = -\frac{1}{2} \quad \pi_{RA}\left(\frac{1}{2}, \frac{1}{2}\right) = 1 \quad \pi_{RA}(1, 0) = -1$$

(*c*) Kantian Altruist:

$$\pi_{KA}(0, 1) = -\frac{1}{2} \quad \pi_{KA}\left(0, \frac{1}{2}\right) = 0 \quad \pi_{KA}(0, 0) = 0$$

$$\pi_{KA}\left(\frac{1}{2}, 0\right) = -\frac{1}{2} \quad \pi_{KA}\left(\frac{1}{2}, \frac{1}{2}\right) = 1 \quad \pi_{KA}(1, 0) = 0$$

(*d*) Superkantian Altruist:

$$\pi_{SKA}(0, 1) = -1 \quad \pi_{SKA}\left(0, \frac{1}{2}\right) = -\frac{1}{2} \quad \pi_{SKA}(0, 0) = -\frac{1}{2}$$

$$\pi_{SKA}\left(\frac{1}{2}, 0\right) = 0 \quad \pi_{SKA}\left(\frac{1}{2}, \frac{1}{2}\right) = 1 \quad \pi_{SKA}(1, 0) = \frac{1}{2}$$

(*e*) Pure Egoist:

$$\pi_{PE}(0,1) = 1 \quad \pi_{PE}\left(0, \frac{1}{2}\right) = 1 \quad \pi_{PE}(0, 0) = 1$$

$$\pi_{PE}\left(\frac{1}{2}, 0\right) = -\frac{1}{2} \quad \pi_{PE}\left(\frac{1}{2}, \frac{1}{2}\right) = -\frac{1}{2} \quad \pi_{PE}(1, 0) = -1$$

(*f*) Egoist with Regret:

$$\pi_{ER}(0,1) = 0 \quad \pi_{ER}\left(0, \frac{1}{2}\right) = \frac{1}{2} \quad \pi_{ER}(0, 0) = 1$$

$$\pi_{ER}\left(\frac{1}{2}, 0\right) = -\frac{1}{2} \quad \pi_{ER}\left(\frac{1}{2}, \frac{1}{2}\right) = -\frac{1}{2} \quad \pi_{ER}(1, 0) = -1$$

Notice that this numerical representation for ER implies that *I*'s negative 'pay-off' caused by the observation of the (positive) contribution of others is substantially less than the negative 'pay-off' caused by her own contributing.

The formal description of the contribution game is thus complete. In the next section we derive best reply strategies for each type of player depending on the opponent's type.

7. Best replies

SA vs. SKA

Playing against a SKA, a SA will never choose to contribute 1; the reason is simple: since a SKA will contribute something anyway, contributing 1 for a SA becomes a dominated strategy. Thus the choice for a SA is restricted to contributing 0 or $\frac{1}{2}$. In the first case, a SKA's best response is contributing 1; in the second, a SKA's best response is contributing $\frac{1}{2}$. On the other hand, provided that a SKA contributes 1($\frac{1}{2}$), a SA's best response is to contribute 0 ($\frac{1}{2}$ or 0). We have therefore two possible Nash equilibria: (SA = 0, SKA = 1); (SA = $\frac{1}{2}$, SKA = $\frac{1}{2}$). On the other hand, there is a strong incentive for a SA to play 0 anyway, since even provided that a SKA intends to play $\frac{1}{2}$, a SA gets in this case the same 'pay-off' by playing 0 or $\frac{1}{2}$, i.e. SA = $\frac{1}{2}$ is a weak best response to SKA = $\frac{1}{2}$. On the other hand, if a SKA plays 1, a SA is strictly better. We can therefore conclude that, provided that a SA and a SKA meet, the natural outcome to predict is (SA = 0, SKA = 1).

SA vs. KA

As before, a SA knows that, playing against a KA, the latter will always choose to contribute something. Therefore, SA = 1 is ruled out. Now, irrespectively of whether SA = $\frac{1}{2}$ or SA = 0, a KA's best response is playing $\frac{1}{2}$. A SA is indifferent between these two options: provided that a KA plays

$\frac{1}{2}$, a SA gets $\frac{1}{2}$ anyway. This choice, however, does make a difference for a KA: if a SA plays $\frac{1}{2}$, by playing $\frac{1}{2}$ a KA gets 1, whereas if a SA plays 0, a KA gets only $\frac{1}{2}$. To sum up, in this case there are two Nash equilibria: (SA = 0, KA = $\frac{1}{2}$), (SA = $\frac{1}{2}$, KA = $\frac{1}{2}$). Neither of them can be ruled out, so both outcomes are possible.

SA vs. RA

In this case, a SA knows that a RA will never play 1. If a RA plays 0, a SA is indifferent between playing 1 and playing $\frac{1}{2}$. However, provided that a SA plays $\frac{1}{2}$, a RA prefers to play $\frac{1}{2}$ as well. Now, if a RA plays $\frac{1}{2}$, a SA is again indifferent between playing 0 and playing $\frac{1}{2}$. Therefore, the only reason why a SA may be induced to play 1 is the belief that a RA will play 0. In this case, however, a SA will be indifferent between playing $\frac{1}{2}$ and playing 1. But if a RA is not going to play 0, playing $\frac{1}{2}$ is definitely better for a SA since she will be strictly better off provided that a RA plays $\frac{1}{2}$. As for a RA, if a SA plays 1 a (weak) best response for a RA is to play 0; if instead a SA plays $\frac{1}{2}$, a RA will surely play $\frac{1}{2}$. Finally, notice that a SA will never play 0 in equilibrium. In conclusion, there are two Nash equilibria: (SA = $\frac{1}{2}$, RA = $\frac{1}{2}$) and (SA = 1, RA = 0). As in the case SA vs. SKA, the second Nash equilibrium may be ruled out. We are therefore left with a unique prediction.

SA vs. PE

In this case, a PE unambiguously plays 0. A SA is then indifferent between playing $\frac{1}{2}$ or 1. We therefore obtain the two Nash equilibria (SA = 1, PE = 0), (SA = $\frac{1}{2}$, PE = 0) , none of which can be ruled out.

SA vs. ER

In this case also a ER unambiguously plays 0, and a SA is therefore indifferent between $\frac{1}{2}$ and 1. This choice, however, now makes a difference for a ER; if a SA plays 1, a ER gets 0, whereas if a SA plays $\frac{1}{2}$, a ER gets $\frac{1}{2}$. (Notice the analogy with the case SA vs. KA.)

RA vs. KA or vs. SKA

These cases are relatively straightforward. A RA knows that a KA will play $\frac{1}{2}$ anyway, so she will play $\frac{1}{2}$ as well; the same reasoning holds *a fortiori* for the SKA. Therefore, in both cases the natural outcome to predict is (RA = $\frac{1}{2}$, KA = $\frac{1}{2}$), resp. (RA = $\frac{1}{2}$, SKA = $\frac{1}{2}$). (In the case of a SKA, (RA = 0, SKA = 1) would in principle be a Nash equilibrium as well but, since RA = 0 is a weak best response, it can be ruled out by the same line of reasoning set out above.)

RA vs. PE or ER

Here also the analysis is straightforward. Both a PE and a ER will always play 0. Consequently, a RA will surely play 0 as well.

KA vs. SKA

Provided that the KA will play $\frac{1}{2}$ anyway, the SKA will play $\frac{1}{2}$ as well. Once again the natural outcome to predict is (KA = $\frac{1}{2}$, SKA = $\frac{1}{2}$). (Here too there exists another Nash equilibrium which can be ruled out by the usual argument, namely (KA = 0, SKA = 1).)

PE vs. KA or SKA

Provided that PE = 0, a KA will surely play $\frac{1}{2}$, whereas a SKA will surely play 1.

ER vs. KA or SKA

Similarly a ER will surely play 0. However, if facing a KA (who will play $\frac{1}{2}$), a ER gets $\frac{1}{2}$, whereas if facing a SKA (who will play 1), a ER gets 0.

ER vs. PE

Clearly, both will play 0 reaching their bliss outcome.

The only cases left are now those where players face opponents of the same type.

SA vs. SA

When two SA meet, it is easy to check that three Nash equilibria are possible: (i) one of the two contributes 1 whereas the other does not contribute; (ii) both contribute $\frac{1}{2}$; (iii) one of the two contributes $\frac{1}{2}$ whereas the other does not contribute. At the last two equilibria, both players get the same pay-off; at the first, the one who leaves the burden of contribution on the shoulders of the other is better off.

RE vs. RE, SKA vs. SKA, KA vs. KA

In all three cases, the natural outcome to predict is clearly that at which each player contributes $\frac{1}{2}$.

PE vs. PE, ER vs. ER

In both cases, the natural outcome to predict is clearly that at which each player contributes nothing.

8. Evolutionary dynamics: basic assumptions

In this section we move one step further to analyse the following model. We start from a continuous population in which players of two different types initially coexist. Time is continuous. Players are randomly matched to play the contribution game discussed earlier. Players' types are perfectly observable, as well as the actual distribution of types within the population. When matched to an opponent of a certain type, a player acts according to the theory of strategic rationality set out in the previous section, i.e. they play their best response strategy to the opponent's type. It is moreover assumed that, at each given time t, a negligible fraction of players is prompted to revise their strategy choice, according to the following criterion: a player decides to change her type if and only if the strategy that characterizes the other type yields a higher expected 'pay-off', i.e. behaviours that look more rewarding are imitated at the expense of others. In other words, the timing of players' decisions is asynchronous and players are boundedly rational in the sense that their strategy choices may (temporarily) not be best responses to the observed distribution of types. Notice, however, that the actual best response strategy depends on the distribution of types itself; this means that a given strategy may be effective in some situations but not in others. In spite of players' bounded rationality, if a stationary distribution of types is ever reached, it should have the property that players eventually learn the corresponding best response strategy.

The set of assumptions just introduced is summarized by the following dynamic model, known as pay-off-monotonic dynamics (see e.g. Samuelson and Zhang 1992), which states that if a strategy is more rewarding given the current distribution of types it will spread over the population at the expense of the other:

$$\dot{q} \propto \Delta\,\tilde{\pi}(q)$$

Here $q \in (0, 1)$ denotes the proportion of players of type α (say) in the population; the proportion of players of type β is clearly $1 - q$. $\Delta\tilde{\pi}(q)$ is the (expected) 'pay-off' differential between type α and type β players, which depends on q.

It can be shown (see e.g. Friedman 1992, Ritzberger and Weibull 1992) that when there are only two strategies to choose between, all possible pay-off-monotonic specifications are dynamically equivalent up to a reparametrization of time, i.e. different specifications entail different speeds of adjustment towards stable states which are, however, common to all (together with the corresponding basins of attraction). Therefore choosing one particular specification does not entail any real loss of generality in this context. To simplify the exposition, in the remainder of the chapter we will always refer to the best-known example of pay-off-monotonic dynamics, namely replicator dynamics (see e.g. Hofbauer and Sygmund 1988):

$$\dot{q} = q(1 - q)\Delta\tilde{\pi}(q) \tag{1}$$

It is apparent from (1) that $q = 0$ and $q = 1$ are always stationary points for (1), that is, if the population is entirely made up of players of a same type, it will stay homogeneous as long as no exogenous perturbation occurs. Finally, a type's proportion increases if and only if it performs better than the other, as required above. It is easy to check that equation (1) is equivalent to postulating that $\dot{q}$ is positive if and only if players of type α earn a 'pay-off' that is higher than the population average 'pay-off' $q\tilde{\pi}_\alpha(q) + (1 - q)\tilde{\pi}_\beta(q)$.

In our context, players' strategy choices are whether to be altruist or egoist, and of which type. This clearly implies that players' altruistic (egoistic) attitudes are to be seen as the object of a purposeful choice rather than as a basic, immutable feature of their personality over which they have no control. Players are assumed to be ready to choose a certain altruistic (egoistic) attitude whenever their observation of other individuals reveals that people behaving that way look 'happier' than others. Of course, players' 'happiness' (namely 'pay-offs') has to be perfectly observable; one can for example think that the level of 'happiness' may be unambiguously inferred from the intensity of an individual's 'smile' (or 'frown'). This is the mechanism through which players' experience is assumed to feed back on the respective motivational systems. Moreover, notice that the diffusion of a certain kind of altruistic (egoistic) attitude within the population may be easily read as the emergence of a social convention in the sense of Lewis (1969): given that people tend to behave in a certain way, each individual finds it convenient to behave in the same way and expects the same to hold for all others. In fact, it is possible to show that all asymptotically stable states of the evolutionary dynamics (1) (i.e. all possible social conventions in the sense of Lewis) are evolutionary stable Nash equilibria.[10]

In the following section we will study the conditions under which such social conventions emerge, starting from an initial distribution of types. In this chapter we limit our attention to two-type populations; however, there is nothing that prevents the extension of our analysis to higher-dimensional cases. This endeavour, which is clearly of great interest, is left for future research.

9. Selection of conventions: the relative 'fitness' of altruistic and egoistic attitudes

The order with which the various possible cases are analysed in this section is different from the one followed earlier. In both cases, it has been chosen for expositional convenience; no confusion should arise from this.

[10] This result no longer holds when more than two types of players interact, as far as the evolutionary stability part of the statement is concerned; see Hofbauer and Sygmund (1988).

SKA vs. ER

We begin by analysing the case of an initial population made up of SKA and ER players (briefly, a SKA–ER population). We denote by q the proportion of SKA players. Their expected 'pay-off' is then given by

$$\tilde{\pi}_{SKA}(q) = q\pi_{SKA}\left(\frac{1}{2}, \frac{1}{2}\right) + (1-q)\pi_{SKA}(1, 0) = \frac{1}{2}q + \frac{1}{2} \tag{2}$$

Accordingly, the expected 'pay-off' for ER players is

$$\tilde{\pi}_{ER}(q) = (1-q)\pi_{ER}(0, 0) + q\pi_{ER}(0, 1) = 1 - q \tag{3}$$

One therefore has that

$$\Delta\tilde{\pi}(q) = \frac{3}{2}q - \frac{1}{2} \tag{4}$$

from which it follows that $\Delta\tilde{\pi}(q) = 0$ for $\hat{q} = \frac{1}{3}$. More specifically, for $q > \hat{q}$ one has that $\Delta\tilde{\pi}(q) > 0$, whereas for $q < \hat{q}$, $\Delta\tilde{\pi}(q) < 0$. It is then easily checked that the following holds:

PROPOSITION 1. *Consider a SKA-ER population. If the initial proportion q_0 of SKA players is larger than one-third, then all players will eventually become SKA. If conversely q_0 is less than one-third, all players will eventually become ER.*

What Proposition 1 says is that, in order to observe a stationary population entirely made up of SKA players when the alternative for players is to be of the ER type, a large enough initial proportion of SKA players is necessary (see Fig. 14.2). The critical threshold which qualifies the 'large enough' clause clearly depends on the numerical specification of 'pay-offs'. Assume, for example,[11] that instead of $\pi_{SKA}(1, 0) = \frac{1}{2}$ one has $\pi_{SKA}(1, 0) \equiv \phi$, where $\phi \in [0, 1]$. Then one has that $\tilde{\pi}_{SKA}(q) = q + (1-q)\phi$ and $\hat{q} = (1-\phi)/(2-\phi)$. As $\phi \to 0$, i.e. SKA players get little pleasure from carrying the whole burden of the contribution alone, $\hat{q} \to \frac{1}{2}$, i.e. the minimal initial proportion of SKA players needed to bring the SKA convention about increases. On the other hand, as $\phi \to 1$, i.e. as SKA players tend to find their bliss in carrying the burden alone, $\hat{q} \to 0$, i.e. the population is eventually all made up of SKA players as long as a positive initial proportion of SKA players, however tiny, is present in the population. Notice that, however little pleasure SKA players get from carrying the burden alone (as long as $\phi > 0$), if SKA players are initially the majority within the population, everybody will be a SKA eventually.

[11] Here and in the following we assume that, when one or more 'pay-offs' are allowed to vary, other 'pay-offs' vary accordingly if necessary in order to ensure that the selected actions are still best responses.

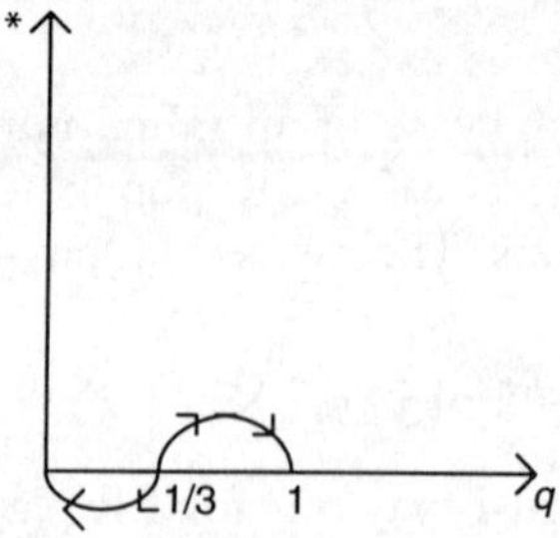

FIG. 14.2. *Bistable dynamics: the SKA-ER case*

PE vs. ER

We now pass to a population where players are all egoists, although of different types. It is clear that, in this case, both types of players attain the same 'pay-offs' whatever the initial distribution of types since they will always play exactly the same way. As a consequence, the initial distribution of types q_0 will not be altered as time unfolds: players have nothing to learn from experience. Every possible q_0 is therefore a social convention here. In other words, in this case (1) gives rise to a neutral dynamics.

SKA vs. PE

Denoting again by q the proportion of SKA players, one has

$$\tilde{\pi}_{SKA}(q) = q\pi_{SKA}\left(\frac{1}{2}, \frac{1}{2}\right) + (1-q)\pi_{SKA}(1, 0) = \frac{1}{2} + \frac{1}{2}q \tag{5}$$

On the other hand, it is easily checked that $\tilde{\pi}_{PE}(q) = 1$, i.e. PE players reach their maximum attainable 'pay-off' anyway. Consequently, we have

PROPOSITION 2. *Consider a SKA-PE population. Unless the population is initially entirely made of SKA players* (i.e. $q_0 = 1$), *all players will eventually become PE.*

Notice the difference between the results of Proposition 1 and those of Proposition 2. The fact that egoist players may regret, i.e. may be disturbed by the generosity of Superkantian players, gives Superkantian Altruism a (pretty large) chance to survive in equilibrium. On the other hand, Pure Egoists are not affected at all by the behaviour of their opponents, however altruistic it is. Therefore, they will always be happier than SKA altruists and Pure Egoism will prevail (see Fig. 14.3). If, however, SKA players attain a 'pay-off' of $\phi \to 1$ when carrying the whole burden of the contribution, they end up as happy as PE players. In other words, Superkantian Altruism is

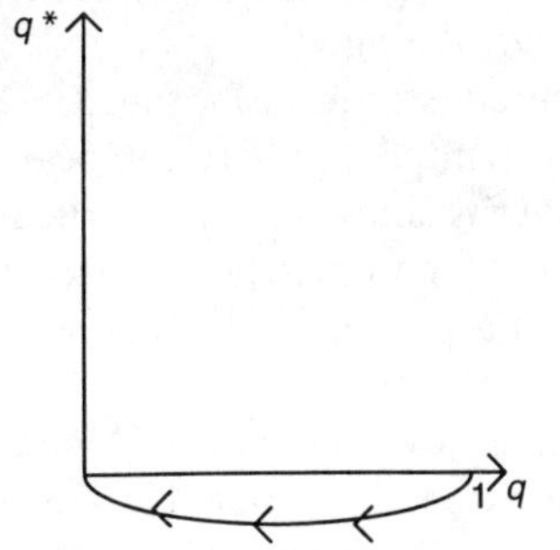

FIG. 14.3. *Globally stable dynamics; the SKA-PE case*

not wiped out by Pure Egoism in its 'pure' form, i.e. when SKA players reach their bliss when carrying the whole burden of the contribution, valuing altruism *per se*. In this latter case, a neutral dynamics results once again, that is, the initial distribution of types is preserved: both Pure Egoists and altruists stay of the same mind, learning nothing new from experience.

KA vs. ER

Denoting by q the proportion of KA players and computing 'pay-offs' by the usual procedure, we have

$$\tilde{\pi}_{KA}(q) = q\,\pi_{KA}\left(\frac{1}{2}, \frac{1}{2}\right) + (1-q)\pi_{KA}\left(\frac{1}{2}, 0\right) = \frac{1}{2}q + \frac{1}{2} \tag{6}$$

$$\tilde{\pi}_{ER}(q) = (1-q)\pi_{ER}(0, 0) + q\pi_{ER}\left(0, \frac{1}{2}\right) \tag{7}$$

from which it follows

$$\Delta\tilde{\pi}(q) = q - \frac{1}{2} \tag{8}$$

As in the case of SKA vs. ER, it is easily checked that $\Delta\tilde{\pi}(q) > 0$ for $q > \hat{q} = \frac{1}{2}$ and $\Delta\tilde{\pi}(q) < 0$ for $q < \hat{q}$. Therefore:

PROPOSITION 3. *Consider a KA-ER population. If the initial proportion q_0 of KA players is larger than one half, then all players will eventually become KA. If conversely q_0 is less than one-half, all players will eventually become ER.*

Notice the difference w.r.t. the case SKA vs. ER. Being less generous than those of SKA players, the choices of KA players are less disturbing for ERs. Therefore, the minimum initial proportion of KA that is necessary to bring Kantian Altruism about eventually is larger than that for Superkantian

Altruism. Clearly, as KA players get more satisfaction from their partial contribution to *P*'s well-being (in spite of its inadequacy), i.e. as $\pi_{KA}(\frac{1}{2}, 0) \equiv \alpha \to 1$, such constraint is loosened, i.e. $\hat{q}$ decreases. Unlike the case of SKA players, it is improper here to speak of pure altruism, in that in this case the KA player is simply not concerned at all by the fact that the needs of *P* have not been completely fulfilled, i.e. she reaches her bliss despite this. Rather than a pure altruist, such a player seems rather a pure philistine.

More generally, assume now that $\pi_{KA}(\frac{1}{2}, 0) \equiv \alpha, \pi_{ER}(0, \frac{1}{2}) \equiv \beta, \alpha, \beta \in [0, 1]$. β clearly measures the extent to which ER players are disturbed by the altruism of KA players; the closer β is to 1, the less ER players are disturbed. In this case, $\hat{q} = (1 - \alpha)/(2 - \beta - \alpha)$. As α and β both tend to zero, $\hat{q} \to \frac{1}{2}$. On the other hand, if $\alpha \to 0$ whereas $\beta \to 1$, $\hat{\mu} \to 1$ (i.e., all players are eventually ER for $q_0 \neq 1$); if instead $\alpha \to 1$ whereas $\beta \to 0$, $\hat{\mu} \to 0$ (i.e. all players are eventually KA for $q_0 \neq 0$). Finally, if both α and β tend to 1, the limit value of $\hat{q}$ depends on the relative speeds of α, β.

KA vs. PE

Denote by q the proportion of KA players. It is easy to check that $\tilde{\pi}_{PE}(q) = 1$, as above. As to KA, we have

$$\tilde{\pi}_{KA}(q) = q\pi_{KA}\left(\frac{1}{2}, \frac{1}{2}\right) + (1 - q)\pi_{KA}\left(\frac{1}{2}, 0\right) \tag{9}$$

Therefore,

$$\Delta\tilde{\pi}(q) = \frac{1}{2}q - \frac{1}{2} \tag{10}$$

from which follows

PROPOSITION 4. *Consider a KA-PE population. Unless the population is initially entirely made of SKA players* (*i.e.* $q_0 = 1$), *all players will eventually become PE.*

Analogously to the case SKA vs. PE, for $\pi_{KA}(\frac{1}{2}, 0) \equiv \delta \to 1$ one obtains a neutral dynamics which preserves the initial distribution q_0 whatever it is. As observed above, this sort of behaviour cannot be interpreted as an instance of pure altruism.

KA vs. SKA

This case is very easy to deal with, since starting from any initial distribution of types, players' behaviour is the same irrespective of the actual type of the opponent with which they are matched, provided that the Nash equilibrium (KA $= \frac{1}{2}$, SKA $= \frac{1}{2}$) at which both types reach their bliss is played. If instead the other Nash equilibrium (KA = 0, SKA = 1) is played, all players are eventually SKA since $\pi_{KA}(0,1) < 0 < \pi_{SKA}(1, 0)$. This latter possibility is, however, somewhat unlikely for the reasons explained earlier.

RA vs. PE or ER

Here also the analysis is very simple, since RA players always choose to contribute nothing against egoist types of players. As a consequence, RA players achieve a low level of 'pay-offs' whenever they meet egoist players, whereas the latter always get their maximum attainable 'pay-offs' (no matter whether they meet RA players or players of their same type). Thus, unless the initial population is entirely made of RA players, everybody will eventually be an egoist here. Notice in particular that Reciprocal Altruism is the only sort of altruism that is not disturbing for ER players.

RA vs. KA or SKA

When RA players meet KA or SKA players, each subject chooses to contribute one-half, no matter her type. As a consequence, players always reach their bliss independently of the identity of the opponents with which they are matched. Once again we therefore have a neutral dynamics that preserves the initial distribution of types q_0, in which players have nothing to learn from experience.

Egoist players with probabilistic regret We have so far only considered egoist players who either feel no regret or always regret when meeting players who choose to contribute. We now consider the case of egoist players who regret with a fixed probability $\theta \in (0, 1)$ provided that their opponents choose to contribute, or of egoist players who regret with a probability q, increasing in the proportion q of altruistic players (with θ still belonging to the interior of the unit interval). It can be checked that, in the former case, the critical threshold $\hat{q}$ for a KA – ER(θ) population, beyond which all players eventually become KA, is equal to $\hat{q} = 1/(1 + \theta)$. For a SKA – ER(θ) population, the threshold is now equal to $\hat{q} = 1/(1 + 2\theta)$. In the latter case, the critical threshold becomes $\hat{q} = (1/2\theta)[\sqrt{2\theta + \frac{1}{4}} - \frac{1}{2}]$. Notice that $(1/2\theta)[\sqrt{2\theta + \frac{1}{4}} - \frac{1}{2}] < 1/(1 + 2\theta)$, i.e. the survival chances of egoist behaviour are enhanced when they regret with probability q since, as q is close to zero (i.e. as there are few SKA players around) egoist players ar eless likely to regret. More generally, the case of egoist players who regret with a certain probability (no matter whether fixed or density dependent) is intermediate between the case of PE and that of ER players; the survival chances of egoist behaviour vary accordingly.

SA vs. KA

We have observed earlier that when two SA players meet there are three possible Nash equilibria: (0, 1), (0, $\frac{1}{2}$), ($\frac{1}{2}$, $\frac{1}{2}$). In order to determine how two SA players choose their strategy when meeting each other, we assume that they play a correlated equilibrium that prescribes to play with probability 1– γ and 0 and 1 with probabilities $\gamma/2$ each; this is equivalent to a prescription to play the equilibrium ($\frac{1}{2}$, $\frac{1}{2}$) with probability 1 – γ and the equilibrium (0, 1) with probability γ, with the assignment of roles randomized with equal probabilities. Notice that the equilibrium (0, $\frac{1}{2}$) has been ruled out here since at this equilibrium players get at most as much as they get at the equilibrium (0, 1) (and strictly less when they are not prescribed to contribute).

At the correlated equilibrium (*c*), players expect to get

$$\frac{\gamma}{2}\pi_{SA}(0, 1) = \frac{\gamma}{2}\pi_{SA}(1, 0) + (1-\gamma)\pi_{SA}\left(\frac{1}{2}, \frac{1}{2}\right) = \frac{1}{2}$$

We have moreover seen that, when playing against KA players, SA players have two possible best responses: playing 0 or playing $\frac{1}{2}$. We denote by q the proportion of SA players and assume that they choose to play 0. Then we have

$$\tilde{\pi}_{SA}(q) = q\pi_{SA}(c) + (1-q)\pi_{SA}\left(0, \frac{1}{2}\right) = \frac{1}{2} \tag{11}$$

$$\tilde{\pi}_{KA}(q) = (1-q)\pi_{KA}\left(\frac{1}{2}, \frac{1}{2}\right) + q\pi_{KA}\left(\frac{1}{2}, 0\right) = 1 - \frac{1}{2}q \tag{12}$$

from which it follows

$$\Delta\pi(q) = \frac{1}{2}q - \frac{1}{2} \tag{13}$$

Following the usual line of reasoning, it is easy to check

PROPOSITION 5. *Consider a KA–SA population. Unless the population is initially entirely made of SA players (i.e. $q_0 - 1$), all players will eventually become KA.*

The rationale behind Proposition 5 is clear: when two SA players meet, they cannot simultaneously reach their bliss; on the other hand, when two KA players meet, they always reach their bliss. On the other hand, when meeting an opponent of the other type, both types of players get the same 'pay-off'. Therefore, Kantian Altruism spreads over the population because of its superiority w.r.t. Subsidiary Altruism in cases where players of the *same* type meet.

Consider now the more general case where $\pi_{SA}(0, \frac{1}{2}) = \varepsilon$, $\pi_{KA}(\frac{1}{2}, 0) = \eta$. Then one can check that there exists a critical threshold $\hat{q} = (1 - \varepsilon)/(3/2 - \varepsilon - \eta)$ beyond which all players will eventually be SA. $\hat{q}$ lies in the interior of the unit interval if $\eta < \frac{1}{2}$. In this case, Subsidiary Altruism has a chance to survive provided that the initial proportion of SA players is large enough; the less KA players are happy to carry the burden of contribution alone, the less this constraint is binding.

If on the other hand SA players choose to play $\frac{1}{2}$, the 'pay-off' for the two types is now independent of the actual distribution of types and is given by $\tilde{\pi}_{SA}(q) = \frac{1}{2}$, $\tilde{\pi}_{KA}(q) = 1$. We are therefore led to an interesting conclusion: although playing 0 or $\frac{1}{2}$ is indifferent from the point of view of SA players facing a KA player, the latter choice makes KA players definitely happier and thus leads to the eventual disappearance of Subsidiary Altruism (independently of the actual 'pay-off' specification for SA players). In other words, even if playing 0 does not give SA players a direct advantage in terms of 'pay-offs', it gives them an evolutionary advantage (in the sense of the survival possibilities of Subsidiary Altruism). More generally, if SA players randomize between playing 0 and playing $\frac{1}{2}$ with probabilities ρ and $1 - \rho$, respectively, it turns out that $\hat{q}$ lies in the interior of the unit interval if $\rho > \frac{1}{2}$ and $\eta < 1 - (\frac{1}{2}\rho)$, a more binding condition than $\eta < \frac{1}{2}$. Clearly, the larger ρ, the more the survival possibilities of Subsidiary Altruism.

SA vs. SKA

Once again there are two possible Nash equilibria when a SA player meets a SKA player: both playing $\frac{1}{2}$ or the SKA player carrying the whole burden of the contribution. We consider first this latter equilibrium and denote by q the proportion of SA players. In this case, it is easy to check that

$$\tilde{\pi}_{SKA}(q) = \tilde{\pi}_{SA}(q) = 1 - \frac{1}{2}q \tag{14}$$

Since both types get exactly the same 'pay-offs' independently of the actual distribution of players' types, it follows that $\Delta\tilde{\pi}(q) \equiv 0$, i.e. the dynamics preserves the initial distribution of types. KA players have therefore an evolutionary advantage w.r.t. SKAs when playing against SAs: unlike SKAs, they contribute only their fair part of the overall burden, thus making SA players relatively worse off. Notice moreover that, in this case, SA players (expect to) get $\frac{1}{2}$ when playing against themselves and 1 when playing against SKAs; SKA players, on the other hand, get 1 when playing against themselves and $\frac{1}{2}$ when playing against SA. An immediate corollary is therefore that if $\pi_{SKA}(1, 0) < \frac{1}{2}$, all players will eventually be SA, whereas if $\pi_{SKA}(1, 0) > \frac{1}{2}$, all players will eventually be SKA. In other words, if SKA tend to be pure altruists, Superkantian Altruism spreads throughout a SKA–SA population.

As to the other Nash equilibrium where both SKA and SA players contribute one-half, it is easily checked that now $\tilde{\pi}_{SKA}(q) = 1$. As a consequence, all players will eventually be SKA now. Once again, then, although the two possible options for SA players are indifferent in terms of 'pay-offs', they are definitely not indifferent in terms of the survival chances of Subsidiary Altruism.

Finally, if SA players randomize between playing 0 and playing $\frac{1}{2}$, with probabilities σ and $1 - \sigma$, respectively, it can be checked that all players are eventually SKA unless $\pi_{SKA}(1, 0) \equiv \chi < \frac{1}{2}$ and σ is large enough, more precisely $\sigma > \frac{1}{2}(1 - \chi)$.

SA vs. PE or ER

For a SA–PE population, it is very easy to check that all players will eventually be PE. As to a SA–ER population, there are once again two possible Nash equilibria when a SA player meets a ER player: the one at which the SA player contributes one-half and the one at which she contributes 1. Clearly, ER players are more disturbed when SA players contribute 1; more specifically, in this latter case both the SA and the ER player get a 'pay-off' of 0. However, even so all players will eventually be ER since ER players perform better than SA players when playing against an opponent of their same type.

SA vs. RA

In this case, all players will eventually be RA since $\tilde{\pi}_{SA}(q) = \frac{1}{2}$ whereas $\tilde{\pi}_{RA}(q) = 1$. This is due to the fact that, when playing against RA players, SA can do no better than playing $\frac{1}{2}$. Thus RA players here do better than SAs both when playing against opponents of their same type and against opponents of the other type.

10. Conclusion: a few 'stylized facts' and directions for future research

We conclude our formal analysis with a list of the most important 'stylized facts' that can be extracted from the conclusions reached in the previous section.

(*a*) Pure Egoism can never be wiped out provided that it is initially present in the initial distribution of types. There are some forms of altruism, namely Kantian and Superkantian Altruism, that can survive against Pure Egoism even if only in extreme cases (i.e. when players are 'pure altruists' or 'pure philistines').

(*b*) If egoist players are disturbed by the altruism of their opponents, egoistic behaviour can be wiped out under certain conditions. The sort of altruism that performs better against Egoism with Regret is

Superkantian Altruism. Some sorts of altruism, like Subsidiary or Reciprocal Altruism, are instead systematically wiped out by egoistic behaviour of any sort.

(*c*) There are some forms of altruism, like Kantian or Superkantian Altruism, that, although performing relatively well against egoistic behaviour, can be wiped out by other forms of altruism, specifically Subsidiary Altruism, at least under certain conditions.

(*d*) There are many cases in which players cannot learn from experience and the initial distribution of players' types reproduces itself perpetually. This happens whenever the types that make up the population behave homogeneously (but can also happen when types do not behave homogeneously, as in the SA vs. SKA case).

Our analysis may be extended in several different directions. One could study higher-dimensional population dynamics with more than two behavioural types. Also, one could interestingly extend our results to more general game-theoretic contexts; it is not excluded that further relevant variants of selfish and altruistic behaviour may then emerge. At a more fundamental level, our results, in line with some other recent game-theoretic literature, call for a deep rethinking of the methodological individualism postulates on which the standard theory is built. It is not intended to abandon methodological individualism, but rather to go beyond it: we have argued that the core elements on which purposeful individual choices are based (i.e. preferences) may themselves evolve as a consequence of repeated social interaction. Therefore, a true understanding of the nature and structure of social institutions calls for a redistribution of emphasis away from the individual level and towards the relational level. Economic phenomena have a primary social dimension. Individual behaviours are embedded in a pre-existing network of social relations which cannot be thought of as a mere constraint; rather, they are one of the driving factors that prompt individual goals and motivations (see Granovetter 1985). People's aspirations are deeply conditioned by the conventional wisdom about what makes life worth living. What we need is a new organizing principle, that we could provisionally call methodological relationism, to throw light on the interplay between individual behaviours and the architecture of society. Several interesting contributions which point in this direction have appeared recently; see for example von Foerster (1984) and Alexander and Giesen (1987). This is of course a very complex and far-reaching set of issues, which the current literature has just begun to explore; as a consequence, there is not yet a satisfactory theoretical framework that allows us to address them in full generality. Despite this, the evolutionary approach to altruism set out in this chapter seems to us a promising point of departure for further thought in this vein.

To conclude, the main message we would like to convey through this chapter is that the attempt of relaxing the assumption of selfishness in favour of a notion of altruism appears to us as the most promising research strategy in coping with several present-day economic problems. After all, it is not at all clear why rationality should not involve the intelligent pursuit of *all* one's goals and values, properly weighted, rather than sticking only to a particular class of goals, i.e. self-interested ones.[12] Indeed, by not taking goals seriously, the standard concept of rationality has offered an impoverished view of human behaviour. An extended view of rationality, one which recognizes people's ability to think about their goals, emerges as a superior alternative to the standard, instrumental view.

REFERENCES

Alexander, J. C., and Giesen, B. (1987), 'From Reduction to Linkage: The Long View of the Micro-Macro Link', in J. C. Alexander *et al.* (eds.), *The Micro-Macro Link* (Berkeley, Calif.: University of California Press, 1–42).

Argyle, M. (1991), *Cooperation: The Basis of Sociability* (London: Routledge).

Axelrod, R. (1984), *The Evolution of Cooperation* (New York: Basic Books).

Becker, G. (1976), 'Altruism, Egoism, and Genetic Fitness: Economics and Sociobiology', *Journal of Economic Literature*, 14: 817–26.

Bernheim, D., and Stark, O. (1988), 'Altruism Within the Family Reconsidered: Do Nice Guys Finish Last?', *American Economic Review*, 78: 1034–45.

Bicchieri, C. (1990), 'Norms of Cooperation', *Ethics*, 100: 838–61.

Boyer, R., and Orlean, A. (1992), 'How Do Conventions Evolve?', *Journal of Evolutionary Economics*, 2: 165–77.

Bromley, D. W. (1991), *Environment and Economy: Property Rights and Public Policy* (Oxford: Basil Blackwell).

Broome, J. (1978), 'Rational Choice and Value in Economics', *Oxford Economic Papers*, 30: 313–33.

Collard, D. A. (1978), *Altruism and Economy* (Oxford: Martin Robertson).

—— (1991), 'Love is Not Enough', in G. Meeks (ed.), *Thoughtful Economic Man* (Cambridge: Cambridge University Press, 17–28).

Cooper, R., and John, A. (1988), 'Coordinating Coordination Failures in Keynesian Models', *Quarterly Journal of Economics*, 103: 441–63.

Damme, E. Van (1987), *Stability and Perfection of Nash Equilibria* (Berlin: Springer Verlag).

Dawes, R. M., van de Kragt, A. J., and Orbell, J. M. (1988), 'Not Me Or Thee But We: The Importance of Group Identity, in Eliciting Cooperation in Dilemma Situations: Experimental Evidence', *Acta Psychologica*, 68: 83–97.

Dawkins, R. (1976), *The Selfish Gene* (Oxford: Oxford University Press).

Downs, A. (1956), *An Economic Theory of Democracy* (New York: Harper and Row).

[12] For a general discussion of this issue see Zamagni (1991), where morality is seen as an element in an extended preference function.

Elster, J. (1984), *Ulysses and the Sirens* (rev. edn.), Cambridge: Cambridge University Press).

Eshel, I. (1972), 'On the Neighborhood Effect and the Evolution of Altruistic Traits', *Theoretical Population Biology*, 3: 258–77.

Fikentscher, W. (1983), *Wirtschaftsrecht*, (Munich).

Foerster, H. von (1984), *Observing Systems* (Seaside, Calif: Intersystems Publishing Co).

Frank, R. (1988), *Passions Within Reason* (New York: Norton).

—— Gilovich, T., and Regan, D. (1995), 'Does Studying Economics Inhibit Co-operation?', *Journal of Economic Perspectives*, forthcoming.

Friedman, D. (1992), 'Economically Applicable Evolutionary Games', CentER Working Paper, no. 9226 (Tilburg University).

Gallino, L. (1980), 'Oltre il gene egoista', in *Sociobiologia e natura umana* (Turin: Einaudi, pp. vii–xlvi).

Granovetter, M. (1985), 'Economic Action and Social Structure: The Problem of Embeddedness', *American Journal of Sociology*, 91: 481–510.

Hamlin, A. P. (1985), *Ethics, Economics and the State* (London: Wheatsheaf).

Hardin, G. (1968), 'The Tragedy of the Commons', *Science*, 162: 1243–8.

Harris, M. (1989), *Our Kind* (New York: Harper and Row).

Hicks, J. R. (1941), 'Education in Economics', *Manchester Statistical Society*, 1–20.

Hirschleifer, J. (1977*a*), 'Economics from a Biological Viewpoint', *Journal of Law and Economics*, 20: 1–52.

—— (1977*b*), 'Shakespeare vs. Becker on Altruism: The Importance of Having the Last Word', *Journal of Economic Literature*, 15: 500–2.

—— (1982), 'Evolutionary Models in Economics and Law: Cooperation Versus Conflict Strategies', *Research in Law and Economics*, 4: 1–60; repr. in id., *Economic Behavior in Adversity* (Brighton: Wheatsheaf, 1987).

Hirschman, A. O. (1984), 'Against Parsimony: Three Easy Ways of Complicating Some Categories of Economic Discourse', *Bulletin: The American Academy of Arts and Sciences*, 37: 11–28.

Hofbauer, J., and Sygmund, K. (1988), *The Theory of Evolution and Dynamical Systems* (London: Cambridge University Press).

Jencks, C. (1979), 'The Social Basis of Unselfishness', in H. J. Gans *et al.* (eds.), *On the Making of Americans: Essays in Honour of David Riesman* (Philadelphia: University of Pennsylvania Press, 63–86).

Khalil, E. L. (1990), 'Beyond Self-interest and Altruism', *Economics and Philosophy*, 6: 255–73.

Kirzner, I. (1990), 'Self-interest and the New Bashing of Economics: A Fresh Opportunity in the Perennial Debate', *Critical Review*, 4: 27–40.

Laffont, J. J. (1975), 'Macroeconomic Constraints, Economic Efficiency and Ethics: An Introduction to Kantian Economics', *Economica*, 42.

Lattimore, R. (1992), 'Is it Rational to be "Rational"? The Case of Economists', *Economic Notes*, 21: 395–417.

Lewis, D. (1969), *Convention: A Philosophical Study* (Cambridge, Mass.: Harvard University Press).

Lunati, M. T. (1992), 'On Altruism and Cooperation', *Methodus*, 4: 69–75.

Mansbridge, J. (ed.). (1990), *Beyond Self-interest* (Chicago: University of Chicago Press).

Miller, D. (1989), *Market, State and Community* (Oxford: Clarendon Press).
Mueller, D. (1986), 'Rational Egoism vs. adaptive egoism', *Public Choice*, 51.
Ochs, J., and Roth, A. E. (1989), 'An Experimental Study of Sequential Bargaining', *American Economic Review*, 79: 355–84.
Ritzberger, K., and Weibull, J. (1992), 'Evolutionary Selection in Normal Form Games', Industriens Utredningsinstitut Working Paper no. 383 (Stockolm).
Robson, A. (1990), 'Efficiency in Evolutionary Games: Darwin, Nash and the Secret Handshake', *Journal of Theoretical Biology*, 144: 379–96.
Roth, A. E. (1991), 'Laboratory Experimentation in Economics: A Methodological Overview', in A. J. Oswald (ed.), *Surveys in Economics*, ii (Oxford: Basil Blackwell, 90–147).
Samuelson, L., and Zhang, J. (1992), 'Evolutionary Stability in Asymmetric Games', *Journal of Economic Theory*, 57: 363–91.
Sacco, P. L. (1993), 'Selection Mechanisms in Economics', mimeo (European University Institute).
Schultze, W. (1987), *Vom Gemeinnutz Eigennutz*, Vorträge 13 (Munich).
Selten, R. (1991), 'Evolution, Learning and Economic Behavior', *Games and Economic Behavior*, 3: 3–24.
Sen, A. (1967), 'Isolation, Assurance and the Social Rate of Discount', *Quarterly Journal of Economics*, 81: 112–25.
—— (1977), 'Rational Fools: A Critique of the Behavioural Foundations of Economic Theory', *Philosophy and Public Affairs*, 6: 317–44.
—— (1987), *On Ethics and Economics* (Oxford: Basil Blackwell).
Seneca, *De beneficiis.*
Stark, O. (1989), 'Altruism and the Quality of Life', *American Economic Review*, 79: 86–90.
Steedman, I. (1989), *From Exploitation to Altruism* (London: Polity Press).
Stigler, G. (1981), 'Economics or Ethics', in S. M. McMurrin (ed.), *The Tanner Lectures in Human Values*, ii (Cambridge: Cambridge University Press).
Sugden, R. (1982), 'On the Economics of Philanthropy', *Economic Journal*, 92: 341–50.
—— (1984), 'Reciprocity: The Supply of Public Goods through Voluntary Contributions', *Economic Journal*, 94.
—— (1989), 'Spontaneous Order', *Journal of Economic Perspectives*, 3: 85–97.
Trivers, R. (1971), 'The Evolution of Reciprocal Altruism', *Quarterly Review of Biology*, 46: 35–57.
Tullock, G. (1976), *The Vote Motive* (London: Institute for Economic Affairs).
—— (1978), 'Altruism, Malice and Public Goods', *Journal of Social and Biological Structures*, 1: 3–9.
Ullman-Margalit, E. (1977), *The Emergence of Norms* (Oxford: Clarendon Press).
Wicksteed, P. H. (1933), *The Common Sense of Political Economy* (London: Macmillan).
Wilson, E. (1975), *Sociobiology* (Cambridge, Mass.: Belknap Press).
Zamagni, S. (1991), 'Extended Rationality, Altruism and the Justification of Moral Rules', mimeo (University of Bologna).

15

Social Ethics and Implementation Theory

STEFANO VANNUCCI[1]

1. Introduction

Game theory and ethics provide us with reasons for choosing in certain ways amongst alternative actions, outcomes, rules, or institutions. The emphasis of game theorists is on 'rational' and 'self-interested' choice in an interactive environment, where the relevant notion of 'self-interest' is in principle amenable to a broad interpretation which does not rule out altruistic or 'higher-level' preferences. On the other hand, ethical analysts dispute over—but insist upon—criteria of 'rightness', 'goodness', or 'morality' of choice. All in all, the scope for potential conflict between 'rational strategic' and 'ethical' prescriptions is large enough, especially when it comes to assessing basic social arrangements, institutions, and rules of conduct. Prisoner Dilemmas and other sorts of co-ordination failures are the most typical examples of those potential conflicts.

At least two distinct—and in my view complementary—research programmes in game theory address issues of relevance to the solution of that potential conflict. Since ethics is after all about individual behaviour in a social interactive context, it can be plausibly argued that any admissible ethically motivated 'social norm' must have a proper game-theoretic justification. (Perhaps different 'social norms' will turn out to admit different game-theoretic justifications.) But then one should simply identify the game and the solution concept which are most relevant to human moral dilemmas, since to the game-theoretically minded 'reductionist' only choices which are consistent with some appropriate solution concept as applied to the 'right' game can ultimately count as morally sound. This is the research programme pursued by Binmore (1984; 1989; 1990*a*), building upon and

[1] This chapter was partly written while the author was visiting the Department of Economics at Georgetown University. Thanks are due to M. Dore, P. Hammond, H. Moulin, and other participants at the 1991 Siena Workshop on 'Ethics and Economics' for useful discussions on an earlier version of this chapter. Detailed comments by F. Farina and F. Hahn on a later draft are gratefully acknowledged. The usual disclaimer applies.

criticizing previously proposed 'contractarian' approaches as diverse as those put forth by Rawls (1971), Harsanyi (1955; 1977*a*; 1977*b*), Buchanan (1975), and Gauthier (1986) among others. Under this game-theoretic view of moral behaviour, it can even be maintained that human rational strategic behaviour evolves within games which are substantially different from Prisoner Dilemma-like situations, but can possibly be exported to the latter resulting in strategically 'irrational' but socially beneficial behaviour. In any case, this approach suggests that, in principle, any 'conflict' between game-theoretic and ethical prescriptions might be resolved by focusing on the 'right' game and—accordingly—on the 'right' application of the relevant solution concept.

The present chapter will focus on another research programme which addresses a related but distinct issue pertaining to game-theoretic implementation—as opposed to justification—of 'social norms'. Let us suppose that the members of a certain human society have reached a large agreement about the proper (i.e. morally 'right') general 'social norms' which should be obeyed by their social interaction (a better understanding of the naturalistic foundations of ethics through game theory along the lines of the first research programme sketched above might conceivably help to explain or even to establish that agreement). The practical import of such an agreement lies, however, in the subsequent specialization and implementation of those general 'social norms' within several ongoing interactive decision problems. But these decision problems are typically distinct from the stylized 'moral' games (if any) which can be used to justify those 'social norms' via rational strategic behaviour. Assuming that moral behaviour will generally prevail—to the effect of inducing a plain implementation of the 'social norm' under consideration—would amount to a naïve and unacceptably *ad hoc* way to sidestep the issue of compliance. Therefore, the following question naturally arises: is the agreed-upon 'social norm' implementable through rational strategic behaviour on the part of the players if their prevailing motivation may but need not be 'moral' compliance with the prescriptions of the given 'social norm'?

Under this implementation-theoretic approach, the ethical criteria advanced in order to evaluate the performance of a system of social interaction are best seen as 'memes' that have somehow evolved within a given culture, and can be combined to formulate alternative 'social norms'.

A first test which any such set of criteria or 'social norms' should pass is obviously 'internal'—i.e. logical—consistency (we have learnt from a myriad of social choice-theoretic impossibility theorems that this test may well turn out to be a very stringent one as far as our uneducated intuitions are concerned: see e.g. Arrow 1963, Sen 1970, Suzumura 1983).

Implementability provides a second test for any logically consistent 'social norm'. It amounts to a sort of 'external' consistency test: i.e. consistency between the given 'social norm' and a compound theory concerning both the structure of the players' relevant individual characteristics and their rational strategic behaviour. As we shall see in more detail below, implementation theory tells us—for any such compound theory of individual characteristics and rational strategic behaviour—whether a given 'social norm' is implementable or not. Briefly, implementation theory purports to establish whether a certain 'social norm' is consistent with rational strategic behaviour.

However, the ultimate Game Theory Textbook is yet to be written. In the meantime, there remains scope for considerably different views concerning the 'right' theory of rational behaviour—or solution concept—for certain interactive environments. Thus, by establishing the consistency of any proposed 'social norm' with alternative theories of rational strategic behaviour as applied to suitable interactive environments, implementation theory offers a very useful test of its 'strategic robustness'.

Therefore, the relevance of implementability tests is twofold. If the focus is on a particular theory of rational strategic behaviour as applied to a specific interactive environment (maybe because one is persuaded that he can anticipate the content of the Game Theory Textbook's chapter on the relevant games), then implementation theory partitions the collection of conceivable 'social norms' into implementable and non-implementable ones. While the implementable 'social norms' qualify for further scrutiny and perhaps serious consideration, the non-implementable ones can be discarded on the grounds of their strategic inconsistency. On the other hand, if a more sceptical attitude is taken, and different theories of rational strategic behaviour are considered, then implementation theory can still inform us about the strategic 'robustness' of alternative 'social norms' with respect to changes of the solution concept. Furthermore, when a 'robust social norm' is identified, implementation theory may offer us some supplementary information on the strategic robustness (or lack of it) of the institutions or mechanisms which can be employed to implement that norm.

The aim of the present chapter is to provide a selective survey and a critical discussion of a few relevant results from some areas of implementation theory, that are at the interface of game theory and normative (ethical, political, economic) system evaluation.

Two kinds of normative evaluation criteria will be considered, namely (i) welfarist consequentialist criteria and (ii) rights-oriented (non-welfarist) criteria.

Two basic kinds of 'social norms' defined by combining some of those criteria will then be singled out for an implementation-theoretic analysis:

(*a*) 'democracy plus efficiency' of collective decision-making procedures, i.e. Pareto optimality of outcomes as achieved through an equal allocation of a priori voting power among players, and

(*b*) 'fair sharing of the surplus from co-operation', i.e. social choice rules which specify a 'fair' and Pareto optimal division of the benefits which the players can enjoy if (and only if) they agree on a certain outcome and on the actions to take in order to bring it about.

The choice of 'social norms' concerning points (*a*) and (*b*) above needs little justification. The principle of democratic choice, a respect for unanimous preferences, and a quest for distributive justice are essential components of any plausible contemporary view of social ethics.

Furthermore, I shall adopt an unconventionally broad view of implementation theory, taking into consideration two main objects of mechanism design, namely (i) standard coalitional, strategic, and extensive game forms and (ii) some abstract game forms first introduced by Greenberg (1990), and called situation-forms.

It will be argued that (1) generally speaking, the typical 'social norms' mentioned above under (*a*) and (*b*) turn out to be implementable, i.e. consistent with rational 'self-interested' strategic behaviour on the part of individual players and/or coalitions. Namely, the relevant incentive constraints—perhaps unexpectedly—are not really binding with respect to the implementability of most ethically significant performance criteria: a clever mechanism design activity can, in principle, guarantee the required consistency between rational 'self-interested' strategic behaviour and the systemic performance prescribed by the relevant 'social norm'.

(2) By contrast, significant restrictions on the range of implementable 'social norms' may arise when rational 'self-interested' strategic behaviour is coupled with further assumptions reflecting 'factual' realities—such as informational decentralization or bounded rationality and their extent—or prevailing institutions (e.g. specific voting methods or bargaining procedures). These assumptions amount to implicit restrictions on the class of institutions which are taken as feasible, and/or on the acceptable rational solution concepts, so that it should be no surprise that significant impossibility—i.e. non-implementability—results obtain.

To put it in other terms, it turns out that (at least some of) the most appealing 'social norms' for collective decisions and fair distribution are largely consistent with rational strategic behaviour on the part of the players, whatever the (not necessarily moral) prevailing motivations of the latter: the incentive constraints only restrict the choice of the institutions by which a certain 'social norm' can be implemented, as opposed to the choice of the 'social norm' itself. But then it seems reasonable to conclude that it is just this sort of 'factual' restrictions (which may well be, at least in some cases, context dependent or historically contingent) that precipitates apparent inconsistencies between 'ethical' performance criteria for institutions and rational 'self-interested' strategic behaviour.

The chapter is organized as follows: section 2 outlines the 'ethical' criteria to be used; section 3 provides a detailed description of the implementation-theoretic framework; section 4 is a critical survey of some relevant results concerning implementation of 'social norms'; section 5 offers some concluding remarks.

2. Social ethics and performance criteria

As mentioned in the introduction, we shall consider instances of both welfarist consequentialist criteria and rights-based criteria (see e.g. Sen 1987 for a thorough discussion of the main issues related to such a classification of normative evaluation criteria).

Consequentialist criteria assess the performance of the relevant system by focusing on outcomes or end-results, as opposed to the processes or procedures which bring them about (for a given convenient description of the outcome space).

Welfarist criteria assess the performance of the relevant system according to some direct welfare indicator of the relevant social units (e.g. individual preferences or utilities as opposed to, say, educational level, income, or health care).

Rights-based criteria assess the performance of the relevant system in terms of fulfilment of a certain set of individual or collective rights: e.g. the right to choose freely among options pertaining to a suitably defined 'personal' sphere, the right to a maximal equal freedom, or the right to an equal a priori voting power on matters of common concern. Rights-based criteria are perhaps best viewed as non-consequentialist in character, but they can also be given a consequentialist formulation. Also, they typically embody a kind of information (on the relevant social units) which is in principle publicly observable or verifiable (as opposed to welfarist criteria, which typically rely on the elicitation of some essentially private information).

The performance criteria we shall take into considerations are the following:

(*I*) *Efficiency, or Pareto Optimality* (*PO*). The outcomes of the given interactive system should be such that feasible changes making some player better off should only be possible at the cost of worsening the condition of someone else. This is the prototype of a consequentialist and welfarist criterion, and the core of current welfare analysis in economics and related disciplines. Efficiency is consistent with many ethical principles, including utilitarianism. To be sure, if one subscribes to conventional Bayesian expected utility theory under uncertainty and to Harsanyi's version of the contractarian 'moral game', then it can be shown that efficiency is essentially equivalent to utilitarianism (see Harsanyi 1955). However, it should be immediately noticed that these are no minor requirements. Moreover, it has been shown that this equivalence result does not hold if a more general skew-symmetric bilinear utility theory is used (see Fishburn and Gehrlein 1987).

(*II*) *Individual Rationality* (*IR*). The outcomes of the given system should be such that each player is at least as well off as she would have been by not taking part in the relevant social interaction. This is another consequentialist and welfarist criterion, which requires the specification of a *status quo* and amounts to a necessary condition for voluntariness of social interactions. Therefore, IR also expresses—in an indirect way—a minimal requirement of freedom of choice among the available options.

(*III*) *Symmetry or Anonymity Criteria* (*S*). This is a generic label for a family of criteria requiring the invariance of the outcomes of the relevant collective decision procedure with respect to all the permutations of the players (see e.g. Campbell and Fishburn 1980, Moulin 1983; 1988). We shall focus on (i) a symmetry requirement for simple games, which amounts to a rights-based criterion requiring the allocation of an equal decision power to each player,[2] and (ii) a symmetry requirement for economies with private goods, namely symmetry of individual preferences with respect to the group of all permutations of the personal bundles of goods at a suitably selected reference allocation (if the reference allocation is the final allocation itself the resulting criterion is envy-freeness: see e.g. Thomson 1983, Thomson and Varian 1985).

(*IV*) *Neutrality* (*NT*). This is a sort of 'dual' criterion to S above which requires the invariance of the outcome of the relevant collective decision procedure with respect to the labelling of the alternatives (see e.g. Moulin 1983; 1988). Briefly, the social outcome must not depend on parameters different from those explicitly modelled in the profile of individual characteristics: no a priori discrimination among alternatives is allowed.

Indeed, we are going to disregard in this chapter those welfarist criteria which require interpersonal comparisons of well-being. The main reason for that is our persuasion that those criteria require a measurement and elicitation technology which is much more sophisticated than that required by most typical non-welfarist criteria and by those welfarist criteria which do not require interpersonal comparisons of well-being. As a result, it seems to us that those criteria which invoke such interpersonal comparisons are more likely to be controversial (but see Harsanyi 1955; 1977*a*; 1982, Sen 1987, and some of the contributions in Elster and Roemer 1991 for other somewhat more optimistic views on the feasibility and significance of interpersonal comparisons of well-being).

3. Implementation theory

Implementation theory is best viewed as a representation theory. It deals with the representability of performance-related objects by means of game-

[2] This is so regardless of the power-index chosen, since virtually all the relevant power-indices reflect all symmetries of the simple games they refer to: see e.g. Owen (1982).

theoretical objects. Its main ingredients may be described as follows: the environment, the objects to be represented (i.e. the 'social norms'), a theory of rational strategic behaviour, and a suitable class of games to be used in the representation exercise.

A. The environment

The environment—or domain—is a description of the entire class of conceivable states of the world to be taken into consideration. The choice of the relevant environment may reflect a concern for the 'realism' of assumptions and/or elements of a prescriptive theory of rational behaviour (the latter most typically consists of restrictions imposed upon admissible individual preferences), or technical considerations of mathematical tractability. In any case, the environment typically includes a space consisting of admissible profiles of individual characteristics (e.g. preferences, endowments, information structures, and so on), and is sufficiently 'rich', in order to represent a reasonably large set of contingencies. These profiles of individual characteristics are then used as constitutive elements for the definition of the relevant implementing games to be described below.[3]

The environments we shall take into consideration include the following:

(i) *The Linear Ordering Domain.* The characteristics of each player reduce to her preferences on the set X of all conceivable alternatives. The preferences of each player i are represented by an arbitrary linear ordering r_i (i.e. a total, transitive, and antisymmetric binary relation) of X. A profile of individual characteristics is therefore the assignment of a linear ordering to each player: if N is the set of all players, and $L(X)$ the set of all linear orderings of X, a linear N-profile is a function $r{:}N \to L(X)$. The linear domain for (N, X) is the set of all such profiles, to be written $\mathsf{L}(N, X)$ (a strictly related and very much studied environment, the Total Preordering Domain, obtains from the foregoing definition by dropping 'antisymmetric' from the definition above).

(ii) *The Finite von Neumann–Morgenstern Domain with or without an Exogenous Status Quo.* Each player $i \in N$ is characterized by a von Neumann–Morgenstern utility function u_i representing her preferences on the set L of lotteries defined over a finite set X of outcomes:

$$u_i(\ell) = \sum_{x \in X} \ell(x) u_i(x).$$

[3] It is assumed that any given domain is common knowledge among the players who are part of it (we shall disregard here all the subtleties and difficulties attached to such a notion, as lucidly discussed in Binmore and Brandenburger 1990). By contrast, the (true) individual characteristics of any player are typically meant to be the private information of that player, unless otherwise specified.

If a *status quo* x^* is exogenously fixed a reservation utility level $u_i(x^*)$ also obtains. The Finite von Neumann–Morgenstern Domain with (respectively without) exogenous *status quo* for (N, X) is the set of all the resulting N-profiles and is denoted $\mathsf{U}^*(N, \mathcal{L}(X))$ (respectively $\mathsf{U}(N, \mathcal{L}(X))$). We shall occasionally refer to the restricted version of this domain which obtains by requiring that each player has a unique strictly preferred lottery.

(iii) *The Quasi-linear Surplus Sharing Domain with or without an Exogenous Status Quo*. Given a compact set x of public decisions, each player $i \in N$ is characterized by a utility function u_i: $\mathrm{X} \times \mathsf{R} \to \mathsf{R}$ which is separable and linear in a perfectly divisible private good (i.e. $u_i(x, y) = v_i(x + y)$. A *status quo* x^* may be exogenously fixed to the effect of inducing a reservation utility level. Any resulting N-profile $u = (u_i)_{i \in N}$ of such utility functions implicitly determines a surplus:

$$S(u) = \max \left\{ \sum_{i \in N} u_i(x, y_i) : x \in \mathrm{X}, \sum_{i \in N} y_i = 0 \right\}, \quad \text{or}$$

$$S(u) = \max \left\{ \sum_{i \in N} u_i(x, y_i) - u_i(x^*, 0) : x \in \mathrm{X}, \sum_{i \in N} y_i = 0 \right\} \quad \text{respectively.}$$

The Quasi-linear Surplus Sharing Domain with (respectively without) exogenous *status quo* for (N, X) is the set of all the resulting N-profiles and is denoted $\mathsf{Q}^*(N, X)$ (respectively $\mathsf{Q}(N, X)$).

(iv) *The Neo-Classical Domain with Undefined Property Rights*. The characteristics of each player $i \in N$ amount to her preferences and her (net) consumption set X_i (a bounded from below, closed, convex subset of the l-dimensional space R^l of (private) goods, which contains the origin). The preferences of each player i are selfish and represented by an arbitrary continuous, convex, strictly monotonic total preordering r_i (i.e. a total transitive binary relation) defined on the set of all feasible (net) consumption assignments

$$\mathcal{A} \subseteq \prod_{i \in N} X_i \quad .$$

A neo-classical profile of individual characteristics for a finite set N of players is then a neo-classical pure exchange economy with undefined property rights $e = e(N, \mathcal{A})$. The neo-classical domain of N is the set of all such economies, to be written $\mathscr{E}(N, \mathcal{A})$.

B. The performance-related objects: social norms

As mentioned above, the 'social norms' are the objects to be represented, i.e. implemented. They typically embody the relevant—ethically motivated—prescriptions, or part of them. We shall take into consideration the following objects:

(i) *Symmetric Proper Simple Games.* A symmetric proper simple game is a pair (N, W), where N is the set of the players and $W \subseteq \mathcal{P}(N)$ the (non-empty) set of winning coalitions, which satisfies the following restrictions: (*a*) (monotonicity): a coalition which admits a winning subcoalition is winning; (*b*) (properness): the complementary coalition of a winning coalition cannot possibly be winning; (*c*) (symmetry): any two coalitions with the same number of players are bound to be either both winning or both losing. A symmetric proper simple game is a model of a democratic collective decision procedure, in that it embodies an equal-decision-power requirement.[4]

(ii) *Anonymous and Efficient Social Choice Correspondences.* A social choice correspondence for a fixed (finite) set N of players, a fixed set

$$\Theta' \subseteq \prod_{i \in N} \Theta_i$$

of admissible profiles of individual characteristics for players in N (the domain), and a fixed set X of outcomes (or alternatives), is a function $F\colon \Theta' \to \mathcal{P}(X)\setminus\{\varnothing\}$ mapping profiles into non- empty sets of alternatives such that any outcome in X is uniquely selected for some profile in Θ'; single-valued social choice correspondences are called social choice functions. Obviously, any profile $\theta \in \Theta'$ is meant to include a profile $r = r(\theta)$ of individual preferences defined on X. The social choice correspondence F is anonymous or symmetric (S) iff for any permutation σ of the player set N and any profile $\theta \in \Theta'$,

$$F(\theta_\sigma) = F(\theta) \text{ where } \theta_\sigma = (\theta_{\sigma(i)})_{i \in N} ;$$

F is efficient or Pareto optimal (PO) iff for any profile $\theta \in \Theta'$, any alternative selected by F is Pareto-Optimal w.r.t. $r(\theta)$ (i.e. $F(\theta) \subseteq \mathrm{PO}(r(\theta))$) where $\mathrm{PO}(r(\theta))$ is the set of Pareto-Optimal alternatives in X, according to $r(\theta)$). An anonymous and efficient social choice correspondence models a collective decision procedure which ensures equal treatment of players and respects (local) unanimity of preferences. Occasionally, we shall focus on social choice correspondences which are also individually rational, in order to require that participation be voluntary and rational when a *status quo* is exogenously fixed (e.g. standard bargaining solutions) or neutral, in order to ensure an equal treatment of alternatives otherwise (e.g. surplus sharing rules or modified bargaining solutions with endogenous *status quo*).

4 The concept of a symmetric proper simple game is amenable to several interesting extensions, the most widely used among them being anonymous, neutral, regular, and monotonic effectivity functions (see Abdou and Keiding 1991); libertarian criteria for collective decision procedures as introduced by Sen (1970) can also be modelled by means of objects of a similar kind, namely as suitable non-neutral effectivity functions: see e.g. Deb (1989).

(iii) *'Fair' and Efficient Social Choice Correspondences.* Several notions of 'fairness' have been proposed following the pioneering definition of 'fairness as no-envy' from Foley. The common aim of those 'fairness' criteria consists of attempting to introduce prescriptions related to some notion of 'distributive justice' without invoking interpersonal comparisons of utility. We shall focus on (Pareto efficient) envy-free (POEF) and on (Pareto efficient) egalitarian-equivalent allocations (POEE) for economies of the neo-classical domain with free disposal. An allocation is POEF if it is efficient and no agent prefers the allocation bundle of another agent to her own, and POEE if it is efficient and such that for some egalitarian (possibly not feasible) allocation each player is indifferent between that allocation and the bundle of goods she receives according to the allocation under consideration (see Pazner and Schmeidler 1978, Suzumura 1983, Thomson and Varian 1985).

Two remarks on the foregoing sample list of performance-related objects are in order. First, it should be noticed that a sharp distinction can be drawn between symmetric proper simple games (and related notions) and the other objects considered above (e.g. social choice correspondences). In fact, the former class of objects is defined with respect to a set of players, without any reference to spaces of individual characteristics. By contrast, all the other objects of our list do refer to such spaces. This distinction can be sensibly summarized by defining the objects of the first class as pure rights-based objects, i.e. objects embodying (only) rights-based performance criteria. On the contrary, the other objects may embody welfarist performance criteria, and definitely represent criteria of a consequentialist kind.

Second, proper simple games (and related notions) can be attached in a natural way to objects from the other classes listed above (e.g. a proper simple game is defined out of a social choice correspondence by defining as winning the coalitions that can force—at any profile—the choice of whatever alternative they agree upon, by means of a suitable co-ordination of their members' behaviour: see Peleg 1978; 1983). As a result, symmetric proper simple games and similar rights-based objects can be related in a natural way to welfarist objects. This makes it easier to combine several performance criteria of a different nature into the same implementation test.

C. *Theories of rational strategic behaviour*

That is where game theory enters. As models of strategic interaction, games come in a large variety of formats (e.g. abstract, coalitional, strategic, and extensive games).

Theories of rational strategic behaviour—or solution concepts—refer to classes of games. They prescribe the rationally admissible solutions of games in a certain class (obviously, they also purport to predict the possible outcomes of such games if the players are rational in the relevant sense).

However, a theory of strategic rationality may fail on certain games in its domain, giving rise to an empty set of solutions: we shall call it partial in that case, and complete otherwise. There are many available theories of rational strategic behaviour, though some theories are more popular than others. This plurality of theories reflects both differences among various game-theoretical formats and substantial disagreements.

We shall focus on the following theories (which are by no means intended as constituting an exhaustive list):

(i) *von Neumann–Morgenstern Stable Sets and Related Solution Concepts.* This is a theory of rational strategic behaviour which is defined on the class Γ of abstract games or 1-digraphs. A von Neumann–Morgenstern (henceforth VNM) stable set of an abstract game $g = (X, R) \in \Gamma$ is a set of states $Y \subseteq X$ satisfying the following requirements:

(*a*i) (internal stability): for any $x, y \in Y$, $(x, y) \notin R$ (two states of a stable set cannot be related by dominance);

(*a*ii) (external stability): for any $x \notin Y$, a $y \in Y$ exists such that $(y, x) \in R$ (any state outside a stable set must be dominated by some state of this stable set).

The VNM solution attaches to any abstract game g the collection VNM(g) of its VNM stable sets (a VNM selection VNM* attaches to any abstract game g at most one of its VNM stable sets, denoted-if it exists—by VNM*(g)). It is well known that any strictly acyclic abstract game (X,R) admits exactly one VNM stable set ((X, R) is strictly acyclic iff $R^k = \emptyset$ for some positive integer k, where R^k is the k-th composition of R with itself): hence the VNM solution is a complete theory for the class of strictly acyclic abstract games, coinciding thereupon with its unique VNM selection (see von Neumann and Morgenstern 1953). Both refinements and extensions of VNM stable sets have been proposed. Strictly stable sets (see Harsanyi (1974)) are sets of states $Y \subseteq X$ satisfying external stability and a strengthened version of (*a*i), namely

(*a*i′) (strictly internal stability): for any $x, y \in Y$, $(x, y) \notin \bigcup R^k$.

Sub-stable sets (or subsolutions, according to the original terminology of Roth (1976)) are sets of states $Y \subseteq X$ satisfying internal stability and

(*a*ii′) (self-protective maximality): for any $x \in X$, $x \in Y$ iff for any $z \in X$, $(z, x) \in R$ entails (y, z) for some $y \in Y$.

(ii) *Core.* This is another theory of rational strategic behaviour which refers to the entire class of abstract games. The core of an abstract game $g = (X, R)$ is the set of R-maximal states. Of course, strict acyclicity of g (see the definition above) is sufficient to guarantee that Core$(g) \neq \emptyset$. Other, weaker, versions of acyclicity are also sufficient to ensure a non-empty core.

(iii) *Nash Equilibrium*. This is a non-cooperative theory of rational strategic behaviour (i.e. it implicitly refers to games which do not allow for binding agreements). Hence its ultimate aim is to identify the class of self-enforcing agreements. It can be referred both to the class Γ' of games in strategic form and to the class Γ'' of games in extensive form.

For any strategic (extensive) game g with preference profile r, a strategy profile (a behavioural strategy profile) $s = (s_i)_{i \in N}$ is a Nash equilibrium to g if and only if for any player $i \in N$ and any $s'_i \in S_i$ $(s, (s_{-i}, s'_i)) \in r_i$.

A similar definition applies to games induced by the profiles of a Bayesian domain with explicit information partitions (see e.g. Jackson (1991)). In that case, a Nash equilibrium is sometimes referred to as a Bayesian (Nash) equilibrium (see Dasgupta, Hammond, and Maskin 1979, Palfrey and Srivastava 1989).

The Nash equilibrium theory of a certain class G of games attaches to any game $g \in G$ the set $NE(g)$ of its Nash equilibria. Nash equilibrium theory is a complete theory for several large classes of games, including the standard domain of finite strategic games with a finite set of outcomes and von Neumann–Morgenstern utility functions (see Nash 1951).

(iv) *Refinements of Nash Equilibrium*. It is well known that for certain games some Nash equilibria entail an unreasonable choice of strategy on the part of some players: for example, some Nash equilibria of certain normal and extensive games are weakly dominated (a player can do better and cannot do worse by changing her strategy, whatever the reactions of the other players), other Nash equilibria of certain extensive games involve non-credible (i.e. self-damaging) threats. A refinement of Nash equilibrium is a theory of rational strategic behaviour which is aimed at a systematic elimination of any such unreasonable equilibrium while retaining the nice existence properties of Nash equilibrium (hence selecting a suitable non-empty subset of Nash equilibria for every relevant game). Two general principles seem to be essential to any such attempt at defining a good refinement of Nash equilibrium. Those are the 'backward induction principle' (an agreement is self-enforcing only if it is consistent with deductions about the present behaviour of rational players, which are based on their predictable future rational behaviour) and the 'forward induction principle' (an agreement is self-enforcing only if it is consistent with deductions about the future behaviour of rational players, which are based on their past rational behaviour). The weakest refinement of Nash equilibrium for extensive form games are subgame perfect equilibria: Nash equilibria which induce a Nash equilibrium on any subgame of the given game. This is perhaps the most obvious example of a refinement which is tailored to satisfy the backward induction principle.

It turns out that the backward and the forward induction principles are not easy to reconcile with each other. As a matter of fact, most proposed refinements (including subgame perfect equilibrium, sequential equilibrium, and trembling-hand perfect equilibrium) are somehow tilted towards the 'backward induction principle' and thus tend to perform quite poorly with respect to the 'forward induction principle' (we refer the reader to Van Damme (1987) or Kohlberg (1990) for excellent and comprehensive surveys of the entire topic). Currently, the best compromise between the two principles seems to be the notion of stable sets of equilibria, a solution concept due to Kohlberg and Mertens (see Kohlberg, and Mertens 1986, Van Damme 1987, Mertens 1988, Kohlberg 1990). A stable set of equilibria of a normal or extensive game g is a closed set $s(g)$ of Nash equilibria of g which is minimal with respect to the following property: for each suitably defined 'perturbation' of the reduced normal form of g a Nash equilibrium of g exists which is arbitrarily close to $s(g)$ (the reduced normal form of a game g is the game which obtains after deleting from the normal form of g all the strategies which are duplicates or mixed combinations of other strategies).

(v) *Coalitional Nash Equilibrium.* This is a theory of rational strategic behaviour which implicitly assumes a high potential for co-ordination as made possible by unlimited communication among the players (this solution concept was first introduced in Aumann 1959). A coalitional (or strong) Nash equilibrium of a strategic game $g = (N, (s_i)_{i \in N}, r)$ is a strategy profile $s = (s_i)_{i \in N}$ such that for any coalition $T \subseteq N$ and any strategy profile s' with $s'_i \neq s_i$ iff $i \in T$: $(s, s') \in r_j$ for some $j \in T$ (the definition can be extended to strategic and extensive form games).

The main problems with a coalitional Nash equilibrium are, arguably, a certain lack of internal consistency (why coalitional deviations which are vulnerable to further deviations by some subcoalition should be taken into consideration?) and, above all, the stringent conditions which are needed in order to ensure its existence (see e.g. Ichiishi 1982). Thus, a coalitional Nash equilibrium is at best a very partial theory of rational strategic behaviour. On the other hand, coalitional Nash equilibria enjoy a very nice property in that their outcomes are, by definition, Pareto optimal. In the social choice-theoretic literature a refinement of a coalitional Nash equilibrium—called exact coalitional Nash equilibrium—is sometimes used when analysing revelation games in strategic form (i.e. games with strategy sets consisting of spaces of admissible individual characteristics). Namely, a coalitional Nash equilibrium r' of a game g with (true) preference profile $r = r(\theta)$ and outcome function h is exact if $h(r) = h(r')$ (see e.g. Peleg 1984, Holzman 1986*b*).

(vi) *Admissible and Iterately Admissible Strategy Profiles.* A strategy profile $s = (s_i)_{i \in N}$ of a given extensive or strategic game g with strategy sets $(S_i)_{i \in S}$ and preference profile is (weakly) admissible—or undominated—if for each player $i \in N$, s_i is not (strictly) dominated by another strategy $s'_i \in S_i$ (i.e. for each $s'_i \in S$, if an

$$s'_{-i} \in \prod_{j \neq i} S_j \text{ exists s.t } ((s'_i, s'_{-i}), (s_i, s'_{-i})) \in r_i$$

then an

$$s''_{-i} \in \prod_{j \neq i} S_j \text{ exists s.t. } ((s_i, s''_{-i}) (s'_i, s''_{-i})) \in r_i).$$

It should be recalled that a Nash equilibrium needs not be undominated. While admissibility is largely regarded as a minimal requirement for rational behaviour (see e.g. Kohlberg and Mertens 1986, Palfrey and Srivastava 1991, Börgers 1991, Jackson 1992), it is also usually viewed as an exceedingly weak criterion to qualify as a full-fledged solution concept. It could perhaps be argued that, generally speaking, the latter view should not be taken for granted (in fact, Binmore and Shin 1992 provide some arguments which might be used to defend the plausibility of admissibility as a solution concept for large and complex games played by algorithmic players). Moreover, in games where each player is completely informed about the pay-off-relevant characteristics of her opponents, the admissibility criterion can be iterated, in order to select (algorithmically) the set of iterately admissible profiles. As a solution concept, iterated admissibility is obviously much more powerful than admissibility (see e.g. Moulin 1983 for some conspicuous applications) but is not consistent with common knowledge (see Samuelson 1992). On the other hand, iterated weak admissibility can be easily axiomatized for a large class of games in terms of common knowledge of rationality (see Bernheim (1986), in which it is also shown than rationalizability obtains by the further assumption of independent choices on the part of the players).

D. The implementing games

As mentioned above, we shall take into consideration two main classes of implementing games, namely the games induced by a game form (for a given environment) and the games of a 'social situation'.

(i) *The games induced by a game form and an environment.* As mentioned above, game forms model institutions, i.e. rules for strategic interaction. We recall here that a (strategic) game form for a set N of players and a set X of outcomes consists of an array $G = (N, (S_i)_{i \in N}, h)$ where S_i is the set of strategies of player i, and

$$h\colon \prod S_i \to X$$

is the outcome function (extensive game forms are similarly defined). Thus, a game form is a sort of game 'without preferences'. It represents a scheme of strategic interaction whose specification is independent of any information about (essentially) private individual characteristics: it can work for any profile of such characteristics. In fact, for any given environment Θ and any profile $\theta \in \Theta$, a game in strategic form $g = (G, \theta)$ can be attached in a natural way to G (this is the game induced by G on θ).

(ii) *The games of a 'social situation'*. Social situations are a model of strategic interaction recently introduced by Greenberg (1990). A social situation consists of a set of grand coalitional games called positions, that are endowed with a set of game-specific admissible inputs (consisting of a proposed outcome and an 'active' coalition), and a non-deterministic dynamics—called the inducement correspondence—which maps 'feasible' position-input pairs into sets of positions (the positions which are reachable from the given position by a move of the input-specified coalition when the input-specified outcome is proposed). Namely, a social situation is a pair $\mathcal{G} = (\Gamma, d)$ where Γ is a class of grand coalitional games, and d a correspondence mapping each triple (g, x, T) such that $g \in \Gamma, x \in X = X(g)$, $T \subseteq N = N(g)$, into a set $d(g, T, x) \subseteq \Gamma$ of positions having a set of players included in $N(g)$. Notice that the games in Γ may have distinct sets of players. A social situation form is a 'social situation without preferences' i.e. it is a pair $\mathsf{S} = (\mathsf{G}, d')$ where G is a class of grand coalitional game forms (including a grand coalitional game form consisting of the $\subseteq$-greatest player set in G and the $\subseteq$-greatest alternative set in G) and d' a non-deterministic dynamics defined along the same lines of the dynamics of a social situation (provided that G is substituted for Γ). A social situation procedure for a set of alternatives Y is a social situation form $\mathsf{S} = (\mathsf{G}, d')$ endowed with an outcome function $\mu: X[\Gamma] \rightarrow Y$.

If the inducement correspondence d of a social situation $\mathcal{G} = (\Gamma, d)$ is independent of the preference profile of the relevant positions (i.e. $d(g, x, T) = d(g', x, T)$ for any $g, g' \in \Gamma$ such that $N(g) = N(g')$ and $X(g) = X(g')$) then the social situation $\mathcal{G} = (\Gamma, d)$ is uniquely determined by the environment $\Theta = \Theta(\Gamma)$ consisting of preference profiles of games in Γ, and the social situation form $\mathsf{S} = (\Gamma', d')$ (where $\Gamma' = \{(N, X)/ (N, X, r) \in \Gamma$ for some $r \in \Theta\}$ and for any $(N, X) \in \Gamma'$ and $r \in \Theta(\Gamma)$ $d'((N, X), x, T)) = d((N, X, r), x, T)$ if (x, T) is an (N, X, r)-admissible input for d, and undefined otherwise; such an S will be referred to as a situation form for (N, X)). It should be noticed that a situation form amounts to an abstract game form, i.e. a most general model of mechanisms (or institutions). In particular we shall say that a social situation is *non-sequential* if no position can be induced from an induced position, and *non-cooperative* if the only 'active' coalitions are trivial i.e. single players.

It should be noticed that an abstract game $g(\mathcal{G}) = (X(\mathcal{G}), R(\mathcal{G}))$ can be attached in a natural way to any social situation $\mathcal{G} = (\Gamma, d)$ by the following definitions: $\mathrm{X}(\mathcal{G}) = \{(g, x)/g \in \Gamma, x \in X(g)\}$, and for any (g, x), $(g', x') \in \mathrm{X}(\mathcal{G})$ $((g, x), (g', x')) \in \mathcal{R}(\mathcal{G})$ if and only if $g' \in d(g, x, T)$ for some $T \subseteq N(g)$ s.t. for any $i \in T$ $u_i(g')(x') > u_i(g)(x)$ (where $u_i(g)$ and $u_i(g')$ are utility functions representing the preference relations r_i, r'_i of i in g and g', respectively). In words, a feasible position-outcome pair '(optimistically) dominates' an alternative position-outcome pair if the former position-outcome pair is unanimously preferred by the members of a coalition that has the power to induce it starting from the latter position outcome. Another abstract game $g^*(\mathcal{S})$ embodying a related notion of 'cautious dominance' can also be attached in a natural way to any social situation $\mathcal{S}$ (see Greenberg 1990).

The foregoing definitions implicitly refer to a complete information setting, but are amenable to quite natural extensions to other informational environments (see Vannucci 1993). In any case, it follows that the solution concepts defined for abstract games (see points C (i) and (ii) above) apply to social situations as well: in particular, it can be shown that any VNM-stable set of the abstract game $g(S)$ of a social situation $\mathcal{S}$ is the graph of a correspondence which is—according to Greenberg's suggestive terminology—an optimistically stable standard of behaviour. By analogy, we shall also refer to (optimistically) sub-stable standards of behaviour and to cautiously stable standards of behaviour.

E. The implementation problem

We are now ready to describe a general implementation problem.

Let F be a social choice correspondence for a set N of players and a set X of alternatives, defined over an environment Θ. Let P be one of the performance-related objects described above under section B such that it 'represents' F in a suitable sense (i.e. $\mathsf{P} = f(F)$ for a suitably defined function f: f may be the identity function, or the function mapping F to its simple game, or its effectivity function). Furthermore, let $\Gamma = \Gamma(\Theta)$ be the admissible class of implementing games, T a theory of rational strategic behaviour defined on Γ, $\mathsf{X}\,[\Gamma] \supseteq \mathsf{T}[\Gamma]$ the class of T-relevant solution objects (e.g. strategy profiles for normal or strategic games, states or sets of states for abstract games), and H a suitable function mapping solutions into alternatives (e.g. the function selecting the outcome induced by—or the utility profile attached to—a strategy profile of the relevant game). Then P is T implementable on Θ by means of Γ if and only if the triangular diagram in Fig. 15.1 commutes.

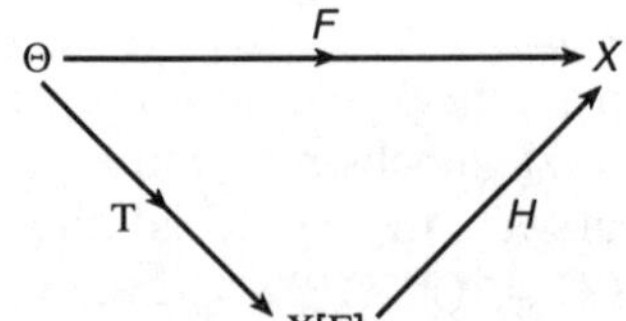

FIG. 15.1.

Obvious specializations of the involved objects by suitable selections from the lists presented above under sections A, B, C, and D result in the typical implementation problems studied in the game-theoretic literature. As mentioned above, an implementation problem amounts to a sort of conditional consistency test between a theory of rational strategic behaviour (T) and a (composite) criterion of good performance for a system of social interaction (P). That test is conditional upon the general hypothesis that only states of the world which are consistent with domain Θ may obtain. Thus, if it turns out that P is T implementable on the domain—or environment—Θ, then one may conclude that the prescriptions embodied in P and in T are consistent, as long as Θ is a good (partial) description of the state of the world.

To be sure, other—weaker—notions of implementation are available (and sometimes used in the literature). In fact, the implementation test can be weakened by requiring that the triangular diagram in Fig. 15.1 commutes when some subcorrespondence $F' \subseteq F$ is substituted for F (i.e. weak implementation: this weakening of the implementation concept is mandatory if one is interested in a single-valued solution concept as advocated by Harsanyi and Selten (1988) and not willing to restrict her attention to social choice functions), or when some supercorrespondence $F' \supseteq F$ is substituted for F (i.e. partial implementation). Also, the implementation test can be weakened by requiring that the triangular diagram in Fig. 15.1 commutes when some correspondence F' which is 'close to F'' (in a suitably defined sense) is substituted for F (this is the notion of virtual implementation, which has been shown to result in very permissive implementability theorems: see Matsushima 1988, Abreu and Sen 1991, Abreu and Matsushima 1992). However, each of those weakened versions of the implementation problem has clear drawbacks of its own and adds a degree of arbitrariness into the problem, resulting in a somewhat less significant consistency test.

4. Some implementation results

This section is devoted to a sample of implementation results. The implementation theorems described below are chosen in order to make clear the following point: most impossibility theorems can be turned into possibility results (i) by relaxing restrictions on the class of acceptable (available?) institutions, as opposed to the environment (i.e. the class of admissible individual characteristics) and/or (ii) by varying the assumptions about the prevailing information structures. The chosen theory of rational strategic behaviour can also be consequential in that respect, but only to a smaller extent.

4.1 Symmetric simple games and efficiency: capacity theory

As mentioned above, (proper) simple games can be represented in a natural way by social choice correspondences having the same set of winning coalitions (see e.g. Peleg 1978; 1983). Social choice correspondences are to be considered as a model of the behaviour of a social decision mechanism: hence efficiency and strategic robustness (i.e. existence of some solution of the relevant kind at any possible profile) are natural restrictions to be imposed upon the admissible representations of the given simple game. The capacity of a proper simple game G—for a fixed environment Θ, and a fixed theory of rational strategic behaviour T—is the maximum integer number $c = c(G, \Theta, T)$ such that the following obtains: c is the cardinality of a (finite) set X s.t. for any $Y \subseteq X$ a social choice correspondence $F: \Theta \rightarrow \mathcal{P}(Y|\{\emptyset\})$ exists which is (i) efficient (ii) T implementable on Θ by means of a suitable class Γ of games, and (iii) a representation of G. Moreover, the capacity $c = c(G, \Theta, \mathsf{T})$ is said to be infinite if such a maximum c does not exist (see e.g. Peleg 1978; 1984, Holzman 1986*a*, Vannucci 1991); it should also be noticed that capacities can also be defined for infinite spaces, by substituting 'dimension' for 'cardinality').

Thus, the capacity of a simple game G is a measure of the maximum complexity of the decision problems that a collective decision mechanism with the power structure summarized by G is able to solve whatever the preferences of the players in the environment Θ under consideration (and provided that T is correct).

Obviously, a further restriction to symmetric proper simple games is in order whenever the fulfilment of democratic rights to an equal decision power is the main concern. In that setting, a possibility theorem amounts to the statement that the capacity of some symmetric proper simple game is infinite (for a sensible choice of the environment Θ and of the solution concept T). Following the standard approach, we shall take into consideration the case $\Theta = \mathsf{L}(N, X)$, the linear ordering domain. As it turns out, for several choices of T, a crucial distinction for capacity theory is the one between weak and non-weak simple games (a simple game is weak if and only if it has at least one veto player). Loosely speaking, weak proper simple games happen to have unbounded capacities, whereas non-weak proper simple games need not. Namely, the following holds true:

Theorem 1 *Let $G = (N, W)$ be a proper simple game, X the universal space of alternatives, $\Theta = \mathsf{L}(N, X)$ the linear ordering domain on X, Γ a suitable class of acceptable implementing games, T a theory of rational strategic behaviour defined on Γ, and $C(G, \Theta, T)$ the capacity of G on Θ w.r.t. T. Then:*

(i) (Nakamura (1979)) Let Γ be the set of coalitional games having N as player set, an arbitrary subset $Y \subseteq X$ as alternative space, a linear ordering profile on Y as preference profile, and W as its set of winning coalitions. Moreover, let T be the core as defined on Γ. Then, $c(G, \Theta, \mathsf{T})$ is infinite if G is weak, and bounded otherwise.

(*ii*) (*Peleg 1984, Holzman 1986a, Dutta and Sen 1991a*): *Let* Γ *be the set of strategic games induced by arbitrary social choice functions* $F: \Theta(Y) \rightarrow Y$ *and linear preference profiles* $\theta \in \Theta(Y)$ (*where* $Y \subseteq X$, *and* $\Theta(Y)$ *is the linear ordering domain on Y with N as player set*). *Moreover, let* T *be an arbitrary selection of exact coalitional Nash equilibria* (*or the coalitional Nash equilibrium solution concept*) *defined on* Γ. *Then* $c(G, \Theta, \mathsf{T})$ *is infinite if G is weak, and bounded otherwise.*

(*iii*) (*Greenberg 1990, Vannucci 1992*): *Let* Γ *be the collection of grand coalitional games attached to some non-cooperative and non-sequential situation form* $\mathsf{S} = (\mathsf{G}, d)$ *for* (*N, Y*) (*see the definition above*) *and the corresponding linear ordering profiles defined on Y* (*where Y is an arbitrary subset of X*). *Moreover, let* $\mathsf{T} = \mathsf{T}(d)$ *be any selection of sub-stable sets as defined on* Γ (*thus* T *may be any selection of VNM-stable sets as defined on* Γ). *Then* $c(G, \Theta, \mathsf{T})$ *is infinite if G is weak, and bounded otherwise.*

In particular, the foregoing theorem holds true if G is a symmetric (proper) simple game. Also, it should be noticed that unanimity simple games are both weak and symmetric. They represent the power structure attached to decision mechanisms based on a suitable allocation of some (typically limited) veto power to every player (see e.g. Moulin 1983, and Abdou and Keiding 1991). On the other hand, symmetric non-weak simple games typically arise from majoritarian decision mechanisms. It follows that the foregoing theorem can be regarded as a positive result as far as democratic and efficient performance criteria are concerned. Their restrictive implications only refer to the institutions that can be used in order to satisfy the 'social norm' of democratic decision. In fact, an impossibility theorem obtains if—and only if—one insists that a majoritarian decision method should work. It should also be mentioned that (essentially) the same result holds true when shifting the focus on smooth representations of simple games and to finite-dimensional manifolds of alternatives (a version of Theorem 1 above can in fact be obtained working along the lines of Schofield 1985: see also McKelvey 1990).

Much more permissive results obtain under the assumption of complete ignorance on the part of each player about the individual characteristics of the opponents, when combined with admissibility as the relevant theory of rational strategic behaviour. This has been shown by Jackson (1992), while Vannucci (1993) shows that under a quite natural extension of social situations to a complete ignorance setting, the same result can be replicated with respect to implementation by means of situation-forms. In fact, the following theorem holds true:

Theorem 2 (*See Jackson 1992, Vannucci 1993*). *Let* $G = (N, W)$ *be a proper simple game, X the 'universal' set of alternatives, and* $\Theta = \mathsf{L}(N, X)$, *the linear ordering domain on N and X. Moreover,* (*i*) *Let* Γ *be the collection of strategic games induced by some linear ordering profile in* Θ *and some game form for N and X, and* T *admissibility. Then the capacity* $c(G, \theta, \mathrm{T})$ *is infinite.*

(*ii*) *Let* Γ *be a set of positions induced by a suitable situation form for* (*N, X*) *and by linear ordering profiles in* Θ, T *any selection of sub-stable standards of behaviour, and* $\mathcal{I}$ *the coarsest information correspondence profile* (*i.e. at any position-outcome pair, each player regards as possible any position that is consistent with her component of the proposed outcome*). *Then, the capacity* $c(G, \Theta, \mathrm{T})$ *is infinite.*

On the other hand, the prospects get slightly worse if one (implicitly) assumes a complete information setting *and* shifts to Nash equilibrium. Namely, the following theorem holds true:

Theorem 3 (*Ferejohn, Grether, and McKelvey 1982; see also Vannucci 1991*). *Let* $G = (N, W)$ *be a proper simple game, X the* (*universal*) *alternative space,* Θ *the linear ordering domain on X,* Γ *the set of games in strategic form induced by some strategic game form with outcome set Y at linear preference profiles on Y* (*where Y is an arbitrary subset of X*), *T the Nash equilibrium solution concept, as defined on* Γ, *and* $c(G, \Theta, \mathrm{T})$ *the capacity of G on* Θ *with respect to* T. *Then* $c(G, \Theta, \mathrm{T})$ *is infinite if G is either weak and s.t.* $\#N \geqslant 3$ *or dictatorial, and bounded otherwise.*

Thus, choosing Nash equilibrium as the relevant theory of rational strategic behaviour implies an additional structural limitation on the capacity of any symmetric proper simple game, to the effect that only committees with at least three players can solve efficiently decision problems of any size by means of some democratic method (when the linear ordering domain is the predictably prevailing environment): see also Maskin (1977; 1985), McKelvey (1989), and Moore and Repullo (1990) or Sjöström (1991), for a complete solution of the Nash implementation problem, including the two-player case. On the other hand, it turns out that a moderate amount of refinement of the Nash equilibrium solution (either for extensive or for strategic games) is powerful enough to produce a substantial improvement of the situation (see e.g. Moore 1992 for a detailed survey). This is summarized by the following theorem.

Theorem 4 (*Moore and Repullo 1988, Abreu and Sen 1990, Palfrey and Srivastava 1991*). *Let* $G = (N, W)$ *be a proper simple game, X the* (*universal*) *alternative space, and* Θ *the linear ordering domain defined on X. Then the following holds true:*

(*i*) *if* Γ (*the set of implementing games*) *is the set of games in extensive form induced by some extensive game form with outcome set Y on the corresponding linear ordering domain* $\Theta(Y)$ (*where Y is an arbitrary subset of X*), *and T is the subgame perfect equilibrium solution concept as defined on* Γ*, then* $c(G, \Theta, \mathsf{T})$ *i.e. the capacity of G on* Θ *w.r.t.* T *is infinite for both weak and (some) non-weak symmetric G, provided that* $\#N \geqslant 3$ *(see Moore and Repullo 1988, Abreu and Sen 1990).*

(ii) if Γ *is the set of games in strategic form induced by some strategic game form with outcome set Y on the corresponding linear ordering domain* $\Theta = \mathsf{L}(N, Y)$ *(where Y is an arbitrary subset of X),* $\#N \geqslant 3$*, and* T *is the undominated Nash equilibrium solution concept then* $c(G, \Theta, \mathsf{T})$ *is infinite for both any weak and some non-weak symmetric proper simple game G (see Palfrey and Srivastava 1991).*

Thus, a theory of rational strategic behaviour which is only slightly more stringent than Nash equilibrium enables (if correct) even majoritarian methods to work properly on the linear ordering domain (provided that there are at least three players; with two players, a restriction to domains allowing for a universally bad outcome seems to be unavoidable: see Moore and Repullo 1988; 1990, Dutta and Sen 1991*b*). Results in a very similar spirit have been obtained by Herrero and Srivastava (1992) and Dutta and Sen (1993) for implementation in subgame perfect equilibrium and iterate admissibility by finite extensive game forms, and by Sjöström (1993) for implementation in trembling-hand perfect equilibrium. Generally speaking, the price to be paid for such an improvement on Theorem 3 is a further enlargement of the strategy spaces of the relevant mechanisms. That is quite definitely a cost. A more precise evaluation of that cost and of the ensuing trade-offs has, however, to wait for further developments in the theory of 'bounded rationality' (see e.g. Simon 1978) and for a detailed analysis of the role of mixed strategies in implementation theory (see the observations of Jackson 1991; 1992, on this point).

Be it as it may, it is quite clear that the 'social norm' of democratic and efficient collective decision-making is implementable under a large set of theories of rational strategic behaviour. However, certain institutions or decision procedures do the job better—i.e. in a more robust manner—than others. In particular, voting by veto procedures are better suited than majoritarian ones to the task of achieving democratic and efficient decisions under complete information and coalitional strategic behaviour (see Theorem 1).

4.2 Dividing the surplus from co-operation: implementable social norms of fair distribution

Identifying fair 'social norms' to decide how to share the benefits from co-operation has always been the benchmark problem for any approach to the issues of distributive justice. Two main subproblems should be distinguished in that setting, according to the presence versus absence of an exogenous fixed *status quo* or conflict point. In fact, the presence of an exogenously fixed *status quo* gives rise in a natural way to the imposition of individual rationality requirements upon the social choice correspondence which represents the sharing rule, as a necessary condition for voluntary participation. This amounts to a version of the bargaining problem, as introduced by Nash (1950). Obviously, the existence of an exogenous *status quo* destroys the neutrality of any such individually rational sharing rule (see e.g. Sen 1970 for an early discussion of this point). On the other hand, whenever the conflict point is endogenous neutrality qualifies as a sensible requirement for an acceptable sharing rule.

A major standard assumption underlying the bargaining approach to distributive justice and sharing rules is the implicit 'welfaristic' principle owed to Nash, which allows the reduction of the outcome space to the set of feasible pay-off vectors. A number of well-known social choice rules have been proposed in this 'welfaristic' setting as solutions to the sharing problem both in the *status quo* and in the no-*status quo* case. They typically satisfy Pareto optimality (perhaps in a weak form) and (conditional) symmetry plus neutrality (in the no-*status quo* case) or individual rationality (in the bargaining or *status quo* case). Further requirements are usually added to the foregoing list in order to characterize each specific proposed rule. Thus, the Nash rule (i.e. select an alternative which maximizes the product of net pay-offs w.r.t. the—exogenous or endogenous—conflict outcome) as defined on the von Neumann–Morgenstern domain may be characterized by a contraction consistency property requiring invariance of the optimal choice with respect to deletion of sub-optimal alternatives (the so-called Nash's independence property). (Of course, many other axiomatizations of the Nash rule are now known: some of them rely on consistency properties concerning bargaining games with variable sets of active players, others on consistency properties regarding changes of the exogenous conflict point; see e.g. Thomson and Lensberg 1989, Peters and Van Damme 1991.)

Similarly, the (generalized) Kalai–Smorodinsky rule (i.e. select an alternative which maximizes the minimal actual-net-pay-off/ideal-net-pay-off ratio across players) has been characterized through continuity and a population monotonicity property forbidding the possibility of gains arising from the mere arrival of newcomers (see e.g. Thomson and Lensberg 1989).

In the context of discussions on the principles of distributive justice, versions of the Nash rule and of the Kalai Smorodinsky rule have been advocated, among others, by Binmore (1984) and Gauthier (1986), respectively. Whatever the merits of these rules, a word of caution about the foregoing characterizations is in order here. Indeed, it has been persuasively argued that those axiomatizations of sharing rules which implicitly rely upon the 'welfaristic' reduction of the outcome space are far from compelling, since they characteristically combine requirements that receive their appeal from specific intuitions regarding the allocation of economic resources (e.g. Nash's independence, population monotonicity, and so on) and a principle—the 'welfaristic' reduction mentioned above—which makes this sort of intuition essentially irrelevant (see e.g. Roemer 1986; 1990). In fact, this criticism has prompted some researchers to focus on alternative characterizations of bargaining solutions as defined on smaller domains with constant feasible pay-off set and variable conflict point, and based upon criteria concerning changes of the optimal solution in response to changes of the conflict point (see e.g. Peters and Van Damme 1991). While one may conjecture that this ongoing debate will end up with the eventual diffusion of a more sceptical attitude towards the real scope of 'traditional' bargaining solutions, the details of this controversy need not detain us here, given our present concerns for implementability—as opposed to a more general assessment—of proposed sharing rules.

Generally speaking, sharing rules seem to be on a firmer ground when defined on some specific 'economic' domain. For instance, on the quasi-linear domain $\mathsf{Q}(N, X)$ both egalitarian and utilitarian surplus sharing rules can be defined without any need to invoke interpersonal comparisons of well-being, and are amenable to very simple characterizations within the class of anonymous and efficient social choice rules (see e.g. Moulin 1985). Moreover, on the neo-classical domain $\mathsf{Q}(N, X)$—where egalitarian and utilitarian surplus sharing are not generally definable—one may define (selections of) the efficient envy-free (POEF) social choice correspondence and (selections of) the efficient egalitarian equivalent (POEE) social choice correspondence.

As it turns out, virtually all of the surplus sharing rules mentioned above are implementable with respect to many different theories of rational strategic behaviour. This fact can be summarized by the following results.

Theorem 5 (*Howard 1992*): *The Nash rule—both with endogenous and with exogenous conflict outcome as defined on the 'welfaristic' reduced VNM domain with unique individual maxima—is implementable w.r.t.* (*subgame and trembling-hand*) *perfect equilibrium, by means of an extensive game form specifying rules for proposal and approval and resulting either in unanimous approval or in the conflict outcome* (*which is the 'random dictator' outcome, whenever endogenously fixed*).

Theorem 6 (*Van Damme 1986*): *The Nash rule for two players with exogenous conflict point as defined on the 'welfaristic' reduced vN–M domain is implementable w.r.t. Nash equilibrium* (*and in maximin strategies*), *by means of a strategic game form whose strategies are those bargaining solutions for the same domain which satisfy Pareto optimality and conditional symmetry.*

Theorem 7 (*Moulin 1984a*): *The Kalai–Smorodinsky rule with exogenous conflict outcome as defined on the vN–M domain is implementable w.r.t.*

subgame perfect equilibrium by means of an extensive game form (consisting of a sealed-bid auction for the leadership followed by a proposal by the leader to be enforced against the status quo with a probability proportional to the winning bid if and only if it is unanimously approved).

Theorem 8 (*Moulin 1981, Moulin 1984b, Chun 1989*): *(i) The egalitarian surplus sharing rule with exogenous conflict point as defined on the quasi-linear domain is implementable w.r.t. subgame perfect equilibrium and iterate admissibility by means of an extensive game form consisting of a sealed-bid auction for the leadership followed by transfer payments performed by the leader according to her winning bid, and by a proposal by the leader to be enforced against the status quo if and only if unanimously approved: see Moulin (1981)*

(ii) Similarly, an egalitarian surplus sharing rule with an endogenous conflict point as defined on the quasi-linear domain is implementable w.r.t. subgame perfect equilibrium and iterate admissibility by means of an extensive game form relying on announcements of personal preferences, on estimates of the surplus available, and on a suitable tie-breaking device. This game form selects the leader among the players who announce the highest estimate of the surplus, then allows the leader to choose the public project and enforces her to pay the other players a compensation equal to their pro capita shares of the surplus—as estimated by the leader—over and above their respective self-announced utility gains from the chosen project: see Moulin (1984b).

(iii) Moreover, the egalitarian surplus sharing rule (with exogenous conflict point)—as defined on the quasi-linear domain—is implementable w.r.t. Nash equilibrium by means of a strategic game form whose strategies amount to proposed Pareto optimal, (weakly) progressive, and (weakly) monotonic sharing rules (see Chun 1989).

Theorem 9 (*Crawford 1979, Demange 1984*): *The social choice correspondence that selects for any economy of the neo-classical domain $\mathscr{E}(N, X)$ the efficient allocations which are—for any player—equivalent (i.e. indifferent) to the maximal feasible egalitarian allocation is implementable w.r.t. subgame perfect equilibrium by means of an extensive game form: such game form consists of a sealed-bid auction for the leader's role, followed by the leader's proposal of an allocation which is enforced (if unanimously approved) or rejected and replaced with the allocation resulting from the appropriation by each player of a quota proportional to her own initial bid (or of any remaining lesser quota), in an (otherwise prefixed) order starting with the first 'rejecting' player and ending up with the leader.*

Theorem 10 (*Palfrey and Srivastava 1991*): *Moreover, all of the sharing rules mentioned above, the utilitarian rule as defined on the quasi-linear domain, and* *every sharing rule selecting envy-free and efficient allocations as defined on the neo-classical domain $\mathscr{E}(N, X)$ are implementable w.r.t. undominated Nash equilibrium (by means of a strategic game form relying on individual messages consisting in the announcement of a point of the graph of the relevant rule, of a preference profile, and of an integer number which is used to define the outcome of an integer subgame that is activated whenever (quasi-)unanimity in the former messages is lacking: see e.g. Palfrey and Srivastava 1991).*

The previous implementability results—which refer to theories of rational strategic behaviour under complete information—can be replicated for theories regarding the case of complete ignorance, as testified by the following propositions.

Theorem 11 (*i*) (*Jackson 1992*): *The Nash rule, the Kalai-Smorodinksy rule (both either with exogenous or with endogenous conflict outcome), the egalitarian and the utilitarian (quasi-linear) sharing rules, the efficient egalitarian equivalent correspondence, and the efficient envy-free correspondence are implementable w.r.t. undominated—or admissible—strategy profiles, by means of a strategic game form relying on the announcement of some preference orderings, of a proposed outcome, and of an integer number.*

Theorem 11 (*ii*) (*Vannucci 1993*): *All the sharing rules mentioned above under Theorem 8(ii) are implementable w.r.t. optimistically and cautiously stable standards of behaviour and w.r.t. optimistically sub-stable standards of behaviour by means of a situation form for generalized social situations when the players are endowed with the coarsest information correspondences (this situation form is an abstract counterpart of Jackson's strategic game form mentioned above).*

Summing up, it seems to me that—while some relevant details are still lacking—the foregoing implementability results make the general picture sufficiently clear. Namely, the typical 'social norms' of fair distribution are implementable with respect to several theories of rational strategic behaviour (and the implicitly attached informational scenarios).

5. Conclusions

The results surveyed in section 4 offer a very positive picture. Virtually every 'social norm' we have considered passes some (in fact, many) crucial implementation tests. This is a piece of most valuable information since its main implication is that the ethical performance criteria embodied in those 'social norms' can be met through rational strategic interaction on the part of the individual players. To put it in other terms, a lot can be achieved—at least in principle—through decentralization, provided that the relevant institutions are cleverly designed. Thus, the first question asked in the introduction can be answered in the positive: most 'social norms' for fair distribution and collective decision-making procedures are consistent with rational strategic behaviour (or, rather, can be made consistent with the latter through mechanism design).

Moreover, the implementability results mentioned above provide some relevant information concerning the relative performance of different mechanisms or institutions. Thus, voting mechanisms endowing voters with limited veto rights exhibit more strategic 'robustness' than majoritarian mechanisms do when it comes to implementing democratic and efficient decision-making. Similarly, mechanisms relying on a predictable conflict outcome and on unanimous approval with or without an auction for the leader's role can be used in order to implement fair sharing rules (the conditional auction mechanism mentioned above under Theorem 8 (ii) is in fact an exception in that it amounts to an auction for the leader's role while dispensing with unanimous approval of the leader's proposal: it should be noticed, however, that at the equilibrium being the leader does not matter at all, under this mechanism). Summing up, it seems that mechanisms of a definitely consensual sort—as opposed to more unilateral decision schemes including majoritarian mechanisms—are bound to be the rule rather than the exception when it comes to reconciling fairness with efficiency under rational strategic behaviour (but see Mueller 1978, Moulin 1983, Peleg 1984, Abdou and Keiding 1991, for a general analysis and discussion concerning the properties of consensual decision mechanisms).

On the other hand, the impressively long list of positive implementability results surveyed in this chapter should not be taken, in my view, as conclusive theoretical evidence that—as far as implementability is concerned—'everything goes' or even that virtually all of the relevant 'social norms' are on an equal footing. In fact, I am persuaded that one should distinguish between 'implementability in principle' and something like 'implementation in practice', whatever it might mean. On this last issue, implementation theory is admittedly still in its infancy. Satisfactory notions of 'practical implementation' are presumably to arise from a better understanding of procedural aspects of rational strategic behaviour (see e.g. Simon 1978 for an early advocacy of models emphasizing procedural aspects of rationality, and Binmore 1987/1988—among many others—for a similar emphasis in the context of game-theoretic models). Moreover, a more realistic view of mechanisms should consider mechanism design as part of a broader process of 'endogenous' mechanism selection (see e.g. Holmström and Myerson 1983, Crawford 1985, Kalai and Samet 1985, Vassilakis 1990, Lagunoff 1992). It seems fairly obvious, then, that dramatic progresses concerning 'implementation in practice' have to wait for better models of procedural aspects of rational strategic behaviour and of mechanism selection processes.

REFERENCES

Abdou, J., and Keiding, H. (1991), *Effectivity Functions in Social Choice* (Dordrecht: Kluwer Academic Publishers).

Abreu, D., and Matsushima, H. (1992), 'Virtual Implementation in Iteratively Undominated Strategies: Complete Information', *Econometrica*, 60: 993–1008.

—— and Sen, A. (1991), 'Virtual Implementation in Nash Equilibrium', *Econometrica*, 59: 997–1021.

—— and —— (1990), 'Subgame Perfect Implementation: A Necessary and Almost Sufficient Condition', *Journal of Economic Theory*, 50: 285–99.

Arrow, K. J. (1963), *Social Choice and Individual Values* 2nd edn., New Haven: Yale University Press).

Aumann, R. J. (1959), 'Acceptable Points in General Cooperative n-Person Games', in Tucker and Luce (1959).

Bernheim, D. S. (1986), 'Axiomatic Characterizations of Rational Choice in Strategic Environments', *Scandinavian Journal of Economics*, 88: 473–88.

Bicchieri, C., and Dalla Chiara, M. L. (1992) (eds.), *Knowledge, Belief, and Strategic Interaction* (Cambridge: Cambridge University Press).

Binmore, K. (1984), 'Game Theory and the Social Contract', Part I, ST/ICERD Discussion Paper 84/108.

—— (1987/1988), 'Modeling Rational Players', Parts I and II, *Economics and Philosophy*, 3 and 4: 179–214 and 9–55.

—— (1989), 'Social Contract I: Harsanyi and Rawls', *Economic Journal*, 99: 84–102.

—— (1990*a*), 'Evolution and Utilitarianism: The Social Contract III', *Constitutional Political Economy*, 1(2): 1–26.

—— (1990*b*), *Essays on the Foundations of Game Theory* (Oxford: Basil Blackwell).

—— and Brandenburger, A. (1990), 'Common Knowledge and Game Theory', in Binmore (1990*b*).

—— and Shin, H. (1992), 'Algorithmic Knowledge and Game Theory', in Bicchieri and Dalla Chiara (1992).

Börgers, T. (1991), 'Undominated Strategies and Coordination in Normalform Games', *Social Choice and Welfare*, 8: 65–78.

Buchanan, J. (1975), *The Limits of Liberty* (Chicago: University of Chicago Press).

Campbell, D. E., and Fishburn, P. C. (1980), 'Anonymity Conditions in Social Choice Theory', *Theory and Decision*, 12: 21–39.

Chun, Y. (1989), 'A Noncooperative Justification for Egalitarian Surplus Sharing', *Mathematical Social Sciences*, 17: 245–61.

Crawford, V. P. (1979), 'A Procedure for Generating Pareto-Efficient Egalitarian Equivalent Allocations', *Econometrica*, 47: 49–61.

—— (1985), 'Efficient and Durable Decision Rules: A Reformulation', *Econometrica*, 53: 817–35.

Danilov, V. (1992), 'Implementation via Nash Equilibria', *Econometrica*, 60: 43–56.

Dasgupta, P., Hammond, P., and Maskin, E. (1979), 'The Implementation of Social Choice Rules: Some General Results on Incentive Compatibility', *Review of Economic Studies*, 46: 185–216.

Deb, R. (1989), 'Rights as Alternative Game Forms: Is There a Difference of Consequence?', Working Paper 8955, Department of Economics, Southern Methodist University.

Deistler, M., Furst, E., and Schwödiauer, G. (1982) (eds.), *Games, Economic Dynamics, Time Series Analysis* (Vienna: Physica Verlag).

Demange, G. (1984), 'Implementing Efficient Egalitarian Equivalent Allocations', *Econometrica*, 52: 1167–77.

Dutta, B., and Sen, A. (1991*a*), 'Implementation under Strong Equilibrium: A Complete Characterization', *Journal of Mathematical Economics*, 20: 49–67.

—— and —— (1991*b*), 'A Necessary and Sufficient Condition for Two-Person Nash Implementation', *Review of Economic Studies*, 58: 121–8.

—— and —— (1993), 'Implementing Generalized Condorcet Social Choice Functions via Backward Induction', *Social Choice and Welfare*, 10: 149–60.

Elster, J., and Roemer, J. E. (1991) (eds.), *Interpersonal Comparisons of Well-Being* (Cambridge: Cambridge University Press).

Ferejohn, J. A., Grether, D. M., and McKelvey, R. (1982), 'Implementation of Democratic Social Choice Functions', *Review of Economic Studies*, 49: 439–46.

Fishburn, P. C., and Gehrlein, W. V. (1987), 'Aggregation Theory for SSB Utility Functionals', *Journal of Economic Theory*, 42: 352–62.

Gauthier, D. (1986), *Morals by Agreement* (Oxford: Oxford University Press).

Greenberg, J. (1990), *The Theory of Social Situations: An Alternative Game-Theoretic Approach* (Cambridge: Cambridge University Press).

Harsanyi, J. C. (1955), 'Cardinal Welfare, Individualistic Ethics, and Interpersonal Comparisons of Utility', *Journal of Political Economy*, 63: 309–21.

—— (1974), 'An Equilibrium-Point Interpretation of Stable Sets and a Proposed Alternative Definition', *Management Science*, 20: 1472–95.

—— (1977*a*), *Rational Behavior and Bargaining Equilibrium in Games and Social Situations* (Cambridge: Cambridge University Press).

—— (1977*b*), 'Morality and the Theory of Rational Behaviour', *Social Research*, 44: 623–636 (reprinted in A. K. Sen and B. Williams (1982) (eds.), *Utilitarianism and Beyond* (Cambridge: Cambridge University Press)).

—— and Selten, R. (1988), *A Theory of Equilibrium Selection in Games* (Cambridge, Mass.: MIT Press).

Herrero, M. J., and Srivastava, S. (1992), 'Implementation via Backward Induction', *Journal of Economic Theory*, 56: 70–88.

Holmström, B., and Myerson, R. (1983), 'Efficient and Durable Decision Rules with Incomplete Information', *Econometrica*, 51: 1799–1819.

Holzman, R. (1986*a*), 'The Capacity of a Committee', *Mathematical Social Sciences*, 12: 139–57.

—— (1986*b*), 'On Strong Representations of Games by Social Choice Functions', *Journal of Mathematical Economics*, 15: 39–57.

Howard, J. V. (1992), 'A Social Choice Rule and its Implementation in Perfect Equilibrium', *Journal of Economic Theory*, 56: 142–59.

Hurwicz, L., Schmeidler, D., and Sonnenschein, H. (1985) (eds.), *Social Goals and Social Organization: Essays in Memory of Elisha Pazner* (Cambridge: Cambridge University Press).

Ichiishi, T. (1982), 'Non-cooperation and Cooperation', in Deistler, Furst, and Schwödiauer (1982).

—— Neyman, A., and Tauman, Y. (1990) (eds.), *Game Theory and Applications* (New York: Academic Press).

Jackson, M. O. (1991), 'Bayesian Implementation', *Econometrica*, 59: 461–77.

—— (1992), 'Implementation in Undominated Strategies: A Look at Bounded Mechanisms', *Review of Economic Studies*, 59: 557–75.

—— Palfrey, T. R., and Srivastava, S. (1992), 'Undominated Nash Implementation in Bounded Mechanisms', (Dept. of Economics, North Western University, Mimeo).

Kalai, E., and Samet, D. (1985), 'Unanimity Games and Pareto Optimality', *International Journal of Game Theory*, 15: 41–50.

Kohlberg, E. (1990), 'Refinement of Nash Equilibrium: The Main Ideas', in Ichiishi, Neyman, and Tauman (1990).

—— and Mertens, J. F. (1986), 'On the Strategic Stability of Equilibria', *Econometrica*, 54: 1003–37.

Laffont, J. J. (1992) (ed.), *Advances in Economic Theory: Sixth World Congress*: (Cambridge: Cambridge University Press).

Lagunoff, R. (1992), 'Fully Endogenous Mechanism Selection on Finite Outcome Sets', *Economic Theory*, 2: 465–80.

McKelvey, R. (1989), 'Game Forms for Nash Implementation of General Social Choice Correspondences', *Social Choice and Welfare*, 6: 139–56.

—— (1990), 'Game Theoretic Models of Voting in Multidimensional Issue Spaces', in Ichiishi, Neyman, and Tauman (1990).

Maskin, E. (1977), Nash Equilibrium and Welfare Optimality, mimeo (MIT).

—— (1985), 'The Theory of Implementation in Nash Equilibrium: A Survey', in Hurwicz, Schmeidler, and Sonnenschein (1985).

Matsushima, H. (1988), 'A New Approach to the Implementation Problem', *Journal of Economic Theory*, 45: 128–44.

Mertens, J. F. (1988), 'Stable Equilibria: A Reformulation', CORE Discussion Paper 8838.

Moore, J. (1992), 'Implementation, Contracts and Renegotiation in Environments with Complete Information', in Laffont (1992).

—— and Repullo, R. (1988), 'Subgame Perfect Implementation', *Econometrica*, 56: 1191–220.

—— and —— (1990), 'Nash Implementation: A Full Characterization', *Econometrica*, 58: 1083–99.

Moulin, H. (1981), 'Implementing Just and Efficient Decision-Making', *Journal of Public Economics*, 16: 193–213.

—— (1983), *The Strategy of Social Choice* (Amsterdam: North Holland).

—— (1984*a*), 'Implementing the Kalai-Smorodinsky Bargaining Solution', *Journal of Economic Theory*, 33: 32–45.

—— (1984*b*), 'The Conditional Auction Mechanism for Sharing a Surplus', *Review of Economic Studies*, 51: 157–70.

—— (1985), 'Egalitarianism and Utilitarianism in Quasi-linear Bargaining', *Econometrica*, 53: 49–67.

—— (1988), *Axioms of Cooperative Decision Making* (Cambridge: Cambridge University Press).

Mueller, D. C. (1978), 'Voting by Veto', *Journal of Public Economics*, 10: 57–75.

Nakamura, K. (1979), 'The Vetoers in a Simple Game with Ordinal Preferences', *International Journal of Game Theory*, 8: 55–61.

Nash, J. F. (1950), 'The Bargaining Problem', *Econometrica*, 28: 155–62.
—— (1951), 'Noncooperative Games', *Annals of Mathematics*, 54: 289–95.
Neumann, J. von, and Morgenstern, O. (1953), *Theory of Games and Economic Behavior* (3rd edn., Princeton: Princeton University Press).
Owen, G. (1982), *Game Theory* (2nd edn., New York: Academic Press).
Palfrey, T., and Srivastava, S. (1989), 'Mechanism Design with Incomplete Information: A Solution to the Implementation Problem', *Journal of Political Economy*, 97: 668–91.
—— and —— (1991), 'Nash Implementation Using Undominated Strategies', *Econometrica*, 59: 479–501.
Pattanaik, P. K., and Salles, M. (1983) (eds.), *Social Choice and Welfare* (Amsterdam: North Holland).
Pazner, E., and Schmeidler, D. (1978), 'Egalitarian Equivalent Allocations: A New Concept of Economic Equity', *Quarterly Journal of Economics*, 92: 671–87.
Peleg, B. (1978), 'Representations of Simple Games by Social Choice Functions', *International Journal of Game Theory*, 7: 81–94.
—— (1983), 'On Simple Games and Social Choice Correspondences', in Pattanaik and Salles (1983).
—— (1984), *Game Theoretic Analysis of Voting in Committees* (Cambridge: Cambridge University Press).
Peters, H., and Van Damme, E. (1991), 'Characterizing the Nash and Raiffa Bargaining Solutions by Disagreement Point Axioms', *Mathematics of Operations Research*, 16: 447–61.
Rawls, J. (1971), *A Theory of Justice* (Cambridge, Mass.: Harvard University Press).
Ricci, G. (1991) (ed.), *Decision Processes in Economics*, LNEMS 353 (Berlin: Springer Verlag).
Roemer, J. E. (1986), 'The Mismarriage of Bargaining Theory and Distributive Justice', *Ethics*, 96: 88–110.
—— (1990), 'Welfarism and Axiomatic Bargaining Theory', *Recherches Economiques de Louvain*, 56: 287–301.
Roth, A. E. (1976), 'Subsolutions and the Supercore of Cooperative Games', *Mathematics of Operations Research*, 1: 43–9.
Samuelson, L. (1992), 'Dominated Strategies and Common Knowledge', *Games and Economic Behavior*, 4: 284–313.
Schofield, N. J. (1985), *Social Choice and Democracy* (Berlin: Springer Verlag).
Sen, A. K. (1970), *Collective Choice and Social Welfare* (San Francisco: Holden Day).
—— (1987), *On Ethics and Economics* (Oxford: Basil Blackwell).
Simon, H. A. (1978), 'Rationality as Process and as Product of Thought', *American Economic Review*, 68: 1–16.
Sjöström, T. (1991), 'On the Necessary and Sufficient Conditions for Nash Implementation', *Social Choice and Welfare*, 8: 333–40.
—— (1993), 'Implementation in Perfect Equilibria', *Social Choice and Welfare*, 10: 97–106.
Suzumura, K. (1983), *Rational Choice, Collective Decisions, and Social Welfare* (Cambridge: Cambridge University Press).
Thomson, W. (1983), 'Equity in Exchange Economies', *Journal of Economic Theory*, 29: 217–44.

—— and Lensberg, T. (1989), *Axiomatic Theory of Bargaining with a Variable Number of Agents* (Cambridge: Cambridge University Press).
—— and Varian, H. (1985), 'Theories of Justice Based on Symmetry', in Hurwicz, Schmeidler, and Sonnenschein (1985).
Tucker, A. W., and Luce, R. D. (1959) (eds.), *Contributions to the Theory of Games*, iv (Princeton: Princeton University Press).
Van Damme, E. (1986), 'The Nash Bargaining Solution is Optimal', *Journal of Economic Theory*, 38: 78–100.
—— (1987), *Stability and Perfection of Nash Equilibria* (Berlin: Springer Verlag).
Vannucci, S. (1991), 'Noncooperative Capacities of Simple Games', in Ricci (1991).
—— (1992), 'Stable Standards of Behaviour and Capacities of Simple Games', paper presented at the VII CITG Conference on Game Theory and Applications, Pisa.
—— (1993), 'Generalized Social Situations and Admissible Implementation', mimeo (University of Siena).
Vassilakis, S. (1990), 'Rules for Changing the Rules', Working Paper 265 (Department of Economics, University of Pittsburgh).

16

Remarks on Rationality and Morality

MENAHEM E. YAARI

1. Introduction

Can conflict ever arise between rationality and morality? According to prevailing thinking, it never can. Why? Because morality (so the story goes) has to do with what your goals are, whereas rationality has to do with how effectively you are pursuing your goals, be they what they may. To quote Bertrand Russell (1954: 8): 'Reason . . . signifies the choice of the right means to an end that you wish to achieve. It has nothing whatever to do with the choice of ends.'

In other words, the dictates of rational decision-making can only lead to immoral action when ends, i.e. pay-offs, are inconsistent with moral tenets. When pay-offs are morally correct, how can pay-off maximization be morally incorrect?

To see more clearly what is being asserted here, think of a game-form G, with just two players, for simplicity. Let us write $G = (S, T; H)$, where S and T are the players' respective strategy sets and where H is the outcome function. We have $H : S \times T \to Z$ and $H(s, t) = z$ is the assertion that $z \in Z$ is the physical outcome of the interaction when the players' respective actions are $s \in S$ and $t \in T$.

In order to convert the game-form G into a game, say G^*, we must endow the two players with evaluation functions, say E_1 and E_2, where $E_1(z)$ represents the first player's evaluation of the physical outcome $z \in Z$ and similarly $E_2(z)$ for the second player. There is no harm in assuming that the functions E_1 and E_2 are real valued, so that the players' respective pay-off functions, h_1 and h_2 can be defined by writing $h_1 = E_1 o H$ and $h_2 = E_2 o H$. The game-form $G = (S, T; H)$ is thus converted into the game $G^* = (S, T; h_1, h_2)$.

The claim that rationality and morality need never come into conflict with each other, i.e. that rationality is ethically neutral, may now be stated as follows:

NEUTRALITY MAXIM. *There exist two evaluation functions, E_1 and E_2, such that the Nash equilibria of the game $G = (S, T; h_1, h_2)$, with $h_1 = E_1 oH$ and $h_2 = E_2 oH$, are always morally sound.*

It looks at first as though the evaluation functions E_1 and E_2 can always be tailored to fit the maxim. Indeed, some of us would no doubt say that this ability to tailor the evaluations to fit the maxim is precisely why morality and rationality never come into conflict. However, this view rests on the false supposition that the choice of evaluation functions is completely unrestricted. The most important restriction of our freedom to pick evaluation functions arises from consequentialism which asserts, roughly speaking, that only outcomes matter and not the institutional arrangements (game-forms) which bring them about. Thus, under consequentialism, the evaluation functions selected for one specific game-form would have to be appropriate also for *all other* game forms. i.e. under consequentialism the Neutrality Maxim would have to be revised as follows:

REVISED NEUTRALITY MAXIM. *There exist two evaluation functions, E_1 and E_2, such that, for all two-person game-forms $G = (S, T; H)$ the Nash equilibria of the game $G*(S, T; h_1, h_2)$, with $h_1 = E_1 oH$ and $h_2 = E_2 oH$, are always morally sound.*

In this form, the Neutrality Maxim is far from innocuous. Consider, for example, the following question, posed by David Hume:

I suppose a person to have lent me a sum of money, on condition that it be restor'd in a few days; and also suppose that after the expiration of the term agreed on, he demands the sum: I ask, What reason or motive have I to restore the money? (1739; Book III, Part II, sect. 1; OUP edn., 479)

We have here a simple game-form. Let us denote: L = amount of loan (principal), I = total interest due, V = value of loan to borrower (all denominated in guineas, say). Then, the game-form in question comes out as in Fig. 16.1. Only the borrower has a move, and outcomes are monetary payments accuring physically to both players, borrower first and lender second.

In considering this game-form, Hume draws a distinction between a collection of individuals interacting in the 'State-of-Nature', and a society

REPAY	$V - I, I$
RENEGE	$V + L, -L$

FIG. 16.1

which emerges when, through education and other evolutionary processes, the State-of-Nature, the borrower would (and should) renege, since 'self love . . . act[ing] at its liberty' constitutes the ethics in that state. In society, however, the borrower's only morally defensible move is to repay, even if 'the loan was secret . . . as when the lender would conceal his riches' (so there is no danger of legal retribution or loss of reputation), even if 'he [the lender] be my enemy', even if 'he be a miser', even if 'he be a profligate debauchee', and even if 'I be in necessity and have urgent motives to acquire something to my family'.

Thus, under the Neutrality Maxim, a society which has progressed beyond the State-of-Nature would be characterized by the borrower having an evaluation function E_B satisfying $E_B\,(V-I,\,I) > E_B\,(V+L,\,-L)$ for all admissible values of V, I, and L. Indeed, by the Revised Neutrality Maxim, an evaluation function satisfying this condition must apply in all of the borrower's potential interactions, and this conclusion is extremely unreasonable. (The inequality $E_B\,(V-I,\,I) > E_B\,(V+L,\,-L)$ for all $V, I, L > 0$ implies that E_B transforms payments to the borrower into payments to the other player at a rate which is less than 1 for 1—'Love thy neighbour *more* than thyself'). It is hard to see how morality should require the borrower to use such a function in all interactions.

But Hume is worried about another difficulty, namely circularity: the borrower is obliged to return the loan because he is in a society which has progressed beyond the State-of-Nature, and a society is said to have progressed beyond the State-of-Nature when returning loans becomes an obligation upon borrowers. Stated in terms of evaluation functions, the problem is that evaluations motivate the actions, but the actions are constitutive in the evaluations. Hume concludes, therefore, that

'tis requisite, then, to find some motive to acts of justice and honesty, distinct from our regard [evaluation] to the honesty; and in this lies the great difficulty.' (1739; OUP edn., 480)

Hume proposes to resolve this difficulty by considering a process in which 'natural virtues' gradually give way to 'artificial virtues'. Now, Hume makes it quite clear that by 'natural virtues' he means virtues existing in the State of Nature. First and foremost among these is self-interest (or self-love in Hume's own words). Natural virtues, according to Hume, will gradually give way to other virtues, which are artificial in the sense that they are not part of man's natural endowment. These artificial virtues come into play not through the formation of moral judgements or evaluations (this would lead to the very circularity that we are seeking to avoid) but rather through the manner in which individuals approach their choices:

This can be done after no other manner, than by a convention enter'd into by all members of the society . . . (1739; OUP edn., 489)

Thus, convention replaces self-interest in the processing of a given problem of choice among actions. In terms of our Neutrality Maxim, what is being proposed here is that Nash rationality be abandoned, in favour of another kind of rationality, namely that of conventions. This point deserves emphasis: in Hume's philosophy, coherence between rationality and morality is achieved not through evaluation functions but rather through the adaptation of the notion of rationality. For Hume, rationality based exclusively on self-interest (i.e. Nash equilibrium rationality) exists only in the State-of-Nature. Indeed, it is precisely this property (self-interest rationality) which defines the State-of-Nature. And the State-of-Nature, as everyone who had read Hobbes knew, was pretty grim: 'And the life of man, solitary, poore, nasty, brutish, and short' (Hobbes 1651; Penguin edn., 186).

Taking my cue from David Hume, I turn now to looking at how departures from Nash equilibrium rationality might help us accommodate certain value judgements within a theory of rational behaviour. Hume himself, as already indicated, proposes not only that the rationality of self-interest be abandoned, but also that the rationality of convention be introduced in its stead. In what follows, I shall take up only the first half of Hume's proposal, leaving the notion of convention (about which I have little to say) completely untouched.

2. Bounded rationality

The idea that a departure from Nash rationality may be required in order to bring equilibrium behaviour into line with prevailing intuitions has been on many people's minds recently. Mostly, this thought has been pursued in connection with examples of interaction where agents would be expected to co-operate with one another, yet Nash equilibrium decrees that they cannot. Celebrated and extensively studied examples of this are the finitely repeated Prisoner's Dilemma and another closely related game, to which K. G. Binmore has given the name the Centipede and which is illustrated in Fig. 16.2, where outcomes are money payments to players *I* and *II*, respectively.

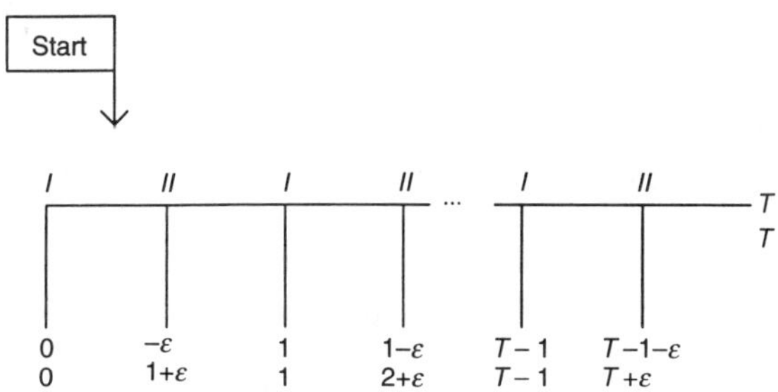

FIG. 16.2

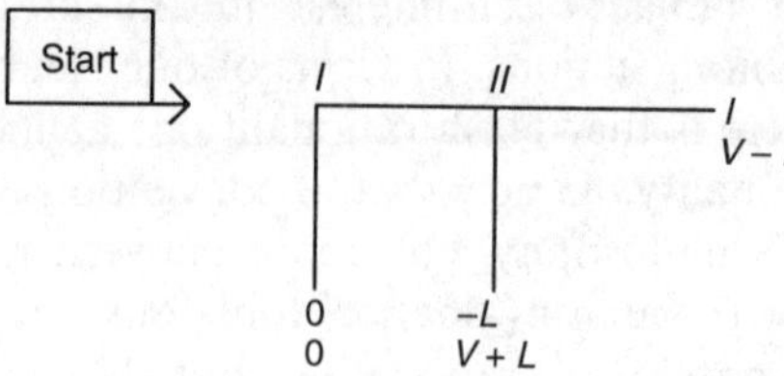

FIG. 16.3

Here, the wages of co-operation are considerable, yet, assuming self-interest, (0, 0) is the unique Nash outcome. The interaction never gets underway and life is indeed 'solitary, poore, . . ., and short' (I don't know about nasty and brutish).

Compare the Centipede with David Hume's game (see section 1 above) between lender (player *I*) and borrower (player *II*), which is illustrated in Fig. 16.3 with the outcomes as in section 1.

There is an obvious similarity between the two games, and this similarity allows us to draw an analogy. Recall that according to Hume, in the State-of-Nature, the borrower would renege, so the lender, anticipating this, would refrain from lending (i.e. both players would move 'down') and the Nash outcome (0, 0), would indeed emerge. In a civilized society, borrowers repay their debts, so both players would move 'right' and the outcome would be $(I, V - I)$. Analogously, for the Centipede, we could describe the Humean view as saying that while the Nash outcome (0, 0) characterizes the State-of-Nature, it is the co-operative outcome (T, T), which would emerge in a civilized society

Now, the teachings of David Hume are unlikely to sway modern game theorists to the point of modifying their theories. What did sway them, however, was empirical evidence. (Indeed, Hume himself would no doubt have exhorted them not to be swayed, *except* by empirical evidence.) Interactions like the one described by the Centipede are easily adaptable to an experimental setting and, in experiments, subjects tend to support Hume more than they tend to support Nash. Co-operation is observed throughout most of the stages of the interaction, sometimes breaking down towards the end, and sometimes continuing all the way to the end. Even in single-stage interactions (as in Hume's lender–borrower example), where each player has but one decision node, co-operation has in many cases been observed.

In order to come to terms with co-operation which, while frequently observed, is unwarranted by Nash Equilibrium Theory, game theorists have recently proposed a number of ideas. It is not my purpose here to discuss these ideas in detail but merely to point out what they have in common. For this purpose, the following brief account will suffice:

(i) *Limited Control* (Rosenthal 1981). Players do not possess perfect control over their actions. With a small but positive probability, a player will 'pull the wrong lever'. Anticipating this, it becomes optimal for players to select co-operation in the early stages of interaction along the Centipede.

(ii) *Limited Information* (Kreps, Milgrom, Roberts, and Wilson 1982). Players are not perfectly sure of the game being played. With a small but positive probability, your opponent is a 'compulsive co-operator'. It then becomes optimal, both for you and for your opponent (even when in fact he is not a compulsive co-operator), to select co-operation in the early stages of interaction along the Centipede.

(iii) *Limited Commonality of Knowledge* (Aumann 1992: 214–27). Players' mutual knowledge of rationality may become imperfect at higher orders. In other words, mutual knowledge of mutual knowledge of . . . of mutual knowledge of rationality may break down when this chain is long. Under these circumstances, any slight irrationality, occurring in some remote and extremely unlikely state, may lead players to co-operate in the early stages of the Centipede.

(iv) *Limited Implementability* (Rubinstein 1986). Players may have imperfect ability to implement their choices. In particular, they may be barred from adopting strategies which are not implementable on a given-sized finite-state machine. Co-operation then emerges in long enough interactions.

(v) *Limited Fastidiousness* (Radner 1978). Players are neither petty nor finicky. Self-interest only goes as far as ε-maximization. With not very fastidious players, co-operation in games like the Centipede may emerge.

(vi) *Limited Recall* (Aumann and Sorin 1989). Players are unable to recall the distant past, so their actions are insensitive to what had happened sufficiently long ago. Admittedly, this feature will not produce co-operation in the Centipede, but in other (rather special) settings it will.

These, then, are six different proposals, all having to do with departures from strict Nash rationality, and all designed to accommodate co-operation within the theory of interaction. At first sight, this seems to be precisely what Hume had argued, namely that self-interest rationality cannot be retained if the moral tenets of a civilized society are to be accommodated. However, a moment's reflection shows this conclusion to be unwarranted: Recent theories of bounded rationality can in no way be viewed as meeting Hume's challenge. There are two reasons for saying this. The first reason is simply that *none* of the six bounded rationality proposals, as outlined above, will do the required job in David Hume's own lender–borrower example. In other words, curious as it may seem, none of these models will produce the pattern of lenders lending and borrowers repaying. Alright, one might say, these six bounded rationality proposals may not do the trick for David Hume's example, but if we keep on exploring bounded rationality, then the next proposal possibly will. Someone, surely, will come up with a version of bounded rationality that will fit the bill. There is, however, a second reason for denying that bounded rationality is capable of meeting Hume's challenge. This second reason applies not only to existing proposals, but to bounded rationality in general. Hume (like Hobbes before him) regarded self-interest rationality as typifying that stark abstract model—the State-of-Nature. Bounded self-interest rationality would therefore characterize, as it were, an imperfect version of the State-of-Nature, which would be completely inappropriate for a description of a civilized society, as Hume saw it. Relying on bounded rationality to justify the moral tenets that Hume was concerned to establish would be like saying that civilization is but the State-of-Nature with a little bit of friction thrown in. Nothing could be farther from Hume's mind, as indeed from the mind of anyone who would view the transition from the State-of-Nature to a civilized society as progress. Thus, if we are to follow in Hume's footsteps, we must look for a model where the departure from self-interest rationality is not just a return to Nash equilibrium with players' faculties beset by imperfections.

3. Surviving response functions: a preliminary proposal

Let us restrict attention to two-person games in normal form. Consider a player with strategy set S facing an opponent with strategy set T. A function f on T, taking values in S, is called a response function for this player, specifying for each $t \in T$ an action $f(t)$ to be taken, if t were known to be the opponent's action. Let the player's pay-off function be denoted h, with $h: S \times T \to R$. A response function f^* for the player will be referred to as a Nash response function if, for all $s \in S$ and $t \in T$, the condition $h(f^*(t), t)$ holds. Nash response functions are also referred to as reaction functions or reaction curves. Response functions have been discussed under different names by many authors, notably by Cournot and by von Neumann and Morgenstern.

Suppose that interaction between two players proceeds as follows. Let the players' respective strategy sets be denoted S and T, and assume that the pair (S, T) is known to both. The first player selects a response function $f: T \to S$ and the second player selects a response function $g: S \to T$. These response functions are submitted to a referee who computes a fixed point—if one exists—of the composition $f_0 g$, i.e. finds an action (or strategy) s^* for the first player such that $f(g(s^*)) = s^*$. (If there is more than one fixed point, the referee uses some arbitrary known rule to select a specific one.) The players are informed and the respective actions, s^* and $t = g(s^*)$, are implemented.

This simple-minded approach to the modelling of interactions suffers from two obvious shortcomings: first, it relies on a fictitious institution, the Referee, to work out a set of mutually consistent actions. In this respect, the approach is similar to Competitive Equilibrium Theory, which relies on a fictitious Auctioneer to announce prices and calculate aggregate excess demands. Secondly, the approach applies to the normal form. Information which may be available in the extensive form, such as the timing of decisions, is liable to be lost.

Weighing against these serious drawbacks are several notable advantages. First, players need not possess forecasts of each other's actions. Secondly, conceptually problematic constructions which rely ultimately on infinite regress are avoided. This applies mainly to Common Knowledge, which is perhaps no less contrived than the notion of a referee. Thirdly, since players can always select Nash response functions, the predictions of Nash Theory can always be accommodated. In this restricted sense, the approach being described here actually contains Nash Theory as a special case. Fourthly, in order to specify a rule of response to your opponent's action, you need not be informed of your opponent's type. In other words, the present approach applies without modification to cases of incomplete information. Moreover, in some cases the approach allows incentive compatible type-elicitation mechanisms to arise endogenously. The following example will serve to illustrate this point.

Consider an auction where a certain object is put up for sale. The auctioneer takes on the referee's role, as described above. (Thus, here the notion of a referee is somewhat less far-fetched.) One player participating in the auction submits a response function specifying his/her bid as a function of the bids of the other players. Suppose, for just a moment, that there are but two players in the auction. Take one of these two players and assume that this player is motivated by self-interest. The response function which this player will submit is $\min(v, b^+)$, where v = the value of the object to the player, b = the opponent's bid, and b^+ = a number which is 'a shade above' b. In other words, the player will seek to outbid his opponent by a hair's breadth, as long as his own value for the object has not been exceeded. When there are more than two players, a self-interested player would still submit the same response function (i.e. $\min(v, b^+)$) except that now b is the maximal bid from the other players. When all players are motivated by self-interest, all response functions are of this form. What will be the fixed point? A moment's thought reveals that the fixed point occurs when all the players bid their values for the object, except for the player with the highest value, whose bid is set a shade above the value of the second-highest bidder. The object is therefore awarded to the player whose value is highest, at a price which is a shade above the value of the second-highest bidder. We thus find the mechanism known as the second-bid auction emerging endogenously.

The foregoing example serves also to highlight another important point. Players in the auction were said to be motivated by self-interest, and this was taken to mean that they always submit Nash response functions to the referee. (The pay-off was $v - p$ for a player who won the object at price p and valued it at v, and 0 otherwise.) Now, in the auction game, self-interest and the use of Nash response functions are indeed synonymous. However, it is easy to produce examples where a reasonable argument may be given to the effect that a player motivated by self-interest would not submit a Nash response function. Indeed, since players are aware of the mechanism being used to process the submitted response functions, they would tend to regard the situation as a game in response functions, i.e. a second-order game in which spaces of response functions play the role of strategy sets and pay-offs are reckoned from the outcomes which arise as fixed points of the submitted response functions, composed together. The picking of Nash response functions by all players is not necessarily a Nash equilibrium in this response function game. In other words, the best (i.e. pay-off maximizing) response to a Nash response function may not be a Nash response function. (For example: consider a symmetric game on the unit square, with pay-off function h. For $0 \leqslant s, t \leqslant 1$, $h(s, t)$ is the pay-off to a player choosing s, whose opponent chooses t. Take h to be given by $h(s, t) = t(1 + s) - s^2$. The Nash response function is $s^*(t) = t/2$. Now suppose that your opponent submits this response function to the referee. If you also submit this same Nash response function, then the fixed point will occur at $s = t = 0$ and your pay-off will be 0. If, however, you submit the response function $s(t) = 1/2$ for all $0 \leqslant t \leqslant 1$, then the fixed point will occur at $s = 1/2$ $t = 1/4$, and your pay-off will be 1/8. Thus, submitting Nash response functions is *not* a Nash equilibrium of the response function game in this example.)

In view of this observation, one may wish to define 'self-interest' not as the adoption of a Nash response function but rather as the adoption of a Nash equilibrium strategy in the response-function-picking game. Having done this, one can then proceed to the next level, by considering the game in which players' actions consist of choosing rules which specify their own response function as a function of their opponents' response functions. Such a rule would be a *second-order* response function, giving rise to a second-order response-function-picking game, in which one can once again look for a Nash equilibrium. In principle, this procedure can be repeated indefinitely, to produce a hierarchy of response functions, of arbitrarily high order, and correspondingly of notions of 'self-interest' and 'rationality' of arbitrarily high order. Examples can easily be given where actions which are out of Nash equilibrium at the first order become 'Nash rational' at higher orders (see e.g. Howard 1971). But this is not the line to be pursued in this chapter. My object here is to concentrate on first-order response functions, among them Nash response functions, and to ask when such functions might be called 'rational'. Nothing will be claimed with regard to the consistency of such response functions with self-interest at higher orders.

Well, then, when shall we say that some given response function is rational? In keeping with modern fashion (but also in keeping, I think, with David Hume's views) I shall adopt an evolutionary definition, linking rationality with ultimate survival.

DEFINITION. *Let G be a two-person game in normal form, with the one-player's strategy sets denoted S and T, respectively. An environment for G is an object of the form* $E = (f, p; g, q)$, *where*

$$f = (f_1, f_2, \ldots, f_n) \text{ with } f_i\colon T \to S \text{ for } i = 1, \ldots, n$$

$$p = (p_1, p_2, \ldots, p_n) \text{ with } p_i > 0 \text{ for } i = 1, \ldots, n \text{ and } \Sigma_{p_1} = 1$$

$$g = (g_1, g_2, \ldots, g_m) \text{ with } g_j\colon S \to T \text{ for } j = 1, \ldots, m$$

$$q = (q_1, q_2, \ldots, q_m) \text{ with } q_j > 0 \text{ for } j = 1, \ldots, m \text{ and } \Sigma_{q_j} = 1$$

In order to interpret this definition, suppose that you were going to play the game G in the role of player I, and that $E = (f, p; g, q)$ was the environment. Then, what E tells you is that, with probability q_j, your opponent (player II) will submit the response function g_j, for $j = 1, \ldots, m$. Similarly, if you were to play in the role of player II, then E would tell you that there is a probability p_i of your opponent submitting the response function f_i, for $i = 1, \ldots, n$. We can think of the player population consisting of n types of player I and m types of player II, with p and q being the respective frequency distributions. The assumption that the number of types on each side is finite (n and m, respectively) is merely a matter of convenience. It should be apparent that environments and Harsanyi systems of incomplete information are, in fact, analogous objects.

Environments are meant to be viewed as dynamic objects, i.e. as evolving over time. Consider the game G with its environment $E = (f, p; g, q)$. As time progresses, the frequency distributions, p and q, of the various types, are subject to change. As for the lists of types, f and g, they are assumed to remain unchanged throughout the process. This assumption rules out mutations or, more precisely, restricts attention to what happens *after* the mutation has occurred, i.e. to whether or not the mutant will survive.

What dynamics shall we put on the frequency distributions, p and q? The idea, sometimes referred to as 'classical dynamics', is to postulate a positive link between the change in a given type's relative frequency in the population and the differential pay-off which this type earns, relative to other types. Consider the environment $E = (f, p; g, q)$ and suppose that i and k are two types of player I, present in E (i.e. f_i and f_k are among the components of f). If type i encounters an opponent (player II) of type j, then an interaction will occur in which player I submits the response function f_i and player II

submits the response function g_j. Let the pay-off to player I from this encounter be denoted $H_j(i)$. Thus, type i's expected pay-off is given by the quantity $H(i) = \Sigma q_j H_j(i)$. The expected pay-off to type k, also in the role of player I, is calculated similarly, and denoted $H(k)$. Now let us write π_i and π_k for the conditional frequencies of the two types: $\pi_i = p_i/(p_i + p_k)$, $\pi_k = 1 - \pi_i$. We shall say that the relative evolution of types i and k is payoff directed at E if there exists a sign-preserving real function D such that

$$\dot{\pi}_i / \pi_i = \Phi(H(i) - H(k))$$

where the dot stands for rate of change over time. The same definition applies also to types of player II.

DEFINITION. *Let G be a two-person game, and let* $E(t) = (f, p(t); g, q(t))$ *be its environment at time t. Suppose that t ranges over the interval* $[0, \infty]$. *We shall say that the process* $\{E(t), t \geqslant 0\}$ *is governed by pay-off-directed evolution if, for all* $t \geqslant 0$, *the relative evolution of any pair of types, whether of player I or of player II, is pay-off directed at* $E(t)$.

It is now possible to formalize the idea that a rational rule of behaviour is one which survives in a world of pay-off-directed evolution.

DEFINITION. *Let* $E = (f, p; g, q)$ *be the environment for a two-person game G. The response function fi (i.e. the i-th member of f) is said to be rational, relative to the environment E, if, for every process* $\{E(t) = (f, p(t); g, q(t)), t \geqslant 0\}$ *governed by pay-off-directed evolution and satisfying* $E(0) = E$, *the condition* $\liminf p_i(t) > 0$ *holds.*

Note that we have not defined rationality *per se*, but rationality relative to a given environment. A rule of behaviour can be rational in one environment and irrational in another. This, I maintain, is very much in keeping with David Hume's thinking. For, in seeking to explain why individuals should behave differently in a civilized society from the manner in which they would behave in the State-of-Nature, Hume argued in effect that rationality in the two environments would be different (see section 1, above).

Another aspect to be noted is that under the foregoing definition, rationality is not exclusive. In a given environment, there may be several different rules of behaviour (response functions) which enjoy long-run evolutionary survival, and are therefore all rational. In particular, suppose that for some game G, a Nash response function is found to be rational, given the environment E. Will this Nash response function always drive all non-Nash response functions to eventual extinction, thus rendering these other response functions irrational? And, conversely, can it ever happen that a non-Nash response function will drive a Nash response function to eventual extinction, thus rendering the latter irrational? In cases where the opposite player's type is observable, even imperfectly, both questions can be answered in the negative (Frank 1987) contains arguments that can be used to establish this claim.) Both questions are open when the opposite players' types are not observable.

4. Conclusion

When rationality and morality clash, one of them has got to yield. There are those who would have us change our moral intuitions: 'Greed is good!', declared the flamboyant Wall Street arbitrageur, just a few months before going to prison. Others would allow that perhaps it is rationality—Nash rationality, to be precise—that ought to give way. Is bounded Nash rationality likely to give us what we need? In this chapter, I have argued that it is not. What is needed, rather, is a more radical departure from Nash. David Hume argued for a notion of rationality based on convention, an idea that has since been explored by many, most recently by David Lewis (1969). The notion of rationality to which I have chosen to refer is one based on survival. There are, and will be, other approaches, and time will tell which, if any, is apt.

REFERENCES

Aumann, R. J. (1992), 'Irrationality in Game Theory', in Dasgupta, Gale, Hart, and Maskin (1992).

—— and Sorin, S. (1989), 'Cooperation and Bounded Recall', *Games and Economic Behavior*, 1: 5–39.

Dasgupta, P., Gale, D., Hart, O., and Maskin, E. (1992) (eds.), *Economic Analysis of Markets and Games: Essays in Honor of Frank Hahn* (Cambridge, Mass.: MIT Press).

Frank, R. H. (1987), 'If Homo Economicus Could Choose His Own Utility Function . . .', *American Economic Review*, 77: 593–604.

Hobbes, T. (1651), *Leviathan* (London: A. Crooke; repr. in Penguin Classics, 1985).

Howard, N. (1971), *Paradoxes of Rationality: Theory of Metagames and Political Behavior* (Cambridge, Mass.: MIT Press).

Hume, D. (1739), *A Treatise of Human Nature* (London: J. Noon; repr. by Oxford University Press, 1978).

Kreps, D. M., Milgrom, P., Roberts, J., and Wilson, R. (1982), 'Rational Cooperation in the Finitely Repeated Prisoner's Dilemma', *Journal of Economic Theory*, 27: 245–52.

Lewis, D. (1969), *Conventions: A Philosophical Study* (Cambridge, Mass.: Harvard University Press).

Radner, R. (1978), 'Can Bounded Rationality Resolve the Prisoner's Dilemma?', unpublished.

Rosenthal, R. W. (1981), 'Games of Perfect Information, Predatory Pricing and the Chain-Store Paradox', *Journal of Economic Theory*, 25: 92–100.

Rubinstein, A. (1986), 'Finite Automata Play the Repeated Prisoner's Dilemma' *Journal of Economic Theory*, 39: 83–96.

Russell, B. (1954), *Human Society in Ethics and Politics* (New York: Simon & Schuster).

Index of Names

Index of Subjects